The Jewish
Community
of
Golders
Green

This is an informative, interesting and entertaining book. It contains huge amounts of information, much of which will be new to readers; it will interest those who are curious about this community, or rather communities, because Pam Fox deftly contrasts their differences, and it is refreshed by insights and anecdotes based on the wide range of people who agreed to talk to the author about their ways of viewing Judaism.

Professor Michael Alpert

This book fills an important gap in our understanding of the history of Jewish Golders Green, and of the impact of Golders Green Jewry on wider society. Grounded in painstaking research and oral history analysis, it covers the full spectrum of Jewish communities in this important area of Anglo-Jewish settlement and growth.

Professor Geoffrey Aderman,
University of Buckingham

Golders Green - the first tube created suburb has for generations been a hub of Jewish life. In this fascinating history Pam Fox through her detailed research has shone light on the story and journey of the Jews who settled in the area. This easy to read book, full of anecdotes, provides readers with hitherto undiscovered stories of Golders Green Jews and their Judaism.

David Jacobs, Chair of the Jewish Historical
Society of England

The Jewish Community of Golders Green

A SOCIAL HISTORY

PAM FOX

The
History
Press

First published 2016

The History Press
The Mill, Brimscombe Port
Stroud, Gloucestershire, GL5 2QG
www.thehistorypress.co.uk

British Library Cataloguing in Publication Data.
A catalogue record for this book is available from the British Library.

ISBN 978 0 7509 6587 3

Typesetting and origination by The History Press
Printed and bound in Great Britain by TJ International Ltd

Contents

 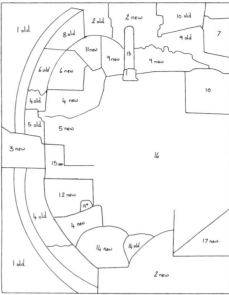

Diagram Explaining Cover Painting of Golders Green Past and Present by Beverley-Jane Stewart

The black and white illustrates the past, and the colour imagery is of the present. The theme of continuous movement was important and starts with the circular motion of the railway line which penetrated the previous rural wilderness. This circuit frames the constant activity of the modern local Jewish community, with their endless rushing to payers, shopping and social chats.

1. (new) – Rural Golders Green.
2. (old) – Golders Green Staton. *c.* 1907.
2. (new) – Present Golders Green Station with the original Edwardian tiles.
3. Hoop Lane Jewish Cemetery opened in 1897, before the arrival of the railways. Cemeteries were often built in rural areas on the outskirts of a town. This chosen location symbolises its remoteness in Victorian Britain. The cemetery now caters for the Reform Movement with a separate area for the Sephardi community.
4. (old) – 1930s houses. A massive growth of redevelopment happened in this period influenced by the railways.
4. (new) – Converted houses between residential homes are modern shtieblech.
5. (old) – North-Western Reform Synagogue, 'Alyth Gardens'. Established in 1933.
5. (new) – Modern service in the North-Western Synagogue.
6. (old) – The original interior of Golders Green Synagogue, Dunstan Road, opened in 1922.
6. (new) – Modern layout of the Golders Green Synagogue.
7. The original red brick railway bridge representing many which are scattered round Golders Green.
8. (old) – Temple Fortune, Golders Green. *c.* 1920.
9. (old) – The shops in Golders Green Road. *c.* 1930.
9. (new) – Present shops with modern kosher outlets.
10. (old) – Local amusements – The Hippodrome and the Ionic.

10. The footbridge at the northern end of Golders Green Road separating it from Hendon.
11. Machzikei Hadath Synagogue, Highfield Road, originally established in 1898 in the East End as Spitalfields Synagogue between Fournier Street and Brick Lane. The building started as Huguenot church. It became a chapel and then a synagogue and is now a mosque. The present building in Golders Green was built in the 1983.
12. (new) – Golders Green Beth Hamedrash, locally known as 'Munks shul' named afer the popular rabbi. Originally established by the German community escaping the Nazi regime. The present building in The Ridings was built in 1959.
13. The War Memorial Cenotaph unveiled in 1923, built opposite Golders Green Station.
14. (new) – Ohel David Eastern Synagogue, established in the 1959.
14. (old) – Iraqi and other Mizrahi Jews in prayer in traditional costume.
15. Modern Jewish communal services – Jewish Care, London Jewish Family Centre, Jewish Learning Exchange (adult education) and Sage Home (elderly care).
16. *Shabbat* scene in Golders Green, this image expresses the diversity of the community.
17. The international influences that have filtered into Golders Green Jewish Community.

Preface

Over the years I have had links with Golders Green through friends and family living in the area. Like many people, I have long been aware of the area's large Jewish population. However, it was not until I moved to Golders Green that I became more interested in the community's origins and development. As a historian recently specialising in Jewish history, I felt impelled to explore the evolution of the Jewish community among whom I was now living. I was amazed to find how little material existed on the Jews of Golders Green. I identified a few general, not very recent, histories of the area like those written by Howkins and by Smith and Hall, a number of pictorial histories of Golders Green, histories covering wider areas, such as Petrie's *Hendon and Golders Green Past and Present* and studies of the development of north-west London (Alan Jackson's *Semi-Detached London, Suburban Development, Life and Transport 1900–39*). These publications all mentioned the rise of the community but did not chart its evolution in any detail. There were no publications dealing exclusively with the Jewish community apart from a brief article on the founding of Golders Green Synagogue.[1]

I delved more deeply into the Jewish history of Golders Green and quickly discovered that there was a rich and fascinating story waiting to be told. So, never being one to resist a challenge, I decided that I would attempt to fill an obvious gap in Anglo-Jewish history. I embarked on the task in the latter part of 2014 and soon came to a view on the type of book that I wanted to write. Being a social historian, I decided to concentrate on recreating the lives of the Jews of Golders Green, exploring their relationships with one another, and to place less emphasis on the geographical and political development of the community.

Prior to the twentieth century, Golders Green was little more than a hamlet and only grew into a major residential suburb after the coming of the underground in 1907. The fact that it is such a recent phenomenon means that there are people still alive whose knowledge of the area dates back to its early development. As a result, the history on which I had embarked clearly lent itself to an oral history approach: my book would not only be about Jews in a particular locality, but Jewish people would help to uncover and tell the story of the community. Although I have drawn on a wide range of sources to produce this book, it is based to a considerable extent on oral history interviews. Some of these already existed but I conducted the vast majority of the interviews used in the book. These conversations took place over a twelve-month period spanning 2014–15 and involved a huge range of people: long-standing and relatively new residents, experts on particular aspects of the community's development, younger and older people and those from across the spectrum of Jewish observance and beliefs.

While I sought to avoid becoming hung up on geographical boundaries, I realised quite early on that I needed to define what I meant by 'Golders Green'. After many discussions, I decided that, for the purposes of this book, the boundary of Golders Green would start where Child's Hill ends, extend eastwards along North End Road as far as the Old Bull and Bush, take in Temple Fortune but end at Henley's Corner with the North Circular Road forming its western extent. I recognise the strong links that exist between the Jews of Golders Green and those living in neighbouring Hendon and that the dividing line between Golders Green and Hampstead Garden Suburb is very hazy. However, I have chosen not to include these areas, firstly because the histories of Hendon and Hampstead Garden Suburb have already been explored in some detail, and secondly to maintain a clear focus for the book. I feared that the larger the geographical area covered, the 'thinner' the material would become. Temple Fortune has its own identity but as far as the history of the Jewish community is concerned, Golders Green and Temple Fortune are fairly inseparable. In recent times this has become even more the case as the roads linking Golders Green with Temple Fortune (notably Prince's Park Avenue) are now mainly populated by Jewish families.

From the outset I knew that I would need to exercise a great deal of sensitivity to avoid offending people. As with other faiths, there is a whole gamut of different interpretations of Judaism. These religious differences are often overlaid by national and ethnic customs and practices that some Jews have acquired as a result of living in countries throughout the world. I was determined to ensure that my book would cover each and every element of the Jewish community, ranging from secular and cultural Jews to the most strictly observant groupings, and that information about the different denominations would be presented in a balanced and non-judgemental fashion.

While the book makes clear the community's enormous strengths and durability, I have not sought to disguise the tensions that have sometimes existed between the different elements of the Jewish community or to avoid mentioning the scandals, of which, as in any community, there have been a number. In my view these tensions and scandals add interest to the story of the Golders Green Jewish community and not to allude to them would detract from the credibility of the history. On the other hand, I have been careful not to over-focus on the controversial aspects of the community's history to avoid giving an erroneously negative impression of the Jews of Golders Green for, above all, I wanted the book to be a celebration of the community and to create a positive awareness of its history.

The book consists of two main parts – a chronological overview of the development of the community from the beginning of the twentieth century until the present day, and a series of chapters on themes that span the community's history, including the synagogues, the shops, leisure pursuits, education and earning a living. However, the history of the community is not considered in isolation but in the context of wider Anglo-Jewish history, in relation to the history of the country as a whole, and alongside the development of the non-Jewish residents of Golders Green. I have sought to cover as much ground as possible but the book is not intended to be either a comprehensive or definitive history. Hopefully it will inspire others to write further histories addressing the topics I have omitted due to lack of space.

Personal testimonies produce rich information but people talk about what they know and what interests them rather than with a view to furnishing a balanced historical account. I have tried to tackle obvious areas of unevenness by a combination of careful editing and drawing on information from other sources. I have also endeavoured to ensure that the content of this book is as accurate as possible, meticulously checking and rechecking information, but I am realistic and know that 100 per cent accuracy cannot be guaranteed when writing history. This is especially the case when one's main source is people's memories, which are sometimes fallible.

Pam Fox, October 2016

Acknowledgements

Producing this book has given me intense pleasure. I hope you will enjoy reading it as much as I have enjoyed researching and writing it. I could not have written it without the help of many people to whom I would like to express my sincere thanks.

First and foremost I would like to thank everyone who contributed their memories and knowledge of Golders Green. I learned a vast amount from those I interviewed and feel greatly enriched as a result of meeting some wonderful people. Some interviewees were kind enough to meet with me on more than one occasion and I would like to thank them for being so generous with their time and their patience in responding to my many questions. Particularly outstanding was the assistance I received from Michael Cohen, Esra Kahn, Gabriel Goldstein, Rabbi Refoel and Loli Berisch. I conducted over a hundred interviews and each and every one provided rich material. I would especially like to thank those whose memories of Golders Green span many years of its existence: Jocelyne Tobin, Barbara Michaels, Naomi Rose, Jeff Alexander, and Hazel and Maurice Sheldon. Readers will see that they have been quoted extensively in the book. Some interviewees asked to remain anonymous. I'd like to thank them; they know who they are!

In addition to interviewees, I would like to thank those who contributed in a variety of other ways: Rosita Rosenberg, who has worked with me on three books, for her research in the *Jewish Chronicle* and for reading numerous drafts of my book; David and Hannah Jacobs for giving me access to their archival material and also for their enthusiasm for my work; Benny and Julia Chain, Jon Epstein, and Monty Frankel, who assisted with my research on particular communities; Hugh Petrie at Barnet Local Studies Centre, who was unstinting with his time and helped me make some amazing discoveries; Pat Hasenson, for the loan of some wonderful historic documents; Selina Gellert, Jean Shindler, Tim Simon and Bernard Benarroch, who put me in touch with contacts who proved invaluable; Helen Fry who helped me source some of the photographs in this book, and Nicola Guy at The History Press with whom it has been a delight to work.

Towards the end of the project, my book was given a 'deep read' by Michael Alpert (who also advised on the use of Hebrew), Geoffrey Alderman, Michael Jolles (who also provided biographical information that had eluded me) and David and Hannah Jacobs. I am indebted to them for their knowledgeable and constructive feedback.

In addition to the photos I have collected from a variety of sources, this book has been enhanced by the artistic talent of Beverley-Jane Stewart, who created the wonderful picture for the front cover, which captures so well the history of the Jewish community of Golders Green. Beverley-Jane also contributed the sketches which have been incorporated into the text.

Producing this book has been quite challenging because of the broad range of topics I had to research, the quantities of information I needed to synthesise and the time necessary to check and double check details. My husband Michael consistently supported and encouraged me. I have promised to leave a decent interval before taking on another book!

Although I have taken every care to ensure that the book does not contain errors, any that nevertheless may have crept in are my responsibility and not that of those who kindly assisted me.

Glossary

Use of Hebrew

In this book, Hebrew words are transliterated from the Sephardi pronunciation, unless the Ashkenazi pronunciation was used orally by the person being quoted (for example, if s/he said *Shabbes* rather than *Shabbat*), or is so common that almost everybody uses it for the word in question, such as *kOsher* rather than the Sephardi *kashER*. Likewise Ashkenazi names of congregations are retained. There are several reasons justifying the use of Sephardi pronunciation as the basis for transliteration. Here are three of them:

Jewish schools, excepting some orthodox ones, teach the Israeli pronunciation, which is Sephardi. It is standard in classes in spoken Hebrew, as well as in secular scholarship and at British and American universities.

Furthermore, not only Sephardi and progressive synagogues (Liberal and Reform) but also Masorti ones and even some constituents of the United Synagogue, at least in part, use the Sephardi pronunciation, especially for Torah reading.

Possibly a greater justification for transliterating Hebrew according to the Sephardi pronunciation is that it is almost always the same irrespective of the speaker. This is not the case for the Ashkenazi pronunciation of Hebrew, which varies depending on the tradition of a community and the origin of the speaker.

List of Hebrew terms

Aliyah (plural *aliyot*): Literally 'going up'. Used to refer to emigration to Israel and also to those called up to the *bimah* (q.v.) to recite blessings before and after the reading of the Torah.

Ark: A cupboard in which the scrolls are placed.

Ashkenazi: Literally 'German' but used to refer to Jews from central or Eastern Europe and the way in which they pronounce Hebrew.

Bar Mitzvah: Literally 'son of the commandment'. Ceremony marking the time at which boys become responsible for their actions in Jewish law, usually

13. Reform and Liberal synagogues add another ceremony at the age of 16, Confirmation.

Bat Mitzvah: As above, usually at 12, for girls. These ceremonies do not take place in the more orthodox synagogues. Some synagogues have ceremonies for girls but they do not have the same status.

Bekeshes (Ashkenazi): Long black coats usually made of silk worn by Hassidic Jews.

Beth Din: Literally 'house of judgement'. Used to refer to a court that adjudicates on Jewish law. In Orthodox Judaism, a *Beth Din* consists of three observant Jewish men, at least one of whom is knowledgeable in *halachah* (q.v.).

Bimah: Literally 'high place'. Used to refer to the reading desk in a synagogue and the platform on which the desk stands.

B'nai Mitzvah: Plural of *Bar* or *Bat Mitzvah* or both.

Challah (plural *challot*): Plaited bread loaf, used to welcome *Shabbat* (q.v.) and festivals.

Chametz: Leavened products, which are forbidden at *Pesach* (q.v.).

Chanukkah: Literally 'dedication'. The eight-day midwinter Festival of Lights commemorating the rededication of the Temple of the Maccabees.

Chanukkiah: A candleholder used for celebrating *Chanukkah* with eight branches, often with a ninth for the servant candle (*shamash*) used to light the other candles.

Chazzan: Cantor.

Cheder: Literally 'room'. Used to refer to a religion school for younger children.

Chevra (plural *chevrot*): A small congregation, frequently established by Jews of Eastern European origin.

Frum (Yiddish): Literally 'observant'. Used to refer to strictly orthodox Jews.

Gemach (plural *gemachim*): Organised act of kindness.

Glatt kosher: The technical definition of *glatt* kosher is meat from animals with defect-free lungs, but glatt is often applied to products that have been processed under the stricter standard of *kashrut* set by the licensing body Kedassia than by the other licensing bodies.

Halachah: Literally 'the way of going'. Used to refer to Jewish law.

Haredi (plural *haredim*): A relatively recent umbrella term for describing Jews who are very punctilious about their Judaism. Its literal meaning is 'the fearful' or 'trembling in the face of God'.

Hassid (plural *Hassidim*): Member of a sect originating in Eastern Europe.

Heimische: Literally 'homely'. Often used as an alternative to *frum* (q.v.).

High Holydays: *Rosh Hashanah* (Jewish New Year; q.v.) and *Yom Kippur* (Day of Atonement; q.v.).

Ivrit: Modern Hebrew spoken in Israel.

Kashrut: Jewish dietary laws.

Kiddush (plural *kiddushim*): The act of declaring a day as holy, accompanied with wine and food.

Kippah (plural *kippot*): Skullcap. Sometimes *cappel* or *yarmulke*.

Kollel (plural *kollelim*): Literally 'collection'. Used for full-time or part-time advanced study for married men.

Kosher: English version of Ashkenazi Hebrew word *kasher* meaning 'fit'. Used to mean food that adheres to Jewish dietary laws.

Mechitza: A screen separating men and women in an orthodox synagogue.

Mikveh (plural *mikvaot*): Ritual bath.

Minyan (plural *minyanim*): A prayer meeting. See appendix for details.

Ner Tamid: Perpetual light that burns above the ark (q.v.) in a synagogue.

Nusach: Form of prayers.

Pesach: Passover, the festival celebrating the freedom gained for Jews with the Exodus from Egypt.

Peyot: Sidelocks worn by some men and boys based on an interpretation of the Biblical injunction against shaving the 'corners' of one's head. There are different styles of *peyot* for Yemenite and Hassidic Jews.

Purim: Literally 'lots'. Minor festival remembering the events described in the book of Esther telling how the Jews were saved from persecution.

Rosh Hashanah: Jewish New Year.

Seder: Literally 'order'. The name of the service for the first night of *Pesach* (q.v.) taking place in Jewish homes using symbolic foods. Orthodox Jews outside Israel observe two nights.

Sefer Torah (plural *sifrei* Torah): Scrolls of the Pentateuch.

Sephardi: 'Spanish'. Used to describe Jews who come from the countries around the Mediterranean and from Islamic countries and to their pronunciation of Hebrew.

Shabbat: Sabbath.

Shacharit: Early morning service.

Shadchan: Matchmaker.

Sheitel (Yiddish): Wig.

Shidduch (Aramaic; plural *shiduchim*): Marital match.

Shiur (plural *shiurim*): Study session.

Shofar: Literally 'ram's horn'. Shaped into a musical instrument that is blown at *Rosh Hashanah* (see High Holydays).

Shtiebl (plural *shtieblech*): Small house of worship. See appendix.

Shtreimel (plural *streimlech*) Fur hats worn by Hassidic Jews from Galicia, Rumania and Hungary. Hassidic Jews from Poland wear spodniks.

Shul (Yiddish): Universal term for synagogue. Used by both Sephardi and Ashkenazi Jews.

Simcha (plural *s'machot*): Celebration, e.g. a *Bar Mitzvah* (q.v.).

Simchat Torah: Literally 'rejoicing'. The festival for celebrating the end of the cycle of scroll readings and the beginning of the new cycle at the end of *Sukkot* (q.v.).

Sukkah: The booths in which some Jews eat and sleep during *Sukkot* (q.v.).

Sukkot: The seven-day harvest festival.

Tallit (plural *tallitot*): Prayer shawl.

Talmud Torah: Schools at which Jewish children are given an elementary education in Hebrew, the scriptures (especially Pentateuch), and the Talmud (boys only) and *halachah* (q.v.).

Tzittzit: Fringes attached to the four corners of the *tallit* (q.v.).

Yeshivah (plural *yeshivot*): A place of study for young Jewish men.

Yom Kippur: Day of Atonement, occurring ten days after Jewish New Year.

About the Author

PAM FOX is an experienced writer living in Golders Green. Surrounded by the history and vibrancy of the Jewish community, she has been inspired to write about its history. In 2008 she conducted a study on the experience of women rabbis, and in 2000 started work on the hundred-year history of the Liberal Jewish Synagogue, which was featured at Jewish Book Week in 2011. During 2012 she contributed to a guide to Jewish London.

Pam is a Research Fellow at Leo Baeck College and in 2014 was awarded a prestigious month-long Fellowship at Hebrew Union College in Cincinnati. Her most recent publication is a biography of Israel Mattuck, which has been favourably reviewed in several journals, including the journal for the Jewish Historical Society of England, the top Jewish history periodical, and nominated for an award by the Jewish Book Council in the US. Pam has spoken at many events and venues about her work.

Sketches by Beverley-Jane Stewart

Plates

The Growth of Golders Green

Historically the hamlet of Golders Green[1] was located in the county of Middlesex and formed part of the manor of Hendon. The name Golders derived from the Godyere family who lived in the area, and Green alludes to the manorial 'waste' (common land) on which the settlement was built.[2] It was established by the time of John Roque's survey of Middlesex in 1756 but was little more than a cluster of cottages and a farm, with the small Brent brook forming its northern boundary. By the end of the eighteenth century several large houses, 'ornamental villas surrounded with plantations', had been erected built with bricks made in the area.[3] It was a place to which people like the poet Arcencide came to convalesce and the artist John Constable visited to capture its idyllic scenery.[4] The earliest reference to adjacent Temple Fortune is on a map of 1754,[5] although the name suggests that its history predates this. The 'Temple' possibly refers to the Knights Templar, a Christian military order holding land in the area in the thirteenth century. 'Fortune' means a small settlement.[6]

The only major change to take place in Golders Green during the nineteenth century was the building of Finchley Road in 1830, upgrading Ducksetters Lane to connect Childs Hill, Golders Green and Finchley. The enclosure of common land commencing in the previous century gathered pace and from the 1880s horse-drawn buses served Golders Green. Towards the end of the century, a laundry and a small hospital for children with skin diseases opened. Given future developments, it is also notable that West London (Reform) Synagogue, in association with the Sephardi community,[7] opened a Jewish cemetery in Hoop Lane in 1895. Changes in Temple Fortune were limited to the opening of a public house, the Royal Oak, and the building of two rows of cottages for labourers in the local brickworks.[8]

At the turn of the twentieth century Golders Green was still a settlement of fewer than 300 people, mainly farmers, farm workers and well-to-do landowners. It lay at the centre of a large tract of undeveloped land and was a place 'where there are roses in the hedgerows and the larks are singing … a place almost unique in its rural character'.[9] Apart from the opening of a crematorium in Hoop Lane in 1902, the only events worthy of reporting in the local newspaper were rick fires, burglaries at the large houses in the area, and horse-stealing in fields bordering the main roads.[10]

The expansion of London had reached the fringes of Hampstead Heath with the settlement of Childs Hill and Cricklewood but the so-called 'Northern Heights' of the Heath had so far protected Golders Green from development by hindering railway traffic.

This protection was not to last much longer; within a few years Golders Green would be transformed from a rural oasis to a bustling suburb. The first portents of change occurred between 1903 and 1905 when gas lamps were installed along Finchley Road and hoardings appeared, advertising land for building purposes. Even more indicative of the transformation about to take place was the announcement that the Underground Electric Railways Company of London Ltd had acquired a large parcel of land in the area for a station. As a contemporary remarked: 'thus the stage was set for one of the most amazing and dramatic developments known in England'.[11]

In 1893 the construction of an underground railway from Charing Cross to Hampstead had been approved by Parliament but the scheme did not proceed due to lack of capital. In 1900 an American syndicate led by the financier Charles Tyson Yerkes[12] revived the plans. Having surveyed the route, the syndicate decided to continue the line from Hampstead to the open area north of the Heath where there was space for car sheds and sidings. From his experience in America, Yerkes was aware of the development opportunities that might abound if the settlements beyond the station were to be connected to it by 'electric cars'. Applications were therefore made to Parliament for both the railway extension and the construction of tramways linking Hendon and Finchley to the new station. Even before the outcome of the applications had been announced, the Finchley Road and Golders Green Syndicate led by Yerkes was formed to develop the fields in the event of the proposals being endorsed.

The railway extension from Hampstead to Golders Green was authorised in November 1902; the tramway scheme was not. Construction of the line commenced almost immediately but the tunnelling was not completed until spring 1906. The line from Charing Cross (later Strand) was opened on 22 June 1907 by the President of the Board of Trade, David Lloyd George. For sixteen years Golders Green station remained the terminus of the 'Hampstead Tube', later a branch of the Northern Line. Initially two-car trains left the station every twelve minutes from early in the morning until after midnight,[13] taking twenty-four minutes to reach Charing Cross. Traffic was heaviest on Sundays when inner-city residents travelled to Golders Green to enjoy the rural atmosphere and the local hostelries. During the first year after the station opened, 1.2 million passengers used Golders Green terminus. By 1914 the total was over 10 million.[14]

Soon after the construction of the railway commenced, estate agents were at work promoting the sale of land for building purposes; these included Ernest Owers, who became a legendary figure locally.[15] Land ownership in the area was concentrated in just a few hands: to the north of the station lay the Beddington estate astride what is now Bridge Lane, and to the east was an extensive tract owned by the Eton College

Golders Green station
Beverley-Jane Stewart

Trustees on which Hampstead Garden Suburb was built. To the south of the station, the Ecclesiastical Commissioners were the main landowners. There were also less substantial land holdings such as those around Woodstock House close to Bridge Lane. As a result of the railway construction, agricultural land that had formerly sold for £150 to £250 an acre soon increased in value eightfold or more.[16] Even before the station had opened, land nearby was sold for shops at £5,500 an acre, while building plots in the same area were changing hands for £10,000 an acre.[17] As the development gained momentum, parcels of land were sub-divided and sold in smaller and smaller lots, which were resold within a few days, often at a considerable profit. Witnessing the profits to be made, some of the owners of large houses sold their property for substantial sums.

The estate agents worked closely with local developers such as Sir Edwin Evans, 'the Napoleon of suburban development', and builders including Edward Streather, who, in partnership with William Turner, built thousands of houses in Golders Green.[18] In 1905 the first new house was completed at the corner of what became Hoop Lane and Wentworth Road (35 Hoop Lane).[19] Work began on 85.5 acres

Golders Green Station

near Woodstock House in 1906 where The Grove, The Drive and parts of Highfield Avenue and Woodstock Avenue were laid out. The following year the Finchley Road and Golders Green Syndicate began building housing south of Temple Fortune, including Templars Avenue and Wentworth Road. Work also started on the Ecclesiastical Commissioner's land where Hodford Road and Rodborough Road were built.[20] In 1909 Golders Lodge was demolished to make way for Golders Gardens, Gainsborough Gardens, and Powis Gardens.[21] While seventy-three houses were ready for habitation in 1907, the following year 340 houses were placed on the market. The rapid development of the suburb reached a peak in 1911 when 744 houses were built.[22] The editor of the *Golders Green Gazette* complained that 'all day long there is continuous hammering which reminds one of distant thunder'.[23] The growth of Golders Green continued well into the First World War,[24] and after a brief hiatus soon picked up again once the conflict was over.

Prospective purchasers and tourists came to marvel at the new houses and in 1911 the *Evening News* published a full-page spread on Golders Green. It included advertisements from several estate agencies selling houses in eight locations in the new suburb at prices ranging from £400 to £1,000. The houses were generally large for speculatively built properties and relatively expensive compared to those in nearby Childs Hill because of the dramatic escalation in land values in the area. The estate agents emphasised the quality of the housing. Half-timbered, tiled, gabled and 'cottagey' in appearance, the rustic design of the new houses set the trend for suburban dwellings for the next three decades.[25]

However, no overall plan was drawn up for developing Golders Green and there was little local authority control of its design or layout beyond requirements on road widths, drainage and compliance with basic building bye-laws. The shape of development was largely determined by land ownership and the desire by speculative builders to build as many houses as possible on a plot of land. The rather haphazard evolution of Golders Green was very different from the carefully laid out Hampstead Garden Suburb being constructed nearby, and this lack of planning was to lead to problems. When the extension of the railway line from Golders Green to Edgware was constructed in the early 1920s, a number of residential roads had to be blocked off and twenty-five houses in Woodstock Avenue, barely ten years old, were demolished.[26]

2

The First Jewish Inhabitants

Even before the opening of the Hampstead Tube, there were Jews living in Golders Green. The very first Jewish resident was Joseph Joel Duveen, a well-known art dealer and benefactor. He was born in Meppel in Holland, which he left in 1866 to settle in Hull. Starting as a general dealer, he later turned to and gained almost a monopoly on sales of Old Masters and *objets de vertu* from private European collections to the burgeoning American millionaire market. In partnership with his brother he opened fine art galleries in Oxford Street and Bond Street and also in New York. As his wealth grew, he bequeathed several paintings to public galleries.[1] He was knighted in 1908 shortly before his death. From about 1890 he lived with his wife and ten children in a large house, The Hawthorns, close to the crossroads of Finchley Road and Golders Green Road.[2] This house and its grounds were purchased by the estate agent Ernest Owers and the first shops in Golders Green, The Parade, were built here.[3]

Samuel Wolff was probably the next Jew to arrive in Golders Green. He was born in Stepney but came to the area with his family from West Ham, where he had worked as a tailor's assistant,[4] to become the superintendent of the Jewish cemetery in Hoop Lane. There was then a pause until after the opening of Golders Green station, when Jews started arriving in increasing numbers. Some histories have suggested that the early Jewish arrivals to the rapidly developing suburb came from the East End of London.[5] However, a detailed analysis of the 1911 census reveals a more complicated picture. The first wave of Jews who came to live in the new suburb in fact came from across London (Stoke Newington, St Pancras, Brondesbury, Willesden and Kilburn), and from provincial cities like Grimsby and Newcastle.

What is particularly interesting is that several of the first Jewish residents of Golders Green were central European in origin – from Germany, Austria and Hungary – who either settled directly in the new suburb or who had moved there having previously lived elsewhere in England. They were mainly traders and business people.[6] There were also a few families who had recently arrived from Eastern Europe, including the eminent scholar Dr Samuel Max Melamed, Jacob Jossern, an artificial teeth manufacturer and a costumier, Philip Kerner.

The families who came from other parts of London included successful traders such as Isidor Keizer, a shoe-trimming manufacturer, who had been born in the City of London but who had lived in Willesden before moving to Golders Green. The music-hall artiste Harry Simms, who had previously lived in Brondesbury, bought a house he named Mizpah (look-out point) in Hamilton Road. While some of the first Jewish inhabitants had come to stay, including Carl Klippstein (later Charles Clipstone), a gentleman's tailor, others were temporary residents, including the barrister Israel Isidore Rubinovitz, who boarded with a family in Golders Gardens. Some early Jewish residents had clearly been attracted by the development activity, including the building contractor Harry Abraham Bernstein, who came to the area from the north-east of England and Sidney Cohen, a house decorator from Essex.[7]

The first Jewish residents of Golders Green were mostly middle class and somewhat different from the small number of Jews who soon started to relocate to the area from the East End of London. By 1910 the Raeburn brothers had opened a hosiery store in Golders Green Road,[8] and Lewis Bercovitz had moved his boot-making dealership from Mile End to The Parade.[9]

However, it was not until the First World War that Jews moved to the area from the East End in significant numbers. Those who did so were mainly the anglicised children or grandchildren of Eastern European Jews who had settled in the East End from the 1880s. They had been educated in English schools, where they had associated with non-Jews and wider social aspirations had penetrated their world.[10] This wave of Jewish arrivals from the East End is said to have been made up of the most affluent, ambitious and determined Jews, who had managed to amass enough capital to secure a comfortable suburban home and were intent on climbing the social ladder.[11] At this time the majority of the East End Jews had neither the means nor the inclination to make the move. The older generation in particular preferred to remain with their families and familiar institutions.

What drew the East End families to Golders Green was the plentiful supply of new housing, which was advertised in the *Jewish Chronicle* as early as 1913.[12] While houses in Golders Green were not inexpensive, they were significantly more affordable than those available in nearby Hampstead and St John's Wood. Some of the early arrivals from the East End were people who had prospered during the war.[13] They purchased some of the large properties in West Heath Drive and other roads adjacent to Golders Hill Park.[14] Those who were not quite so wealthy settled in the new roads to the west of Finchley Road.

Equally important in attracting East End Jews to Golders Green was the station. While a few of the new inhabitants brought with them their trades and professions, initially most travelled daily to inner London to their places of work. The train line also allowed the new residents to stay in touch with family and friends remaining in the East End. The immigrant Jews with their Eastern European ways still settling in the East End may have been an embarrassment to those with the means to make it out of the semi-ghetto, but the new suburban dwellers were not willing to relinquish all of their ties to the area.

Another factor making Golders Green desirable for upwardly mobile East End Jews was the reputation it had speedily gained for the bourgeois respectability to

Beverley-Jane Stewart.   Trams in Finchley Road c. 1915

which the migrants aspired. In 1922 a Royal Commissioner remarked that 'there are some very superior people in Golders Green'.[15] This judgement is confirmed by a review of the 1911 census and street directories for the period. These show that the early residents of Golders Green included many people of independent means, army and naval officers, people with titles, Members of Parliament, Justices of the Peace, doctors and surgeons. Theatrical people including Madame Pavlova, Marie Lloyd and Harry Tate also found Golders Green a convenient place in which to live.

While there were several 'pull' factors drawing Jews to the new suburb, there were also some 'push' factors, the most pressing of which was the increasingly overcrowded and insanitary nature of the East End. Many of the migrants had previously lived in multi-occupancy houses and had dreamed of having a modern home with its own garden. The desire to live in more salubrious surroundings increased during the First World War when the East End was badly damaged by enemy bombing. In addition, the discriminatory 'anti-alien' policies of the London County Council (LCC) had been making it difficult for Jews to obtain housing, education and employment.[16] As Golders Green was situated outside the LCC area, these discriminatory restrictions did not apply.

It is significant that the first Jews to arrive in Golders Green were moving to an area that had not previously been settled to any great extent. It meant that they did not have to carve out an existence alongside an existing non-Jewish community but were able to fashion the lifestyle they were seeking. When they arrived in Golders Green, the former East Enders did not recreate the working-class Yiddish culture with which they had grown up in the East End. However, most of the new residents were not seeking to abandon their faith and Jewish businesses in adjacent areas soon benefited from their presence. As early as 1910 J. Richards of St John's Wood was delivering Passover milk to Golders Green and J. Buckingham & Sons had set up a small local office in Golders Green Road to sell Passover milk.[17] Initially observant Jews used the synagogues in Brondesbury or Hampstead. Maria Alice Philips (née Westell), whose family was among the first to come to Golders Green, recalled walking to Hampstead Synagogue during the First World War despite the aircraft guns on Hampstead Heath firing at German Zeppelins.[18] As the community grew, plans were made to develop a synagogue closer to home but it was not until 1922 that these plans came to fruition and Golders Green Synagogue opened in Dunstan Road.[19]

Not all of the Jews who settled in Golders Green was religiously inclined. In 1917 Dr William Feldman, living in Finchley Road, wrote to the *Jewish Chronicle* protesting that unaffiliated Jews were not represented on the Board of Deputies of British Jews.[20] Pearl Pollack recalled that 'the other Jews in the street were very friendly but none of them kept the Sabbath – we were the only people in the road that did'.[21] As early as 1916 the *Jewish Chronicle* was rebuking Jewish residents of Golders Green for their lack of observance.[22]

The Jewish community was barely established when the First World War commenced. Before 1910 there was just a handful of Jews living in Golders Green, but by 1915 it was estimated that there were 300 Jewish households.[23] Notwithstanding this growth, they saw themselves as 'we Jews of quiet, secluded Golders Green'.[24] Some of the British-born Jewish men who had recently arrived in Golders Green signed up for the armed forces and lost their lives fighting for their country, including 23-year-old Joseph Lewis, whose family lived in Finchley Road. He was killed in action in January 1917.[25]

3

The Community Becomes Established

In 1923 it was estimated that the population of Golders Green was around 10,000, three times what it had been when the underground station opened in 1907. By 1925 an average of 227,000 passengers were using Golders Green station each week.[1] Previously cut off from surrounding areas, at the end of the 1920s Golders Green was connected to a network of major roads. The Hendon section of the North Circular Road was built in 1925.

The rapid growth of the suburb created attendant problems. Hendon Urban District Council (later Hendon Borough Council), which covered Golders Green, struggled to provide adequate sewage facilities for the expanding population.[2] There were frequent complaints about the state of the local roads, which were often 'ankle-deep in mud' because of the building works.[3] Motorists speeding along Golders Green Road became 'a menace',[4] and once the area gained a reputation as an affluent neighbourhood there was a spate of domestic burglaries to which many of the new homes were vulnerable because they backed on to open space.[5]

It was not until the mid-1920s that the Jewish community of Golders Green became firmly rooted in the area. The opening of Golders Green Synagogue in 1922 had made the growth of the Jewish community almost inevitable. In a long-established pattern of Jewish settlement, family members and friends followed those who had already moved to Golders Green. Regular advertisements appeared in the *Jewish Chronicle* specifically encouraging Jewish people to move to Golders Green, 'London's Suburb de Luxe'. They emphasised the area's amenities – its shopping facilities, the Tube service to central London and open spaces – and drew attention to the new synagogue and 'the influential Jewish community'.[6]

The main aim of Jews arriving in Golders Green from the East End was to become part of the community as quickly as possible. They did not want to discuss their origins.[7] This reticence trickled down to the next generation. Selina Gellert remembers that her father, who came to Golders Green with his parents in the early 1920s, never mentioned his parents' origins: 'There were no romantic tales of life in the East End'.[8]

Golders Green
Road in the 1920s

Living alongside Jewish migrants from the East End and from other parts of London, there were now increasing numbers of Jews arriving from Eastern Europe, creating a diverse community. Jocelyne Tobin (née Prevezer) recalls that when they married, her parents, who both originated from Poland, lived in Highbury. After a few years they moved to Golders Green. While the Prevezer family was upwardly mobile, they felt like recent immigrants compared with some of their indigenous neighbours. However, they were also aware of differences between British-born Jewish families: 'some families from the East End were still quite *Yiddishe*'.[9] It was these differences that probably led to a demand for the elocution classes available in Golders Green advertised at this time in the *Jewish Chronicle* by Beatrice Lewisohn and others. A typical advertisement read: 'receives pupils in elocution, voice projection ... special classes for juveniles'.[10] It appears that there was considerable social pressure on the new arrivals to tone down the conspicuous foreignness of their backgrounds.[11]

Although the growing Jewish community was generally ambitious, it was not without its scandals. In 1910 the *Golders Green Gazette* covered the story of Alexander Sharrot, a tailor living at 4 The Parade, who was accused of assaulting the wife of his business partner, Morris Gold. Both parties only spoke Yiddish and relied on interpreters when the matter came to court.[12] In the 1920s a furrier living in The Ridgeway was charged with conspiring to defraud his creditors;[13] Joseph Geiger was granted a divorce against his wife for her infidelity with a neighbour;[14]

and Annie Abrahams, who had left her music-hall artiste husband Alfred Abrahams to live in The Vale with another music-hall artiste, poisoned herself.[15]

Jewish families welcomed the social elevation represented by living in Golders Green. Some of the houses they inhabited were large enough to accommodate a maid, but most were only able at this time to afford occasional domestic help. However, more affluent Jewish households, such as the Townley family who moved to Templars Avenue from South London during the 1920s, employed a live-in maid. She was paid 7s 6d per week and had one afternoon off a week and every other Sunday.[16] Mrs Essex, whose family had moved from Stoke Newington to Sneath Avenue, remembered a maid employed by her mother:

> She came from a comfortable Jewish home in Cricklewood. Her mother had died and her father wouldn't allow her out without a chaperone. She came to work for us and mother being a *Yiddishe* [typically Jewish] mother, got her married off to the man who came to deliver groceries.[17]

By the end of the 1920s employing a maid, and sometimes a nanny, had become more commonplace, even among those families for whom it was a financial struggle, such as Reverend and Mrs Livingstone who employed a maid because they were busy developing Golders Green Synagogue.[18] The maids employed in Jewish households (and middle-class homes generally) often came from the north-east of England where many families had been impoverished by declining wages in the coalfields and sought work wherever it was available.[19]

When they moved to Golders Green, the new residents quickly recognised that some of their values and mannerisms were inappropriate for suburban living. One could no longer cross the road wearing an apron or hang out washing on Sundays. On their arrival in Golders Green, some Jewish households changed the names of the rooms in which they lived: 'We had a sitting room in South London; in Golders Green we had a drawing room'.[20] Notwithstanding the advantages of life in Golders Green, residents sometimes missed the communal atmosphere of the East End: 'it was only when shopping along the Golders Green Parade or when you passed people in their gardens that you actually got to talk to people'.[21] Some families specifically chose not to live in Golders Green because they felt it lacked the vibrancy of the East End:

> We had relations who were looking to move out of the East End and went to visit Golders Green. They saw the open fields, the foundations still being dug for new houses and the lack of employment opportunities and decided it was not for them. Golders Green got crossed off the list and they moved to South London instead.[22]

As the Jewish community expanded, it became possible to consider the establishment of more facilities to support Jewish life, including a kosher butcher.[23] Until then the growing community had been dependent on butchers in surrounding areas such as Barnett's in West Hampstead,[24] and Walsman's in Willesden Lane. However, even after Mr Nathan opened his butcher's shop in North End Road, some families preferred to rely on familiar establishments in the East End.[25]

It was to be several years before all of the services required by observant Jews were available but families found ways of following Jewish traditions despite the dearth of communal facilities. Sometimes assistance in keeping *Shabbat* came from unlikely sources, such as the milkman who delivered milk around Golders Green on a horse-drawn carriage. As a side-line, he lit the gas under the Sabbath kettles for several Jewish families in the area.[26] Other households employed 'housemen' who purchased food on Saturdays for them.[27]

Although Golders Green had seen remarkable development after the opening of the station and many areas of formerly open space had disappeared under a tidal wave of bricks and mortar, there was still a considerable amount of agricultural land that was not built over for another decade. Mrs Sussman, who moved with her parents to Golders Green from the East End in 1927, remembered in her childhood carrying a jug up a track to Hodford Farm to buy milk during *Pesach* (Passover),[28] and Pearl Pollack recollected walking with her father on Saturday afternoons in the open fields adjacent to what is now Hendon Way.[29] The artist Abram Games later recalled that when his family moved to The Vale, there were still green fields opposite the recently erected synagogue in Dunstan Road,[30] across which calls could be heard for the daily *minyan* (prayer meeting).[31] Similarly, although by 1930 Golders Green was already noted for its substantial Jewish population, the community was set to increase even further and become more diverse.

4

Before the Second World War

During the 1930s Golders Green continued to grow and prosper. A number of prestigious properties were completed in roads such as Gloucester Gardens. Most of the remaining large villas were replaced with semi-detached houses or mansion blocks, including Brook Lodge and the Roman-styled Eagle Lodge.[1] The luxury apartment block, Riverside Drive, replaced a row of cottages called Chatterbox Row.[2] The suburbanisation of Temple Fortune also proceeded apace. Work was now complete on Eastfield Crescent, Park Way, and Cranbourne Gardens.

The houses in Cranbourne Gardens were large, some of them being individually designed for Jewish clients such as the Selmans, who commissioned a house to be built on the corner of Cranbourne Gardens and Leeside Crescent.[3] Work started in 1934 on The Pantiles, a Mediterranean-Moderne-style apartment block in Finchley Road.[4]

By the early 1930s more than 600 trains a day were passing through Golders Green station and the local electorate stood at 10,884.[5] The population of the area was becoming increasingly vocal and expressing the need for various amenities and forms of entertainment. The Golders Green Chamber of Commerce demanded: 'we want putting on the map'.[6] These cries were heeded: Golders Green library opened in 1935 and by the mid-1930s there were several cinemas.[7] A *Jewish Chronicle* article declared that 'few districts on the brink of London offer more attractions to houseseekers than Golders Green' and noted that a large proportion of the 'exquisite' properties with 'every possible labour-saving contrivance' had been purchased by Jewish families.[8]

The 1930s saw the rise to power of Hitler and the consequent persecution of Jews in Germany and elsewhere. Britain did not open its arms unreservedly to Jewish refugees fleeing the Nazi regime, but it did allow some 60,000 Jews from Germany, Austria and Czechoslovakia to settle in Britain along with 50,000 Jews from Poland and elsewhere in Eastern Europe. Approximately 10,000 unaccompanied Kindertransport children were rescued just before the outbreak of war.[9] Under the restrictions of the 1919 Aliens' Act the refugees were required to have sponsors willing to provide a guarantee of £250 (later raised to £500) so that they would not be a financial burden on the state.

Those who came as refugees to Britain from Germany and other central European countries (referred to as 'the continental Jews') mainly settled directly in north-west London, bypassing the increasingly well-trodden immigrant routes through the capital. The synagogues already established in Golders Green initially worked with national bodies supporting the continental refugees but soon founded local organisations for channelling their efforts. While a large proportion of the continental Jews found accommodation in Hampstead, Swiss Cottage and Belsize Park, a significant number came to Golders Green, usually due to family connections and friendships. Golders Green was dubbed the 'Fourth Reich' and, according to one refugee, on its streets:

> One heard more 'Guten Tags' and 'Danke schöns' than their English equivalents. And since it was raining often, the careful German Jews always wore their raincoats, which were a good deal longer than those the Londoners wore. The story went that an indigenous Golders Greener had decided that German refugees wore such long coats because they wanted to deprive Hitler of as much cloth as possible so he could make fewer uniforms.[10]

The continental Jews arriving in Golders Green before 1938 generally fared well. A significant proportion were well-to-do professionals, business people and artists who brought with them the resources to buy comfortable homes and to establish themselves economically despite the controls placed on their activities by various professional bodies.[11] A large proportion of the newcomers were well educated and had been highly assimilated in the countries that they had left. Adjusting to new surroundings was not always a smooth process, but the continental Jews generally experienced less difficulty in integrating to English lifestyles than Eastern European Jews had a generation earlier. Many of the continental Jews settling in Golders Green already spoke English. Some of those who did not were aided by the English lessons provided by members of the North-Western Reform Synagogue, which was established in 1933.[12] Rosa Freedman, who led the initiative, later recalled:

> I myself gave a short course in English and at the first class two people turned up – a mother of 70 and her son of 40. Three days later, word had got around and (to my astonishment) fifty German-Jewish refugees turned up. From then on the work snowballed.[13]

By the summer of 1939 over 300 people were attending the synagogue daily for English lessons.[14]

The existing Jewish residents of Golders Green were aware of the differences between themselves and the newcomers:

> Amongst my classmates were Dolly and Harry, refugees from Germany. The Germans were very different culturally both from recent immigrants like my

family who had come from Eastern Europe and the families who had moved from
the East End. The Polish Jews had expected discrimination, that is what they had
grown used to in Poland, but not so the German Jews.[15]

Some of the refugees had belonged to progressive synagogues. On their arrival they
joined either West London Synagogue or the more local North-Western Reform
Synagogue, where they were influential in shaping the congregation.[16] Some were
more traditional in their religious outlook and joined Golders Green Synagogue.
Others had belonged to the prominent orthodox synagogues in Germany and in 1933
a group of strictly observant continental refugees started to meet for religious purposes
and were prominent in forming the Golders Green Beth Hamedrash.[17] Tensions
developed between Golders Green Synagogue (now known as 'Dunstan Road') and
the new orthodox community. Harry Wasser, a member of Dunstan Road Synagogue
who sometimes attended services at the Beth Hamedrash, commented: 'they would
only greet you if you had been born in Frankfurt'.[18] However, as time passed the
different communities became more tolerant of each other's religious perspectives and
the new Golders Green synagogues to the left and right of the 'United' synagogue in
Dunstan Road contributed to the establishment of pluralism in Anglo-Jewry.

   As well as making their mark on the religious life of the local community, the
presence of the continental Jews was reflected in other ways. Hendon Library Service
reported that, in addition to indigenous German writers, translation into German
of the works of such writers as Joseph Conrad, John Galsworthy, Dostoevsky, and
Upton Sinclair were eagerly read by the German members of the newly opened
Golders Green library.[19] The refugees were obviously settling and seeking to engage
with the host culture. Their willingness to integrate may have created the sympathy
that led to the founding in 1934 of the Golders Green Women's Shoppers' League,
which organised the boycotting of German goods and produce.[20]

   What had started as a selective emigration of the intellectual aristocracy and
wealthy families became a mass flight of Jews from Germany. Until March 1938,
when Hitler seized Vienna, the continental refugees coming to Golders Green
were largely from Germany but now they fled in great numbers from Austria,
bringing with them their unmistakeable culture.[21] Eight months later, after the
commencement of a campaign of sustained brutality that followed *Kristallnacht*,[22]
German Jews started to leave *en masse*, mostly headed for north-west London, often
helped by friends and family already living in London such as the Sachs family, who
'spent every penny they had helping relatives restart their lives in the UK'.[23]

   This fresh influx of refugees struggled to a much greater extent to make a living
and to integrate than those who had arrived earlier. Due to restrictions now imposed
by the Nazi regime, they often arrived penniless and British government constraints
on their activities were now much more stringent.[24] Refugee autobiographies
record the difficulties they experienced in adapting to unfamiliar clothes, climate
and customs. The inedibility of the food is also a common theme. Marcelle
Robinson (née Schidowski), whose family came to Golders Green early in 1939,

recalls heating facilities as 'sub-standard' and 'primitive' and that the English seemed to subsist mainly on a diet of cabbage.[25]

The continental refugees could not forget their middle-class backgrounds and preferred a bed-sitting room with a gas ring in a bourgeois neighbourhood like Golders Green to cheaper and roomier accommodation in less well-to-do parts of London.[26] Often living in cramped accommodation, many of the new arrivals had no way of occupying themselves other than to promenade or congregate in public places, lending Golders Green a 'Mitteleuropean' atmosphere and making their numbers appear greater than they were in reality. As the presence of the refugees became more obvious, it gave rise to witticisms regarding the 'Germanisation' of the area; for example, that the British would be prepared to return colonies to Germany if Germany would return Golders Green to England.[27]

Correspondence between Neville Laski, President of the Board of Deputies, and Lord Rothschild in 1939 suggests that, while the continental Jews were greeted with intense compassion, the indigenous Jews were not always comfortable with their Germanic ways. Laski wrote that the Jews of Golders Green had 'a strongly critical attitude to the refugees' and sought to control 'their undesirable Teutonic excesses'.[28] The refugees, who were able to speak up for themselves, occasionally mentioned that the rooms in which they were staying were not quite what they had been accustomed to. They were somewhat taken aback by the reaction this occasionally created. They thought it ironic that people whose parents and grandparents had worked as cabinet-makers and tailors should view it as 'uppity-ness' when former judges and lawyers said they did not like working as servants.[29]

Once the British Jewish Refugee Committee had managed to convince the government to admit children aged 5–17 into the country, adverts were placed in the *Jewish Chronicle* by Jewish families living in Golders Green seeking temporary homes for children from the recently occupied countries of Europe. One advert read:

> Which family would give a home to two Viennese children, girls, aged 14, 10 years, very well educated, speak English and French. Photographs and references willingly sent. Write to Ulman, 31, Dunstan Road, Golders Green, London.[30]

Life was very hard for the unaccompanied young people arriving in Golders Green but even when families arrived together they were sometimes separated. Marian Kreindler and her mother came to Golders Green from Breslau in March 1939. Marian was sent almost immediately to a children's home in Highbury and was only able to see her mother on Sundays, which was a 'terrible wrench'.[31] Renate Daus came on the Kindertransport to live with the Rabson family in Basing Hill in February 1939 just before her 9th birthday. She had been separated from her brother, who was sent to a Christian home outside London, and her 3-year-old sister, who was taken to the Wellgarth nursery training school in North End Road. Their parents escaped from Germany on the eve of war but were interned soon after their arrival.[32]

However, most young people were made to feel welcome. Rachel Konigsberg left Poland for Golders Green in 1938 and found accommodation with family friends, the Jacobs, who lived in The Vale. They were 'a very English family' and 'a religious family'. They arranged for her to attend school locally until the war broke out.[33] Lola Rodin, who lived in Temple Fortune, recalls young refugee girls being taken in by the Caplan family who lived nearby. One of them, Ilse, who came from a wealthy family in Austria, later married into that family.[34] Nicolas Reis, who came to Golders Green on the Kindertransport, was cared for by the Kohn family who lived in Ashbourne Avenue. Although he initially found the country cold and damp, he was delighted by the sights around him and soon forgot about Berlin. Having been taken to cricket and the amusement arcades of Oxford Street he was 'glad but not terribly overjoyed' to be reunited with his mother a year later.[35]

Some Golders Green families would have liked to have cared for refugee children but found themselves prevented from doing so. Placements were mainly arranged by the local synagogues that were sometimes reluctant to lodge children with families they deemed insufficiently Jewish:

> My family belonged to Dunstan Road Synagogue but we hardly ever went there. We didn't keep a kosher kitchen and we had few Jewish friends. This apparently counted against us when it came to placing of refugee children. My mother was very disappointed.[36]

The families who were forced to leave behind their assets found ways to help themselves survive financially. Before fleeing, some Jews often stocked up on clothes for their children, which they could take with them and to wear in future years. Golders Green children who met the offspring of continental refugees when they entered the local schools noticed the different cut and style of clothes they wore.[37]

While the continental refugees arriving during the 1930s were grateful to escape from persecution, the country they came to was not without its difficulties for Jewish people. During the 1930s anti-Semitism, fuelled by Oswald Mosley's British Union of Fascists (the 'Blackshirts'), was making life in the East End uncomfortable for Jews living there by carrying out sporadic acts of violence against them and their property. The East Enders complained that Jews residing in the suburbs were oblivious to the menace of fascism. In November 1938, an editorial in *The Leader* (journal of the Achei Brith Friendly Society) grumbled that 'While you play bridge in Golders Green, old people are living in the shadow of impending terror in Bethnal Green'.[38]

However, the Jewish residents of Golders Green were not unaffected by the rise of anti-Semitism, albeit that the discrimination they encountered was less virulent than elsewhere. Harry Wasser (see page 32) later recalled that in the pre-war years a fascist group would meet close to the Dunstan Road Synagogue on Saturday mornings. Although advised by Reverend Livingstone to ignore the fascists, synagogue members sometimes questioned them leading to 'unpleasant scenes' and the involvement of the police. Congregants volunteered for night duty at the synagogue when attacks seemed likely.[39] Mr Wasser also recalled that, just before the Second World War, the *Hendon and Finchley Times* began reporting on the occasional anti-Semitic remarks made in the area. In 1936 there was a packed meeting of the Hampstead and Golders Green Jewish People's Council, an anti-Fascist group at St Alban's Church Hall.[40]

In addition to the continental refugees, Jewish families from other parts of London were continuing to arrive in Golders Green. While some Jewish families came directly from the East End, others achieved their goal by making a series of moves between the suburbs that were no longer fashionable or were less middle class in character, a route that became known as the 'North-West Passage'. When they first arrived from Eastern Europe in the early 1900s, Viki Minsky's family opened a business in Hoxton. The family later moved to Henley's Corner and from there to central Golders Green. Commenting in 1937 on the shift from north London *The Observer* said that 'Stoke Newington has a large Jewish middle-class population and indeed represents the purgatory stage of the Semite ascent to heaven which is Golders Green'.[41] Some families were only able to make the move to Golders Green because an entire extended family of wage and salary earners shared a house and pooled their resources to pay the mortgage.[42] Some let out parts of their houses to help finance their promotion to the property-owning class,[43] willing to sacrifice space in order to live in a respectable area.

Another common but less chronicled trajectory to Golders Green was via the West End, where many Jewish families involved in the clothing industry lived. Extended families sometimes moved *en masse* from the streets around Soho:

> My parents were born and brought up in the West End. My grandparents, who had a trimmings shop near Goodge Street, moved to Golders Green before the war in 1939. My mother and one of her sisters both set up homes there. We also had various other relations dotted around Golders Green. At that time the 'ghetto mentality' was still intact and families remained pretty much together.[44]

Even when they were not related, some families who had moved to Golders Green knew each other well having previously lived and traded together in the Jewish-dominated Berwick Street area where they had mostly lived over their shops.[45] Living alongside people they knew made them feel secure. One Golders Green resident of the time said: 'I like living here in Golders Green. There's a nice safe and homely feeling'.[46] Golders Green's increasing recognition as a Jewish area attracted people who had achieved a high profile in public life, such as the former Olympic athlete Harold Abrahams, who had become a lawyer after an injury ended his athletic career, and the renowned Russian violinist Michael Zacharewitsch (né Sisserman).[47]

By the 1930s a Jewish 'haute bourgeois' lifestyle had taken root in Golders Green.[48] While immigrant Jewish families had typically arrived in England with six or more children, the new suburban Jewish families were much smaller, mirroring the declining birth rate of the non-Jewish population. Although some residents spoke Yiddish, they regarded it as incompatible with a middle-class suburban lifestyle. Jocelyne Tobin recalls: 'my parents only used Yiddish when they didn't want us children to know what they were saying.'[49] Joan Harris has captured the character of a typical Jewish household in Golders Green in the 1930s:

> I remember birthday parties in the garden, seaside holidays down in Clacton and Cliftonville, my dad's Flying Standard motorcar and his antiquated gramophone, which played all of His Master's Voice records, and mum's pedal-operated Singer sewing machine.[50]

A number of Jews living in Golders Green had anglicised their names. This was sometimes due to the anti-Semitism they had encountered, but also to the general hostility to foreign-sounding names that might be German, which still lingered in the non-Jewish community after the huge loss of life during the First World War.[51]

The predominantly middle-class lifestyle of Golders Green was an anathema to many of those who remained in London's inner city. The move of some East End Jews to north-west London and their increasingly affluent lifestyle created something of a social rift between the new suburban dwellers and those left behind, leading to disparaging remarks on both side. The mutual incomprehension between the suburbanites and the East Enders was captured in Simon Blumenfeld's 1935 novel *Jew Boy*. Alex, the hero, could not understand how any intelligent person could exchange the vitality of the East End Jewish community for the 'anaemic narrow-minded dreariness of suburbia', while his sister showed her contempt for the Jews she had left behind by describing them mockingly as 'Vitechapel Jews'.[52]

Memories of non-naturalised Jews being deported for allegedly engaging in espionage and raids on immigrant political clubs in the East End led many Jews to eschew political involvements, especially those who had left the area and were intent on demonstrating their respectability. However, as early as the 1920s two members of Golders Green Synagogue were councillors,[53] and by the 1930s younger people in particular were beginning to express their support for establishing an independent Jewish homeland. In Golders Green, as in the other middle-class suburbs of north-west London, Zionism was now stronger than in the East End where the Zionist Association had all but collapsed. As early as 1927 the Golders Green Young Israel Society, which had both a junior and a senior section, was formed and met regularly at Dunstan Road Synagogue. A year later the synagogue became the headquarters for the Young Zionist Society of Golders Green and Hendon, which 'proceeded from strength to strength'.[54] Prominent synagogue members included Paul and Romana Goodman. Paul Goodman was vice-president of the English Zionist Federation and editor of *The Zionist Review*.[55] Romana Goodman was one of the founders of the Women's International Zionist Organisation (WIZO). The couple hosted Zionist gatherings in their home, 'Hatikvah', in The Ridgeway.[56]

As the Jewish community grew, its concerns started to become an important factor in local party politics. During the 1930s the Golders Green electoral ward was represented by three Conservative councillors, two of whom were Jewish, reflecting the solid middle-class status of the first Jewish residents of the area. One of the councillors was Albert Abraham Narr, a leading member of the English Zionist Federation[57] and 'respected member' of Dunstan Road Synagogue. When he became chairman of Hendon Urban District Council in 1931, a special service was held at the synagogue to celebrate his appointment.[58]

By this time the political scene in Golders Green was beginning to change. In 1932 a Labour candidate, Mr A.L. Polak, issued a special leaflet addressed to 'Jewish electors' in Golders Green mentioning his twelve years as an officer in the Jewish Lads' Brigade and his committee membership of a Jewish orphanage. Two Jewish brothers, John and Sidney Lewis, who supported the United Front between Labour and the Communist Party, joined the Golders Green ward of Hendon Labour Party in the 1930s. The new Labour Party members were not always received with open arms. During an acrimonious debate about John Lewis's selection in the 1937 local elections,[59] Mrs G.C. Henderson is reported to have said: 'if Hitler has people like Mr Lewis in Germany, no wonder he cleared them out'.[60] An investigation by the national Labour Party concluded that Mr Lewis was 'a little overbearing in his manner', but that Mrs Henderson's statement was 'unfortunate to say the least'. The local party secretary, George Richardson, offered his opinion that there was 'a definite racial problem' in the ward as the result of non-Jews feeling that that they were being displaced by Jewish members.[61]

This shifting political scene can perhaps be attributed to the fact that some of the Jewish East Enders now making their way to Golders Green were not as affluent as those who had moved there in previous decades and that for a number of the incomers, geographic mobility did not necessarily signify the same degree of upward social mobility as it had for the earliest settlers. According to David Cesarani, this accounts for the constellation of Jewish political opinions that existed in the pre- and post-war years in areas such as Golders Green.[62]

5

The Second World War

The continental Jews who had settled in Golders Green before the Second World War had little time to adapt to a new way of life before they faced wartime conditions. In the early part of 1939 there were clear signs that war was looming. The *Hendon Times* started to advertise for shelter construction, and over the summer months precautions against air raids were introduced with increasing urgency. There were frequent Air Raid Precautions (ARP) exercises, which sometimes resulted in real casualties.[1] As the situation in Europe worsened, anxieties increased. The religious institutions in Golders Green reported packed congregations during August 1939.[2]

When a letter appeared in the *Jewish Chronicle* in May 1938 implying that Jews in Golders Green were unenthusiastic about participating in wartime preparations[3] there was a strong rebuttal from 'Jaygee' of Golders Green, saying that he had been attending an ARP class where almost half the members were Jewish and pointing out that Jews made up 20 per cent of the Fire Brigade course.[4] Many Jews became air wardens, like Harry Wasser, whose duties included ensuring that gas masks fitted correctly. He remembered calling on Rabbi Hager from the *shtiebl* (small house of worship) in Highfield Avenue,[5] 'a venerable old man with a nice long flowing beard and sense of humour'. He tried fitting the mask with the rabbinic beard inside and outside the mask but neither worked. He gave it up as 'a bad job' and advised Rabbi Hager that he would have to rely on prayers rather than a mask.[6]

During the so-called 'phoney war' (September 1939 to April 1940) there were a number of false alarms and air-raid sirens were sometimes heard in the area. When bombing began for real, Golders Green was not subjected to the same intensity of bombing as in other parts of London but the area did not escape attack, partly due to its proximity to Hendon Aerodrome. During the war 242 people were killed and 20,000 properties were damaged as a result of bombing in the Borough of Hendon that covered Golders Green. Jewish people who were children during the war retained lasting memories of the air raids:

> There was an air raid shelter in the recreation ground at the bottom of our garden in Dunstan Road. We constructed a ladder against the fence so that we could

climb over to the shelter. When the siren sounded for the first time, we ran down the garden and climbed over the fence only to be told by people coming out of the shelter that what we had heard had been the 'all clear' siren and that we'd missed all the action![7]

And:

When the sirens sounded I was carried downstairs to the Morrison shelter that had been constructed in the rear of the lounge by the French windows. I didn't realise the danger; it was just like camping. All the windows were taped up with blackout curtains but if you lifted the material slightly you could see the lights of the aircraft going over and the searchlights sweeping over the area looking for them.[8]

On the night of what was called 'the Great Fire of London' in December 1940, German aircraft dropped vast numbers of incendiary bombs on the city. Rita Brodie, then living in Golders Green on the other side of London from the target area, remembers that the sky was lit up sufficiently to read a newspaper.[9]

The first bomb to fall on Golders Green was on the night of 30 August 1940. On 23 September 1940, Mrs Naar, Mayoress of Hendon, extinguished a burning incendiary device she discovered on her doorstep.[10] One of the first houses rendered uninhabitable was the home of Reverend Livingstone of Dunstan Road Synagogue. On the night of 24 September a mine fell close to Woodstock Road, demolishing the Livingstone home and several adjacent houses. Just a few nights earlier a bomb had fallen in the area but had not exploded. The Livingstone family, along with eight other households, had been evacuated. This meant that there were no casualties when the landmine demolished their house. Barbara Michaels (née Livingstone) commented that 'We were extraordinarily lucky. If it hadn't been for the coincidence of two bombs falling in the same area, we would all have been killed'.[11] Reverend Livingstone remained in London, sleeping temporarily on a camp bed in a corridor of a local apartment block while his family lived temporarily outside London.[12]

The Hobbins family, German-Jewish refugees who had helped a number of other families to escape from Germany, lived at 44 Ashbourne Avenue, which was 'virtually demolished' by a high explosive bomb in 1941. The family escaped uninjured but had to spend the remainder of the war living in Letchworth.[13] Rabbi Munk from Golders Green Beth Hamedrash was later to speak with emotion about a young congregant who had died even though he had taken cover in an air-raid shelter.[14] Although long-range rockets and flying bombs were often to be seen low in the skies over Golders Green, only one fell in the area. This was a V2 rocket that landed on Golders Green Road in January 1945, resulting in the death of Mrs Nyman in Prince's Park Avenue, the last person to die from bombing in the area.[15]

Notwithstanding his own misfortunes, Reverend Livingstone ensured that Dunstan Road Synagogue played a part in helping those affected by bombing.

Non-Jewish people later recalled how they were accommodated in the synagogue when they were made homeless after bombs dropped in the area.[16] During the seemingly unending nights of the Blitz, Rabbi Munk of Golders Green Beth Hamedrash joined others in fire-watching. He was often to be seen trudging along Temple Gardens in his helmet and boots on his way to collect a companion for night watch.[17]

After one or two 'near misses' when public air-raid shelters threatened to collapse, hundreds of families took to sleeping in Hampstead Tube station, the deepest station in London.[18] Some Jews living in Golders Green during the war recall the camaraderie that existed between the Jewish and non-Jewish families bedding down on the stone stairways and draughty platforms.[19] However, other Jewish families remained steadfastly in their homes, taking cover in their hallways, which they had been advised were the safest part of their homes.[20]

At the start of the war many unaccompanied young people and parentless Kindertransport children living in Golders Green were evacuated to various locations outside London.[21] Two hostels, one for boys in Tylers Green, High Wycombe, and another for girls in Great Chesterton, Essex,[22] were set up under the leadership of Rabbi Munk and Mrs Rosenfeld from Golders Green Beth Hamedrash (now known as 'Munk's shul'). The strictly orthodox way of life at the hostel made it a 'home from home' for many young people. The Sassover Rabbi, Simcha Rubin, religious leader of a *shtiebl* in Finchley Road,[23] opened his own home to child refugees. When the children were moved out of London, he sought to ensure they were accommodated in homes where dietary laws were maintained.[24]

When the bombing was at its height, children from longer-standing Jewish residents were also billeted in various parts of the country. Many were homesick, even when they were sent to live with close relatives:

> My sister and I went to stay with one of my mother's sisters and her family in Little Hayfield, a small village in the Pennines close to Manchester. We hated it there! The environment was very bleak because there were a lot of disused mills and we didn't have many of the things that were available in London even in wartime conditions. One of our jobs was to go out and pick up bits of coal, which made us very grubby. Because we looked different, we became a target for local young people who called us 'dirty Jews'.[25]

Anti-Semitism was a common experience for evacuees. Pearl Dalby remembers witnessing a billeting officer trying to seek a home for a 4-year-old from Golders Green in Leicester: 'She was left standing in the middle of the road. All I could hear was the neighbours saying: "Oh, we can't take her, she's a Jew"'.[26]

It was soon recognised that north-west London was going to survive the war relatively unscathed and families were reunited: 'We skipped with joy up the road when we knew we were going home to Golders Green. We returned for *Pesach* 1941. We had never fitted in. I was a spoilt London girl'.[27]

In 1939 the majority of adult Jewish males living in Britain, with the exception of the recent continental refugees, were eligible for conscription. A large proportion of Jews living in Golders Green were very patriotic. Once war was declared, many did not wait to be called up but immediately volunteered to assist in the war effort, which raised concerns for their families:

> The family story is that although my mother was keen for my brother to join up, she didn't want him to fight in Germany. She went to the recruiting office to plead his case for not being sent there worried he might be captured and tortured for being Jewish.[28]

Another Golders Green resident, Harry Langdon, volunteered for the Territorial Army and operated the anti-aircraft guns sited on Parliament Hill that helped to protect Golders Green during the war.[29] To the chagrin of her parents, Joan Harris also volunteered for the Territorial Army and spent a year in the Royal Army Service Corps distributing food and clothing to units throughout the UK.[30] The immense contribution of Golders Green Jews to the war effort is symbolised by the number of Jewish names engraved on the war memorial that stands at the junction of Finchley Road and Golders Green Road. Throughout the war, Jewish families in Golders Green offered hospitality to American-Jewish soldiers on their way to combat, especially during the Jewish festivals.[31]

Food shortages resulting from the war affected the whole population of Britain but they proved especially difficult for Jews keeping *kashrut* (Jewish dietary laws). To be considered kosher, hindquarter meat had to be porged (removal of the sciatic nerve, blood and suet to make it fit to eat). The work involved in this process was not possible during the war, making hindquarter meat non-kosher. As an alternative to meat, the community became more reliant on fish but the only fish readily available during the war was Icelandic cod, which apparently 'tasted ghastly'.[32] The Hendon Food Committee, which covered Golders Green, reported to the Ministry of Information that Jews were being badly affected by the shortage of fish,[33] but wartime residents of Golders Green recall that, despite the difficulties, they did not starve:

> On Sundays my grandmother cooked for all the family. During the war she was able to serve chicken because the garden was turned into a large chicken run for about 200 birds. The smell and noise was awful but my grandparents kept the neighbours happy by giving them a chicken a month. A chicken was worth a gold bar![34]

Since most Jewish people did not use their bacon ration, they sometimes traded it for chicken feed from a man who had a shop in Hoop Lane.[35] Jews were rarely reduced to using the black market, although an exception was sometimes made for purchasing oil since it was used a lot in Jewish cooking.[36] Wartime shortages impacted Jewish (and non-Jewish) couples marrying during the war. Nancie Craig, who was married in 1942 by her father Reverend Livingstone at Dunstan Road Synagogue, remembered how difficult it was to obtain food for the occasion.[37]

The fall of France and the subsequent evacuation of Dunkirk in 1940 led to panic about the number of Germans living in the country, fanned by the credence the government gave to the possible existence of a 'Fifth Column' in Britain.[38] In Golders Green some continental Jews who had been naturalised prior to the war were dismissed from roles such as voluntary ARP wardens.[39] This antipathy towards the recent arrivals abated for a while when the Blitz commenced and generated greater community solidarity.[40] However, feelings of resentment re-emerged as the war progressed. One memory is that some refugees in Golders Green were able to obtain goods not available to indigenous families, leading to feelings of resentment.[41]

On 16 May 1940 internment measures were applied to so-called 'enemy aliens'.[42] Non-naturalised Jews residing in Golders Green, which included a large proportion of the recently arrived continental Jews, were summonsed to appear before tribunals to determine their alien status. Although they had recently fled from Nazi-occupied Europe, they were not considered to be above suspicion. Sometimes even the older children who had arrived on the Kindertransport were sent to internment camps. Edwin Stanley, who came to Golders Green with his family in 1936, recalls his parents being called to an office in Hoop Lane where they were deemed to be 'enemy aliens' and interned on the Isle of Man. Although eventually reunited with his mother, who was interned in a different camp from his father, Edwin, aged 8, was first sent to live in Macclesfield with his married stepsister who had escaped internment because her husband had already volunteered for the army.[43]

Non-naturalised citizens were considered less of a threat if they were sick or old and those who were considered useful to the economy were sometimes dealt with differently. Herbert and Kathe Trenter came to London from Breslau in 1938. They initially lived with Herbert's brother Bernhard, a refugee already settled in Highcroft Gardens. Bernhard was interned and sent to the Isle of Man but Herbert went to Temple Fortune Police Station and argued: 'Look, there is no point in interning me because I am much more useful to England organising my export business'. The police agreed and allowed Herbert to remain with his wife.[44]

As the result of public protests, internees were released by late 1940 but this did not help those who had already been forcibly deported on specially commissioned liners to Canada and Australia. Martin Sulzbacher, who later opened a bookshop in Sneath Avenue, was fortunate enough to survive the infamous sinking of the *Arandora Star*,[45] which had been carrying many interned Jewish people to Canada. While others perished Martin Sulzbacher managed to survive in the water until he was rescued. He later attributed this to his 'portly' physique allowing him to float for longer.[46] However, his relatives believe that his survival was due to his foresight in identifying the location of the life rafts when boarding the boat and also say that while awaiting help he rescued a fellow passenger.[47] Having survived this horrific incident, Mr Sulzbacher was sent to Australia on the *Dunera*, on which Jews were abused and forced to live in inhumane conditions. His wife and children interned on the Isle of Man were unaware of his experiences.[48] While interned in Australia Mr Sulzbacher's parents and several members of his extended family were killed in the Blitz and when he eventually returned to England in 1942 he found all his property had been destroyed and he had to rebuild his life completely.[49] He brought up not only his own children but also those of an aunt and uncle who had died in the Blitz.

Once they were released from internment many refugees joined the armed forces,[50] and some of those who remained in Golders Green contributed to the war effort in a civilian capacity. Irene White, a German refugee living in Temple Fortune, later recalled taking her turn in fire-watching:

> It was one of our jobs to take the metal dustbin lids and cover the firebombs before they exploded and illuminated everything. The house next door to us caught fire. We formed a bucket chain, and with the help of our neighbours using hosepipes, stirrup pumps and very primitive equipment, the fire was put out.[51]

Despite the major contribution Jewish refugees made to the war effort, anti-alien attitudes continued until the end of the war. In August 1941 a local newspaper reported on the experience of a couple who had moved to Golders Green to escape Nazi persecution. One morning, without warning, six officers from the Home Office descended on their home and took them away to be interned. Although it was quickly recognised that a mistake had been made, they were kept in prison for forty-nine days. To add insult to injury, the local authority claimed that because the couple's furniture had remained in their home while they were detained, they were liable to pay rates. The couple submitted a claim for damages to the Home Office and requested an apology. Neither was forthcoming.[52] However, Jewish communal organisations did their best to help recent refugees settle and feel welcome. In March 1941, the Council for Jewish Education organised a series of lectures in Golders Green to disseminate information on the workings of local and central government.[53]

Compared to the continental Jewish refugees, the longer-standing Jewish residents of Golders Green had a better war. Relations between these families and non-Jews in the area, which had generally been amicable before the war, became even stronger. Jocelyne Tobin recalls that during the war, a non-Jewish couple living a few doors away regularly came to the family home in Dunstan Road to play Solo with her parents. This friendliness dissipated somewhat when the war was over.[54]

During the war there were several changes in the nature of the Jewish community in Golders Green. Migration from east London to Golders Green increased significantly. One of the reasons for this was that the war had depressed rents and house prices across the capital, which meant that families could sometimes move directly to Golders Green, short-circuiting the route via Stamford Hill and other north London suburbs.[55] Jeff Alexander's grandparents, who had settled in the East

End in the 1880s and had built up a business in Mile End Road, had long cherished the idea of moving to Golders Green. In 1939 they realised that as a result of people leaving the area, houses in Golders Green were coming on the market at very good prices. They bought a four-bedroom house in Beechcroft Avenue for £350. His parents subsequently bought a house a few doors away.[56]

However, the main cause of the increase in migration from the East End was the bombing of the London's docklands, which destroyed the housing stock and disrupted the Jewish communal infrastructure of shops, synagogues and schools. This meant that some of the people arriving in Golders Green from the East End in the war years came from necessity rather than by choice. They sometimes felt unsettled by the move and had little affinity with the suburban lifestyle they found in Golders Green. A proportion of the wartime arrivals returned to east London after the war to live in the newly constructed blocks of flats in Stepney. Those displaced by bombing included a number of strictly orthodox rabbis and their congregants who did stay in the area. They joined with the very religious Jews already living in Golders Green to form the first *shtieblech* (small houses of worship) to be established in the area.[57]

As the war progressed and France and Holland were occupied by Germany, a number of Jewish families from these countries were able to find ways round the government's tight restrictions on immigration to come to Britain.[58] Some of these families made their way to Golders Green, where they had relatives. The years between 1939 and 1945 also saw the beginning of a more significant movement of Jews from towns and cities outside London. This was part of a national shift of the Jewish population from the north to the south of the country that was to become even more noticeable in future decades.

The Post-War Years

In the pre-war years the Anglo-Jewish community had experienced steady progress. It had generally (although not uniformly) become wealthier and more middle class. There was hardly a sphere of life to which Jews were not making a major contribution. Leadership of the community was rapidly passing into the hands of people who came to the country as immigrants rather than being dominated by the small circle of acculturated grandees who had all but disappeared from public view. London Jewry retained its predominance in terms of numbers as well as in influence, particularly in the cultural sphere. Most Jewish publications emanated from the capital. By the pre-war years London Jewry consisted of a series of suburban communities rather than the single entity it had been for many centuries.

During the 1940s and 1950s the Anglo-Jewish community continued to flourish economically and socially despite the years of austerity immediately following the war. However, the community remained haunted by the Holocaust. The Jews of Britain now constituted the only intact Jewish community in Europe and the largest in Europe outside the USSR, but feelings of insecurity and of guilt at surviving the calamity of the Holocaust permeated the community. The unique tragedy was particularly poignant for the recent immigrants whose relatives had perished. The violence leading up to and following the establishment of the State of Israel and the wave of anti-Semitism it generated added to the despondency of the community.

The general mood of Anglo-Jewry was reflected in the Jewish community of Golders Green. Although they were rarely mentioned, the spectre of recent events hung over the Jewish homes in the area:

> Unlike some of my mother's Vienna family, we were alive. By the time we moved back to London, the war had been over barely ten years. The 'Holocaust' wasn't even a word used about the slaughter. We seldom talked about it, except for fleeting analogies on Passover and Purim, both commemorating the destruction of early editions of Hitler: Pharaoh, Haman, the perennial *mamzers*, the bastards. There wasn't even much to read until Lord Russell of Liverpool, a lawyer at the Nuremberg trials, published his *Scourge of the Swastika*, which we devoured in the

upstairs synagogue library, aghast and fascinated by the hecatombs of bones; the naked women running before the grinning guards.[1]

In 1947 a packed service led by the local MP, Sir Hugh Lucas-Tooth, supported by Reverend Livingstone, was organised by the Golders Green Memorial Forest Committee at the Golders Green Hippodrome to remember the 6 million Jews who had died during the Holocaust.[2]

After the war ended Rabbi Munk of Golders Green Beth Hamedrash was among the first British Jews to visit the Nazi concentration camps. He spent eighteen months working with survivors, humbly joining other volunteers in menial tasks to make the survivors more comfortable. He was looked upon as 'little less than a Wunder-rebbe'.[3] His contribution spurred members of the community to open a hostel in Golders Green Road to accommodate orphaned young people liberated from concentration camps. Named after its benefactor Osias Freshwater, the hostel at 833 Finchley Road was run along strictly orthodox lines by Mrs Leo Feuchtwanger. Kurt Klappholz, a young Polish man who stayed in the hostel during 1946, recalled walking up and down Finchley Road and around the clock tower with a feeling of wonderment:

> As a child, my father often talked to me about the Western countries, namely England, France, perhaps also Holland – countries whose political set up he admired – and I am sure that he wished that that particular set up had prevailed in Poland … I was extremely lucky.[4]

Due to the difficulty in obtaining construction licences and to the shortage of builders and building materials, it took some time for war-damaged property in Golders Green to be repaired.[5] Rationing continued until 1954 and the way in which the rationing of meat operated disadvantaged Jewish households. While most rationed food was controlled by weight, meat was controlled by price. Since kosher meat was more expensive than non-kosher meat, Jewish families had to manage with less meat. However, Naomi Rose recalls that 'If you registered as being Jewish, you received extra cheese and margarine instead of bacon'.[6]

Jews who came to the area from abroad were struck by the depressed nature of post-war Golders Green:

> It seemed so bleak after the places where I'd lived before. Rationing was still in force and bomb damage was evident in the streets. I found the existing Jewish community very bourgeois and very gloomy.[7]

A number of continental refugees who had been interned did not return to Golders Green and a few of those who did return, together with some of those who had remained in the area during the war, subsequently relocated elsewhere, mainly to America or to Israel. However, the majority chose to stay and, once repatriation had been ruled out, they quickly became part of the local community and began to make a contribution to its social and economic life. Between 1946 and 1950 most became naturalised, and some took English and elocution lessons to help the process of integration. Many changed their names to make a clean break, to reduce complications in their adopted country or to fashion a new identity for their families.[8] Miriam Levene (née Bentley) recalls that when she was growing up in Golders Green, it was not uncommon for young people to have grandparents and parents with different surnames because the younger generation had anglicised theirs.[9]

Although the former refugees tended to be concentrated in certain parts of Golders Green, such as in Eagle Lodge,[10] they socialised with the British-born Jewish residents of Golders Green,[11] and with continental Jews who had settled in Britain prior to those fleeing Nazism. Naomi Rutstein recalls:

> We didn't consider ourselves Germans. We were Jews living in England. We knew people who had come from Germany, but we also had lots of other friends. We wanted to be part of the community.[12]

Some former refugees became very prominent in the area, such as Clement Krysler, a dentist with a surgery in Hodford Road: 'He was a real character; he knew everyone and everything that was going on in Golders Green'.[13] Despite their often painful experiences, many remained committed to creating a better world and ensuring the continuation of the Jewish people by dedicating themselves to communal life, including Ruth Sachs who, over many decades, led British Emunah, and her husband Jakob, who was a member of the Board of Deputies.[14] However, even when they assimilated, some former refugees never felt totally secure: 'my parents were uncomfortable about owning property in case they had to move again'.[15] Others found integration very difficult, especially some older people who remained wedded to the lifestyles of their native countries, and some of the youngest who had been traumatised by their experiences. In addition, while they were keen to integrate, most did so while preserving their distinct continental culture that they kept alive via various social clubs and cultural societies.[16] This meant that post-war Golders Green had a definite continental feel to it that is still recalled by those that lived in the area at that time.[17]

The number of continental Jews living in the area was increased by the arrival of Holocaust survivors. Although they were keen to put the past behind them as quickly as possible, their presence brought home the devastating reality of the concentration camps. Hazel Sheldon, whose family owned Franks outfitters in Golders Green Road, recalls noticing that some of the Holocaust survivors who were now coming into the shop and trying on clothes had concentration camp numbers tattooed on their bodies, which she found 'very, very sad'.[18] The Holocaust survivors were often strictly orthodox in their outlook. They mainly settled in the roads beyond Hoop Lane and became members of Munk's shul, often joining family members who had settled in the area before the war.[19] For example, Rachel Deutsch's mother came to Golders Green when she was released from a Westerbork concentration camp to join her brother Dr Avraham Adler (see page 188).[20]

Holocaust survivors holding progressive views also settled in Golders Green, including Rabbi Georg Salzberger who moved to Hodford Road in 1946. In 1938 Rabbi Salzberger was interned in Dachau until he obtained papers to allow his family to come to England. Having been a rabbi in the German *Liberale* movement, Frankfurt am Main, Rabbi Salzberger was appointed as the rabbi for the refugee congregation, the New Liberal Jewish Association, that took forward the German modern traditions and became Belsize Square Synagogue in 1971.[21]

The new arrivals would probably have been deeply unsettled by an ugly incident that occurred in Golders Green in January 1947. Following the flogging of British Army servicemen by Jewish extremists in Palestine, some local non-Jews incensed by the incident, daubed paint and chalk notices on the premises of Jewish firms in Golders Green. This desecration, which placed 'a small and nasty blemish on the relationship between Jew and non-Jew',[22] was totally out of keeping with the general tolerance that hitherto epitomised social relationships in the area.

Tensions between Jews and non-Jews may have been exacerbated by the mushrooming of Zionist bodies in Golders Green that took place in the post-war years. All three of the larger synagogues in the area organised events to raise money to help establish the State of Israel and they also co-operated in staging larger events, such as the series of bazaars held at Dunstan Road Synagogue, that were overseen by a joint committee composed of representatives of the three synagogues.[23] In 1948 Barclay House[24] at 783 Finchley Road became the base for the Golders Green Zionist Society and the merged Golders Green and Hampstead Garden Suburb Federation of Zionist Youth Groups,[25] and a centre for Zionist work generally. Later it housed the Zionist school, Mathilda Marks-Kennedy.[26]

When the State of Israel was established in 1948, one of the repercussions was a wave of anti-Jewish feeling that swept across Arab countries. Jews were forced to leave many Arabic countries including Iraq, Iran, Yemen, Tunisia, Algeria, Morocco, Libya and Syria.[27] While most went to Israel, a significant number came to Britain, some of whom came to Golders Green, which was by then internationally known as an area of Jewish settlement. Unlike most of the earlier groups of settlers, the new arrivals were Sephardi rather than Ashkenazi in origin.[28] They were joined by Baghdadi Jews, who came to Golders Green from a number of different places to which they had relocated over the centuries in search of trading opportunities, such as Shanghai,[29] Burma and Singapore.

However, Jews from India, who had started to leave following the granting of independence by the British in 1947, formed the largest element of the new Sephardi community. Although there was no history of anti-Semitism in India, the Second World War had unsettled the Indian Jewish community. They had prospered in India under the Raj and were uncertain of their political and economic future under the new Indian government. With increasing opportunities for the immigration of Indian citizens to Britain during the 1950s, many chose to make a new life here.

A group of inter-related Jewish families who had lived in Calcutta relocated to Golders Green and extended family members and friends soon followed them.[30] As a result, by the end of the 1950s there were said to be more Jews from Calcutta living in Golders Green than in Calcutta itself.[31] They had been part of Calcutta's wealthy and cosmopolitan social milieu,[32] and had family ties to the Iraqi Jews who had come to Golders Green from elsewhere. They generally adapted well to English life due to the fact that in India they had spoken English as their first language and had been exposed to English culture in their schoolbooks and the cinema.[33] Dissatisfied with the disintegrating Jewish community life in Calcutta, Mary Shooker Abraham came to Golders Green in about 1960, where she met up with some members of her mother's family who had arrived from Shanghai and been settled comfortably in the area for a number of years.[34] However, there were some aspects of life in Golders Green that the Calcutta Jews initially found difficult:

> Things were cleaner when we came here, but it was a harder life because, you know, we were not used to being without servants. Slowly we got used to the life and things became easier later on when there were washing machines and launderettes.[35]

When they had been in Britain for a few years, the Calcutta Jews became increasingly concerned about the number of young people from the community who were 'marrying out' (both marrying Ashkenazi Jews and non-Jews). David Elias came to England in 1950 with his wife and four children. In India he had been a vice-chairman of the Zionist Federation, working with both Gandhi and Nehru, and had gained a reputation for effective leadership. He was approached to take on the task of helping to organise Indian Jews living in Golders Green (and also in Stamford Hill and Ilford). Although he accepted the task somewhat reluctantly, he was highly successful in reviving a community that had been on the point of rapid decline.[36]

After the Suez Crisis of 1956, Egyptian Jews started to come to Golders Green. They were generally highly educated, having attended French *lycées* or English schools in Egypt. They initially formed their own community, the Maimonides Society, with the support of the Spanish and Portuguese Synagogue in Lauderdale Road.[37] Maurice Sabah, one of its founders and former head of ICI in Cairo, recalled that 'we would meet for a cup of tea and help people to trace long-lost brothers and sisters'.[38] However, over time this group, along with Jews arriving from Aden after Britain gave up the colony,[39] allied itself with the Calcutta Jews to form Ohel David Eastern Synagogue,[40] the first Sephardi synagogue in Golders Green.[41] The synagogue, of which David Elias (mentioned above) became the secretary, was known for its warmth and ebullience. It was not a wealthy congregation but it drew Sephardi families from Stamford Hill to live in Golders Green.[42] Although

Ohel David became the main focal point for Indian and Middle Eastern Jews, a small number also joined other synagogues in Golders Green like North-Western Reform Synagogue (known as 'Alyth Gardens' or just 'Alyth').[43]

The Middle Eastern Jews coming to Golders Green were culturally a world apart from another group of Jews who settled in Golders Green after the war. From the mid-1940s onwards there was a fresh influx of Jewish East Enders, this time in far greater numbers than previously. The impetus for the new wave of migration was the break-up of the Jewish community in the East End. The community had been steadily declining for two decades due to the impact of the Aliens' Act, but the Second World War exacerbated the process. The evacuation of women and children from the East End in 1939 and 1940 had scattered the Jewish population previously living in areas such as Stepney, which never recovered their pre-war population levels.[44] The impact of bombing and, after the war, the conversion of former residential areas to offices, factories and warehousing reduced the Jewish population of the East End even further. By 1950 it was mainly older people who remained and there were few Jewish goods and services left that could not be obtained elsewhere.[45]

There was now a quest for homes with 'the right address' and for many East Enders Golders Green was the place to be; NW11 apparently sounded more 'high-class' than E15.[46] It became common parlance in the Anglo-Jewish world that a person was a failure if they could not even get themselves out of the East End.[47] The historian Simon Schama, who lived in Golders Green in the 1950s, recalls:

> The oldest of my father's twelve siblings were still stuck in the East End and when we went to see them it was like a trip to some sort of mournful immigrant antiquity: their dreaded sponge cake, and the tall glasses of lemon tea, sipped with spoons of plum jam.[48]

In the immediate post-war years a number of properties were standing empty in Golders Green because people (Jewish and non-Jewish) had not returned, having been evacuated during the Blitz. Younger people in particular had become accustomed to living in the country.[49] Some Jewish families who had remained in or who had returned to Golders Green did not have the resources to rehabilitate houses that had become run down or had been damaged in the war.[50] A number of properties became available at low prices because their owners had failed in their business dealings and had become bankrupt.[51] When Nancie Craig (née Livingstone) married, she bought a house in Golders Green from the trustees in the bankruptcy of a Mr Epstein, who had 'done a bunk, which was quite common in this area then'.[52] Pearl Pollack recalled that many dilapidated or empty properties were 'snapped up by the middle-class and upper-class people from the East End'.[53] However, by the end of the decade houses in Golders Green were in very short supply. There was now a national housing shortage and properties that came on the market were likely to be requisitioned by the council. As a result, for a while many Jewish arrivals and newly formed households acquired their homes by 'word of mouth'.[54]

The fresh influx of Jews from the East End gave Golders Green a more leftward-leaning political outlook than had existed in the pre-war years. It has already been mentioned that, during the 1930s, a number of left-wing Jews had made their way to Golders Green, but the number of Jewish socialists now increased significantly.[55] In July 1945 the Conservative Sir Hugh Lucas-Tooth won the new parliamentary seat of Hendon South into which Golders Green had been incorporated, but the Labour Party captured Golders Green ward in the local elections in November of the same year.[56] Cesarani has explained that although the Jewish immigrant working class had broken up, 'it enjoyed a remarkable after-life amongst those who moved to the leafy suburbs'.[57]

However, the leftwards shift in the Jewish community of Golders Green was only partly the result of demographic changes. It was also due to the indifference of post-war Conservative Party members both nationally and locally, who were seemingly unsympathetic to the interests of Jewish voters. In 1964, Mr C.H. Sheil, the candidate for the Central Ward of Hendon Borough, announced that he stood for a 'Christian approach' and following the elections, Louis Levy resigned from the Golders Green Conservative Party, alleging that his failure to secure election to the Borough Council had been due to the lack of support from his local party during the campaign.[58]

In addition to the former East Enders, Jewish households also continued to arrive in Golders Green from other Jewish enclaves. They were mainly households with young families seeking a larger house with a garden, which they had been unable to afford in locations closer to central London where property prices were rising rapidly.[59] While the majority of new residents saw locating themselves in Golders Green as a positive move, others who had moved to the suburb from necessity rather than choice saw it as a 'come down' and found it hard to come to terms with semi-detached suburbia:

> We were in Golders Green in the early 1950s because my father, Arthur, had come down in the world a bit; taken one of his periodic falls from grace in the *schmatte* [clothing] trade, steep enough for us to have to sell off, in a hurry, the Tudor-ish villa by the sea … My mother Trudie, in shock, railed at my pa for his commercial failings … When he couldn't take any more, Arthur would march off down the hill, coming home slightly tiddly, playing worryingly with the soup noodles at supper.[60]

Pamela Nenk, who had been brought up in the West End, initially regarded Golders Green as 'the back of beyond': 'For a while she used to push the big Silver Cross pram all the way back to her former haunts in West Hampstead where she felt more at home to meet friends and family'.[61] Within just a few years of her arrival, Mrs Nenk was fully involved in the bridge-playing network of Jewish families that had become such an important feature of life in Golders Green.[62]

As the size of the Jewish community increased and Golders Green came to be referred to as a 'gilded ghetto',[63] some existing inhabitants began to see it as a less attractive place to live;'the wrong sort' of Jews were making it not such a marvellous place to be. People began to grumble. 'You know what they are calling it now? Goldstein Green'.[64] Just as previous generations had thought that they had 'got beyond' Stepney and Stamford Hill, there were now people who had 'got beyond' Golders Green and were casting their eyes around looking for new locations. Areas such as St John's Wood and Hampstead were the destination of choice for those who could afford the move. Beatrice Franks, who ran a successful outfitters in Golders Green Road,[65] had for many years set her heart on living in an area with a view of Regent's Park. In the 1950s she achieved her dream.[66]

This ambivalence towards Golders Green was not shared by some young people of the time:

> When a bus conductor shouted, 'Gol-ders Green: get yer passports out!' I chuckled along with everyone else. I loved being one of Them: the loudmouths, the violinists, the wide boys with the sharp suits, the showmen. I didn't want to blend in with the tea-cosy people of Macmillan's Britain, shuffling patiently forward in the bus queue, muttering about the weather. I was happy to be a Brylcreem boy, a jiving Jew of the Green, from my gleaming winkle-pickers to the white knitted ties and the snap-brim trilby, worn with an attitude on the way to shul.[67]

However, young people were now discovering that when they were seeking to establish homes of their own, house prices in Golders Green were beyond their reach. Some young married couples moved across the North Circular Road to Hendon, where there were a greater number of affordable houses. The short move meant that they were able stay in touch with their friends and relatives but rising house prices in Hendon soon made it necessary for young couples to look even further afield.

Although Jews were leaving Golders Green, their numbers were far outweighed by the numbers of those still arriving. By the end of the 1950s the Jewish community had grown so much that approximately one quarter of Golders Green residents were Jewish.[68] However, even more striking was the diversity of the community. Jews from many backgrounds and countries and holding different Jewish beliefs now lived in Golders Green. This diversity added zest to the community overall, but also led to some religious and social tensions between the Jewish sub-communities. Stereotypical views about the temperament of the continental Jews persisted for some time after the war and some of the more orthodox former refugees who belonged to Munk's shul continued to frown on what they saw as the religious laxities of Dunstan Road Synagogue:

> My grandparents used to have their Shabbos [Sabbath] lunch in the front room of their home in Woodstock Avenue. Reverend Livingstone would often walk past as

we were eating. He always carried with him his umbrella whether it was raining or not. To see him carrying on *Shabbos* really irritated my grandfather. He gritted his teeth when Reverend Livingstone walked by with his umbrella.[69]

They were also inclined to look down on the Anglo-Jewish pronunciation of Hebrew used in Dunstan Road Synagogue and were appalled that the Dunstan Road male congregants wore their prayer shawls folded, which looked like an imitation of the attire of the Church of England.[70] They deplored the synagogue's apparent lack of concern for the education of young people. Ian Torrance, a young member of Dunstan Road in the 1950s, recalls:

One day I was walking down the road and met Mr Schwab, one of our neighbours in Gresham Gardens, who was a member of Munk's shul. He asked where I was going and I told him I was going to Hebrew classes at the synagogue. He was incredulous. In his strong German accent he asked: 'Dunstan Road has Hebrew classes?'[71]

Apparently some Munk's shul members would walk on the other side of the road from Dunstan Road Synagogue to avoid it.[72] While these largely cultural tensions receded over the next few decades, new challenges were emerging, as we shall see in the next chapter.

7

The 1960s and 1970s

In the 1950s the Anglo-Jewish community rose to an estimated all-time high of 425,000.[1] Over the next two decades, Anglo-Jewry expanded geographically in urban centres, but it began to decline in numbers. The decline was due to a combination of factors: an excess of deaths over births, increasing intermarriage that was making communal leaders concerned about the erosion of Jewish identity, and emigration to Israel.[2] A predominantly middle-class Jewish suburban lifestyle was now fully developed. This was not the result of the merger between the rapidly shrinking 'old community' and the immigrant culture, but a distinctive social formation forged by people with changed aspirations, who moved in new social circles and made their living in different ways.[3] Equally apparent were signs of the segmentation of the community and growing secularisation.

The changes taking place in Anglo-Jewry nationally were reflected in the development of the Golders Green community. By 1960 the 'age of affluence' could be seen in many facets of life, such as in increased car ownership, which both served to make suburban living possible for those who travelled for work purposes and supported an enhanced social life.[4] Commenting in the *Jewish Chronicle* on increased Jewish car ownership, Chaim Bermant said:

> Missing a bus is a slight matter in Golders Green for here most people are car-borne – in fact, so much car-borne and so little leg-borne that one wonders how all the shoe shops there get their custom. Under Milkwood there is Evans the post, Jones the milk, so in Golders Green there is Zederblaum the Zephyr and Jacobs the Jag.[5]

At home, the better-off Jewish families in Golders Green were among the first to invest in the new technologies of the day like private telephones, which were said to have been a 'wonderful improvement' on the telephone cubicles in Hoop Lane, where people had queued to make calls.[6]

During the 1960s and 1970s the commercial areas of Golders Green blossomed and Jewish-owned businesses and those catering specifically for the Jewish community flourished.[7] Although some commentators were now predicting that areas such as Stanmore, Edgware and Finchley might overtake Golders Green as the foremost Jewish community in London, it was still widely noted for its vibrancy and cosmopolitanism. In fact during the 1970s Golders Green became an even greater focal point for Jewish life when a number of Jewish organisations moved to the area.

In 1976 two *kashrut* licensing bodies, the London Board for Shechita, licensing kosher slaughterhouses, and the Kashrus Commission, licensing caterers and hoteliers, were united under one roof (physically if not administratively) in Bridge Lane.[8] In the same year, the Mizrachi Federation (the Orthodox Zionist movement, a branch of which had been very active in Golders Green for many years) together with the World Zionist Organisation's Torah department, obtained premises at 2b Golders Green Road. The premises also housed the Women's Mizrachi Society, later British Emunah. When the Aida Foster Theatrical School closed in 1970, Jews' College purchased the building as a base for various educational activities.[9] In 1979 the Jewish Welfare Board (JWB), in collaboration with the Jewish Blind Society (JBS), established the Sobell Community Centre on the site of the former La Sagesse Convent on the corner of Golders Green Road and Limes Avenue. The premises housed a daycentre (formerly in Swiss Cottage) and provided space for other community projects. The daycentre developed a relationship with the local community from which it drew many of its volunteers, including a number of young people.

As in previous decades, newly arriving Jewish residents were quickly absorbed into the community. Some of the small number of Jewish families left in the East End made the move across London and, as a result of national patterns of change in education and employment, Jews came in greater numbers from towns and cities across Britain, including Manchester, Liverpool, Dublin, Leeds and Glasgow.

However, particularly noticeable in the 1960s and 1970s was the increasing arrival from Stamford Hill of strictly orthodox Jews, mainly those with a Germanic background. The population movement had started as a trickle in the late 1940s, but became much more discernible over the next two decades. There were several reasons for this: Golders Green was seen as being a more prestigious area than Stamford Hill; there were individual houses with gardens rather than the multi-occupied properties that typified Stamford Hill; the rapid influx of new minorities to Stamford Hill had made it feel less secure; and the Germanic orthodox community was feeling 'swamped' by the large Hassidic community that had grown up in the area.[10] Those who made the move were largely business people working in the property sector and professionals such as doctors and university professors.[11] Close behind them were Jews with a Lithuanian but non-Hassidic background (the *Litvishe*).[12] Initially whole families moved but subsequently it was only younger people who set up their homes in Golders Green. The rise in house prices had slowed the pace of migration.[13]

The arrival of strictly orthodox families did not yet have a significant impact on the character of the Golders Green Jewish community, but their presence did not go unnoticed. Some existing residents were not comfortable with the newcomers:

I didn't want to be in the company of the *frum* ... the ultra-orthodox with
their deep swaying and knee-bobbing, the corkscrew sidelocks and fringed *tzitzit*
[knotted ritual fringes]; the pallor peeping from beneath the homburgs.[14]

While some found the very observant Jews 'a bit alien', early preconceptions often
proved to be unfounded:

When shopping for my sister's *Bat Mitzvah* outfit we went to a shoe shop run by
a very orthodox woman, M&M Shoes. We entered the shop in some trepidation
thinking that we wouldn't be welcomed. It felt like stepping into another world.
We were wrong. The woman was wonderfully helpful and when she heard that
we were shopping for a *Bat Mitzvah* she was really interested in what portion my
sister would be reading and said that it was the same as her son had read for his
Bar Mitzvah.[15]

Also new to Golders Green in these years were Jewish families from South Africa,
who had mainly emigrated for ideological reasons and because of the political
situation in South Africa:

The Nationalists got stronger and stronger and the country less and less palatable.
My husband, Hans, said that he had escaped Nazi Germany and didn't want to
end his life living in another fascist country.[16]

Robert Papier, whose family owned Kendrick's toyshop in Temple Fortune and
who grew up in the area, recalls that one of the South African political exiles was
Esme Goldberg, wife of Denis Goldberg, who was imprisoned at the same time as
Nelson Mandela. She lived for a time in Hoop Lane:

Her daughter was in the same class as me and I got to know Esme quite well; she
politicised me in respect of the unjustness of apartheid and the barbaric treatment
of non-whites in South Africa.[17]

The South African Jews tended to arrive after particular events: the Sharpeville
Massacre and the Soweto riots. For most it was a difficult decision to leave South
Africa because they were leaving behind close family members. As with previous
groups of immigrants, they gravitated to Golders Green because they knew somebody
already living in the area, but they did not seek to establish a closed community even
though a number of them originated from the same village in South Africa.[18] Lucille
Sher, who came to Golders Green after the Soweto riots, recalls:

I joined Alyth and made a conscious effort to become part of the community and
to make friends with existing members. I had been a teacher in South Africa and I
decided that I could contribute my skills to the community. I became involved in

the *cheder* and later, after I had taken a course in pre-school teaching, in the Alyth Kindergarten. My husband also became very active in the community, especially with the Monday Club, which he has been running for over twenty years.[19]

A notable cluster of Jews who came from South African established itself in Dunstan Road: the Freund, Ackerman and Adelstein families, who mainly had a progressive Jewish outlook and who became the backbone of Dunstan Road Residents' Association.[20] South Africans living in other parts of the area were prominent in establishing cultural activities, such as the Hart family in Golders Green Road, who in 1962 set up an amateur dramatic society.[21]

In addition to the South Africans, Jewish people of Middle Eastern origin continued to settle in Golders Green. Monazzam Samyah came as a refugee from Iran in 1974 accompanied by her daughter and mother. They settled in Temple Fortune, having left behind their family and friends, but felt lucky to have escaped as many Jews who remained in Iran were executed. Monazzam's daughter and granddaughter both established successful careers in this country and Monazzam continues to be very involved in Alyth Gardens Synagogue.[22]

Following the Six Day War in 1967, the small Jewish community remaining in Iraq, now concentrated in Baghdad, was used as a scapegoat for Iraq's losses in the war. Jews were falsely accused of having acted as spies. They were persecuted and some were murdered, leading to another wave of departures. While many escapees settled in Israel, some made their way to England to join the Iraqi Jewish community already established here. Nadia Nathan, who had a traumatic escape from Iraq in 1970, initially found work in Israel but while visiting an aunt in Golders Green Road she met her future husband and came to live in Golders Green. She became an active member of Ohel David Synagogue and helped to shape the close and mutually supportive Iraqi Jewish community in the area.

> Ninety-nine per cent of my friends are from Iraq. When there is a big celebration, a large proportion of the Iraqi Jewish community will be there. We all know each other. We are mostly not related but we all grew up together. I know the community here better than I know my actual relatives living elsewhere.[23]

Although the Jewish community was continuing to evolve, some young people growing up in Golders Green in the 1960s and 1970s found it 'very ordinary' and 'not very exciting'. They only realised its benefits when they left the area: 'I encountered anti-Semitism for the first time at university'.[24] At this time a large proportion of young people in Golders Green attended non-Jewish day schools[25] where Jews and non-Jews co-existed quite harmoniously and Jews did not feel the need to hide their Jewish identity: 'I always wore my Star of David without worrying it could get me attacked'.[26] However, some young people unwittingly raised the hackles of their non-Jewish peers:

Frankly, I blamed my mum. Smoked salmon sandwiches for lunch every day: how was that going to square me with the gentiles? There were days when I envied the *goyim* their mince, and their frogspawn tapioca; and hungered for the dark and dirty freedom from kosher … It never occurred to me that a daily smoked salmon lunch, worse, complaining about having to eat it all the time, might get up the nose of boys doomed to Shipman's shrimp paste, or the steak'n'gristle glop served by Doris in the hairnet.[27]

Not everyone felt comfortable with being Jewish. Peter Englander, who attended a school with very few Jewish pupils and who was less part of the local 'Jewish scene' because his family were members of the Liberal Jewish Synagogue in St John's Wood, felt 'very aware of being a member of a minority group'. Although he never experienced aggressive or violent anti-Semitism, he perceived tensions between Jews and non-Jews that were 'quite palpable' and felt stigmatised by living in 'a core Jewish area'.[28] Similarly, Benjamin Sachs, who was raised in Munk's shul but attended non-Jewish schools, did not feel at home in either situation. At school he was embarrassed that he had 'a different war narrative' from that of his schoolfriends. This led to his decision to emigrate to America to pursue his career in academic medicine.[29]

Traditionally Judaism had been passed down from one generation to the next, but by the 1960s young people in Golders Green, like those in other areas, wanted to make their own religious choices. While some families were more liberal, within the community generally there remained considerable pressure to 'marry in'.[30] Most young people of this era did find Jewish partners, but it has been suggested that was less the result of parental influence than for pragmatic reasons: 'living in Golders Green meant that a large proportion of your friends and contacts were Jewish so there was a high likelihood that you would meet a Jewish partner'.[31] Jeff Alexander was among the few young people in Golders Green who at this time chose to reject the orthodoxy of his parents and grandparents and to 'marry out':

Although they were very observant, my family accepted I had a right to make my own religious choices. I always turned up for Friday night dinners at my grandparents' house because I could drink wine! However, I married a Catholic woman from Sardinia who was training to be a nurse at New End Hospital. I was reticent about telling my grandmother, but they got on well. Because she had dark hair, my grandmother always said that she looked Jewish![32]

Later, some of the more rebellious young women chose Jewish partners who were not quite what their parents might have expected. One interviewee said: 'they rebelled by marrying Sephardi Israelis who they met while on a kibbutz experience in Israel, or in one of the Finchley Road nightclubs where they used to 'hang around'.[33] Ashkenazi/Sephardi unions were not welcomed by some parents because they were seen as threatening the different customs and practices.

Any worries that Jewish parents might have had about their children's tenuous links to their religion and their involvement in the various left-wing causes that were a feature of the early 1960s, such as nuclear disarmament, were abated by the advent of the Six Day War of 1967. In Golders Green, as elsewhere, the war was a 'wake-up call'[34] leading to a sudden upsurge of pride in being Jewish. The *Jewish Chronicle* noted that young boys were walking the streets of Golders Green wearing 'miniature crocheted *yarmulkes* dangling precariously from a clip'.[35] Parents who previously would never have entertained the thought of their children attending the Jewish schools that had opened in Golders Green and nearby, increasingly wanted their children to know what it meant to be Jewish. The schools had long waiting lists. Zionism, always strong in Golders Green, now became for many people the focal point of their Jewish lives, sometimes being more important than religious observance. This was illustrated one Saturday in 1967 when members of Finchley Jewish Youth Club organised a collection for Israel. They stationed themselves at various points along Golders Green Road, angering more observant Jews walking to synagogue.[36]

Over the years the Golders Green Jewish community had raised huge sums of money for the Zionist cause. However, few people had been interested in giving up their comfortable suburban life for a pioneering existence. After the Six Day War the situation changed dramatically. There was a sudden rise in the number of young people deciding to make *aliyah* (literally 'going up' but meaning going to live in Israel), including those who had previously had no interest in the fate of Israel. To aid the emigration process, in 1969 the Jewish Agency opened an *aliyah* information desk in Golders Green providing information on housing, employment and education.[37] The information desk later sited itself more permanently at the premises of the Mizrachi Federation at 2b Golders Green Road.[38]

During the 1970s there was a renewed emphasis on Jewish cultural activities and the number of Zionist groupings in the area began to grow again. For example, in 1978 a British Na'amat group for younger women was formed in Golders Green, similar in purpose to the WIZO Aviv group that had begun a few years earlier to fight for Jewish women's rights in Israel.[39]

However happy their childhood and teenage years in Golders Green, and no matter how connected they were to their Judaism and Jewish causes, once they reached adulthood, fewer and fewer young people were able to stay in the area. Due to spiralling house prices, there was a marked exodus of young married couples to areas such as Bushey, Shenley, Radlett, Elstree and Borehamwood.[40] Worried about the impact on religious life that would be caused by people moving to places where there were no synagogues, national communal leaders appealed to them to 'come back to Golders Green' where they could be close to the synagogues.[41] Locally, Rabbi Eugene Newman, now the rabbi at Dunstan Road Synagogue, complained publicly about the shortage of purpose-built flats in the area suitable for young couples.[42]

The loss of the younger generation was not the only worry for the Jewish community. During the 1960s and 1970s there were periodic outbreaks of anti-

Semitism across London, involving the daubing of synagogues with swastikas and attempted arson. When these attacks were at their height, members of Alyth Gardens Synagogue took it in turns to sleep in the synagogue to keep watch but the synagogue was unaffected.[43] In August 1965 Dunstan Road Synagogue was warned that it might be harmed. A scuffle occurred outside, but no actual damage was caused.[44] Despite the recent establishment of a Golders Green branch of the Council of Christians and Jews,[45] in 1965 Reverend John Pearson, vicar of St Michael's parish church in Golders Green, unsettled the Jewish community by commenting in the *Hampstead and Highgate Express* that 'if a Christian moves out, his house is nearly always bought by Jewish people, because they are the only ones who can afford the present exorbitant prices'. He was also on record as saying: 'Golders Green might become a community without a church if Jewish people continue to move in in place of Christians'.[46]

In previous decades the Labour Party had benefited when anti-Semitism had disturbed the equilibrium of the Jewish community, but in the 1960s the Liberal vote rose in Golders Green, reflecting the national Liberal revival at this time. However, few Jews in the area were willing to challenge anti-Semitism openly. In 1964 John Shock, Mayor of the Borough of Hendon and member of Alyth Gardens Synagogue, took his fellow Jews to task for being 'apathetic'.[47]

Notwithstanding the attacks from outside the community and the insensitive words of some local people, like their children, adult Jews generally had good relations with the non-Jewish residents of the suburb. Jews who lived in the area during this period speak with warmth of their non-Jewish neighbours and some tell of how they developed lasting friendships with non-Jews. Pamela Nenk became friendly with Sister Catherine of La Sagesse[48] Convent School: 'She told my mother how much she admired her independence, so my mother taught her to drive'.[49] However, some Jewish families were more self-contained. Ian Torrance, who came to Golders Green as a child in 1950, recalls that his life revolved round his many aunts and uncles who regularly visited the family home in Gresham Gardens. He had a close relationship with them all, sometimes confusing him about who his parents were.[50]

Many people who lived in Golders Green in the 1960s and 1970s describe it as 'comfortable', 'unthreatening' and 'religiously easy going'. Peter Gilbey who had an off-licence in Temple Fortune during these years remembers that the secretary of Alyth Gardens Synagogue used to come into the shop on Saturdays to buy kosher wine and Mr Coffer, the director of Palwin,[51] who lived in the area, would walk past the shop on *Shabbat* and raise his hat.[52] However, other people found the atmosphere of Golders Green 'raving mad'.[53] In his poem, 'Odd',[54] the Jewish poet Dannie Abse, who lived in Hodford Road and was a familiar local figure, captured what he saw as the spirit of the suburb in the 1960s:

Its unusual to meet a beggar,
You hardly ever see a someone drunk.
It's a nice clean, quiet religious place.
For my part, now and then, I want to scream;
Thus by the neighbours, am considered odd.

Golders Green also sparked the poetic imagination of Jonathan Treital in his 'The Golem of Golders Green' in which he has Rabbi Yehuda Loew saunter through Golders Hill Park admiring 'the impertinence of the snowdrops' after which he 'drops into Grodzinski's for a kilo of Israeli couscous'.[55]

During the 1960s there grew up what was termed the 'Golders Green Novel' penned by 'Anglo-Jewry's angry young men'. Included under this heading were novels such as Brian Glanville's *The Bankrupts* (1958), Frederic Raphael's *The Limits of Love* (1960) and Chaim Bermant's *Jericho Sleep Alone* (1964), *Berl Make Tea* (1965) and *Ben Preserve Us* (1965). The subject of these novels was what was seen as the uncultured superficiality of the 'centrally-heated, wall-to-wall carpeted Judaism' of the north-west London suburbs, particularly Golders Green. The writers railed against an 'ill-defined, half-forgotten Jewishness, institutionalised into a hypocritical weekly or yearly synagogue attendance'.[56]

The 'Golders Green Novel' never became a vibrant genre in Jewish literature in the same way as books on life in the East End, and was generally deeply unpopular in Anglo-Jewry, especially in Golders Green where some found it too accurate for comfort. The books written by Brian Glanville (a Golders Green resident) in particular prompted so many letters of complaint to the *Jewish Chronicle* that they had to be published in a special supplement.[57] The historian Cecil Roth was moved to defend Golders Green Jewry, saying:

> [It] possesses abundant vitality, which brought it out of east London in the course of one generation; it has strong Jewish consciousness, and the desire to do what is right. It is in rapid evolution.[58]

Despite their unpopularity, the Golders Green novels do provide insights into life in Golders Green during the 1960s and 1970s, especially in Gerda Charles's *Crossing Point* (1960), dealing with controversial aspects of Jewish life such as marrying out and revolt against tradition, trends which were to become more prevalent over the next two decades.

The 1980s and 1990s

Trends in Anglo-Jewry discernible in previous decades reached their zenith in the 1980s. After a period of slow decline, the size of the community now fell dramatically. In 1976 the Board of Deputies had calculated that the level of assimilation through intermarriage was about 20 per cent nationally.[1] This trend increased over the next decade or so due to the large numbers of Jews now going to university.[2] Also worrying to communal leaders was the decreasing number of Jewish marriages and increasing rate of divorce and separation of Jewish couples, which were seen as threatening Jewish family life.[3] The outcome of changes in the religious life of the community was also fully apparent. The number of synagogues and synagogue membership had increased, but this was not matched by attendance of services, especially by younger people. Other signs of falling religious observance included a major decline in the consumption of kosher meat and households keeping a kosher kitchen, and a rise in the numbers driving on *Shabbat* and Jewish festivals.[4]

However, other forces were at play, which counter-balanced and eventually reversed the impact of the trends mentioned above. The arrival in Britain of immigrants from Africa, Asia, the Caribbean and the Middle East gave rise to a multicultural society, which meant that the focus of discrimination was no longer on the Jews alone. Although anti-Semitism resulting from the growth of Arab influence in Britain raised anxieties for Anglo-Jewry, there was sufficient respite to enable the community to make the transition from 'would-be-English' to a successful cultural group. The other main compensating trend was the sharp rise in the number of Jewish day schools, leading to a resurgence of a distinctive Jewish lifestyle.

These shifts in Anglo-Jewry were reflected at a local level in Golders Green but there were also developments that were quite specific to the area. One of the most notable of these developments was the increased rate at which strictly orthodox Jews were moving to Golders Green.[5] The newcomers were still migrating principally from Stamford Hill, but also came (mainly through marriage) from other strictly orthodox communities in New York, Antwerp and Israel. Unlike the strictly orthodox families who came to Golders Green in earlier decades, those now settling in the area largely had a Hassidic background[6] – the Hassidic sects of Gur, Sadigora, Vishnitz, Belz, Sasov and smaller numbers of Satmar, Skolye and Chabad Lubavitch.

The Hassidic Jews moving to Golders Green were generally more affluent, middle class and educated than those remaining in north London. Although deeply observant, they did not want to 'look over their shoulders' in respect of their orthodoxy and, according to one commentator, 'wanted to be able to wear a blue shirt rather than a white one without people looking at them askance'.[7] Their arrival had a much greater impact on the nature of the community culturally, religiously, spatially, socially and physically than any wave of migration to Golders Green since the arrival of the continental refugees in the 1930s.

The most obvious change was that Golders Green became more overtly Jewish. Whereas in previous decades the wearing of *kippot* in public places was fairly uncommon, limited mainly to the most orthodox rabbis, traditional dress now became more common: *shtreimels* and spodniks, worn on *Shabbat*, Jewish holidays and festivals; *bekeshes* for men, *tzitzit* for both men and boys; *sheitels* and 'modest' clothing for married women (long-sleeved shirts, skirts and dresses falling below the knee); *peyot* for boys and young men.[8] The sight of a young man in a wide-brimmed hat carrying a tome of the Talmud under his arm as he rushed to worship, and of groups of men in traditional dress silhouetted against the setting sun as they crossed over the bridge spanning the North Circular Road, became defining images of Golders Green. Initially the wearing of *kippot* and other traditional clothes appeared to make orthodox residents an easy target for anti-Semitism,[9] but while periodic attacks on Jews unsettled the community, they did not curtail the wearing of traditional garb.

A second clearly discernible impact of the expansion of the strictly orthodox community in Golders Green was that the area became much more religiously observant. This was evident in the increased closing of Jewish shops on *Shabbat*, the opening of new *mikvaot* (ritual baths), the rapid expansion in the number and size of strictly orthodox Jewish schools serving Golders Green,[10] the more public celebration of Jewish festivals, especially *Purim, Sukkot* and *Chanukkah*[11] but, above all, by the appearance of numerous *shtieblech* of various descriptions.[12] In the latter part of the twentieth century the number of houses of prayer and strictly orthodox shuls in Golders Green more than doubled and it became possible to pray or study at any time of day or night. One long-standing resident said:

Following the influx into the street of much more orthodox residents,[13] a dear friend was wont to say: 'When I married in Golders Green in the 1950s I was the only Jew in my street. I am now the only 'gentile'!'

The religiosity of the newcomers served to suppress the secular Zionism that had preoccupied the Jewish community in previous decades. There was now a distinct shift in focus from Israel to Jewish belief and Jewish learning.[14]

We have seen that when Jewish families first came to Golders Green they had clustered in the roads close to Finchley Road. Over subsequent decades they spread throughout the area, but the hub of the community remained near to Golders Green station. By the 1980s and 1990s there was a greater concentration of Jews in the streets close to the North Circular end of Golders Green (referred to as 'down there' or 'the *frum* end') such as Woodlands, Prince's Park Avenue and Highfield Avenue, which came to be referred to as 'B'nei Brak'.[15] Whereas previously there were up to six Jewish families living in some roads, now certain streets were almost exclusively Jewish.[16]

The newly arrived families not only lived geographically apart from the established Jewish community, they also carved out a separate social niche for themselves consistent with their religious beliefs. When there were fewer strictly orthodox families living in Golders Green, the impression was that they were more integrated into the local Jewish community but that as their numbers increased they became more separatist:

> When I was young my grandparents had neighbours who were very orthodox but they were quite outgoing – their children and I played together and when they were older they went to university and became professionals. Afterwards the community became much more closed.[17]

This separatism was reinforced by the fact that a large proportion of the strictly orthodox taking up residence in Golders Green, especially those from Hassidic sects, spoke Yiddish as part of their identity: 'The only language you could hear was Yiddish. It felt just like being in a foreign country'.[18]

One of the prime motives for the strictly orthodox moving to Golders Green was the type of housing available, but the houses they purchased were used very differently from previously.[19] Many houses were extended; adjoining houses were sometimes knocked into one; garages were converted into extra accommodation; front gardens were paved over to provide parking for the estate cars and people-carriers used by the large families now living in the houses.

Some existing residents enjoyed the tone and colour added by the new arrivals and admired their religious intensity and unselfconscious Jewishness.[20] They also enjoyed the hustle and bustle of families shopping for *Shabbat* followed by the sense of calm that came over the area once *Shabbat* arrived.[21] Many welcomed the feeling of safety created by the close-knit community: 'in Golders Green you feel that people will look out for you'.[22] However, others thought that the strictly orthodox community gave the mistaken impression to outsiders that Jews were 'more exotic than they really are',[23] and regarded the appearance of the *glatt* kosher establishments as divisive since they implied that 'kosher is not really kosher at all'.[24] Some Jews of German origin also thought the traditional clothing 'unnecessary',[25] subscribing as they did to the dictum 'Be a Jew in your home and a *mensch* (human being) on the street'.[26]

Many people were saddened by the splits they saw appearing in the community. However, the community remained quick to unite around issues impacting on Jews regardless of their religious outlook. This was clearly demonstrated in 1989 when a messianic sect located itself in Bridge Lane seeking to convert Jews to Christianity. All the religious leaders in the area delivered the same warning messages, advising congregants to be alert to the activities of the sect and to watch over those who might be vulnerable to their missionary intent.[27] It was also demonstrated when there were developments abroad to which the whole community responded such as the experience of the Refuseniks in the former Soviet Union.[28] In addition to the campaigns mounted by individual congregations, Golders Green was the location of the high-profile and very influential Women's Campaign for Soviet Jewry ('The 35s'), whose initial members largely came from Golders Green and Hampstead Garden Suburb.[29] It occupied a series of not very salubrious offices the women were able to 'beg, borrow and steal' from various benefactors:

> We first worked from some nasty damp rooms in a basement with a dripping lavatory. We worked surrounded by buckets to catch the leaks from the ceiling. Our next premises above a hairdressers shop were even worse.[30]

Many of the rallies organised by the group commenced from Golders Green and attracted a great deal of support from across the Jewish community, including a number of Holocaust survivors living locally.[31]

While the existing Jewish community soon adapted to the ways of their observant neighbours, it took non-Jews a little longer to understand the religious rules by which the strictly orthodox lived. One of the roads in which they had coalesced was Gresham Gardens, where on the first day of *Pesach* in 1989 free packets of Kellogg's cornflakes were delivered for advertising purposes through the letterboxes of *chametz*-free homes.[32] Within a short time, the roadway outside was littered with unopened packets of the offending grain.[33]

The differences between the newcomers and the existing community were illustrated during the course of the long debate over the introduction of an *eruv*, an area demarcated by a wire (or other device) within the confines of which observant Jews can carry or push objects such as prams and wheelchairs on *Shabbat*. Because of the controversy it created, it took fifteen years from the time that *Ner Israel*'s Rabbi Alan Kimche commissioned an American expert to draw up a map for what is known as the North-West London Eruv, until it went live in 2003 covering Golders Green and a number of adjacent districts – Hendon and Hampstead Garden Suburb together with parts of Child's Hill, Cricklewood, East Finchley, Finchley and Mill Hill.[34]

Opposition to the *eruv* came from several directions. Some secular and non-orthodox Jews talked about 'ghettos',[35] arguing that the *eruv* would encourage separateness and discourage assimilation. Some non-Jewish residents protested against the erection of what they feared would be intrusive religious symbols.

Rumours circulated about Jewish vigilante groups being set up to guard the *eruv* against vandals. While Dunstan Road Synagogue fought hard for the introduction of the *eruv*, many of the local rabbis from the Union of Orthodox Hebrew Congregations disputed its validity under *halachah* (Jewish law), forbidding followers to use it. Some families were torn between support for the *eruv* and loyalty to their religious leaders. A member of Munk's shul was quoted as saying that she would leave the community if its leader, Rabbi Feldman, opposed the *eruv*,[36] which he did. According to newspaper reports, some young families left congregations opposing the *eruv* to join more 'eruv-friendly' synagogues.[37]

The other group of Jews coming to Golders Green who helped to change the 'feel' of Golders Green in the 1980s and 1990s were Israeli Jews. Small numbers of Jews from Israeli had been arriving in Golders Green since the 1960s. Typically they came as families who tended to settle for substantial periods of time. Initially they were significantly outnumbered by British Jews who were moving to Israel.[38] The reason why numbers were so small during the 1960s and 1970s was that Zionist ideology demanded that Israelis must live in and identify with Israel to protect the identity of the Jewish people. Those who left were seen as violators of this belief and as a potential threat to the nation. They were referred to as *Yoredim* (literally 'those who come down').[39]

However, by the end of the twentieth century the number of Israelis living in Golders Green had risen so dramatically that their presence became unmistakeable.[40] A few who came to the area were studying in London, but Golders Green was usually too expensive for those not earning. Most Israelis were coming for economic reasons. During the 1990s Israel's significant economic and demographic growth, its relatively peaceful relations with neighbouring countries, but above all its increasingly globalised economy, had the effect of reducing the stigma attached to Israelis working abroad. Having Israeli citizens employed in other countries became essential to the continued expansion of the economy.[41] Many of the Israelis who arrived in Golders Green in the 1990s worked in IT, venture capital markets and education.[42]

As the number of Israelis living in Golders Green increased, several falafel bars and other eateries catering particularly for the Israelis opened. The new infrastructure attracted more Israelis to Golders Green but they continued to feel ambivalent about staying in Britain. They socialised almost exclusively with other Israelis, and rarely engaged with the indigenous Jews. They often talked about returning home and many actually did so, usually as their families were starting to grow up. According to one commentator, young people preferred Israel to London and their parents developed concerns about the national identity of their offspring once they became teenagers.[43] However some Israelis did come with the intention of remaining in Britain. This small group were mainly Sephardi Jews originating from Middle Eastern countries who had found it difficult to settle in Israel. They arrived with the aim of making a better living than they had been able to in Israel. Some were very observant and were prominent in setting up new

Sephardi shuls like Menachem Haziza who established a *glatt* kosher[44] butchers in Russell Parade.[45]

While a large proportion of the Israeli migrants of the 1980s and 1990s saw themselves as temporary residents, the third group of Jews arriving in Golders Green at this time – another wave of South African Jews – came to stay. The South Africans settling in the area in the latter part of the twentieth century migrated for different reasons from those who had arrived during the 1960s and 1970s. They were no longer mainly political émigrés, but had left South Africa principally for economic reasons: 'They could see that the Apartheid regime was crumbling and that they were unlikely to fare well under a black majority government'.[46] Although not all of them were Jewish, the number of South Africans living in Golders Green doubled between 1991 and 2001.[47] This wave of Jewish South Africans tended to be more orthodox than those who had settled in Golders Green during the 1960s and 1970s since by the 1990s the South African Jewish community had experienced a rightward shift in Jewish outlook similar to that of Anglo-Jewry.

In contrast to general trends in Anglo-Jewry, the inward movements described above served to change the balance in the Jewish population of Golders Green between those born in this country and those born abroad and also between those Jews who used English as their first and only language of social intercourse and those who used other languages such as Yiddish and *Ivrit* (Modern Hebrew). The demographic changes also helped to maintain the size and viability of the Golders Green Jewish community as other groups of Jews were leaving the area. Some older Jewish people who had arrived in the area in the post-war years and whose offspring had left home were now finding their properties too large and were moving to areas where there were a greater number of smaller properties, such as Hendon and Finchley. Others were selling their property and using the equity to move closer to central London, particularly St John's Wood where certain blocks of flats were popular with former Golders Green Jewish households that were 'downsizing'.[48]

However, a number of older people also moved from larger properties into the apartment blocks in the area. One such woman was Miriam Burke (née Karbatznick) who, according to her relatives,[49] loved living in Golders Green with all its Jewish people and shops, and who epitomised 'the type of Jewish lady for whom Golders Green had been invented'. Her relatives have recalled:

> She opened her flat … to all who came with a warmth and genuine pleasure in the company of her family and friends, either round the dining or Kalooki table. A sumptuous spread and unending gifts were her hallmark … She delighted in giving in abundance. Long before the contemporary discussion of genetically enhanced foods, Auntie Miriam's produce was outsize – grapes the size of plums, plums the size of oranges. I recall the story of a plumber who had already paid her a visit to complete an odd job being asked to return by a family member and replying to the request, 'This time I'd better not eat anything before I go'.[50]

While during the 1980s young families continued to leave Golders Green, by the 1990s the move out of London had tailed off and there were even signs that some families were beginning to move back to Golders Green having spent several decades in the Hertfordshire suburbs. With fewer family responsibilities, some 'empty-nest' couples were willing to trade space for the convenience of being closer to the facilities of central London.[51] Others were attracted back by the increasing religious atmosphere of the area discussed earlier in this chapter.

Not only was the Jewish community of Golders Green changing significantly at the end of the twentieth century, the wider population of the area was also becoming more diverse. From the inception of the suburb at the beginning of the twentieth century there had been people from minority groups other than Jews living in Golders Green, including students and teachers from the Indian sub-continent attached to one of the universities in London.[52] In the 1970s Indians from Uganda started to move into the area in substantial numbers and Golders Green became noticeably more multicultural. When Indians first began to buy property and to establish communal buildings, a few Jews felt slightly uneasy about developments, not with any thought of discrimination, but simply because the people and their culture were an unknown entity.[53]

However, any unease was momentary and most Jewish families rapidly became accustomed to their new neighbours. Viki Minsky devoted time to working in a tuition school set up to teach Indian children to speak English so they could make the most of the education system.[54] Steven Derby, who went to school and made friends with several Indian children, recalls: 'We used to play cricket together on the Heath Extension. They were very good and much better than me!'[55]

During the 1980s and 1990s, the Indians were joined by other ethnic and national groups such as Japanese people, who had mainly came to England to work in the banking sector, and also Koreans and South-East Asians. Some of the new residents opened businesses and restaurants catering both for their own and for the Jewish community including many kosher establishments.[56] As a result, by the 1990s the Jewish community of Golders Green now existed in a culturally diverse area.

9

Recent Years

For the first time in Anglo-Jewry's existence, at the beginning of the twenty-first century reliable statistics became available on the community when a question on religious affiliation was included in the 2001 census. Until that time Jewish policymakers and service providers were reliant on data with major shortcomings. The information became even richer when the 2011 census yielded comparative data that confirmed that, compared with other religious groups, Jews are relatively old but that, between 2001 and 2011, the community became younger. Given that Anglo-Jewry had been ageing since the 1950s onwards, this was a major turnaround.

The key driver of the change was the growth in the strictly orthodox section of Anglo-Jewry (now referred to collectively as *haredi* rather than ultra-orthodox, which was seen as pejorative) among whom there was a preponderance of large families.[1] The trend was particularly pronounced in Golders Green with its large *haredi* community. In 2011 the Jewish population of Golders Green was 7,661, an increase of 35 per cent since 2001,[2] making Golders Green electoral ward the most Jewishly populous neighbourhood in the country. Jews formed 37 per cent of the total population of the ward and had become the largest population group.[3] This considerable growth resulted partly from continued migration to the area but more from the increasing family size of the *haredim*. It is now common for *haredi* couples in Golders Green to have upwards of six children.

This change alongside an increasing number of Jews living into their 90s might have presented major problems for communal organisations had they not been prepared for the demographic shifts. During the 1980s, a number of Jewish welfare agencies relocated to Golders Green to premises adjacent to the Sobell Community Centre. As a result of their co-location, the various bodies (the Jewish Welfare Board, the Jewish Blind Society and eight other smaller charitable organisations) combined to form Jewish Care, producing an organisation equipped to provide comprehensive and integrated services for Anglo-Jewry. Working in close proximity to a large Jewish population enabled Jewish Care to reach out into the community and gain a detailed understanding of its support needs.

The growth in the haredim in Golders Green is indicated by the dramatic increase in the number of *haredi* shuls that have opened in the area in the last ten years. For a time many strictly orthodox Jews, especially the *Hassidim* who had relocated to Golders Green, returned routinely to Stamford Hill to attend specific shuls, often taking rooms in hotels over *Shabbat*. They walked to shul there and returned to Golders Green on a Saturday evening or, during the summer months when *Shabbat* ended late, on a Sunday.[4] By 2000 most members of the *haredi* community had at least one shul in Golders Green in which they felt at home. Remarking on this development, one interviewee said:

> When I came to Golders Green in 1964, on *Shabbat* I could walk to 40 places to *daven* [pray] within an hour. Now I can walk to forty *minyanim* [prayer meetings] within 15 minutes.[5]

The growth in shuls is not the only indication that the *haredi* community is becoming more firmly rooted in Golders Green. There is now also a highly developed social infrastructure to support *haredi* life. This infrastructure includes an ambulance service, Hatzollah, based in Highfield Road. Hatzollah is run by volunteers and has three ambulances providing a responsive emergency service. It is mainly funded by private donations, but also raises income by selling its skills (for example, running first-aid courses for Jewish Care staff).[6] One Golders Green resident recounted how, when she called Hatzollah, an ambulance arrived within minutes to take her sick child to the Royal Free Hospital. Once the child was well enough to leave hospital, Hatzollah arranged a taxi to take them home, all at no expense.[7] Hatzollah also deals with people who have mental illnesses and dementia as well as responding to emergencies in the non-Jewish population.[8] Linked to Hatzollah is a group providing facilities (a relatives' room and kosher food) for the families of patients at the Royal Free Hospital.

Shomrim [watchmen] London NW is part of a network of mobile neighbourhood watch schemes set up by *haredi* communities across Britain and the United States. The local branch was established by Gary Ost in 2008 and covers Finchley, Hendon and Child's Hill as well as Temple Fortune and Golders Green, where it has a base from which it operates around the clock. Its volunteers, who have all had police training, are proactive and intervene when members of the community feel unsafe or threatened. They are particularly effective in tracking down and detaining suspects until the police arrive. However, Shomrim's main role is to provide a presence to act as a deterrent to burglary, vandalism, mugging, assault, domestic violence and anti-Semitic attacks. It supports victims of crime, helps locate missing people and liaises between the Jewish community and the Metropolitan Police.[9]

The most remarkable feature of the communal infrastructure is the *gemachim* (acts of kindness). There are *gemachim* to support mothers with newborn babies, to ensure that every family has a chicken to eat on *Shabbat*, to provide wedding outfits for those who are not able to afford to purchase them, to obtain furniture for those without the means to buy it, to supply hospital gowns, to help people fill in forms and to help cook for people on special diets. *Local News* circulated in Golders Green contains a 'Chesed [loving kindness] Corner' listing help needed and support available locally. *Shomer Shabbos* (those who keep the Sabbath), a directory covering the area, lists *gemachim* for every conceivable eventuality. It also lists *chaverim* (friends) that help people with problems they may face like DIY emergencies and locking themselves out of a house or a car.

The *haredi* community, which prides itself on being self-sufficient, is also involved in an immense amount of fundraising and charitable giving. During *Purim* the community raises large sums of money for various charities such as Camp Simcha, which provides respite care, and for Kisharon School.[10] More affluent members of the community regularly make major donations to individuals and to communal causes such as the *haredi* schools.[11] The Freshwater family are well-known local benefactors who over the years have funded numerous community projects. Benzion Dunner, a property magnate who described himself as 'God's Postman', regularly made generous donations to both individuals and institutions. Shortly before he was killed in a car crash in 2008 he had signed cheques totalling £2 million at one of the 'open houses' for dispensing charity held at his Golders Green home. He often worked into the early hours to ensure that no deserving cause was neglected.[12] Maurice Wohl, owner of United Real Property Trust, made donations to various communities and communal buildings in Golders Green (notably the Maurice and Vivienne Wohl Campus in which Jewish Care and other organisations are housed).[13] Each week Mr Reich, the well-known Golders Green caterer, provides food for struggling families.[14]

As well as monetary giving, members of the *haredi* community donate large amounts of their time to community support activities. One woman has turned a room of her house into a storeroom for the goods that she collects that people might need, such as a car seat for a visiting family or crockery for a major event.[15] Another woman has established a free postal service. She receives invitations for celebrations and passes them on to distributors appointed for each of the roads in which there are concentrations of *haredi* families.[16] Yet another woman works on a voluntary basis several days a week for an organisation that distributes food for members of the community who cannot afford to support their large families.[17]

Family life is paramount in the *haredi* community, and people who do not have children can become very isolated. A fertility service has therefore been set up to help couples experiencing difficulties in conceiving.[18] The Club House in Woodstock Avenue, founded by Rabbi Refoel Berisch, offers a refuge and support for vulnerable young people from *haredi* families such as drug users and truants. Rabbi Berisch provides 'hands-on' help at the Club House but also devotes time to fundraising for its activities.[19]

In addition to the *glatt* kosher shops and restaurants that are now such a feature of Golders Green,[20] the last ten years has seen the development of a number of facilities on which the *haredi* community relies: a new communal *mikveh*, a crockery and cutlery *mikveh*[21] and a Shatnez Centre based nearby in Hendon, where garments are tested to ensure that they are kosher – that is, that they do not contain a prohibited mixture of wool and linen.[22] The *Shomer Shabbos* directory lists numerous *mohalim* (those who perform the rite of circumcision on male infants).

As previously mentioned, the *haredim* of Golders Green are generally more affluent and educated than the *haredim* of Stamford Hill. The Golders Green *haredi* community is also more diverse than the Stamford Hill community, which is now almost exclusively composed of *Hassidim*. While the Golders Green *haredim* remain strictly religious and observance is increasing because of the prevalence of *yeshivah* (place of study for young men) education,[23] the differences between the Golders Green and the Stamford Hill communities are becoming more accentuated. A *haredi* man living in Golders Green who formerly travelled regularly to Stamford Hill to study said, 'It's like going to a foreign country when I go there these days'.[24]

The unifying body of the *haredi* community in Britain is the Union of Orthodox Hebrew Congregations ('the Adath').[25] However, the *haredi* community of Golders Green has recently begun to demonstrate its divergence from the thinking of the Adath on some communal issues. In his column in the *Jewish Chronicle* in March 2015, Geoffrey Alderman has suggested that, whereas after the Second World War the Adath became increasingly dominated by deeply conservative Hassidic sects who were more ultra-conservative than its founders, this situation may be changing as a result of the geographical dispersal of the Union's membership.[26] A prominent member of the Golders Green *haredim* believes that 'In Golders Green we are much more independent and able to look after ourselves. The Adath has less influence here than it does in Stamford Hill'.[27] Located in a temporary building in Golders Green Road, the *haredim* of Golders Green have set up their own *Beth Din*[28] to take decisions on religious matters, including Jewish divorce certificates, licensing of restaurants and shops, conversions to Judaism and the maintenance of *mikvaot*.

The *haredi* community has made an impact on life in Golders Green, but Golders Green also appears to have influenced the *haredi* community. In comparison to Stamford Hill, the Golders Green *haredi* community is increasingly ambitious and there is said to be a certain amount of 'keeping up with the Cohens'.[29] The listings for expensive holidays, upmarket catering services and beauty salons contained in a local Jewish advertising circular aimed mainly at the orthodox community suggests that the consumerist lifestyle in the surrounding population is finding its way into *haredi* community. In their Golders Green setting, the traditionally isolationist *Hassidim* are becoming more open to the outside world and taking on the bourgeois lifestyle long accepted by *Litvishe* and German *haredim* and are seemingly more prepared to adopt some aspects of modern society as a means of survival.[30] Although some Jews who become more orthodox in their religious beliefs and some newly religious Jews have elected to speak Yiddish as a means of identification, a number of *haredim* have decided not to transmit the language to their children.[31]

Living in a less closed environment has opened the younger generation to new possibilities. Some young *haredi* men are aspiring to a better standard of living and are seeking to achieve social standing through their earning ability rather than through intensive learning.[32] Occasionally young *haredim* choose to pursue totally different lifestyles. Henry Stimler (who, as a child, was, in his own words, 'a wandering spirit and a dreamer') grew up as the second of five children in a strictly orthodox home in Golders Green. He now works as a creative director in a nightclub in New York rather than in his father's successful commodities business, which he was expected to enter. Although he no longer lives within the *haredi* community, his Jewish faith remains very important to him.[33]

There are some signs that women are becoming more liberalised and are 'pushing at the boundaries' in respect of the traditional roles of women in the *haredi* community.[34] *Haredi* marriages also appear to be changing. Not only is the dynamic between couples closer and more equal, but young people are also having more input into their choice of partners. There are paid and free Jewish dating services geared towards strictly orthodox Jews, but they are very much frowned upon by the *haredi* community, and it remains very rare for *haredi* couples to select their own partners.[35] Even in more liberal Golders Green the mingling of the sexes is strictly regulated and boys and girls have little contact with the opposite sex outside their families. The vast majority of potential couples do not meet until after extensive research and negotiations have been carried out by a *shadchan* (matchmaker).[36] However, some young people are meeting more often with prospective partners before making a decision on their suitability.[37]

Although *haredi* schools continue to promote the ideal of a husband who is in full-time learning, this stereotype is no longer totally prevalent across the Golders Green *haredim*. However, there remain strongly held views on what constitutes a 'suitable' partner, chief of which is that a young man must be *yeshivah* educated and young women must have attended a ladies' seminary. Some families are unable to finance extended education for their children and bursaries have been established to sponsor the education of young people so that they are not disadvantaged in the 'marriage market'.[38]

Some matchmakers are becoming increasingly sophisticated in their research activities, often employing information technology to work on a global basis.[39] However, others adhere to more traditional methods. Rabbi Refoel and Loli Berisch have been involved in matchmaking for thirty-six years and are now arranging marriages for the children of couples they matched. They have extensive knowledge of the community and their services are very much sought after. They mainly deal with matches for the 25 to 40 year olds, but there is a growing demand for matches for older people. Rabbi Refoel and Loli Berisch arrange Monday 'get togethers' because they prefer matches to result from face-to-face meetings.[40]

International *shidduchim* (arranged marriages) are particularly common among the Gur and Satmar *Hassidim* due to the fact that the movements' centres are in Israel and there are also large communities of both sects in New York. Although outsiders may consider it a major move for a young person to make a shift to another country when they are married, the transition is not as great as it might appear because, as one member of the Golders Green *haredi* community pointed out, people from the same sect will instantly understand the community to which they move.[41]

As well as forging an identity that diverges from that of the community of Stamford Hill, the Golders Green *haredim* appear to be increasingly confident about their identity in relation to the non-Jewish world, especially younger people. Whereas most *haredi* men unselfconsciously wear traditional clothing in Golders Green, many young men now do so wherever they are. One man commented:

> My sons are much more confident about displaying their Jewishness than I am. I am still cautious about wearing a *kippah* [skull cap] if I am travelling into central London, but they don't think twice about it. They say: 'What's the problem?'[42]

Some people have attributed this growing confidence to the arrival of Israelis in the area who are less self-conscious about displaying their Jewishness, having been brought up in a Jewish state.[43]

The *haredi* community in Golders Green has a close relationship with strictly orthodox Jews in Hendon. However, Golders Green is generally regarded as being more religious. Some Jewish families living in Hendon would prefer to live in Golders Green but are unable to afford the higher house prices. There is therefore quite a flow of people from Hendon across the road bridge over the North Circular Road to attend shuls in Golders Green. There is also a flow in the opposite direction but it is not nearly as pronounced.[44]

With its many shuls and a *haredi* community that is rapidly expanding, Golders Green is now regarded as a centre of strict orthodoxy of global significance. It is often likened to Borough Park in New York. With its *Hassidim* becoming increasingly wealthy and influential, world-famous Hassidic rabbis regularly visit Golders Green from Israel and America, often seeking financial support for their causes. It is sometimes a matter of contention that money is taken from the Golders Green community for projects abroad.[45]

For many years Rabbi Chuna Halpern was a legendary figure in Golders Green and it was generally understood that 'the Halperns ruled Golders Green'.[46] It has been suggested that Rabbi Halpern's death in 2015 marked the passing of an era in terms of the development of the Golders Green *haredi* community.[47] However, even before Rabbi Chuna's death, the Halpern family was losing its currency, mainly as a result of the allegations against a leading family member.[48] Today there are indications that new leaders may be emerging. For example, the launch of a rabbinical helpline by Rabbi Greenberg of Munk's shul has been seen as a sign of broader ambitions. However, one commentator has suggested that individual rabbis in Golders Green may be content to 'operate as masters of their own houses without any alpha-rabbis blowing a louder *shofar*'.[49]

Some *haredi* young couples are prepared to live quite frugally in small flats, but there is a limited amount of property that they can afford to buy in Golders

Green. Over the last decade there have been discussions about setting up a *haredi* community outside of London where property is more affordable (for example, in Canvey Island, Borhamwood, Hadley Wood and Milton Keynes). So far, these plans have not come to fruition because too few young couples are willing to leave their wider families to form a viable community.[50]

As significant as changes occurring in the *haredi* community are the developments among Israeli residents. Around the turn of this century, the number of Israelis coming to Britain rose rapidly. This was partly the result of the opening of stalls in shopping malls across the country selling Middle Eastern goods for which there was a major recruitment drive in Israel. However, the main impetus was a major downturn in the Israeli economy, especially in the field of information technology, exacerbated by a deteriorating political situation. This wave of migration was largely made up of young, single, predominantly male Israelis, many of whom had just completed their army service.[51] Compared to Israelis who came to Golders Green in previous decades, the new migrants were settling for shorter periods of time, often staying for only a year or so before either returning to Israel or moving on to other parts of London. In the latter case, this was often because they had met a partner, started a family and wanted access to a different range of facilities from those available in Golders Green.[52] This made the Israeli Jews living in Golders Green an even more transient group than it had been previously. Dov Softi, an Israeli who previously lived in Golders Green said:

> Many Israelis would really like to go to America but they can't gain entry. The UK is a second choice destination because it's much closer than the US. Some Israelis come because they have joint nationality passports or European passports. Some don't have the proper paperwork and leave again quite quickly! Even when they are here for a short time they return to Israel at regular intervals for weddings, a *Bar Mitzvah* or other celebrations.[53]

Although the prime reason for the increase in younger Israelis coming to Golders Green is economic, they are often motivated by other reasons – they do not like the political situation in Israel, do not feel safe there, dislike the growth of strict orthodoxy and, as they see it, the intrusion of rabbinical law into private lives. Many of those arriving would prefer to live closer to central London but they cannot afford to do so. They recognise that Golders Green works well as a 'first port of call'[54] and often they know people living in the area who can show them around, give them advice and pass on useful contacts.[55] The migrants also see Golders Green as convenient for accessing the plentiful supply of jobs in inner London and because of the availability of rental property, even if it is quite expensive, creating the need for many Israelis to share accommodation.[56] The tendency of Israelis to cluster has led to *Ivrit* becoming one of the main languages in some roads.[57]

Few of the new wave of Israeli migrants have come for religious reasons and many are secular Jews, making them very different culturally from the increasingly observant Jewish population of the area. The Israelis generally do not attend services in the local synagogues or participate in their communal activities, of which they would probably be unaware, since synagogues in Israel do not provide the same social function as they do in England.[58] Many cannot understand why Jews in a free country would willingly go to synagogue without being obliged to do so by the state or for celebrations.[59] Nor do they understand why indigenous Jews who associate mainly with other Jews do not go and live in Israel. It has been suggested that religiously observant Israelis tend to join Alyth Gardens (Refom) Synagogue or New North London (Masorti) Synagogue rather than an orthodox synagogue, where most would be uncomfortable.[60] In 2008 Anat Koren, the publisher of London's main Hebrew-language magazine *ALondon*,[61] commented that 'We are two communities who share the same religion but have completely different cultures.'[62] While Israelis define themselves in national terms, British Jews define themselves religiously.

Since they do not intend to stay for long, a large proportion of the Israelis now coming to Golders Green do not attempt to put down roots or to assimilate. According to Dov Softi, although the Israelis engage with the Golders Green Jewish population at festival time and especially on Israel's Independence Day, they generally 'hold themselves aloof'.[63] Despite the efforts made by the Israeli consulate, which at one time convened a weekly *bayit* (gathering) in Golders Green,[64] the Israelis have not become organised or formed societies or cultural bodies. They do, however, socialise in certain cafés and restaurants, which has contributed to Golders Green's reputation for its 'pavement café society'. JW3, a Jewish cultural centre in nearby Hampstead, is promoting some activities specifically aimed at Israelis, which could aid their integration into local life.[65] However, although the number of Israelis in Britain has grown as a number of Israeli families[66] have joined the younger migrants due to the continuing deterioration of the Israeli economy, the migrants have been unsettled by the recent rise in anti-Semitism and anti-Israeli sentiment in Britain. This has hindered bridge building between local Jewish and Israeli residents in areas like Golders Green.[67]

Paralleling the change in the profile of Israelis coming to Golders Green, there has been a change in the type of Jewish resident leaving Golders Green for Israel. In the 1960s and 1970s those making *aliyah* from Golders Green were mainly younger people who thought it was the right thing to do for religious or political reasons. More recently an increasing number of retired people have made their home in Israel to achieve an improved quality of life. Several retirement complexes have opened to cater for older people from across Europe making *aliyah* and the United Synagogue's decision to purchase land in Israel for burials and its willingness to allow United Synagogue members to transfer their burial rights has made the move easier.[68]

Some of those who have made the move to Israel are long-standing members of Dunstan Road Synagogue, which since its inception, has been very Zionist in its orientation. The older people who made *aliyah* include Zena and David Clayton, who left Golders Green to live in Herzliya in 2010. Writing from Israel in 2013 about their experiences they said that coming from Zionist families they had often thought about making *aliyah*, especially after two of their three daughters and several other family members and friends settled in Israel. The proximity of a shul with an 'Anglo corner' in the retirement complex they had identified was pivotal in their decision to make the move.[69] In addition to those leaving the UK permanently, there are also an increasing number of older people from Golders Green who live in Israel for large parts of the year.[70] There is a particular exodus around *Pesach* and *Sukkot*.

While Israelis have been coming to Golders Green for some time, in the last five years a completely new group of Jewish migrant has been settling in the area: French Jews. It was recently estimated that there are between 10,000 to 20,000 French Jews living in London. They started to come to England in the early 2000s, often taking up highly paid jobs in the City of London. They usually returned home on Friday afternoons on the Eurostar to spend *Shabbat* with their friends and family. However, the increase in anti-Semitism in France meant that going home was no longer an attraction and the French Jews began to settle in London.

Initially the French-Jewish community, which is largely made up of Sephardi Jews originating in Morocco, Tunisia or Algeria, found accommodation in central London. Having lived mainly in Paris and other large French cities, they associated the suburbs with poverty and tracts of unattractive housing. They gradually realised that London's suburbs were very different and started to settle in areas such as St John's Wood, West Hampstead and Maida Vale. Until recently Golders Green, which the French Jews refer to as the *Quartier Noir* because of the large number of orthodox Jews wearing traditional dress, was regarded only as a destination for kosher food and restaurants. However, young couples have recognised that housing in Golders Green is more affordable than elsewhere in London and are moving to the area in increasing numbers.[71] The long-term goal of a large proportion of the French-Jewish community, which is 'tight-knit and cliquey', is to go to Israel but for now they are educating their children here, mainly in the *haredi* schools serving the area.[72]

In addition to the French Jews, in the last ten years there has been a steady flow to Golders Green of Sephardi families from many different Middle Eastern backgrounds, attracted by and expanding the Sephardi shuls that have been established in the area.[73] Sephardi families are arriving not only from across London but also from outside the capital, particularly Manchester. The recent arrivals are concentrated in roads such as Sneath Avenue, Ambrose Gardens, Woodstock Avenue and The Drive, but especially in Cranbourne Gardens, which has been dubbed 'Sephardi Road'.[74]

Existing alongside these newer elements of the Golders Green Jewish community are rare vestiges of the community in bygone days. There are still a number of former continental refugees living in care homes in the area, and for several years a distinguished group of war veterans, both men and women, have met monthly under the auspices of the Association of Jewish Refugees (AJR) at the Imperial Café in Golders Green Road to reminisce about the experience they gained as 'enemy aliens'.[75] Their numbers are gradually dwindling.[76]

Over the last decade the number of Jewish institutions located in Golders Green has increased. The premises occupied by Jewish Care and the Sobell were

Golders Green 2016.

demolished and totally rebuilt during 2008–10. The Maurice and Viviennne Wohl Campus now provides the base for an even wider range of welfare activities, including a dementia unit and care-assisted-living flats. It is also used as a venue for many communal activities, local organisations including several *minyanim* and Jewish learning sessions and cultural events.[77] In 2013 it was announced that the *Jewish Chronicle* would be relocating to Golders Green, which was greeted with enthusiasm by many people but questioned by others. The criticism is that too many communal bodies are situated in Golders Green or nearby, which is not convenient for Jews living and working in other parts of the capital, has made the area more 'ghetto-like' and has had a deleterious impact on other Jewish communities.[78]

Many people interviewed for this book said that 'Golders Green is not what it used to be'. This is undoubtedly true. Its Jewish shops and kosher restaurants attract Jews from all over the world; many families have links to Jewish communities in other countries, especially those in Belgium,[79] Israel and New York; people spend significant periods of time in Israel; many Jews living in Golders Green are engaged in occupations with international horizons. Information technology has hastened internationalism. Even *haredim* who officially frown on the Internet are not unaffected by it. Some *haredi* men use the Internet in the local library, which they feel is a controlled and safe environment where they will not have to mix with those with whom they might feel uncomfortable.[80] The Golders Green Jewish community is no longer part of a cosy middle-class suburb; it is a major feature of international Jewry.

Places of Worship: The Larger Synagogues

Over the last hundred years many Jews have left Judaism, come to regard themselves as secular or cultural Jews, chosen not to affiliate to a Jewish community, or elected to worship informally. Nevertheless, the synagogue remains the core institution of Jewish life. This and the next chapter explore the history of the Golders Green synagogues. This chapter outlines the history of the larger synagogues – the strictly Orthodox Golders Green Beth Hamedrash ('Munk's shul'), the progressive North-Western Reform Synagogue ('Alyth') and the United Synagogue, 'middle-of-the-road' Golders Green Synagogue ('Dunstan Road') – drawing out common themes and significant differences between them. Chapter 11 will focus on the smaller synagogues. Some readers may find it helpful to refer to the explanation of the various Jewish denominations provided in the appendix.

The founding of the synagogues

In the early years of the twentieth century it was not uncommon for Jews to walk several miles to a synagogue.[1] The first Jewish residents of Golders Green walked to the existing synagogues in Brondesbury and West Hampstead (Hampstead Synagogue). However, as the number of Jews moving to the area increased, there was a growing demand for a synagogue to be established locally. A 1911 edition of the *Jewish Chronicle* included a statement recognising the obligation of communal bodies to provide religious services in Golders Green.[2] Two years later Mr Elsley Zeitlyn, a barrister living at Carmel Lodge, Hampstead Way,[3] wrote to the newspaper expressing regret that no action had been taken. He had been attempting to fill the gap himself by leading services, and given the apparent lack of interest of communal bodies, the Jews of Golders Green had decided to take matters into their own hands.[4]

A group of twenty people secured a room in the premises of the Middlesex Auto-Car Company Ltd in West Heath Drive to celebrate the High Holydays (*Rosh Hashanah*, Jewish New Year and *Yom Kippur*, the Day of Atonement) of 1913.[5]

Shortly afterwards, the nascent congregation was contacted by the Jewish Religious Union (JRU), which had recently established the Liberal Jewish Synagogue (LJS) near Baker Street and was seeking to foster more Liberal communities. The JRU was deeply unpopular and the brand of Judaism promoted by its religious leader, the Lithuanian-born, Harvard-educated Rabbi Israel Mattuck, was creating controversy in the Jewish press because of its radical departure from traditional Judaism.[6] In May 1914 Rabbi Mattuck, who lived in nearby Wildwood, addressed a meeting at the Willifield Club House in Temple Fortune.[7] It was agreed to establish what was known as Golders Green and District JRU.

Rabbi Mattuck preached at a choral service of the new JRU branch on 17 October 1914,[8] which followed well-attended High Holyday services. However, the report of the occasion contained a hint of what was to come. It mentioned that current and prospective members of the branch were being consulted on the type of services they wished to hold. It emerged that only a few families had supported services being held 'on Liberal lines', and there was a greater demand for traditional forms of worship.[9] Many of the Jewish residents of Golders Green had only recently left behind *chevrot* (small, traditional houses of worship) in the East End of London and possibly found a shift to progressive Judaism too great. Several families were on their way to becoming prominent members of the Anglo-Jewish community and wanted to be seen as part of 'the establishment'.[10]

In July 1915 a public meeting was held in the recently opened Ionic cinema,[11] at which a community consisting of twenty members was established. Benjamin

Building of
Golders Green
Synagogue

Drage[12] (later Sir Benjamin) was elected as its president. In his address he pronounced it a vindication of the 'might and beauty of Judaism' that the Jews of Golders Green were 'gathered in glorification and unity of our ancient faith' during wartime.[13] The embryonic community set about organising regular services and religion classes. Arrangements were made with Reverend Trundle to use St Alban's church hall, the only part of the church to exist at that time.[14] The various signs of Christianity were covered to protect the sensibilities of the Jewish worshippers,[15] but nothing could be done about the 'cold winds ascending through the floor'.[16] A Ladies' Canvassing Committee was formed to recruit children to religion classes.[17]

At the end of 1915 Reverend Nathan Levine[18] was employed as temporary 'Reader' for services and to teach the religion classes,[19] but the growing community soon decided to recruit a permanent rabbi. Reverend Isaac Livingstone, who had been serving Bradford Hebrew Congregation, was appointed as 'Minister, Superintendent and Teacher of the Religion Classes'.[20] At this point the membership of the community was still fewer than thirty,[21] and the salary offered was very low. However, as one of Reverend Livingstone's daughters later explained, he could see that the community would grow and that the position would 'turn into a decent job':[22]

> Mummy said the move to London took all their savings ... Sir Benjamin Drage, who was a rich man, said to my mother one day after a meeting: 'Who provides the tea and the biscuits?' So she said, 'Well who do you think? It's me.' He said: 'You must be barmy.' He immediately got them a £50 rise.[23]

Shortly after his arrival, Reverend Livingstone set out in search of congregants. He obtained a directory, identified the Jewish-sounding names and knocked on their doors. He later admitted: 'I had some terrible disappointments, and I may have missed some Jewish Browns or Smiths'.[24] Not all of those who joined the community were orthodox in their outlook or even particularly observant, but they nevertheless worked hard to develop the community.[25] Reverend and Mrs Livingstone initially visited people on Saturday afternoons to help consolidate the congregation. They subsequently only did so by invitation to avoid embarrassing those who were less observant in their post-service activities.[26] Many years later Nancie Craig (née Livingstone) told the story of being taken as a child to a service at St Alban's Hall. Her parents had forgotten to explain that Reverend Livingstone would be wearing the canonical robes for which he became noted:

> I saw my father who was reading the prayer for the king. I shouted out at the top of my voice: 'You look funny in those clothes'. I was taken home and didn't go back for several months because my mother was so embarrassed.[27]

Reverend Livingstone took out advertisements in the *Jewish Chronicle* to encourage attendance at services, welcoming people from Hampstead Garden Suburb, Finchley, Hendon, Childs Hill and Cricklewood as well as from Golders Green.[28] However, in these early days, attendance was not high and Friday night services were soon dropped. Nevertheless, plans to build a synagogue went ahead. Several possible sites were identified; the one eventually selected was in Dunstan Road, which was still in the process of being constructed. It took seven years for the building to be erected due to delays created by the war, including when the chosen site was reserved by the government to grow food.[29] In October 1921 Lionel de Rothschild, President of the United Synagogue, finally laid the foundation stone for the synagogue. The ceremony was attended by Chief Rabbi Hertz, who gave a stirring address on the importance of Jewish education. The report of the event in the *Jewish Chronicle* expressed surprise that the foundation stone omitted the names of Benjamin Drage and Reverend Livingstone.[30]

An imposing synagogue building was built and partially equipped during 1922. Some of the funds for the building were raised locally from concerts, productions and social events organised by the community. The remainder was provided by the United Synagogue which, after a period of negotiation, had accepted the Golders Green community as a constituent member.[31] The leading spirit during the building process was Benjamin Drage, who was determined to ensure that the Jews of Golders Green had a synagogue 'commensurate with the growing needs of the district'.[32] With its cathedral-style interior and throne-like seats, the synagogue was to become the 'flagship' of the United Synagogue[33] and a symbol of its 'eminently respectable suburban surroundings'.[34]

In May 1924 Reverend Livingstone was confirmed as the permanent minister of the new synagogue.[35] The following year the building was completed following further fundraising. It now included purpose-built classrooms, and marble steps leading to an ornate *bimah* (raised platform), gifted by the Drage family.[36] Due to its location the synagogue was soon known as 'Dunstan Road'.

By the time that the new building was fully operational, another community was already in the making. The roots of what eventually became Golders Green Beth Hamedrash can be traced back to the 1920s when a group of strictly orthodox men, mainly of German origin, started to attend regular *shiurim* (study sessions) led by Rabbi Dr Avigdor Schonfeld from North London Adath Yisroel synagogue.[37] They were held in the home of Reuben Lincoln, a member of the Dunstan Road community.[38] The group dissolved after the death of Rabbi Schonfeld in 1930, but in 1933 Salo Schwab and some of his friends started to meet on *Shabbat* in the library of King Alfred School in North End Road.[39] The *minyan* (prayer group) held High Holyday services in a rented flat.[40]

In 1934 Rabbi Eliyahu Munk, who had come to England from Berlin,[41] completed his time as temporary rabbi at the North London Adath Yisroel, and moved to Golders Green. The *minyan* invited him to help them form a new community. The *minyan* moved to Rabbi Munk's home in Temple Fortune and on 25 February 1934 Golders Green Beth Hamedrash came into being.[42] At first it was not always possible for Rabbi Munk to gather a *minyan* so he and its other members sometimes attended services at Dunstan Road. However, during 1934 increasing numbers of continental refugees arrived in Golders Green, some of whom joined the struggling *minyan*. They were looking for something that avoided the Hassidic atmosphere of the *stieblech* of Stamford Hill, what they saw as the 'disorderliness' of Federation shuls, and the rarefied Anglicism of United Synagogue. The president of the fledgling community was Albert Lehman.

When the *minyan* became more viable and outgrew Rabbi Munk's house, it moved to the Spiritualist Hall in Broadwalk Lane, off Golders Green Road. The growing community was apparently taken by surprise in autumn 1934 when Reuben Lincoln renovated premises he owned adjacent to the Spiritualist Hall for use by the developing community[43] and to house a library, classrooms and study space. The premises, named the Lincoln Institute,[44] were occupied for several years by the shul, but not without controversy. The Lincoln Institute was donated to communal life in Golders Green on the understanding it would not be used to establish a congregation rivalling the existing synagogue. As a result, for many years the Chief Rabbi refused to grant the shul the necessary certification for conducting marriages and the United Synagogue refused to recognise it. The religion classes established by the community, initially held in the Beeches School in Bridge Lane, moved into the Lincoln Institute.[45]

At the same time as the strictly orthodox Golders Green Beth Hamedrash (known as 'Munk's shul') was being established, efforts were being made to set up in the area a very different type of synagogue – a progressive one. The 'founding fathers' of what became North-Western Reform Synagogue (Hebrew name, *Shaare Tsedek*, Gates of Righteousness) were E.L. ('Len') Mendel, Ralph Nordon and Henri Silbert.[46] They had hoped to establish a congregation associated with the LJS, but their overtures to Rabbi Mattuck apparently met a cool response. Their approach to Rabbi Reinhart at West London (Reform) Synagogue was apparently greeted more enthusiastically.

The first meeting of the community was held on 24 May 1933 at 17 Templars Avenue at which Alan King Hamilton was appointed as acting chairman.[47] The first service was held on 16 June in Henri Silbert's home at 2 The Meadway. Rabbi Reinhart officiated at the service, which was attended by about fifty people. Afterwards nineteen people signed up as members of the community, pledging support sufficient to cover expenses for six months.

Over the next few years West London Synagogue acted as a 'parent' to the developing community, lending its ministers and prayer books and providing advice and guidance. As with Dunstan Road Synagogue and Munk's shul, education was an immediate priority and religion classes were established at the Hawthorn Hall in Bridge Lane.[48] By the end of 1934 membership had risen to 190 and continued to rise rapidly over the next twelve months. The remarkable growth was partly due to the appeal of the progressive nature of services, which attracted some members of Dunstan Road, including Jeffery Rose's family who became leading members of the new community.[49] A number of previously unobservant Jews also joined, their Jewish consciousness having been raised by events in Europe.

Early services were makeshift. Friday evening services were held in private homes, *Shabbat* morning services were held at Hawthorn Hall and High Holyday services were held at the Free Church Hall in Hampstead Garden Suburb using a portable ark (cupboard for housing the scrolls).[50] The community's finances were 'precarious'. Rena Salinger, secretary to Rabbi Starrels who had been appointed to lead the community (see page 86), was later to recall that she worked in the 'office' – a corner of Rabbi Starrels' sitting room – for 12*s* 6*d* a week, usually paid several months late.

Despite its shaky foundations, the community decided that it should have a home of its own and a building committee was set up to fundraise. West London Synagogue offered the community a site bordering Alyth Gardens in Temple Fortune that was part of the Jewish cemetery in Hoop Lane. In addition to its cost of £3,000, a major challenge was that a Private Member's Bill had to be passed by Parliament for the land to be released for building purposes. The ambitious community was not daunted, despite the misgivings of a few members. Their commitment endured even when West London Synagogue wavered in its support. The focus of everyone involved was on raising money. Even the children attending religion classes were expected to donate a penny each week to contribute to the purchase of the *Ner Tamid* (the everlasting light that hangs above the ark).[51]

This determination paid off; in January 1936 the foundation stone was laid for the new building. The ceremony, attended by a 'crowd of top-hatted gentlemen', was an important one because what had already become known as 'Alyth' was only the second Reform synagogue in London. The synagogue, with seating for 370, was consecrated on 12 July 1936 at a service attended by several local dignitaries, including Alderman A.J. Reynolds, Mayor of Hendon.[52]

Among those present at the Alyth consecration service were Sir Benjamin Drage and Reverend Livingstone from Dunstan Road Synagogue. This was despite the fact that some Dunstan Road members had apparently been unsettled by the setting up of a Reform synagogue with lower seat rentals. In a long letter to the *Jewish Chronicle* in 1934, Sidney Ellis, 'a very outspoken character',[53] railed against the new synagogue, which he said was 'making religion easier'. He spoke disdainfully of 'the services run by private individuals who advertise High Festival services on dustbins' (probably referring to the newly established *shtiebl* in Finchley Road),[54] and regretted that a rabbi of 'eminence and undoubted sincerity' (Rabbi Munk) was involving himself in a movement likely to lead to 'the splitting of the orthodox forces in the locality'.[55] He called upon orthodox Jews to combine their efforts in resisting the tide of progressive Judaism rather than forming new congregations that would encourage 'chevraism' (that is, recreating the network of small religious societies in the East End).

Although Rabbi Munk was to develop good relationships with the Alyth rabbis, he never attended events held at the synagogue. He politely declined the invitation to the Alyth consecration service because of 'a fundamental divergence of religious views'.[56]

The first rabbis

Often referred to as the 'Bishop of Golders Green', Reverend Livingstone led Dunstan Road Synagogue for approaching forty years. At a time before the welfare state existed, he devoted a great deal of energy to pastoral activities.[57] He was also a good administrator and an accomplished preacher. According to his daughter, 'he wasn't an outstanding intellectual but loved being a minister. He had a lovely speaking voice and his sermons were always well received. His diction was excellent and everybody could hear him'.[58]

Reverend Livingstone was involved in many external activities. He had a good relationship with the Golders Green Christian clergy, particularly with the vicar of St Alban's.[59] He addressed gatherings of Christians and Jews who met in Golders Green prior to the Second World War.[60] He was also prominent in a number of Anglo-Jewish communal organisations, including Jews' College and the Anglo-Jewish Association, and was the Jewish chaplain to Maidstone Prison and Broadmoor Asylum. He was a member the Education Committee of Hendon Borough Council. By the time he retired, he held more honorary offices than any other Jewish cleric apart from the Chief Rabbi.[61]

In 1922 Dunstan Road Synagogue appointed Reverend Asher Littenberg as Reader of the Congregation. He had previously worked with Reverend Livingstone in Bradford[62] and the two ministers worked well together. However, they had different religious outlooks. Whereas Reverend Livingstone was tolerant of progressive Judaism, Reverend Littenberg was more *frum* (orthodox).[63] Nancie, one of Reverend Livingstone's daughters, later recalled that when Reverend Littenberg visited their home, he refused to accept refreshments because the household was not sufficiently kosher.[64]

Although the two men had a good professional relationship Rabbi Munk was very different in character and outlook from Reverend Livingstone. Initially Rabbi Munk's position with the congregation he was to lead for over thirty years was somewhat ambiguous as he still held no formal paid role. Not all members of the community conformed to the standards of practice he thought appropriate, but he felt he had no remit to instigate a discussion of the rules that should govern the community before he was officially appointed as its leader. In August 1935 he became head of the Lincoln Institute, rather than the shul, because of its unofficial status. His salary was 'meagre' but some members of the community made additional contributions so he could maintain a reasonable lifestyle. Rabbi Munk was generally regarded as somewhat remote and academic, but his relationship with his congregants had its lighter side. For instance, he felt the cold and preferred the window near his seat on the *bimah* to be closed. However, one prominent shul member liked a constant flow of air and occasionally services were enlivened by the spectacle of the two men alternately opening and closing the window.

Unlike some shul members, Rabbi Munk was not an isolationist and was prepared to collaborate with the wider Jewish community, providing that it did not compromise the shul's independence, which he was intent on maintaining in keeping with the ways of the German strictly orthodox community from which he emanated. The shul never affiliated to the Union of Orthodox Hebrew Congregations (UOHC) and Rabbi Munk objected when, in error, it was once listed in the *Jewish Year Book* as a UOHC member.

Despite his strict orthodoxy, Rabbi Munk, like Reverend Livingstone, had no difficulty in relating to non-Jews. He welcomed non-Jews to the shul, apparently enjoying lecturing them on Jewish practices and customs, and non-Jews often attended his *shiurim*. He had a good relationship with the vicar of the Golders Green parish church.[65] In contrast to Reverend Livingstone, Rabbi Munk kept his external involvements to a minimum, refusing to act as a spokesperson for groupings of rabbis or Jewish pressure groups. His attitude towards the Chief Rabbinate was a mixed one: he accepted its primacy in communal organisations but strongly objected to the Anglo-Jewish concept of ministers being subservient to the Chief Rabbi.

Unlike Dunstan Road Synagogue and Munk's shul, Alyth was initially led by rabbis who stayed for relatively short periods. The first religious leader was American-trained Rabbi Solomon Starrels. In America he had served communities in New Orleans and Nebraska,[66] but prior to his appointment to Alyth he was an assistant rabbi at the LJS. With war looming, in 1938 Rabbi Starrels decided to return to America. For several months the ministers of West London Synagogue led services until Reverend Maurice Perlzweig, also previously at the LJS, was appointed. Reverend Perlzweig is said to have shown 'boundless energy' in developing the congregation. He was an ardent Zionist and frequently devoted his sermons to the subject of Palestine.

Early developments

While the synagogue in Dunstan Road was being planned and erected, the community continued to develop.[67] By the early 1920s there were well-attended religion classes,[68] a Ladies' Society had been formed, which involved itself in charitable activities as well as promoting the religion classes, and there were successful literary and social circles that were open to the wider community.[69] When the synagogue opened, it became the venue for additional societies, many of which were Zionist in nature.[70] The synagogue's Executive Committee held regular 'open meetings' for young people living in the area interested in becoming involved.[71]

By 1930 membership of Dunstan Road exceeded 800,[72] and with the aid of a generous donation the synagogue constructed the Joseph Freedman Hall, named after the father of its main benefactor. It was used for communal functions – meetings of the various societies that now existed, receptions for weddings and *B'nai Mitzvah*.[73] Whereas during the 1920s attendance of services was not always good, the congregation on *Shabbat* was now usually large and there were sometimes as many as five celebrations.[74]

In 1934 Reverend Littenberg retired and was succeeded by Reverend Moise Taschlicky, the son of a Ukrainian cantor who had 'vocal attainments of the highest order'.[75] He was famed for his 'phenomenal top C' even when he was an older man.[76] One long-standing synagogue member recalls that many congregants attended services to be entertained by Taschlicky rather than to pray, looking forward to a cantorial rendition to rival the best opera performances of the day.[77]

The Dunstan Road congregation was generally quite affluent. An editorial note in the *Jewish Chronicle* in 1932 described the long black coats and silk top hats worn by its lay and religious leaders, suggesting that the congregation paid more attention to *Shabbat* attire than to religious matters.[78] However, not everyone dressed up for services. Nancie Craig (née Livingstone) recalled that one congregant came to services wearing jodhpurs having been riding in Rotten Row; his Rolls-Royce car would be waiting for him outside.[79] Synagogue members made 'a special thing' of dressing up for *Kol Nidre* (service on the eve of *Yom Kippur*) when some women were 'dripping with furs' and the most affluent women wore 'beautiful white dresses'.[80] Fashion photographers stood outside the synagogue to take pictures of the women's attire.[81] A correspondent to the *Jewish Chronicle* commented that on *Kol Nidre* the synagogue looked more like the first night at the opera than a place of devotion.[82]

The congregation at Dunstan Road included a disproportionate number of leaders of Anglo-Jewry and people active in wider public life. Paul Goodman, chairman of the Classes Committee, was prominent in the Zionist movement and a distinguished author; Israel Cohen was a member of the Board of Deputies and an authority on Zionism; Aaron Wright was President of the Jewish National Fund; Alfred Woolf, senior warden (later president) of the synagogue, served on the councils of Jews' College and the Anglo-Jewish Association and later became President of the United Synagogue; Mr S. London was Treasurer of the London Board of Jewish Religious Education; Charles Barclay was president of the Golders Green Zionist Society.[83] Several prominent synagogue members were councillors, some becoming mayors, including Sidney Bolsom, who was Mayor of St Pancras in 1933.[84]

Unlike at Dunstan Road Synagogue, in Munk's shul there were few communal activities for adults apart from study sessions, but youth activities were set up.[85] Due to the continued arrival of refugees from Germany, by 1937 the shul's membership had risen to 100 and the premises at the Lincoln Institute were extended. The shul organised a kosher milk delivery for Golders Green and in 1937 Rabbi Alexander Carlebach from Cologne was appointed as secretary, teacher and *chazzan*,[86] roles previously performed in a voluntary capacity by Hermann Schwab, a well-known writer, who had become second president of the shul. According to one commentator, Munk's shul was founded and developed by 'a remarkable generation of survivors who learnt to thrive in a totally new world'.[87]

In Alyth's early years Rabbi Starrels was 'tireless' in recruiting new congregants and membership soon grew to over 300. Like Munk's shul many of those who joined the synagogue were continental refugees. However, unlike the refugees who joined Munk's shul, they had been members of progressive synagogues in Germany. Known initially as 'the group', they not only increased the size of the community, but also gave it a cosmopolitan culture.

Many activities were set up at Alyth to attract young people, including a Girl Guide company and a Brownie pack, both of which were to run for over sixty years. A Scout troop was established a few years later. From the beginning the Women's Society, which had many name changes over the years, was very active. Initially its members met in each other's houses to make garments for Jewish charities and organised events held at the synagogue. Kathe Trente, one of the German refugees who had joined the congregation, recalled her early impressions of synagogue life:

> Everybody dressed down and the functions at the synagogue, the dances and even the *Bar Mitzvahs*, were very modest. If you couldn't afford to pay for a ticket for a dance at the synagogue, you were always welcome anyhow.[88]

Apart from its informality, what distinguished Alyth from the other two synagogues was its egalitarianism. One of its early council members was Mrs M. Carmel, and a motion was passed to increase the participation of women in the leadership of the community.[89] At Rabbi Starrels' insistence, there were no reserved seats in the synagogue, not even for the wardens, a policy that has remained unchanged.

Before and during the Second World War

In the lead-up to the Second World War all three synagogues became focused on supporting those affected by the rise of Nazism. Reverend Perlzweig from Alyth took the lead in setting up the Jewish Emergency Committee for Refugees, covering Finchley and Hendon, in which the Golders Green synagogues participated. At Dunstan Road, the Ladies' Society organised house-to-house collections to pay for the accommodation and living costs of refugee children and made clothes for them.[90] The synagogue supported the Central British Fund for German Jewry (CBF) set up to assist refugees from Nazism and was vocal in its criticism of the United Synagogue for failing to support the CBF.[91]

Since both Munk's shul and Alyth had high numbers of refugee members, they were particularly alert to the situation in Europe. As a general rule Rabbi Munk preferred not to be disturbed after 10 p.m. However, in the years preceding the war he was always available when urgent action was required, such as making alternative arrangements for refugee children faced with being placed in a non-Jewish environment. Alyth was 'a hive of activity on behalf of refugees', and many people came to the synagogue seeking help for themselves or for their friends and relatives. By the time war commenced Alyth was supporting three children at the Wittingham Farm School in Scotland,[92] as well as contributing £400 per year towards the maintenance of the North London Refugee Boys' Hostel Fund. Ten days after *Kristallnacht* in November 1938, Reverend Perlzweig conducted a moving service during which a charred scroll rescued from Germany was re-consecrated. Raymond Goldman, then aged 8, later recalled:

> It was the first time that I had seen my father cry ... On the *bimah* stood a party of English ex-servicemen wearing their war medals and bearing the Union Jack and beside them a party of twelve German-Jewish ex-servicemen, all wearing Iron Crosses. The Germans were carrying the *Sefer Torah* [scroll].[93]

In February 1939 Reverend Perlzweig invited to Alyth the eminent American Zionist Rabbi Stephen Wise, who spoke on the place of refugees in the consciousness of Jewish people. The synagogue was packed to hear 'his superb eloquence, unmatched among preachers in his generation'.[94] Refugees were invited to the synagogue's first communal *seder* (service for the first night of *Pesach*) in April 1939.

Once the war began, many activities at Dunstan Road were suspended as families were evacuated. As Jews started to trickle back to Golders Green after the Blitz, new activities were established, including a Cadet Battalion and the successful Golders Green Jewish Youth Club.[95] The involvement of people from the East End who came to Golders Green having lost their homes in the bombing helped to maintain communal life. However, this did not improve the synagogue's financial situation since most of the temporary residents retained their membership of East End *chevrot* rather than joining the synagogue due to its higher membership fees.[96]

Like Dunstan Road, the congregations of Alyth and Munk's shul were greatly depleted by the war, but communal life was affected to an even greater extent because of internment.[97] At Alyth the small proportion of members who remained in London became involved in wartime activities such as helping with the local Red Cross Working Party. Reverend Perlzweig represented a number of German refugees living in Golders Green in their dealings with local police and sought help on their behalf through the Home Office. In 1941 Rabbi Dr Werner Van der Zyl, a refugee who had trained at the Liberal rabbinical seminary in Berlin, and who had recently been released from internment,[98] was invited to lead services at Alyth while Reverend Perlzweig was absent on a lecture tour. His brand of progressive Judaism was more traditional and theological than in the other English Reform synagogues at this time. The German refugees who had joined Alyth warmly welcomed him and he took parts of services in German to make refugees feel at home.[99]

When Reverend Perlzweig tendered his resignation in 1943,[100] Rabbi Van der Zyl was appointed as his successor, largely due to the backing of the German members of the congregation. Rabbi Van der Zyl is remembered for his love and understanding of the musical tradition from which he came. He introduced to services the music of Lewandowski and Mombach and established a different form of service for each of the festivals.[101] He had a good voice, which brought warmth to services and encouraged participation.

During the Blitz only seventy members of Munk's shul remained in London. Rabbi Munk campaigned successfully for the release of many members who had been interned.[102] Some congregants were now leaving for safer environments such as America, although the crossing had become increasingly perilous. Shul members Mr and Mrs Guggenheim left for America only to be 'lost at sea' during the Battle of the Atlantic. The scroll they had left behind for safekeeping is still used in the shul today.[103] Rabbi Munk developed a keen interest in the Jewish education of evacuees and, with other shul members, worked to ensure that internees were kept supplied with kosher food. Membership of the shul was boosted when a number of orthodox families who had been bombed out of their homes in north and east London joined the community.[104] On High Holydays a series of services took place in members' homes so that the whole congregation was not put at risk.

The post-war years

After the war, pre-war activities were quickly re-established at all three synagogues and their regular *Shabbat* services were well attended.[105] This was partly the result of raised Jewish consciousness following the Holocaust, but also because of the large number of Jews now moving to the area.[106] Attendance of High Holyday services was so high that 'overflow' services had to be organised. Dunstan Road Synagogue held additional services at St Alban's Hall and later in the Ionic cinema.[107] The Alyth High Holyday services held at the synagogue and Hodford Hall were each attended by 700 worshippers. At Munk's shul seats were full throughout the year, not just on High Holydays and festivals.[108] Attendance at Alyth *Shabbat* services dropped off somewhat after just a few years as some members became preoccupied with earning a living. However, by the 1950s the congregation had become predominantly a young one and a high proportion of its membership was attending and taking an active part in services.

In the post-war years the three synagogues gave particular attention to maintaining the involvement of young people. In 1948 Dunstan Road Synagogue appointed a dedicated youth minister, Reverend Myerovitch, who organised services for young people.[109] They were modelled on the adult services with young wardens and boys and girls sitting separately.[110] While some people recall these services with enthusiasm,[111] others were less taken with their formality and found more exciting things to do:

> My grandfather often took me to the Dunstan Road Synagogue. He went to the main service, and I was supposed to go to the children's service. But sometimes instead I got a bus up Brent Street to the Classic Cinema in Hendon to see Laurel and Hardy, Flash Gordon, and the like. There was just enough time to get back to Dunstan Road before the service came out. One day I got caught out. My grandfather asked me how the children's service had gone. I said: 'OK, the same as usual'. My grandfather said: 'That's funny, I heard that there wasn't one today!'[112]

At Munk's shul, the pre-war youth activities developed into a youth club known as Ezra in which Rabbi Munk took a personal interest, and which ran a full programme of social and educational activities. Rabbi Van der Zyl at Alyth made activities for young people a priority and said that young people 'should have their own rooms where they can feel at home and the synagogue is a proper place for them'.[113] He held 'at-homes' for young people and led study sessions for 'the more serious-minded youth'. It was many years before he succeeded in establishing the young people's centre for which he campaigned tirelessly, but he did set up a Junior Youth Club in 1946; it soon had a membership of over seventy.[114] He also established the Alyth Fellowship for over-16s and monthly children's services led by young people, providing them with 'a useful and relatively painless introduction to the art of public speaking'.[115]

Despite their shared emphasis on young people, the congregations of three synagogues evolved very differently after the war. Until the early 1950s, Dunstan Road Synagogue retained the anglicised atmosphere that had prevailed since its inception, as recalled by the historian Simon Schama who spent his teenage years in the area:

> In Golders Green, our oak-panelled and stained-glassed synagogue had an air of late Victorian ecclesiastical grandeur about it: 'wardens' in ceremonious top hats, installed in a special boxed-in pew at the front of the congregation. High up above the ark behind a metal screen, a massed choir, featuring my cousin Brian as the star tenor, poured the operatic melodies out on to the congregation.[116]

The ladies' gallery of the synagogue was described as 'a sight to compete with Ladies' Day at the Royal Ascot'.[117]

However, by the end of the decade the synagogue was changing, and the now-retired Reverend Livingstone found it difficult to understand pressure within the congregation for the introduction of more traditional rituals. According to his daughter, 'it looked as if he was going to have a stroke when he saw all the ritual dancing in the shul, which he thought was undignified'.[118] When he was still able to walk, he attended services at Hampstead Synagogue, which were still conducted to his liking. In his final years he attended services at Munk's shul,[119] but remained Emeritus Minister at Dunstan Road Synagogue until his death in 1979. He preached at Dunstan Road on his 90th birthday wearing his long robes and, as one congregant recalls, 'looking like the Pope'.[120]

At Munk's shul a Ladies' Guild and what was known as 'the YMCA', the Young Married Couples' Association, were set up. In 1948 Dr Israel Brodie became Chief Rabbi, and developed a close relationship with Rabbi Munk based on their shared ideological outlook. Dr Brodie granted the shul a certificate to conduct marriages, ending the era of the shul not being officially recognised by some Jewish communal authorities.[121]

With the rise in its membership, Munk's shul outgrew its accommodation at the Lincoln Institute and larger premises were sought. An early member of the shul,

Sam Kahn, identified the site for a new synagogue. While out walking he noticed a disused orchard behind what was then St Michael's parish church (now a Greek cathedral). He thought the location would suit the congregation well, being 'tucked away out of the public eye'.[122] With the aid of German reparations money, a new building was constructed.[123] The congregation took up residence in September 1959 following a ceremony involving the scrolls being processed across Golders Green Road to the consecration service attended by the Chief Rabbi.[124]

Due to lack of space at the Lincoln Institute, two *Shabbat* services had been held. This had sometimes led to dissension when the first service overran.[125] The practice continued in the spacious new shul, grieving Rabbi Munk, who felt it detracted from the cohesion of the congregation. However, the new building did allow Rabbi Munk to fulfil his ambition of expanding the shul's study activities. In 1944 the shul had joined a committee led by the Chief Rabbi to set up and run the north-west London communal *mikveh* in Shirehall Lane, Hendon. The new premises included a *mikveh*, and amid a storm of protest in the *Jewish Chronicle*, Munk's shul withdrew from the communal facility.[126]

As a student the Alyth rabbi, Rabbi Van der Zyl, had been inspired by the famed theologian Rabbi Leo Baeck. While Rabbi Baeck was incarcerated in Theresienstadt concentration camp, Rabbi Van de Zyl paid homage to his teacher by organising a function at Alyth to celebrate his 70th birthday. After his liberation, Rabbi Baeck came to England to live with his daughter and her husband, Dr Berlak, who were active in the congregation. He was made an honorary member of the synagogue and in 1947 became its first president. Widely respected in the Jewish world, Rabbi Baeck brought dignity and stature to the synagogue and left a lasting legacy. In 1951 an extension to the synagogue was completed and consecrated by Alderman Joseph Freedman, Mayor of Hendon and former synagogue chairman. It was dedicated in honour of Rabbi Baeck.

Although progressive Judaism in England was still generally anti-Zionist in the years following the Second World War, the Alyth congregation, perhaps as a legacy from Reverend Perlzweig, took a keen interest in developments in Palestine. In the summer of 1948, just after the State of Israel came into being, the distinguished scholar Professor Norman Bentwich was invited to Alyth to deliver a notable lecture, 'From Herzl to the Jewish State'. During the debate that followed many shades of opinions were expressed and to this day synagogue members have held a range of views on Israel.

From the mid-1950s onwards, Alyth became an increasing force in Anglo-Jewry. It played an active part in both the Board of Deputies and in the youth movement for Reform synagogues, the Youth Association of Reform Synagogues of Great Britain.[127] Alyth was particularly influential in respect of training new ministers. The founding of Leo Baeck College in 1956[128] owed a great deal to Rabbi Van der Zyl's vision and support from Alyth's congregation.[129] Rabbi Van der Zyl was the first Director of Studies at the college. The synagogue's increasing profile attracted many new members. Fresh activities were introduced and a new building to house the ever-expanding religion school was planned.[130] Social functions of the synagogue became much more elaborate. Dinners and balls were held in central London hotels, replacing the 'hops' of synagogue's early days.

In recognition of his achievements, in 1958 Rabbi Van der Zyl was appointed Senior Minister at West London Synagogue, the 'cathedral synagogue' of the Reform movement. He was succeeded by Reverend Philip Cohen (the third minister to join the synagogue from the LJS), who brought to fruition an ambitious building programme. In June 1959 the Leo Baeck Centre for young people was finally completed and three months later a new Scout headquarters opened.

1960s and 1970s

During the 1960s Rabbi Eugene Newman (later Rabbi Dr Newman),[131] who had succeeded Reverend Livingstone on his retirement from Dunstan Road Synagogue in 1953, faced many challenges, including a damaging debate about the installation of an ornate Torah reading desk in the centre of the synagogue designed by Rabbi Newman's son. Moving the reading desk was an indication of an increasing desire by some members of the congregation for a more traditional approach,[132] but there was strong resistance from long-standing members like Alfred Wolfe, who said that he would be 'carried out dead rather than allow the change'.[133] Nevertheless, after a discussion lasting nearly ten years, the installation went ahead.

Rabbi Newman died unexpectedly in office in 1977. The increasing traditionalism apparent at Dunstan Road Synagogue during his twenty-three-year tenure continued under the leadership of Rabbi Jonathan Sacks (1978–82), who later became Chief Rabbi.[134] He was knighted in 2005 and made a life peer in 2009. With the 'sheer force of his personality', he helped to revive the ageing congregation[135] and estabished 'a thirst for learning'.[136]

From the mid-1970s the synagogue started to lose about thirty members a year.[137] At its height, membership of the synagogue had been about 1,500 but, over time it declined to around 500. Some members were joining the more orthodox shuls now established in Golders Green, some joined progressive synagogues and others discontinued synagogue membership. People were also attracted to the modern and refurbished synagogues that had opened in Hendon and Edgware. Whereas it had once been the only synagogue in the area, there was keen competition for members.[138] The synagogue was never full, not even on High Holydays.[139] It gained a reputation for being old fashioned and for its unchanging, cathedral-like atmosphere, which made it difficult to attract new members. To add to the feeling of decline, the building was deteriorating rapidly. Many members were now single-practice professionals or owned small businesses rather than the wealthy merchants who had dominated the early congregation, which meant that the congregation did not have the means to repair the building.[140]

In contrast, Munk's shul was flourishing. By the 1960s it had become a well-known community with a distinctive style and culture shaped by the background of its members. Many strictly orthodox Jews had moved to the area because of its reputation. While a few members were British-born, most came from Germany where they had belonged to *Austrittsgemeinden*, secessionist communities.[141] The congregants often knew each other from Germany, sometimes having lived in the same street.[142] Sermons were delivered in German and the community was imbued with German thinking. The congregation developed a clear sense of purpose, set out in its 1963 publication, 'Our Kehilla' (community). Rabbi Munk might have preferred to model the shul on the Berlin community from which he hailed, but since congregants came from many different parts of Germany where they had followed slightly different traditions, what had emerged was a form of observance that was an amalgamation of the varying practices. However, the congregation was united on the overriding principles of discipline and decorum, both of which were jealously guarded by Rabbi Munk,[143] differentiating the shul from Hassidic *shtieblech* where, as many from Munk's saw it, there was 'a lot of shouting'.[144]

Munk's shul continued to grow and new premises were acquired at 678 Finchley Road for communal activities. With funding provided by Mr Wohl, a new communal hall was added to the shul.[145] Although the congregation was solidly middle class and mainly made up of professionals and business people, some families struggled to make a decent living.[146] Due to the impact of the Holocaust, many families had relations living in other countries, which gave the congregation a more international flavour than the largely indigenous Dunstan Road.[147] Prior to the Second World War Rabbi Munk had given many of his addresses in German as a large proportion of the congregation did not yet speak English well.[148] By the 1960s English was the main medium.[149]

While Munk's shul was widely respected for its 'impeccable orthodoxy', it was also seen by some as 'rigid', as epitomised by an anecdote appearing in the *Jewish Chronicle* in 1964:

> A few months ago a young doctor of impeccable orthodoxy tried to join the [Munk's] congregation and he was required to appear before a tribunal. The conversation went something like this:
> 'You are a doctor, are you not?'
> 'Yes.'
> 'Supposing you were called out on an emergency case some distance away on Shabbat, would you use your car?'
> 'Naturally.'
> 'And would you then leave your car where it was or would you drive back?'
> 'I would drive back. I'm a doctor, and I cannot be parted from my car.'
> 'Quite so. But I am afraid in the circumstances you cannot join our congregation.'[150]

The author of the article commented that while Dunstan Road Synagogue was becoming more 'sacred', Munk's was 'glatt sacred'.[151] Rabbi Munk was not embarrassed to admit that he had become more doctrinaire as he grew older. He believed that young people needed a more intensive Jewish education than a generation earlier due to counter-pressures in the wider environment.[152] On reaching 60 he perceived that his skills were no longer equal to the shifting needs of young people whose standards of Torah study continued to rise. He persuaded the shul's lay leadership to appoint an assistant rabbi to take over his teaching responsibilities.

Rabbi Hyman Israel Feldman, head of the Gateshead Boarding School, was the successful candidate. He knew the shul well because his parents had attended services there.[153] His appointment enabled Rabbi Munk and his wife to take extended leave in 1965.[154] Rabbi Feldman's success in covering Rabbi Munk's duties and striking up a relationship with the congregation contributed to Rabbi Munk's decision to retire in 1968. Rabbi Feldman was appointed as his successor and Rabbi Munk was given the title of Founding Rabbi.[155] He moved to Israel where he devoted his remaining years to studying, writing and teaching. He died there in 1978.

Rabbi Feldman was more anglicised than Rabbi Munk but, as a result of his *yeshivah* education, he was also more orthodox than his predecessor. In the shul's early days only Rabbi Munk was allowed to wear his *tallit* over his head, but gradually other men now adopted the practice. Similarly, until the 1960s only Mrs Munk and the *chazzan*'s wife wore *sheitels*, but by the end of the 1970s, *sheitels* were commonplace. Rabbi Feldman insisted on the separation of the sexes for social, cultural and educational activities.[156]

The shul was apparently not changing quickly enough for some of the younger generation. By the mid-1960s a few young men who had been born and educated in Britain started to seek slightly different approaches. They formed informal study groups and attended *Shabbat* services in other local shuls where they acted as prayer leaders, their communal ties having been loosened by attending *yeshivot* (plural of *yeshivah*). On the other hand, for some of those families whose children had not been *yeshivah* educated, the increasing orthodoxy of the shul was alienating and they left to join more progressive shuls.[157] A number of older members also went to live in Israel. These departures were matched by families joining the shul attracted by its forms of worship, including a number who were not German in origin.[158]

By the 1960s Alyth had lost the intimate and family atmosphere of its early days and Reverend Cohen inaugurated a Social Services Committee. Its members visited people who were sick, organised transport for older people and congregants with disabilities, supported people suffering from mental illnesses and helped with household tasks. In 1957 Professor Norman Bentwich, who had been a 'good friend' of the synagogue over the years, succeeded Rabbi Leo Baeck as Alyth's second president.[159] Under his leadership support for Israel increased. An active branch of the Friends of Hebrew University was formed and the synagogue made generous donations to Israeli causes. Following the 1967 Six

Day War, over £45,000 was raised by the congregation for the Joint Palestine Appeal Emergency Fund.[160]

In 1972 Reverend Cohen retired and Rabbi Dow Marmur became the senior minister. Over his long tenure he introduced a more traditional and participative approach to services. Talmud as well as the Torah was now studied in the synagogue. In the same year as Rabbi Marmur was appointed, the Alyth Youth Centre, planned for several decades, eventually became a reality. Under Rabbi Marmur's leadership, the synagogue's ties to Israel became even 'closer and deeper' and during the 1973 Yom Kippur War, Alyth raised sums of money 'of unequalled proportions'. In the spring of 1974 Rabbi Marmur led a solidarity tour of Israel and in 1976 an Israel Committee was re-formed which organised a series of cultural and fundraising events.

In 1963 Alyth began to participate in the activities of the Council of Christians and Jews and five years later the Women's Guild 'extended the hand of friendship' to Christian women in the area, organising an interfaith tea that became an annual event. Rabbi Rodney Mariner, Director of Youth at the synagogue during the 1970s, established close links with the Hindu community. In 1977 the synagogue joined Barnet's Community Relations Council and formed its own Anti-Fascist Committee that took an active stance against racism, writing to the press, distributing leaflets and picketing.

From the outset Alyth had been international in its outlook. In the 1970s this was epitomised by the synagogue's Soviet Jewry campaign instigated by Ruth Langdon, who travelled alone to the Soviet Union to meet with Refuseniks.[161] When asked if she had been frightened of being followed by the KGB, she replied: 'I didn't look back'.[162] The Alyth campaign helped to raise the profile of the plight of Jews in the Soviet Union both in Anglo-Jewry and among the general public by organising exhibitions, lectures and public meetings.

Since its inception, the Alyth Women's Guild had made a major but largely unsung contribution to the synagogue. As well as arranging flowers, looking after the vestments and catering for events, the guild raised large sums for charitable and communal causes, including Leo Baeck College and the Reform Synagogues of Great Britain (RSGB). By the 1970s women were playing a more prominent role in both the religious life and leadership of Alyth. There were many trailblazers: the women who were the first to carry a scroll, to do *Hagbaah* (raise the scrolls), to be given an *aliyah* (invited up to the *bimah* to participate in services), to be *Kallat Torah* (asked to read the scroll at the *Simchat Torah* service).[163] In 1978, after twenty years of involvement in synagogue life, Joyce Rose became the first woman Alyth chairman and the first woman chairman of a UK synagogue.[164]

The end of the twentieth century

In 1983 Rabbi Ivan Binstock, who had recently been ordained at Mir *yeshivah* in Jerusalem, took over from Rabbi Sacks at Dunstan Road Synagogue. He quickly immersed himself in communal life and made strong links with other local rabbis, forging a particularly close bond with Rabbi Rubin of the Sassover *shtiebl*.[165] The much-reduced congregation he led was deeply divided on the future direction of the synagogue. While some congregants wanted to keep things as they were in the synagogue's heyday, others wanted a more participative approach. New activities were introduced to help attract young people, but services changed little. After Rabbi (now Dayan) Binstock left to join St John's Wood United Synagogue in 1996 there was a long leadership gap because the congregation could not agree on the type of rabbi they wanted to replace him. Some members wanted an 'old-style rabbi' while others wanted one who would inspire. The differences were largely generational – younger people with a better Jewish education wanted 'something more intellectual'.[166] A series of temporary rabbis were appointed to provide religious leadership.

Although in some respects change was slow, in others the synagogue evolved with the times. In its early days, women played a very traditional role in synagogue life, mainly through their involvement in the highly stratified Ladies' Guild. After the Second World War women became involved in more aspects of synagogue life, often using the skills they had developed in their increasingly diverse careers.[167] However, their involvement in services remained limited.

By the 1990s there was a growing nucleus of members who wanted change, particularly in respect of services to make them more welcoming and more participative and for there to be less talking in services. They were bitterly opposed:

> Some people didn't understand why we wanted services that would involve young people. They argued: 'Why would you call up a young person when there are experienced older people around?' They seemed to have a real fear of change.[168]

Faced with this resistance, members seeking change set up an alternative *minyan*. It was initially agreed that the *minyan* would meet monthly in the synagogue hall, but the first service was so popular that there was a call for weekly services. When this was refused, the *minyan* started to meet at the premises of the nearby Jewish Vegetarian Society (JVS):

> We were squashed into a small room. It was very cosy! The services were very informal. We didn't have a *chazzan* [cantor] but Daniel Greenberg had a beautiful voice. The feeling of being rebels was quite exciting. The *minyan* was very successful although some members were upset that they couldn't have herrings for *kiddush*! [small meal after a service] [169]

About sixty people attended the alternative *minyan*, which was maintained by a group of families who wanted services that would engage their children. Until then some young people had been refusing to come to services they saw as being dominated by 'a lot of old men'.[170] Services in the main synagogue were attended by just a handful of people but the wardens continued to wear their top hats.[171] An 'official minyan' was formed, reinforcing the divisions between the synagogue and those meeting at the JVS. Although members of the alternative *minyan* continued to pay synagogue fees, at one point it looked as if a new congregation might be formed.[172] The synagogue was losing members and no new ones were joining. Horrified by what was happening, Nancie Craig (née Livingston) wrote to the *Jewish Chronicle* beseeching the factions to resolve their 'senseless quarrelling' to prevent 'United Synagogue Judaism' disappearing from Golders Green.[173]

In the end a rift was avoided. People with new ideas stood for and were appointed to the synagogue board and gradually introduced changes. They were helped by the fact that some of the most vociferous opponents had left the congregation or changed their mind.[174] The *minyan* returned to the synagogue and the fortunes of the congregation began to improve.

Both Munk's shul and Alyth continued to thrive. Under Rabbi Feldman's leadership the congregation (still known as 'Munk's') supported the setting up of a Hospital Kosher Meals Service and also sheltered flats (Wohl Lodge) for older people in Ravenscroft Avenue. It disposed of a number of community assets that it no longer required and became more economically stable. To reflect the ageing profile of the community, a new weekday morning *minyan* and a study session for older people were introduced. However, the community remained wedded to two *Shabbat* morning services.[175] At the turn of the twenty-first century Munk's shul was a vibrant and world-famous congregation with a membership in excess of 400. Although many of its original members had died, younger generations of some founding families remained deeply committed to the shul and occupied leadership positions.[176]

By the 1980s the Alyth congregation was largely made up of professional middle-class Jews, including many who participated in wider public life: several mayors, local councillors, MPs, a knight and a number of CBEs. Alyth members Harold Langdon, Jeffery Rose and Jerome Karet had served as chairmen of RSGB. The emphasis on communal welfare continued, relying on the efforts of volunteers supported by a part-time welfare officer. A number of initiatives, such as a befriending scheme, were launched to involve and keep in touch with members now living not just in the surrounding area but also across north-west London.[177]

There was a growing involvement in social issues reflecting a trend in RSGB. The Alyth Social Issues Group (later the Social Action Group) launched initiatives ranging from food collection for the homeless, recycling projects and support for Bosnian refugees to fundraising events for deprived South Africans, the Monday Club (a club for people with learning disabilities) and fundraising 'sleepouts' held at *Sukkot*.[178] Adult members and children from the religion school took part in *Chanukkah* marches to Golders Green clock tower in support of the Refuseniks, Prisoners of Zion and non-Jewish prisoners of conscience, sometimes accompanied by celebrities such as Maureen Lipman. The Soviet Jewry Committee adopted a number of prisoners of conscience and helped to support those who succeeded in establishing new lives in Israel and elsewhere by writing, sending parcels, and visiting them. Links were made with the Jewish community in Rostov-on-Don in Russia.[179]

From the 1970s onwards, an increasing number of South African Jews had joined Alyth,[180] who, like the continental refugees before them, played a prominent role in shaping congregational life.[181] By the 1990s South African members were serving on Alyth committees and reaching leadership positions. Many had brought professional expertise to synagogue activities, including the kindergarten and youth work. Outside Alyth, South African members were active in communal bodies including the Board of Deputies and Jewish Care. Peter Galgut has explained that the South Africans had brought the pioneering attitude of their parents and grandparents to the community and put it into practice.[182] South Africans continue to make up about 10 per cent of the Alyth's membership.[183]

As the Alyth community embarked on its fifty-year anniversary celebration, Rabbi Marmur announced his resignation. His departure was seen as a loss to the synagogue and to Anglo-Jewry generally. He was replaced by American-trained Rabbi Charles Emanuel who had been working in Leeds. Although he was regarded as more 'traditionalist' than his predecessor, over the twenty-two years of Rabbi Emanuel's leadership, the synagogue saw a great deal of experimentation. Changes included new seating arrangements, enabling services to be led from among the congregation rather than from the *bimah*, the convening of *minyanim* with more traditional approaches and using what became the new Reform prayer book and *shacharit* services (early morning services) on Sunday mornings. The number of girls choosing to have a *Bat Mitzvah* grew significantly and it became 'almost the norm' for *B'nai Mitzvah* children to chant rather than read their portion. A number of different ways of involving young people in the religious life of the synagogue were pursued (for example, Tiny Tots and Kuddle up *Shabbat* for young children and their families and the leading of certain services by young people). New services became part of the annual cycle such as *Yom HaShoah* (service to remember the Holocaust).

Recent years

After a drawn-out recruitment process due to Dunstan Road Synagogue's poor reputation, Rabbi Harvey Belovski (later Rabbi Dr) was appointed in 2003. Although he came from a more traditional background than some synagogue members might have desired, he adapted to the needs of the congregation.[184] He divided his time between the different services including at High Holydays: 'He gave the impression that he was working with mirrors because he always arrived in the right place at the right time'.[185] While he insisted on decorum in services, 'he was not dogmatic'.[186]

In partnership with the synagogue's lay leadership, Rabbi Belovski set about developing a range of activities covering every facet of communal life. Particularly crucial in reviving the synagogue was the establishment of a new primary school,

Rimon, attached to the synagogue.[187] Its opening led to several young families joining the congregation. As well as helping to meet escalating demand for school places in north-west London, the school partly funded the renovation of the synagogue. This was now a priority as the roof was no longer watertight and plaster was falling away from the ceiling, creating a safety hazard.[188]

In 2011 a major funding appeal was launched. The United Synagogue was not initially supportive of the initiative, believing that the valuable site should be sold and a smaller synagogue built elsewhere. However, by then the synagogue had a clear vision for what it wanted to achieve, backed by an energetic marketing strategy.[189] In the end the United Synagogue agreed to support the project. The Joseph Freedman and the Lebetkin halls[190] were both demolished, making way for the new school where space could be used for communal purposes when not required for school activities. In addition to essential renovation works in the synagogue, the prayer space was reconfigured and the ladies' gallery was abandoned. Women now sit downstairs, separated from the men by a *mechitza* (partition). Some women find this arrangement makes them feel more spiritual; others would prefer to have kept the traditional ladies' gallery.[191]

The 'user-friendly' building has made possible an ambitious programme of communal activities. Rabbi Sam Fromson and his wife Hadassah were appointed to work with young people for whom there are now many different services and activities. The *minyanim* have been combined and more participative services have been introduced.[192] The synagogue has extended its social action activities and outreach work in the local community, and uses social networking to engage with a wide audience.[193]

Over the last decade women have been playing an increasing role in the lay leadership of Dunstan Road Synagogue. For six years Jacqui Zinkin was vice-chairman and acting chair of the synagogue.[194] More recently there has been a growing demand, particularly among younger women, for greater involvement in services.[195] Some women from the synagogue participated in the Golders Green 'partnership minyan' (part of a global movement), which met at the JVS.[196] At its meetings women were able to officiate at certain points in the service. While Rabbi Belovski was not supportive of the partnership minyan,[197] it appears to have prompted changes within the synagogue. There is now women's *hakafot* (circulating around the synagogue with the scrolls) on *Simchat Torah* and women offer *divrei Torah* (giving an explanation of a Torah passage). Women speakers are regularly invited to the synagogue and a women's *minyan* is held once a month.[198] However, some people believe that there is still some way to go in persuading young women in the congregation that Judaism can satisfy them intellectually.[199]

In June 2015 the synagogue celebrated its centenary. It was marked by a special service held on 20 June attended by Chief Rabbi Mirvis and local dignitaries.[200] At this celebration it was apparent that the major renovation project had not only rejuvenated the building but also the congregation. Membership is rising and its age profile reducing rapidly. Despite its turbulent start and the divisions it had sometimes created within families and among friends, the alternative *minyan* succeeded in breathing new life into the synagogue.[201]

When in 2001 Rabbi Feldman announced his intention of retiring, Munk's shul encountered difficulties in recruiting a replacement, despite its continuing vibrancy. The shul was led on a temporary basis by Rabbi David Cohn of North Hendon Adath Yisroel shul. Rabbi Yisroel Meir Greenberg was eventually appointed in September 2006. The shul celebrated both its 75th and 80th anniversaries, by which time it was offering more than ten men's *shiurim* a week, numerous *chavurot* (social learning groups) and women's *shiurim*. There were now also many social activities ranging from a mother and toddler group to a 'friendship zone' for older members. A re-established youth movement, Mooth, was led by the assistant rabbi, Rabbi Zvi Zimmels.[202]

Today, descendants of its founding members still daven (pray) at Munk's shul and continue to play major roles in the community. It has lost some younger members to the less formal shuls in Golders Green and many long-standing members have moved to Israel. However, its membership has remained fairly stable as newcomers to Golders Green have joined the community. The shul has attracted a number of South Africans, mainly those of German descent, as well as some from mainland Europe. People who have become observant as a result of the activities of various *kiruv* (literally 'gathering in') bodies in Golders Green, especially the Jewish Learning Exchange, have also joined the congregation.[203] Some of the newcomers have become active in the governance of the shul. Although the shul's German roots are fairly distant, certain practices originating in Germany, such as the lighting of eight candles at circumcisions, are proudly maintained.[204]

Some commentators feel that the shul has lost its *raison d'etre* and will gradually fade away, but for the present it has a very loyal congregation, including a number of younger families drawn in by recent initiatives[205] such as the successful retreats for young men and the 'simple' alternative services held in the shul hall.[206] The congregation is not as large as it once was, but there is a strong community atmosphere.[207] The discipline and decorum cherished by Rabbi Munk are still very much in evidence and Munk's shul is one of the few orthodox synagogues to retain a *chazzan*, which draws many visitors to daven at the shul. Four decades after his death, a candle burns in memory of Rabbi Munk.

Rabbi Emanuel retired from Alyth in 2006. Reviewing his time at the synagogue, he highlighted his trips to the Soviet Union and Alyth's links with Israel (twinning with a Reform congregation in Ramat Gan) but above all, Alyth's welcoming atmosphere: 'Alyth represented for me an oasis where it was understood that the business of a synagogue is people'.[208]

During the course of Alyth's history there had been a number of changes to enhance the synagogue building, including the installation of windows designed by Roman Halter.[209] After twenty years of consideration and a number of abortive schemes, in 2003 Alyth embarked on an extensive remodelling of the building to make the synagogue 'a Centre for Living Judaism in the Twenty First Century'. The project included an improved synagogue area, a new façade,[210] a larger reception area, a new kindergarten and library and an upgraded kitchen and offices. The Leo Baeck Centre now opens onto a garden that converts into a *sukkah*.

For over twenty-five years membership of Alyth has remained relatively stable at around 3,000 adults and children.[211] Since 2004 non-Jewish partners of Alyth members have been able to become 'associates' and several have played an active part in synagogue life. There are now services ranging from the Classical Shabbat Service to the highly experimental *Tefillah* (prayer) Laboratory. There is also a lay-led *minyan* and an informal participatory *minyan* called *Kollot* (voices). There are many study activities: a Rosh Chodesh (literally 'head of the month') Women's Group, frequent *shiurim*, a Talmud class, educational activities for young people and special learning events. However, the synagogue is not resting on its laurels; discussions are already taking place on how the building can continue to be used effectively to meet both current and future needs.[212] The current rabbinic team is Rabbis Goldsmith and Levy and two part-time rabbis, Maurice Michaels and Colin Eimer.

Places of Worship: The Smaller Synagogues

Over the last twenty years Golders Green has become known for its thriving *haredi* community and an abundance of strictly orthodox shuls and *shtieblech*. What is less widely known is that *haredim* have lived in Golders Green since the early years of the twentieth century and the first *shtieblech* were established during the 1930s. As a background to this history of the smaller shuls of Golders Green some readers may find it helpful to have a brief explanation on the composition of the *haredim* and the general characteristics of their houses of worship.

The *haredi* community is very diverse, composed of a number of groups and sub-groups, some tracing their origins back many centuries. However, there are four main *haredi* groupings, largely identified by their national origins: Jews of German origin, sometimes referred to as 'Yekkes',[1] who follow the practices established in the mid-nineteenth century in Frankfurt by Rabbi Samson Raphael Hirsch, as a counter to the German Reform Movement, seeking to blend a religious life with measured integration into the world of modern education and employment; Hassidic Jews, who are followers of the populist pietist movement that grew up in the Podolia area of Ukraine in the eighteenth century; non-Hassidic Jews from Lithuania, who are known as *mitnaggedim* (those opposed to Hassidism) or *Litvishe* (Yiddish for Lithuanian); and strictly orthodox Sephardi Jews, largely from Middle Eastern and North African countries, who often use their mother tongues – Farsi, *Ivrit* and French – in daily conversation.

A feature the smaller shuls and *shtieblech* share, and one that distinguishes them from the larger shuls, is that they are mainly focused on prayer and learning. Very few organise communal activities other than services and study sessions. Charitable activities are generally pursued by individual members of the shuls rather than communally. Another difference between the smaller shuls and those that are less orthodox is the high proportion of members who attend services and the frequency of attendance. However, the smaller shuls do not involve women to any great extent. Women attend services on the main Jewish festivals and during the High Holydays and also for family celebrations such as a *Bar Mitzvah*. At other times they mainly pray at home.

In contrast to other types of shul, the rabbis in *haredi* shuls are less active in leading services, often moving around the congregation encouraging worship and study. As well as the local rabbis who play a pastoral role, some of the Hassidic shuls also have a grand rabbi (the '*rebbe*'), the head of a particular dynasty, to whom they hold an allegiance and who live outside the UK (for example, the Sadigur and Alexander *rebbes*, both of whom live in Israel). Young *yeshivah*-educated men in particular are in frequent contact with the *rebbes* seeking their guidance.

Early shtieblech

The first strictly orthodox *shtiebl* to be established in Golders Green was the **North–West London (Golders Green) Synagogue.** It grew out of the informal *minyan* known as Golders Green and Hendon Hebrew Congregation, which was established in 1932 and met in the home of Reverend Baruch Azulay at 45 Sneath Avenue.[2] Reverend Azulay was born in Jerusalem, a member of the famous Azulay-Rivlin family descended from Spanish exiles.[3] The decision to set up a formal community was taken at a meeting held in the home of Mr L. Gulperta in October 1933.[4] Many members enrolled at a follow-up meeting at the Brent Bridge Hotel.[5] The congregation quickly expanded and started to hold services in St Alban's Hall.[6]

Reverend Azulay was joined by Reverend (later Rabbi) Joseph Rosenfeld, whose family came to England from Palestine in 1929.[7] For a few years Reverend Rosenfeld practised as a *shochet* (someone licensed to slaughter animals humanely according to Jewish tradition) for the Federation of Synagogues[8] before joining the new congregation as *chazzan* and Reader. By 1939 the community, now numbering seventy, had acquired 89 Woodstock Avenue and adapted it for use as a *shtiebl*. Religion classes commenced and a literary and debating society for young people[9] and a Ladies' Guild were also formed.[10] The *shtiebl* was initially affiliated to the UOHC, but by 1945 it had become affiliated to the Federation of Synagogues and Reverend Rosenfeld had been elected as its rabbi.[11] Rabbi Rosenfeld is remembered as a very warm man and a good teacher.[12]

The atmosphere of the *shtiebl* appealed to Jews who had grown up in 'Federation-type' synagogues in other parts of London and, according to Rabbi Rosenfeld, people liked the fact that 'they could become someone without having to give a fortune to the JPA (Joint Palestine Appeal)'.[13] Gerald Peters, who was brought up in a family with moderate orthodox observance, felt 'out of place' at Munk's shul, where he attended *cheder* until his *Bar Mitzvah*. This was not just because of its German character, but also because of its strict orthodoxy.[14] However, Gordon Greenfield, who also grew up in the community, recalls being 'very uncomfortable' with the 'blind following of tradition' at the *shtiebl* and preferred the services at Dunstan Road Synagogue to which he was occasionally taken by an uncle.[15]

The *shtiebl's* premises at 89 Woodstock Avenue consisted of a living room that had been knocked through to the dining room to accommodate the men while the women prayed in the converted kitchen that went off at a right angle. A window was removed and a curtain inserted to provide a *mechitza*. During the 1940s about twenty-five men and six women davened there on *Shabbat*.[16] High Holyday services, which had initially been held in the Methodist church in Hodford Road, were transferred to The Refectory Ballroom in Finchley Road.[17] Since the *shtiebl* did not have facilities for its own marriage ceremonies, some of its early members were married at Dunstan Road Synagogue, either by Reverend Livingstone or by the *chazzan*, Reverend Taschlicky.[18]

In 1938 the first Hassidic *shtiebl* was established in Golders Green. It was initially known as **North-West Sephardish Synagogue**.[19] The initiative to establish the *shtiebl* was taken by Meshullem Scharfstein supported by Rabbi Yehuda Hirsch Hager from Stamford Hill. At a meeting held in August 1938 in the home of Dr and Mrs Kirsch, Mr Scharfstein drew attention to the increasing number of Jews living in Golders Green who had been accustomed from their childhood to praying according to the *Hassidic Nusach* (liturgy and style) and needed their own shul.[20]

The *shtiebl* initially rented premises above a shop in Russell Parade (later Flax's delicatessen), where a Talmudic study group was formed. The *shtiebl* moved to 4 Highfield Avenue in 1940.[21] The first rabbi was Rabbi Issachor Dov Berish Hager, the son of Yitzak Hager, a scion of Kossov and Vishnitz,[22] who lived in Vienna. Rabbi Berish Hager, who in 1932 had succeeded his father as rabbi of Storzhinetz, was invited to lead the new *shtiebl* by people living in Golders Green.[23] He came to London with his wife and mother at the end of 1938, and his two sons followed shortly afterwards.[24]

The congregation, known as 'Hager's', grew steadily and in 1960 its premises were extended to accommodate an increasing number of worshippers.[25] On principle Rabbi Berish Hager refused to take Austrian restitution money to pay for the works, calling it 'blood money'.[26] He avoided the limelight and spent his years in prayer and study. When he died in 1967, his son Herschel (Zevi) Hager took over and the name of the *shtiebl* was changed to **Beth Yisochor Dov** (House of Issachor Dov) **Beth Hamedrash** in memory of Berish Hager's father. Rabbi Herschel Hager, who combined his diamond business with the rabbinate, is said to have 'kept the seat warm for his son, Gershon'.[27] Rabbi Herschel Hager's brother, Mendel, became the titular head of the Vishnitz community[28] when Herschel died in 1972, while Gershon became the communal rabbi. He was one of the first English-born and educated Hassidic rabbis.[29] The introduction of an 8 a.m. *minyan* in the late 1960s attracted many new worshippers, since its timing was convenient for those on their way to work or study.[30]

In the mid-1970s the shul (now larger than a *shtiebl*) acquired the neighbouring house in Highfield Avenue and relocated temporarily to the Sobell Centre until the enlarged shul was completed in 1980.[31] From then it became mainly focused on study. A *kollel* (Talmudic academy for married men)[32] was opened on the top floor and the shul became very busy. Rabbi Gershon Hager concentrated on building the Hager Hassidic dynasty while his brother Rabbi Yankel Hager focused on maintaining a high standard of learning. He instituted *Daf Hayomi* (a daily regimen of learning the Oral Torah), which takes place three times a day. By the time the shul celebrated its 50th anniversary it was a 'beehive of activity' with four services taking place consecutively every morning and up to twelve *Maariv* (evening services).[33]

After the death in 2012 of Rabbi Mendel Hager, who had been 'a very dominant force', Rabbi Gershon Hager changed the layout of the shul to make it more of a *beth hamedrash*.[34] The pews were removed and replaced with desks at which people could study as well as daven, seeking to appeal to both past and current *yeshivah* students. It is now one of the busiest shuls in Golders Green with up to 1,000 worshippers each day.[35] It operates both a daytime and an evening *kollel*, which, because of their excellence, are attended by men from across London, including from Stamford Hill.[36] People who need a *minyan* for *kaddish* (a prayer for the dead) or because they are flying early or late can always find a *minyan* at Hager's. It is a very participative community: 'everyone is in charge of something!'[37]

A *minyan* led by another rabbi from a major Hassidic dynasty was founded in the home of Rabbi Elchohon Halpern, the Rabbi of Radimshalle,[38] at 5 Oakfields Road in 1942. In 1944 the *minyan* relocated to 18 Alba Gardens before moving in 1947 to 171 Golders Green Road, where two adjoining houses were joined to form a shul named **Beth Shmuel** (House of Samuel) in memory of Rabbi Halpern's grandfather. Following the traditions of the Sanz and Ropczyce sects,[39] the establishment of the shul was seen as 'a landmark in the evolution in Hassidism in North-West London'.[40]

Rabbi Halpern, known as 'Reb Chuna', was born in Kosice in Slovakia in 1922,[41] and came to Britain in his late teens. People who knew Reb Chuna when he first arrived in Golders Green remember him as young and ambitious, with high aspirations for the local *haredi* community,[42] of which he became the chief architect and unofficial leader.[43] He founded Pardes House School,[44] and was its principal along with Rabbi Rubin from the Sassover *shtiebl* (see below).[45] Aged just 30, he became the President of the UOHC and editor of *Yagdil Torah*, then the only monthly rabbinical journal published in Europe.[46]

Over the years, Beth Shmuel ('Halpern's shul') grew to about 200 members. Along with the Sassover *shtiebl* (see below) it absorbed some Holocaust survivors and many of the pre- and post-1956 Hungarian refugees who moved to Golders Green. Today it is one of the leading and most traditional shuls in the area. It is open all day for prayer and study and has its own men's *mikveh*.[47] Rabbi Halpern, described as 'charismatic and caring', died aged 93 in February 2015. An estimated 5,000 people attended his funeral. He was succeeded by one of his five sons, Rabbi Moishe Halpern.[48]

Another well-known Hassidic shul in Golders Green is the Sassover Beth Hamedrash. It was set up in 1943 as **Golders Green S'phardish Synagogue** in the home of Rabbi Simcha Rubin at 843 Finchley Road. Born in 1911, Rabbi Rubin was the oldest son of Rabbi Chanoch Heinoch Dov Rubin, from whom he inherited his title of the Sassover Rabbi while still in his teens.[49] The family emigrated to the East End from Sassov, a small town in Galicia near Lvov. Shortly after they arrived, Rabbi Chanoch Rubin established a Sassover *shtiebl* in Fordham Street subsequently led by his son.[50]

For a while after he moved to Golders Green, Rabbi Rubin maintained the *shtiebl* in the East End. He was also involved in business activities and it was said of him that he was a merchant on weekdays and a rabbi on *Shabbat*.[51] However, from the 1970s he devoted himself full-time to being a rabbi. According to an article in the *Jewish Chronicle*, Rabbi Rubin had 'an open hand and a closed mouth'. By the 1980s he was dispensing charity amounting to £250,000 annually for which he made regular appeals.[52] Just weeks before his death in 2003 he is known to have personally delivered *trousseaux* to impoverished brides and handed over money to those in need. Such visits were often conducted at night to avoid embarrassing the recipients.[53]

Unlike most rabbis from major Hassidic dynasties, Rabbi Rubin engaged with Jews from other backgrounds.[54] However, he was also said to be 'rigid, demanding and severe'.[55] Along with Rabbi Halpern, he was one of the few Jewish men to wear traditional clothing at a time when this was rare in Golders Green.[56] He took a strict line on modest clothing for women and decreed that 'all these modern fashion books and magazines are not meant for the daughters of Rebecca, Rachel and Leah'.[57] He counselled against televisions,[58] mixed bathing,[59] and the employment of au pairs.[60] He frowned on talking and other pursuits during services, saying that 'the less we talk in shul, the more chance our *Tefillot* (prayers) will be answered'.[61]

Rabbi Rubin was succeeded in 2003 by Rabbi Shloime Freshwater,[62] a member of the wealthy Freshwater family and a descendant of the Bobove rabbi.[63] Today the Sassover *shtiebl*, which retained the name of Sassover Finchley Road after it relocated to Helenslea Avenue, remains very traditional and is among the largest and wealthiest Hassidic *shtieblech* in the country. During its existence many prominent men have davened there, including the Schreiber family (founders of the furniture company), Osias Tager (one of the founders of Ravenswood, a charity for people with learning disabilities), and William Stern (a property dealer).[64] On High Holydays *aliyot* (plural of *aliyah*) are auctioned for large sums of money, especially the reading of the Book of Jonah on the Day of Atonement and the opening of the ark at *Neilah* (the final service on Yom Kippur).[65]

The *shtiebl* has its own *mikveh* and is a 'major player' in the Golders Green *haredi* community.[66] The rabbi receives no salary for his leadership, but accommodation is provided by the membership.[67] Approaching 100 people daven at the shtiebl each *Shabbat*, mainly those living close to it. Compared to some other shuls in the area, there are fewer services and *shiurim*.[68] While most small Ashkenazi shuls belong to the UOHC, the Sassover shtiebl has historically been associated with both the UOHC and Federation of Synagogues.

In January 1947 the *shtiebl* **Kol Jacob** (Voice of Jacob) was set up, led by the Gur Hassid, Rabbi Yehuda Chayim Szenfeld (sometimes Jacob Schonfeld). He was born in 1892 in Wloclawek in Poland, and was a descendant of the Peshischa and Radoshitz rabbis.[69] On his marriage he moved to Kielce and became known as the Kielcher Rabbi. After a short stay in Belgium and France, in 1929 Rabbi Szenfeld moved to Fenton Street in Whitechapel where he set up a *shtiebl*. After the Second World War the *shtiebl* moved to Stamford Hill where Rabbi Szenfeld was now living, before transferring to Golders Green.[70]

Rabbi Szenfeld was a 'lovable, easy going and approachable man'.[71] His special concern was *Taharat Mahispacha* (the laws of family purity), which in later years is said to have 'verged on an obsession'. He made regular appeals to the Chief Rabbi on the need for more public *mikvaot*, addressed public meetings on the subject up and down the country and his pronouncements frequently appeared in the columns of the Yiddish newspaper *Die Zeit*.[72] Affiliated to the UOHC, Kol Jacob operated for just under twenty years during which time it remained very small. It closed in 1966 when Rabbi Szenfeld moved to Israel, where he died in 1967. His son Mordechai, a diamond merchant, joined the Sassover *shtiebl*.[73]

Founded about the same time as Rabbi Szenfeld's *shtiebl*, **Adath Yeshurun** had a very different character. It met as an informal *minyan* for several years before being formally opened in 1948. Like Kol Jacob, Adath Yeshurun originated in the East End of London. Its services were first held in the home of Rabbi Jona Ehrentreu at 85 Bridge Lane.[74] It started as an independent *shtiebl* rather than as a member of the UOHC, although it did later affiliate to the movement. It was mainly Germanic in outlook rather than Hassidic, but also catered for the Polish and Russian members of the *shtiebl*, alternating the style of services to suit the mixed composition of the community.[75]

Rabbi Ehrentreu (sometimes known as Aran Treu), the uncle of Dayan Chanoch Ehrentreu, started his career as the rabbi at Ohel Jacob synagogue in Munich. He was sent to Dachau in 1938 but was released later in the year and came to England. On the outbreak of the Second World War he was interned and sent to Australia, leaving behind his wife and six children. The Australian Jewish community secured his release and for seven years he headed a community in Melbourne.[76] On his return to London he founded **Adath Yeshurun** synagogue. Peter Colman, who as a boy and young man davened with his father at the *shtiebl*, remembers Rabbi Ehrentreu as 'very Germanic'. He spoke poor English, wore a long black frock coat and was 'regarded with awe'. He focused on worship rather than other communal activities.[77]

As the *shtiebl* grew, it attracted a number of central European professionals and businessmen, among them the well-known Frohwein family.[78] 85 Bridge Lane was extended into the garden but the premises proved inadequate for the increasing numbers: 'the *minyan* had extended into the entrance hall and even up the stairs; the situation was desperate'.[79] In 1976 the shul moved to 44 Bridge Lane, a former Baptist chapel, which had been secured for the shul by a far-sighted member, Freda

Frankel. By this time the shul had changed its name to Bridge Lane Beth Hamedrash and Rabbi Ehrentreu had retired,[80] which meant that the newly established shul had no rabbi. Services were often led by Yechiel Galas, a local optician with a practice in Temple Fortune. Although he had been ordained at the age of 19 in his native Lithuania[81] he never officially practised as a rabbi but he did give regular *shiurim* in the *Litvishe* tradition and congregants regularly sought his advice.[82] He apparently had 'a wonderful voice for rendering the service and a superb understanding of the texts'.[83]

During the early years at the new location a Ladies' Guild was very active, taking responsibility for the *Shabbat kiddushim* (post-service refreshments), which were very lavish as the food was provided by one of the Grodzinski brothers, owners of the bakery chain, who was a shul member.[84]

Rabbi Shimon Winegarten was appointed as the rabbi of Bridge Lane Beth Hamedrash in 1980 and has continued to serve the community for over thirty years. Rabbi Winegarten, who had studied at Carmel College[85] and taught for several years before becoming a communal rabbi, developed the shul as a 'hub of Torah learning'. Its many activities include a thriving *Avos and Bonim* (father and son) session, held at the end of *Shabbat*. Recently, after the purchase of additional land adjoining the shul, it was totally refurbished and renamed Zichron Kedoshim in honour of the Noe family, who perished during the Holocaust.

The mid-twentieth century

The premises vacated by Bridge Lane Beth Hamedrash were taken over by **Etz Chaim Yeshivah** (Tree of Life Yeshivah), which established a *minyan*. The *yeshivah* was founded in 1903 in London's East End, where it occupied a campus in Thrawl Street, Whitechapel. Its many eminent alumni include former Chief Rabbi Immanuel Jakobovits. However, the *yeshivah* did not succeed in re-establishing the same reputation after the move to Golders Green.[86] It is open day and night for study but the *minyan* remains small. The first religious leader after the move to Golders Green was Rabbi Nathan Ordman, who was very learned but not a prominent communal leader. His successor, Rabbi Rabi, has been described as 'shy and quiet'. Some older men daven at Etz Chaim on Friday evenings but it is not a *minyan* to which younger men are generally attracted.[87]

Another Golders Green shul that originated in the East End is **Machzikei Hadath** (Upholders of the Law). It was founded in 1891 in Brick Lane, made up principally of members of the Lithuanian Machzikei Shomrei Shabbos Synagogue in Booth Street (known as Spitalfields Great Synagogue) and the North London Beth Hamedrash in Newington Green Road. It was mainly established to secure an improvement in standards of *kashrut*. The 'shechita dispute,' which engaged many of the leading sages of the age, commenced in 1891 and raged until 1905 when an agreement was finally reached between the Board of Shechita, Machzikei Hadath and the Federation of Synagogues.[88]

As the Jews migrated away from the East End, the membership of Machzikei Hadath declined and in 1956 a branch of the synagogue was opened at 215 Golders Green Road in the home of Rabbi Simcha Lopian, who was appointed as its rabbi. During the 1960s the Golders Green branch started to function as the main Machzikei Hadath shul. The old building in the East End proved difficult to sell[89] and it was not until 1983 that a purpose-built synagogue was opened at 14 Highfield Road,[90] when Rabbi Dr Ephraim Yehuda Wiesenberg became the communal leader. He was succeeded in 1986 by the current incumbent, Rabbi Chaim Zundel Pearlman, a great-grandson of the famed Kamenitzer Maggid, a founder of Machzikei Hadath and son-in-law of former Chief Rabbi Jakobovits. Machzikei Hadath became a full member of the Federation of Synagogues in 1999 but after the move to Golders Green never regained the status or vibrancy it had in its heyday in the East End. Today its congregation is mainly made up of older people as it is regarded as being 'not serious enough' by the 'yeshivah generation'.[91] Of all the smaller shuls and shtieblech in Golders Green it is the closest to the 'central orthodoxy' of the United Synagogue.

A prominent post-war member of the Sassover shtiebl was Abraham Goschalk, who moved to Golders Green in 1945. He was born in Warsaw where he trained as a porger (a specialist in removing the sciatic nerve from the hind leg of an animal to make it kosher). When he emigrated to London he davened at the shtiebl in Black Lion Yard in the East End and later, after he transferred his butcher's shop to Hackney, at Yavneh Synagogue in Ainsworth Road. He moved to Golders Green after the Second World War and when he lost the use of his legs in the early 1950s he set up a shtiebl in his home at 25 Woodstock Road.[92] Known formally as **Beth Abraham** but popularly as 'Goschalk's shtiebl', it adopted the same S'phard practice followed at the Sassover shtiebl. The shtiebl moved to 46 The Ridgeway in 1957.

Initially the shtiebl had no rabbi but in the 1980s Rabbi S. Schmahl, a teacher at Hasmonean Grammar School, was appointed to lead the community. It has remained a very local shtiebl where about forty or fifty people worship on Shabbat. The congregation is said to have the feeling of a family who meet regularly for a common purpose.[93] Located in what looks from the outside like a normal house, inside it is fairly typical of the smaller shtieblech in Golders Green with the ground floor of the house extended into the garden and partitioned with a glass screen to separate men and women worshippers. According to one observer, at davening times there is a sense of perpetual motion.[94] The 'hallmark' of this (and other) shtieblech is the singing – the joyful Hassidic melodies.

The latter part of the twentieth century

In 1959 North-West London Synagogue moved to purpose-built premises at 54 Woodstock Avenue[95] and changed its name to Sinai Synagogue. When Rabbi Rosenfeld retired in the early 1980s, Rabbi Moishe Leib Flax succeeded him.

The congregation gradually started to wane and by the 1980s its membership had dwindled to a small number of mainly older people and the shul was on the brink of closure. However, it was taken over by a younger generation of men. The group had initially established a *minyan* in 1988 known simply as **Beth Hamedrash** at 137 Golders Green Road, the home of Rabbi Berel Knopfler.[96]

The people who transferred with Rabbi Knopfler to Sinai Synagogue were more orthodox than the original Sinai congregation, and although the move gave new life to the shul,[97] initially there were tensions about the use of space.[98] However, according to one commentator, the shul has never really appealed to *yeshivah*-educated young people because of its somewhat awkward location and its 'church-like' layout.[99] The congregation peaked in about 2005 but in recent years it has started to decline and now stands at about seventy to eighty people, approximately a quarter of whom are in full-time learning.[100]

Some members of Rabbi Knopfler's *minyan* in Golders Green Road objected to moving to a shul that was affiliated to the Federation of Synagogues and formed a congregation located at 35 Highfield Avenue known as **Kehillas Yaakov Beth Hamedrash** affiliated to the UOHC.

The Gerer *shtiebl*, **Beth Hamedrash D' Chasidey Gur** (House of Study of the Hassidim of Gur) was established at 15 The Drive in 1984 in the former home of Menachem Lewinson, a ritual slaughterer. When he became unwell in 1981 he was granted permission by Barnet Council to use his home for private prayer meetings.[101] After his death, his home was acquired by Gur adherents with funding provided by the philanthropist Mr Teitelbaum.[102] When Barnet Council withdrew permission for the house to be used as a shul due to the impact of the rapidly expanding community on neighbouring homes,[103] 98 Bridge Lane was purchased, and later the adjoining building. The houses were demolished and a spacious shul erected. The *shtiebl* attracts many worshippers, both Gur and Gur sympathisers who like the form of services. The shul holds its allegiance to the Rabbi Israel Meir HaKohen in Israel, but has no local rabbi.[104] After *shacharit* Rabbi Israel's works are remembered and a prayer is said for him on *Shabbat*. On his *yahrtzeit* (anniversary of his death) a special collection is made for the maintenance of the rabbi's court in Jerusalem.

In 1990 Rabbi Chuna's son, Rabbi Chaim Halpern, established his own traditional *beth hamedrash*, within walking distance of Beth Shmuel: **Beth Hamaderah Divrei Chaim** (House of Words of Chaim), located at 71 Bridge Lane. It initially thrived as a result of Rabbi Halpern's dynamism but a scandal has caused many members to leave the shul, which apparently now has only thirty or so regular worshippers.[105] A group of those who left Divrei Chaim in 2012 formed **Tiferes Yisroel** (Glory of Israel) **Beth Hamedrash**, in premises at 1 Bridge Lane.

Dedicated on 6 March 1994 by Rabbi Abraham Jacob Friedman, the Sadagora Rabbi of Tel Aviv, **Beth Hamedrash Or Yisroel** (Light of Israel) **Sadigur** opened at 269 Golders Green Road. The community was initially guided by Rabbi Israel's son, Rabbi Moses Freidman. When his father died in 2012, Rabbi Israel Moses

Growth of the
haredi community

returned to Tel Aviv and Rabbi Abraham's grandson, Rabbi A.D. Freidman, now leads the community. The community has grown and has over eighty members who worship in a well-designed building with a men's *mikvah*. It is regarded as 'very much a going concern'.[106]

Recent years

In the last ten years two 'deeply Hassidic' *shtieblech* have been set up. In 2005 **Kehal Chassidim** (Congregation of Hassidim) **Beth Hamedrash** opened at 213 Golders Green Road. The *shtiebl* is led by Rabbi Brief, who is said to be an 'up-and-coming' leader. He has recently been involved in setting up the Penimin Hassidic girls' school.[107] The *shtiebl* has between fifty and sixty members. A few years later **Beis Hamedrash Avreicham** opened at 211 Golders Green Road. It has about sixty or seventy members and is led by Rabbi Y.Y. Lev, who works part-time as a teacher at Pardes House School. It is said to be 'very right-wing', with many of its members wearing *shtreimels* on *Shabbat*. It is currently being rebuilt.

Towards the end of the twentieth century the Chabad Lubavitch movement opened its first shul in Golders Green, **Heichal Menachem** (Temple of Menachem). It was initially located in Highfield Avenue and then at 209 Golders Green Road, but now has premises at 8 Broadwalk Lane. It is a small but growing congregation of around twenty to thirty people led by Rabbi Yitzchok Meir Hertz (also head of the Lubavitch Yeshivah in Temple Fortune, Yeshivah Gedolah),[108] who promotes the Lubavitch *Nusach Ari*. Another *shtiebl* formed at about the same time was **Chovevei Torah** (Lovers of Torah) **Congregation**. Based at 76 Prince's Park Avenue, it was led by the American rabbi Y. Levenberg, previously head of Jewish studies at Menorah Primary School. The *shtiebl* closed in the summer of 2015.[109]

Over the last decade several *shtieblech* have been set up by young men returning to the area from *yeshivot* seeking something different from the shuls in which they grew up. Whereas traditionally the male members of a family davened as a family unit, many young men now prefer to daven with contemporaries who share a similar religious outlook.[110] They generally look for a 'more inclusive setting' and 'a more approachable rabbi'.[111] They are more comfortable davening in an environment that is free from the ornamentation reminiscent of a church.[112] A proportion of the young men who have formed the new wave of *shtieblech* were brought up in United Synagogue shuls or Munk's shul. Most would not regard themselves as being *haredi* but refer to themselves as *yeshivish* (belonging to the *yeshiva* world). The *shtieblech* they have established are generally independent, but the members have private burial rights with the UOHC.

The first of the new wave of *shtieblech* was **Beth Hamedrash Ohr Chodosh** (New Light), which opened in 2001 on the North Circular Road (5 Brentmead Place) under the auspices of Dayan M. Gelley. It places great emphasis on learning and on spiritual growth and unity within its community.[113] It has about 100 members mainly aged between 25 and 40 years.

Shaarei Tefillah (Gates of Prayer) **Beis Midrash** was the next to open. It occupies the upper floor of 281 Golders Green Road. Its *Shabbat* services are led by Rabbi Yeshaya Schlesinger from Stamford Hill. The congregation of **Kehillas Ohel Moshe** (Congregation of the Tent of Moses) at 102 Leeside Crescent was initially part of Ohr Chodesh, but were looking for something 'more intense'.[114] The *shtiebl*'s leader Rabbi David Stern (son of the property dealer William Stern) is 'quiet and unassuming' but a skilled leader and membership has grown to about 150 people.[115] The shul, the premises for which were provided by Mr Posner, is fairly affluent and has a *kollel*. The new generation of shuls also includes the *Litvishe* **Imrei Shefer** (Words of Holiness), temporarily located in the old police station in Temple Fortune (previously at 19 Highfield Road) led by the South African rabbi, Meir Rapoport. Its membership of forty to fifty is mainly young men who are working and learning part-time. In terms of orthodoxy, it sits between Ohr Chodesh and Kehillas Ohel Moshe.

Sephardi shuls

The first Sephardi shul to open in Golders Green was **Ohel David Eastern Synagogue**. It was established in 1958 under the leadership of David Elias who, supported by Rabbi Solomon Sassoon, had already founded a synagogue in Stamford Hill.[116] Rabbi Munk also encouraged David Elias's endeavours and when his shul vacated the premises in Broadwalk Lane in 1959, he arranged for Ohel David to take over the space.[117] The Lincoln family, who owned the premises, let the space at just a shilling a year.[118]

At this time, the membership of Ohel David, which had initially worshipped in the home of David Elias's mother, Rosa Elias,[119] was made up partly of Jews of Baghdadi origin who had settled in Calcutta (and a smaller number from Bombay), and had come to Britain in the late 1940s and 1950s following Indian independence in 1947.[120] However, there were also a significant number of Egyptian Jews. According to one account, the Indian Jews led services in the shul 'because they were more fussy about using their own tunes' (*Minhag Bavel*, the customs that grew up in India), and because 'they had paid for the chandeliers and the carpets'.[121] The Indian Jews had also brought with them a scroll housed in a beautiful silver case.[122]

The synagogue was a community centre as well as a place of worship. Despite the disapproval of the rabbi, parties 'resounding with Indian songs and music and dances' were held at the shul because its members had 'a culture of dancing'.[123] During the early 1960s the shul ran 'Hebrew classes' for about fifty children living in Golders Green and the surrounding area. David Elias personally ensured that the children attended the classes by fetching them and taking them home afterwards.[124]

David Elias, who acted as unpaid secretary of the shul, welcomed anyone who wished to be involved, whether they were Sephardi or Ashkenazi in origin.[125] By the 1970s the community had grown sufficiently to appoint a part-time rabbi. Its early rabbis included Rabbi Sassoon Abraham and Rabbi Toledano. In 1993 Rabbi Abraham Gubbay was appointed, who also worked as a property dealer. He was known for his support of various charities and for seeking good relations between the different streams of Judaism.[126] The congregation was gradually taken over by Iraqi Jews who came to England during the 1970s directly from Iraq rather than from India and other countries.[127] The new members introduced the Babylonian rites and rituals they had practised in Iraq.[128]

Towards the end of the twentieth century the community became less cohesive and members started to join other Sephardi communities being set up in the area. However, under the leadership of Ghassan Cohen who was appointed chairman in 2000, the community has been revived. The congregation has invested significant sums of money to extend its premises, to rebuild it in a Sephardi style and to purchase the freehold. Ghassan Cohen has told the following story:

> Just a few weeks ago, some Israelis walked into the synagogue, had a look around and walked out. One hour later they were back. At the *kiddush* I asked them: 'Why did you leave?' One man told me he had not been to the synagogue for twenty years. He didn't recognise it. He remembered the water leaks, the neon lights and the metal windows and thought he had come to the wrong place.[129]

Since 2009 Rabbi Asher Sebbag has been the rabbi at Ohel David, which now has a membership of around 450 made up of Jews from Iraq, India, Iran, Lebanon and

Syria. Although the community is expanding, there are few younger members as those who grew up in the shul have either moved away from Golders Green due to high property prices or because they are not attracted by the shul's activities.[130] The shul has recently begun to consider holding debates rather than lectures to engage more young people, some of whom now stay with their parents in Golders Green over *Shabbat* so that they can attend services.

The next Sephardi shul to be established in Golders Green was **Knesset Yehezkel** (Assembly of Ezekiel) **Beth Hamedrash**. It was set up in 1987 by Rabbi Aharon Bassous as a *minyan* that met in his mother's home in The Drive on the first anniversary of his father's death. In 1989 it moved to 187 Golders Green Road where the congregation grew steadily. Rabbi Bassous, who is of Iraqi descent, was born in Calcutta. He is a relative of David Elias and was brought up in Stamford Hill. He initially worked as kashrut co-ordinator for *Kedassia*,[131] having studied at *yeshivot* in Gateshead and at Mir *yeshivah*, Israel. He attended Halpern's shul and studied at Hager's before establishing his own *minyan*. Although raised by a family with strong traditions developed in India, his aim was to establish a community that brought together Sephardi Jews with a range of national and cultural backgrounds. The unifying themes are strict orthodoxy and study, distinguishing it from Ohel David.[132]

The shul varies its services to suit the different backgrounds for which it caters. For example, it holds a Moroccan service on Friday evenings. In recent years the congregation has been augmented by French Jews of Moroccan and Tunisian origin who have moved to Golders Green and found a shul in which they have been able to retain their distinctive forms of Judaism.[133] Because of its growing reputation, the shul has attracted people from across London and from Manchester as well as from local Ashkenazi shuls. With over 300 congregants, the congregation has outgrown its premises and has launched an appeal to fund a modern synagogue on the combined sites of 185 and 187 Golders Green Road. The planned new building will have seating for 350 people, a function hall, a large lecture hall, several rooms for smaller *shiurim* and residential accommodation on the top floor.[134] Rabbi Bassous's long-term aim is to make the shul a London-wide centre for Sephardi *halachah*.

Netzach Yisrael Shaarei Chaim Synagogue (Eminence of Israel, Gates of Life), located at 281 Golders Green Road, is a shul with about fifty members, including a number of Israelis attracted by the form of worship (*Netzach Yisroel*).[135] While other Sephardi shuls in Golders Green are independent, Netzach Yisrael Shaarei Chaim has affiliated itself to the Federation of Synagogues. Its part-time rabbi, Rabbi Doron Ahiel, officiates on *Shabbat*. The shul is wedded to the way in which its liturgy is sung and iterated and at High Holydays it employs a professional *chazzan*.[136]

Zichron Shmuel Synagogue (Memory of Samuel) has premises at 1117 Finchley Road in Temple Fortune. It is a Moroccan *minyan* led by Rabbi Don Levy founded by Mr Bendahan, who owns the Kosher Deli store in Golders Green and is of Moroccan descent. The *minyan* is made up of his friends and family.[137]

Mi Kamocha (Who is like you?) **Bet Hamidrash,** is a Baghdadi *minyan* which meets at the premises of Jewish Care, 221 Golders Green Road. It is a *Shabbat minyan* led by Rabbi Binyamin Denderovitz aimed particularly at younger people and newly married couples, encouraging them to remain involved in Judaism. **Kehilat Yacob** (Congregation of Jacob) is another Baghdadi *minyan* meeting at Jewish Care. It is led by Rabbi Mordechai Nissim.

Informal arrangements

There are a number of Jewish organisations in Golders Green that provide opportunities for worship alongside their main activities, including the Jewish Learning Exchange and the Kesher Community Centre.[138] There are also a number of unaffiliated *minyanim* operating for the convenience of their members, including the daily *minyan* that meets at the Sage Nursing Home at 208 Golders Green Road, which is led by variety of people. Its services are very short and informal. Dayan Simon leads a 'right-wing' *Litvishe minyan* which meets at Jewish Care. It has about fifty members who daven and attend *shiurim*, but it is not yet a recognised place of learning. Throughout Golders Green there are several small *minyanim* that meet in private homes such as in Windsor Court and Woodlands. They operate on Friday nights and *Shabbat* afternoons.[139]

The two most recent *Shabbat minyanim* are **Soriano's** *minyan* and the **Alexander** *minyan*. Soriano's *minyan* was set up by a wealthy Argentinian businessman, Mr Soriano. It is a *Litvishe minyan* with a membership of between thirty and forty people.[140] The Alexander *minyan*, set up at the request of the third Alexander Rabbi when he visited Golders Green, has a membership of about twenty Alexander *Hassidim*. It occupies the upper floor of 85 Bridge Lane.[141]

The present position

Although many of the smaller shuls of Golders Green were established for particular groups of worshippers, over the years their congregations have become more mixed and have attracted 'sympathisers' and 'followers' in addition to their core members. This applies both to the Ashkenazi and the Sephardi shuls. A member of one Sephardi shul has reported that an increasing number of *Hassidim* are attending his shul because they like the services. This is leading to concerns that, over time, the distinctiveness of the Sephardi practice in the shul might be diluted.[142]

Another process occurring among *Hassidim* is divestment of their original Hassidic identities. The phenomenon of men who cross from one Hassidic group to another is not new, but in Golders Green there are a number of 'neutral' *Hassidim*, who, while not belonging to a particular Hassidic group, preserve the general framework of Hassidic life. Living in an environment that is more liberal than

Stamford Hill, they are able to be selective about their customs and to adopt a lifestyle that incorporates elements of both Hassidic and *Litvishe* customs.[143] This is particularly the case in respect of studying. While intensive learning was originally the preserve of *Litvishe* men, as they have gravitated towards north-west London, it has also become the ideal of Hassidic men, a phenomenon referred to as 'Litvization'.[144] *Hassidim* are often to be found in non-Hassidic shuls with a reputation for excellent learning.

Among the *haredim* of Golders Green it is becoming very common for people to daven in a number of shuls rather than at only one, varying their attendance depending on the quality of study sessions available, whether there are interesting visiting speakers and rabbis, and what else is happening in their life. One interviewee explained that although a man might usually daven in one place, if he knows that he will be attending a celebration in another location, he may daven close to the celebration.[145] This is a phenomenon that has been referred to by some commentators as 'post-denominational' Judaism,[146] the emergence of a 'new breed' of Jews who are seriously committed to Jewish life within a community structure, but who do not locate themselves within a single institution or ideology. One interviewee said: 'Buildings are not important – people decide who they would like to daven with, then think about a venue'.[147]

The Sephardi congregations of Golders Green sometimes meet together for special events, but they generally maintain a separate existence from each other and also distinguish themselves from the customs and religious observances of the Spanish and Portuguese shuls, which are westernised and have their own traditional melodies. Whereas in Ashkenazi shuls prayers are often silent, in Sephardi shuls every syllable is said aloud. The differences between Sephardi shuls are largely cultural and have less to do with the ordering and form of prayers than the way in which they are expressed.[148]

The Sephardi shuls are 'mainly for men'. Women choosing to daven at a shul are not turned away, but nor are they positively welcomed. Some Sephardi women who want to worship collectively attend Ashkenazi shuls.[149] The Gibraltar Minyan previously located in Golders Green but now in Albert Road Hendon attracts a number of Golders Green residents, including a high proportion of women.[150] Although the Sephardi shuls are generally strictly orthodox, not all members of Sephardi shuls would regard themselves as *haredim*. While the majority of the smaller shuls in Golders Green are Ashkenazi, the Sephardi shuls are increasingly respected and are playing a growing role in communal life in the area.

12

Shopping in Golders Green

Prior to the twentieth century there were few shops and little commercial activity in Golders Green.[1] At the end of the nineteenth century the only businesses apart from the farms and related enterprises, including Mr Suckling the farrier,[2] were a dressmaking business run by Mrs Cornwall, two laundries, two florists, a general store and a grocery shop.[3]

The situation changed dramatically with the coming of the railway. In 1906, even before the station was open, land was being sold for shops at £5,500 an acre. Work started on The Parade at the crossroads of Finchley Road and Golders Green Road in 1908 and a second parade of shops between Hoop Lane and the station, Cheapside, was built between 1911 and 1913.[4] The *Hendon and Finchley Times* calculated that the thirty new shops in Cheapside might realise an annual income of £3,000, a 'veritable goldmine' on land that had once been 'waste'.[5] Two other parades – The Exchange, and further along Golders Green Road, Russell Parade – date from 1912. The main shopping parades in Temple Fortune were completed a year or two later.

Post office facilities and a bank (Parr's) arrived in Golders Green in 1909 together with the grocer J. Sainsbury (later Sainsbury's). The latter found trade so slack in the first year that the shop closed at 4 p.m.[6] However, shops were soon opening at such a rate that by 1910 Golders Green had its own Chamber of Commerce and the long-established drapers, Broadhead and Co., felt sufficiently confident in the future of Golders Green to relocate there from Camden Town.[7] Some of the early businesses opening in the new parades were 'state of the art'. The Refectory restaurant, set up in Finchley Road in February 1916,[8] was the first restaurant in the country to be supplied with electricity.[9] Although it was established during the First World War when food was short, The Refectory offered substantial meals.[10]

The first Jewish families who moved to Golders Green were able to benefit from a flourishing shopping area, but initially few Jewish entrepreneurs opened shops, even though retailing and distribution had been a long-standing occupation in the Anglo-Jewish community.[11] For some years most Jewish shop owners, who had traditionally lived over their shops, travelled from Golders Green to the East End, and the other areas from which they had come, to run their businesses. For example,

Israel Robotkin, a well-known East End butcher, commuted each day from his home in Golders Green Road.[12] There were, however, some exceptions. Ernest and Harry Raeburn, who came to Golders Green from Bow Road in 1910, set up a hosiery store at 25 The Parade.[13] By 1913 Klein and Co. tailors were operating at 2 Cheapside and a Jewish-owned fishmongers, Cope Brothers, had opened at 30 The Promenade in Golders Green Road.[14] Two years later the Copes opened a grocery store in Temple Fortune.[15]

In the early 1920s many Jewish shopkeepers were still commuting to their businesses and there were as yet no shops selling kosher foods. This posed some difficulties for kosher households. It meant that they had to journey to the East End to purchase food and other requirements or to rely on deliveries from kosher businesses in nearby areas such as Walsman's butchers in Cricklewood and Barnett's in West Hampstead.[16] As the community that became Golders Green Synagogue grew,[17] Reverend Livingstone campaigned for the setting up of a kosher butcher in Golders Green. The *Jewish Chronicle* helped to make known the community's need for a kosher butcher by publishing Reverend Livingstone's letters on the issue.[18] The London Board of Shechita was willing to license a butcher in Golders Green, but when Reverend Livingstone approached several possible butchers they were not able to open a business because of the prohibitive cost of leases in the area. At one point Reverend Livingstone suggested that a non-Jewish butcher might sell kosher meat but communal authorities quickly vetoed this proposal.[19] Finally, in January 1922, Mr J. Nathan, a long-established butcher in Kilburn, opened a business at 22 North End Road.[20] This was both a signal and contributed to the viability of the local Jewish community. However, it was still not possible to buy kosher bread in Golders Green during the 1920s. A group of local residents persuaded Cohen's of Petherton Road in Canonbury to deliver bread to Golders Green twice a week.[21]

By the mid-1920s the shopping parades of Golders Green were being described in the *Jewish Chronicle* as 'second to none', and a number of Jewish businesses had opened: Loffler's watchmakers, 20 Cheapside; Leverett and Frye grocers, 4 Temple Fortune Arcade; Appenrodt's delicatessen and caterers,[22] 5 Golders Green Road (later also a popular after-theatre and cinema restaurant, the Continental Café, 10 Golders Green Road); Jacob Kravetsy, costumier, 21 The Parade; Jacob Portnoi's tailors, 16 North End Road. By the end of the decade, the range of Jewish retailers in Golders Green included Mr J. Rosen, 1029 Finchley Road, who was advertising himself as 'the only Jewish Fish Shop in Golders Green', assuring prospective clients that they would receive 'the best quality service than has hitherto existed in this neighbourhood';[23] Mendel Susser's kosher wine merchants, 113a Golders Green Road;[24] Hardyment's Domestic Stores, run by Mr Rosenfeldt and Mr Benjamin at 26–28 Golders Green Road, which sold 'literally everything'.[25] A number of businesses were less obviously Jewish but had Jewish owners, including the Reliance Electrical Company run by George Cohen, a leading member of Dunstan Road Synagogue;[26] Bennos Fancy Galleries, run by Irving Kaufman;[27] and Walker's Ladies Tailors run by Isaac Walker (né Taflowitz), who had been a court tailor in Poland.[28]

An important development in the 1920s was the building of the bridge to enable the extension of the railway line to Hendon to cross Golders Green Road. The road was closed and the bridge was erected 'overnight'. Barbara Michaels recalls being taken by her father, Reverend Livingstone, to see the new construction, which became a landmark in describing the location of shops; they were 'close to' or 'the other side of' the bridge.[29] At this point the shops were mainly concentrated at the Finchley Road end of Golders Green Road and there were very few shops beyond the junction with Hoop Lane apart from the Jewish-owned Pullen's grocery shop.[30]

During the 1930s Jewish-run and -owned shops began to proliferate in Golders Green. The new businesses included Chrystle's newsagents, A.S.J. Woolf chemists, John Israel fruiterers and Leven's fruiterers. There was a particular concentration of Jewish shops in Temple Fortune,[31] including Freier's general stores, Katz the cleaners, Norman's fruit shop and a fur shop run by the Russian immigrant Mr Gilbert, which sold coats made to order.[32] However, a large proportion of the Jewish shops were in the traditional Jewish trading niches of boot and shoe shops (Lusting boot repairers in Golders Green Road), tobacconists (Drapkin in Temple Fortune, Leon in Highfield Avenue and also Golders Green Road, Ferdman in Golders Green Road) and tailoring and outfitting (Maurice Jacobs' drapery in Hamilton Road and his tailor's shop in Station Approach).[33]

Although some of the Jewish tailors and outfitters traded under their own names, others adopted continental names to increase their prestige. Directories for the mid-1930s include listings for Fortuna ladies' outfitters in Temple Fortune, Madame Hélène dressmaker and Valarie costumiers, both in Finchley Road, and Madame René gowns in Russell Parade, some of which are very likely to have been Jewish traders. Bettie's Juvenile Outfitters run by Bettie and Barnett Rubenstein in Golders Green Road sold expensive children's clothing to be worn at weekends and for outings.[34] Upmarket Jewish West End clothing shops had started to open branches in Golders Green. Weiss, 2 Golders Green Road, 'The West End store on your doorstep',[35] was one of the first to relocate. Montague Burton Ltd had opened a branch of the nationwide chain of outfitters established by the Lithuanian émigré Moshe Osinsky.[36]

While never operating on the grand scale of Burton's, one Jewish store that became a local institution was Franks lingerie shop, established in 1929 at 70 Golders Green Road by Mrs Beatrice (Bea) Franks.[37] Her husband's parents had started in business with a store in Berwick Street in Soho.[38] However, Mrs Franks ran the shop in Golders Green.[39] Her daughter recalls:

My father, Philip, paid the bills but my mother was in charge. She was a real businesswoman. She was lively and outgoing and knew everybody in Golders Green. She worked hard but still had energy to play with us when she came home from work. She was a real role model.[40]

Mrs Franks told people that in the early days, trade was so slow due to the Great Depression that 'the greengrocers used to dust the muck off the potatoes for want of something to do'.[41] However, Franks thrived and expanded into 72 Golders Green Road.[42]

The most significant change in the shopping areas during the 1930s was the opening of several kosher food shops including butchers and delicatessens (branches of Walsman's and Cohen's, Golders Green Road; Albert Assan, Russell Parade; Nelson's in Temple Fortune, which also took over Mr Nathan's shop in North End Road);[43] grocers (Homer's, Finchley Road); fishmongers (Levy's, Finchley Road). Despite this, some Jewish families continued to shop in the East End, partly it seems through nostalgia and partly due to the greater range of produce and services still available there. One former resident recalls that the salt beef sandwiches served with pickles taken from a large barrel sold in the East End tasted far better than anything sold in Golders Green,[44] and another recalls that, well into the 1930s, her mother made regular trips to the East End to buy meat she took home to be 'koshered'.[45]

However, a number of East End shops were starting to open branches in Golders Green. In March 1934 Ostwind's bakers, confectioners and pastry cooks of Wentworth Street took out a full-page advertisement in the *Jewish Chronicle* to announce that, 'in response to public demand', it was establishing a branch in Golders Green Road, where it would sell 'guaranteed kashrut' produce.[46] Kramer's,

Franks lingerie shop

also of Wentworth Street,[47] and Monnickendam's,[48] a long-established East End kosher bakery, already had branches in Golders Green Road. Some Jewish shops also moved to Golders Green from other Jewish areas such as Lever's Food Stores which relocated from Stoke Newington.[49]

The kosher businesses opening in the 1930s included a butchers shop run by Fred ('Fritz') Frohwein who had fled to Britain from Frankfurt in 1936. He was a prominent member of Munk's shul,[50] and assisted by Rabbi Munk and Rabbi Solomon Schonfeld,[51] he set up his shop at 1097 Finchley Road, Temple Fortune. When it first opened it was known as the 'Machzikei Hadath shop' because of the traditional approach to slaughtering and testing meat adopted to meet the requirements of the growing number of strictly orthodox Jews in the area.[52] It was later licensed by *Kedassia*, which Fred Frohwein helped to found shortly after the Second World War.[53] Frohwein's introduced Golders Green residents to new types of kosher meat: 'continental cold cuts' and selection of sausages rather than just 'frying sausages'.[54] Fred and his brother Ernest, several family members[55] and a number of assistants were employed in what quickly became a thriving business. Despite several threatened closures, the Temple Fortune store, together with a delicatessen that opened later in Golders Green Road,[56] continued in business until 2007.[57]

During the Blitz the shops of Golders Green were badly affected by air-raid warnings and bombings in the vicinity. Shop windows in Golders Green Road and in Temple Fortune (as elsewhere in London) were boarded over, leaving just a small square uncovered so that people could look in.[58] On the night of 25 September 1940 two landmines fell in Basing Hill, shattering shop fronts and scattering debris the length of Golders Green Road. Almost every shop suffered damage and troops were deployed to prevent looting.[59] When the Blitz ended there were some relaxations. 'Blackout' times became 'dim-out' times and although shops were officially still required to close on the sounding of alerts, shop owners often pulled down their blinds while customers remained inside finishing their shopping.[60]

The Second World War delayed the growth of Franks, but the family had a good reputation for paying promptly and were able to rely on their suppliers to obtain stock to keep the business going. Other Jewish businesses did not fare so well. In 1942 bankruptcy proceedings were brought against Herman Nadler, proprietor of Nadler's Gowns trading at 98 Golders Green Road.[61] However, some new Jewish enterprises opened during the war such as Greenfield's cleaners in Finchley Road, which later specialised in cleaning traditional Jewish garments such as *kippot*.[62]

The period of austerity that followed the Second World War hampered the development of the Golders Green shopping areas. Particularly affected were the food stores like Leven's fruitier, to which deliveries were intermittent. Jewish residents of the time recall queuing along Golders Green Road when there had been a delivery of fruit: 'I would be bundled out of bed early to stand in the long queue as one person was only allowed either one banana or one orange'.[63]

By the beginning of the 1950s the Golders Green shops began to flourish again and some were discovering new markets. Maurice Sheldon, who married Hazel Franks, recalls:

> In the 1950s there used to be a delivery of stockings to Golders Green on a Thursday. They came by taxi from Shaftesbury Avenue where the Franks had a warehouse. They were sub-standard nylon stockings as there was a only a limited supply of perfect ones. People knew that we sold them on a Saturday morning, and they used to queue from six o'clock. In fact some enterprising man used to sell tea and coffee to the people queuing![64]

During the 1950s Franks expanded into part of 74 Golders Green Road and then the other half to become 'a double-fronted lingerie and hosiery emporium'.[65] Franks became the place to go for wedding trousseaux.[66] By the 1960s the shop was employing sixty part-time staff, including specialist window-dressers. Many of the employees were 'Saturday girls' who spent most of their time folding goods and returning them to the shelves. The hosiery department was often 'three-deep' in people waiting to be served.[67] At Christmas additional staff were employed and an extra till opened 'but still the assistants could not take the money quickly enough!'[68] The shop was regularly updated to incorporate modern technology and selling techniques. One resident recalls that she feared entering the shop because 'once inside you always bought much more than you'd intended'.[69] The shop branched out from lingerie and hosiery to knitwear and menswear, but for many years it remained known chiefly for its underwear of which Bea Franks was the doyenne until she retired in the late 1960s. Mrs Franks was very 'hands-on' and some of the sales people felt that their every move was being watched.[70] According to one interviewee, the atmosphere in the shop was 'like the television show *Are You Being Served?*'[71]

Another Jewish-owned shop trading in Golders Green after the war that epitomised Jewish entrepreneurship was Lewis's furniture store. Barnet (Barney) Lewis (né Baruch Karbatznick), grew up in Brick Lane in the East End where he attended the Jews' Free Central School in Bell Lane.[72] He left the school aged 14 and signed up for a seven-year cabinet-making apprenticeship, after which he moved to Hoxton to start his own furniture-making business.[73] Having served in the Royal Fusiliers during the war, Barney Lewis failed to secure a licence from the Board of Trade to restart his furniture manufacturing business. Undeterred, he went into furniture retailing instead. In 1946 he opened a shop at 5 Golders Green Road, where he pioneered the 'take it home and see whether you like it' sales technique, which was apparently highly successful; customers buying furniture 'on appro' rarely brought it back.[74]

The Golders Green shopping parades were given a new atmosphere in the post-war years by the opening of several enterprises by continental refugees and by their patronage of existing businesses.[75] During the 1930s the Viennese refugee Hilda Wolfsfeld started a corset-making business in her home at 3 Powis Gardens and later at 40 Dunstan Road.[76] When the business became more established, she opened an 'exclusive salon de corseterie' at 871 Finchley Road, trading as Madame Leiberg,[77] which was famous across London. Mrs Wolfsfeld is said to have been very stern but 'knew her stuff'.[78] Other businesses established by former refugees when they were more settled included the bookshop run by Martin Sulzbacher in his home at 4 Sneath Avenue.[79] Mr Sulzbacher, who had been a highly successful investment banker in Germany, used an old Morrison air-raid shelter for displaying his books.[80] Benjamin Sachs recalls that the piles of books stretched up to the ceiling behind which Mr Sulzbacher sat hidden: 'I marvelled at how he found specific books amid the clutter. But he never failed'.[81] Mr M. Kerstein had a kosher poulterers at 1029 Finchley Road, Mr Rich ran a shoe repairers in Hamilton Road,[82] and Mr Sweetman opened a radio and television shop in Accommodation Road.[83]

Although there were still businesses that reminded shoppers that Golders Green had once been a rural hamlet, including Suckling's farriers, by the early 1960s the shopping parades were 'buzzing', attracting shoppers from as far afield as Scotland, Leeds and Manchester as well as from across London. There was 'something for everyone'. A *Jewish Chronicle* article captured the essence of the Jewish shops of this era:

> Here the boutique is an essential way of life, more so than it ever could be in Bond Street. Here the *heimische* [homely] vendeuses conducting a family business and shopping is in the way of a social call. They get to know more about you than your hip size and nothing thrills them more than to be able to tell you that they clothed your mother before you.[84]

Jewish traders prided themselves on being on first-name terms with their customers. They often kept lists of their clientele, contacting them when goods arrived they knew their regular customers would want.[85]

When Golders Green was being developed at the beginning of the century, bus crews whose journeys terminated at the station complained that they were 'famishing in a land of plenty' since Golders Green was too aristocratic or concerned with aesthetics to provide a coffee house for workers.[86] However, by the 1960s Golders Green was famed for its cafés, bakeries and delicatessens, most of them Jewish-owned and run:

> The Jewish flavour of the place was no more than just that: the bakeries where you could get gleaming *challah* bread [braided bread eaten on *Shabbat* and festivals] and poppy-seed filled *munn* at Purim; killer strudel, and properly boiled, chewy flat bagels, not the monstrous puffy things that have taken over the world; kosher butchers where the customers haggled about the brisket, and Cohen's, that temple of smoked salmon and pickled cucumbers.[87]

A rival for Cohen (Smoked Salmon) Ltd was Flax's in Russell Parade:

I used to go to Flax's on a Sunday morning to buy smoked salmon. Mr Flax usually stood there with his very sharp knife and cut uniformly wafer thin slices of salmon, which was still very expensive at this time before salmon was farmed. People queued for a long time to get Flax's delicious smoked salmon and you would meet lots of people you knew in the queue.[88]

Many Jewish people who grew up in Golders Green during the 1950s and 1960s recall sights such as the 8ft model Gouda cheese that stood behind the counter at Appenrodt's delicatessen, but a particular source of entertainment was Sainsbury's. At that time goods were set out on a series of white marble counters at which customers queued separately for different types of produce.[89] There were large mounds of butter from which portions would be sliced and shaped using wooden paddles.[90] Naomi Rose remembers being amazed by the accuracy with which the shop assistants were able to gauge the exact amount of butter customers requested.[91] Equally beguiling was Sainsbury's cash-taking system:

There were no cash registers in those days. You gave your money to the shop assistant at the counter who put it in a little bowl guided by a wire that looked like a small cable car. This led to the cashier's office high up over the rear of the shop. You'd see a hand emerge from behind the window, take the bowl and return it with the change back down the wire. You never actually saw the cashier but the process kept us kids amused![92]

There are numerous memories of Importers Retail Salesrooms ('Importers'), which since 1928 had been in business at 76 Golders Green Road, starting as a 'half-shop' and later expanding into neighbouring premises.[93] At a time when coffee was not readily available, Importers stocked dozens of different types from all over the world stored in hessian sacks. The beans were roasted and ground on the premises by a machine located in the front window. Passers-by were able to watch the machine at work and its flume sent out rich aromas that wafted along Golders Green Road as far as the crossroads.[94] Customers' favourite and sometimes exotic blends of beans were sold in paper cones from which 'you savoured the wonderful smell as you walked home'.[95]

Importers also had a small café area partitioned off from the shop. It was apparently 'not very grand', but it was 'almost a ritual' for some families to go there for hot buttered toast and hot chocolate.[96] When he was a boy Jeff Alexander's grandmother took him there for ice cream. Cream had been rationed for a long time and Importers was the first shop in Golders Green to serve homemade ice cream. The indelible memories left by his experience led Jeff Alexander in the 1990s to purchase the business, which was by then one of the longest established shops in the area.[97]

Another Jewish-owned café was Lyons Coffee House in Golders Green Road[98] which, according to one former resident, was an 'old-fashioned shop where you could go and sit and have tea or you could buy your little pastries and things for children's parties'.[99] People who had emigrated from Eastern Europe congregated in Lyons Coffee House (and also the non-Jewish ABC café):

> They gathered to talk about the 'Old Country'. Many of them had moved to the East End together and from there to Golders Green. There was a group who were members of Dunstan Road Synagogue who all knew each other in Poland. My grandfather knew Mr Susser, the kosher wine merchant who he had gone to school with back in Galicia. He also met up with a Golders Green doctor who he knew from Poland.[100]

Appenrodt's Continental Café had a Victorian décor – velvet curtains and aspidistras in pots – and a raised platform on which three ladies played a violin, a double bass and a piano, drawing many customers to the café.[101] Lindy's patisserie in The Parade, a 'plushy time-warp of Austro-German gastronomy', was famous for its Dutch Butter Cake.[102]

Until the 1970s Thursday was half-day closing in Golders Green, but the cafés and bakers stayed open.[103] By the 1960s Grodzinski's (affectionately known as 'Grods'), the Jewish bakers that had originated in the East End, had shops at both ends of Golders Green Road and in Temple Fortune. The shops had a lot of support because they remained open during *Pesach*.[104]

> My grandfather was one of twelve children, and Sunday mornings we'd go to Grodzinski's in Golders Green Road (double-parked of course), and he'd buy a dozen loaves of fresh rye bread to deliver to all his siblings who lived in Golders Green.[105]

Grodzinski's in Finchley Road had an attached café where, according to the comedian Michael McIntryre who grew up in Golders Green, you always saw 'the same collection of Jewish ladies, in the same seats, sipping the same coffee'.[106] The numerous Jewish bakers in the area at this time also included Sharatons, Sherrards and Beecholmes.

Most of the sit-down cafés served traditional English food and people seeking Jewish fare locally were largely confined to the small number of cafés selling salt beef sandwiches and gefilte fish: Godfrey's, which also catered for Jewish functions,[107] Leslie's Salt Beef Bar (in Temple Fortune) and Biedak's, which was a particular favourite with young married couples.[108] For many years Derek Stoller (in partnership with Leslie Godfrey from Godfrey's) ran a fish shop, The Kettle of Fish, opposite the Hippodrome theatre. Decked with sea murals and dramatic menu boards, it did a fine trade with theatre- and cinema-goers.[109]

The dining scene in Golders Green changed with the arrival in 1965 of Bloom's, which is commonly said to have been the first kosher restaurant in the area. In fact a small strictly kosher restaurant, Silver's, operated in Golders Green Road during the

Bloom's restaurant

early to mid-1940s, where the first chef, 'the smiling face of Silver's', was Herbert Bruck, a German refugee.[110] Tucked away in the residential streets, there were two kosher restaurants attached to hotels: Joelson's in Basing Hill[111] and Halberstadt's in West Heath Drive.[112] However, Bloom's was a more elaborate affair than these early kosher eateries. It was a branch of the famous East End delicatessen established in Brick Lane by Morris Bloom in 1920. His son Sidney took over the family business, which in 1952 moved to Whitechapel High Street.[113]

The Golders Green restaurant became even busier than the East End Bloom's. It moved into larger accommodation and the initial premises were used to sell Bloom's canned and packaged products. The restaurant was renowned for its over-familiar and sometimes quite rude waiters. According to one writer, Bloom's employed 'a hilarious cadre of the grumpiest waiters whose irascibility could prick any puffed-up pretensions belonging to the upwardly mobile clientele'.[114] One regular diner recalls hearing a waiter complain to a customer that their tip was inadequate:'I have a family to support,' he said.[115] The longest-standing waiter was Leon Nicholas, who worked in the restaurant for over forty years.

At its height people queued for seats at the restaurant, and a waiter would bring out pickled cucumbers to allay the hunger of the impatient would-be diners. Bloom's was frequented not only by local families but also by well-known people eager to sample its traditional Ashkenazi-style fare:

> Bloom's was always an energetic experience, dodging the waiters carrying soup, catching a boiled gefilte fish in your hand with carrots flying everywhere. It made you feel like you were getting some exercise, a bit like *It's a Knock Out*, when, in reality, you were probably consuming more cholesterol than a sensible person should eat in a year. The food was an affront to man and beast really, but it was always my fall back restaurant.[116]

The restaurant had an idiosyncratic system for dealing with bills. To minimise running costs the waiting staff were self-employed; they paid the kitchen staff for food ordered and the diners paid the waiters.[117] Food was served with startling rapidity and plates were apparently whisked away barely seconds after people had finished eating. Michael Alpert recalls:

> The dishes were heavily loaded and, if you didn't finish what was on them, a woman would come out from the back and tell you off as if she were your Jewish mother. She would say:'So what's wrong with the potatoes, then?' pointing accusingly at the leftover tubers on your plate.[118]

The restaurant was renovated in 2007 and reopened under new ownership,[119] but by then the food no longer appealed to 'the wandering Jewish palate', which had become more sophisticated. Many now regarded the food as 'tasteless stodge'.[120] In addition, the waiters were no longer Jewish and, although pleasant and attentive, the new staff did not convey the flavour of Bloom's.[121] Still spoken of with nostalgia, Bloom's closed in 2010.

It was not the arrival of Bloom's that made the Golders Green shopping parades famous, but the shoe shops. Golders Green Road was described as a 'roll-call of the shoe trade, with shoe shop nudging shoe shop – as if every resident of the suburb was a fashion-conscious centipede'.[122] There were outlets for most of the well-known shoe retailers of the day, most of which were Jewish-owned – Dolcis, Saxone, Trueform, Peter Lord, Stead and Simpson, Lilley and Skinner, Lotus, Bata, Mansfield and Freeman, Hardy and Willis[123] – as well as some family-run shoe shops such as Philip Edwards Ladies' Shoes in Golders Green Road and the upmarket Amandini, operating for many years at 1a Hoop Lane. These shops were a handy source of revenue for young people who worked in them as sales assistants or as window-dressers, advertisements for which roles filled the 'small ad' columns of the

Jewish Chronicle. One regular columnist quipped that in Golders Green 'not only do all God's chillum (children) wear shoes, but all God's chillum seem to sell them'.[124]

Until the 1970s the shops in the West End of London closed on a Saturday afternoon, which provided an opportunity for Golders Green to develop as an alternative shopping venue. There grew up a broad sweep of stylish and expensive clothes shops leading to Golders Green becoming known as the 'Saturday Afternoon Bond Street'. When the West End shops closed at midday, many people boarded the number 13 bus and made their way to Golders Green.[125] Several fashionable stores like Coronel's dress shop, run by the Castle family, that had outlets in Bond Street and Knightsbridge, now opened stores in Golders Green, enhancing its reputation as a 'serious shopping area'.[126] Most of the 'upmarket' womenswear shops were Jewish-owned including Peter Robinson's Ladies' Outfitters, Paige Gowns, Roberta's run by Mrs Nestel, specialising in holidaywear and described by *Harper's Bazaar* as 'one of the best boutiques in England'.[127] Rokay, run by Philip Rosengarten and his daughter Patricia, sold furs and special occasion outfits. The well-known Young Motherhood shop, which also had a branch on Baker Street, sold fashionable maternity wear.

These Golders Green shops were described in New York newspapers as 'not to be missed'.[128] Women came from far and wide, shopping for outfits for special occasions; the expedition was regarded as 'a big treat'.[129] A regular customer at Kit Yorke was a Jewish woman living in Hong Kong. She often arrived looking for clothes that were out of season in Britain and the owner, Josephine Oliver, sometimes had to close the shop and rush around London seeking out creations to please her client. Long-established customers were served with tea and other refreshments to make their shopping expedition a 'home-from-home' experience.[130] The dress shops were also frequented by local Jewish women, with whom Annabelle's is said to have been a particular favourite.[131] Selina Gellert recalls that on one occasion her mother arrived at a function at Alyth Gardens Synagogue to find that 'no fewer than six other women were wearing the same outfit as she was, some in different colours but the same design'.[132]

At the North Circular End of Golders Green was Estelle Fashions (owned by Estelle Simmons), which had opened in Russell Parade in 1953 and had built up a large clientele of women seeking larger sizes and 'modest' clothes. However, orthodox women would also visit other shops. Josephine Oliver recalls that orthodox women sometimes came into Kit Yorke with their husbands, and if it were nearing 5 p.m. the men would go into a fitting room, draw the curtain and daven.[133]

Golders Green also became 'a mecca of fashion' for menswear.[134] It was particularly known for its shops selling ready-made suits made by tailors, many of whom had come to the area from Stamford Hill. The ready-made suits were also sold in the chain stores such as the local branch of the Fifty Shilling Tailor (later John Collier), which provided 'stiff competition' for the made-to-measure tailors in the West End.[135] The other well-known men's outfitters of the 1960s included Geoffrey Davis, Gents' Outfitter, a branch of the Regent Street store, specialising in Chester Barrie suits,[136] the Smart Weston Shops,[137] Cecil Gee, Wiseman's, Alexandre and

Bruno, a branch of a Jermyn Street store run by Emmanuel Sinclair. Commenting on the growth of these shops, Chaim Bermant wrote that 'here the young man about the suburbs aspiring to be a man about town will find his tailored shirts, his mohair suits, and exotic variations on the y-front theme'.[138]

There were also a number of shops selling accessories to go with the smart outfits, including some very upmarket jewellery shops like Dysons (originally in Temple Fortune but later in Golders Green Road), Pullens, run by Sam and Mara Samuel, and Etienne. However the two best-known jewellers were those owned by Leslie Davis and Michael Fishberg. Leslie Davis opened his shop, Design Jewellery, in Golders Green in November 1962, and just a few weeks later it was burgled. A notice in the *Jewish Chronicle* the following week read:

> If the gentlemen who smashed our 'unbreakable' window with a 28lb sledge-hammer one foggy night last week and relieved us of 38 Omega watches worth £2,200 will call in to see us we will give them the free all-risks insurance we always give with our watches. Leslie Davis. PS Other customers wishing to acquire Omega watches in a more conventional manner will be more than welcome in normal business hours.[139]

Michael Fishberg was a fourth-generation craftsman. The traditions he followed dated back to Fabergé's workshops. When he opened his shop at 89 Golders Green in 1971, his father Harry remained for a few more years in Whitechapel but this business eventually moved to the new location.[140]

One of the best-known Jewish-owned accessory shop was Henry's Handbags, which evolved from a general leather dealers established in 1925 by Henry (né Isidore) Falkoff.[141] The shop was passed on to Henry's son, David, and then to his grandson, Jonathan. David Falkner (né Falkoff) was an extremely successful businessman who extended the shop from a double to a quadruple storefront and opened branches in Bond Street and Knightsbridge. The shop 'grew and grew' and diversified into luxury luggage and briefcases.[142] David Falkner bought handbags mainly from Italy and, according to a former salesperson, 'each one was more beautiful than the one before'.[143] The clientele was mainly Jewish, including families who came to buy goods as part of a bridal trousseau, but also included famous non-Jewish people such as the Beverley Sisters.[144] For men, the high-class accessory shop was Cesar, owned by Richard Rubin. As well as shoes selling for up to £200, the shop sold men's jewellery and the Cartier boutique range.[145]

During the 1960s a number of shops opened specifically to cater for young people, several of which were Jewish-owned. Snob and Lady M (run by Viennese-born Freddy Knoller), became the place to 'hang out' for teenage girls.[146] Their counterpart for teenage boys was Fella's in Finchley Road, part of the Ebony of South Molton Street group owned by Jeffrey Kaye, where many of the clothes were designed by his sons John and Robert.[147] In 1971 18-year-old David Krantz opened Belt-Up,[148] and Orange Hand was the shop that 'every Jewish boy loved'.[149] There was also a range of fashion shops for children like Mites, run by Maureen Stern in Russell Parade, and Please Mum, run by Graham Frankel.[150]

In addition to the renowned clothes shops, by the 1960s a number of other Jewish-owned shops had opened, including fruit shops (Hyam's in Temple Fortune and Meyer's in Golders Green Road), specialist shops such as Chinacraft, run by Gerald Lipton in Golders Green Road,[151] and Kendrick's, run by the Papier family in Temple Fortune, which was 'jam-packed with wonderful toys'.[152] There was an ever-increasing number of kosher butchers (J. Cohen in Golders Green Road, G. Odlick in Russell Parade, C.H. Ziff in Temple Fortune), numerous Jewish hairdressers (Percy Kurland 'noted Mayfair and USA Hair Artist'[153] in Golders Green Road, and Mr Norman and Gerrard Phillipe, both in Russell Parade), shops that brought the latest technology to the area (W.H.Vision, television dealers, run by Mr Hersham in Golders Green Road),[154] and stores that reflected the increasing affluence of the 1960s such as Norman Glen at 124 Golders Green Road, which sold fitted kitchens and later also fitted bedrooms.

With business booming, in 1964 the *Jewish Chronicle* pronounced that 'it's a good address, Golders Green, for an ambitious business man'.[155] During the 1960s most of the Jewish shops closed for the main Jewish festivals, but a large proportion traded on *Shabbat*. Apparently it was not uncommon to see signs in shops in Golders Green Road saying 'Closed for the Jewish holiday. Open Saturday as usual'.[156] For some Jewish families it was a regular Saturday afternoon treat go to Appenrodt's to buy fresh baguettes and cakes.[157] Michael Rutstein recalls that 'My family often feasted in Lindy's on a Saturday morning when perhaps we should have been somewhere more spiritual!'[158]

While the Golders Green parades formed a bustling retail area, Temple Fortune retained its village-like ambience. For several years after the Second World War, milk was still delivered to the area by horse and cart. Many of the shops were small and family-owned, which gave it a friendly atmosphere.[159] Although some young people regarded the shops in Temple Fortune as 'unexciting',[160] they were regularly patronised by Jewish families living in their vicinity. Particularly popular were Moshe's the grocers, Simmond's the dispensing chemists, Cohen's the jewellers, Geoff's the florists and a branch of Grodzinski's. Peter Colman, who grew up in nearby Hallswelle Road, has fond memories of going into Grodzinski's in Temple Fortune to buy broken biscuits stored in counter-height, glass-topped tins.[161]

Situated in close proximity to each other in Temple Fortune were two Jewish fishmongers, Sam Stoller & Son (which opened shortly after the Second World War)[162] and J.A. Corney (set up in the early 1960s), both still in existence today run by the owners' sons. The Jewish community has always been divided on which of the two sells the best fish.[163] The kosher delicatessen run by the Masher family from Vienna, Northern Stores, was seen as 'very old fashioned', but people remained loyal to the store when buying their *Pesach* goods.[164] There were also fashion shops in Temple Fortune including a branch of Roberta's run by Mr Nestel where he sold clothes he designed himself,[165] and by Betty Mizzler.

By the mid–1970s the Golders Green shops began to struggle for several reasons. In the early days most people walked or used public transport to go shopping, but the affluence of the 1960s had given rise to the phenomenon of the 'two–car–family', and everyone now wanted to drive to the shops. Since there was limited car parking in Golders Green, shoppers were not able to use their cars, leading to a loss of trade and calls for Golders Green Road to be pedestrianised.[166] According to Maurice Sheldon, then chairman of the Golders Green Chamber of Commerce, the problem was compounded by shop owners encouraging their staff to park close to the stores where they worked, and the reductions in public transport accompanying increased car ownership.[167] In his view, the lack of parking was a particular problem for the Jewish community:

> Jews like to park right outside the shop they're visiting rather than walk for three or four minutes. If you go to the West End you've got to get rid of your car and walk. So why not Golders Green? But apparently attitudes are different in Golders Green.[168]

Franks lost some passing trade but retained most of its regular customers, including well-known people such as Cissie Cohen, the wife of Jack Cohen, the founder of Tesco's. Cissie Cohen visited Franks to purchase the 'high-class, pure silk underwear' stocked by the store and sold by the 'local legend' Miss Ford.[169] By the late 1980s a large proportion of clothes marketed in Britain were made abroad, leading to the demise of Britain's clothing industry. It was a particular concern to Jewish firms that much of the competition came from Germany. For a while Franks refused to buy German goods but in the end had to capitulate: 'It was going to be commercial suicide if we didn't'.[170]

Golders Green was also adversely affected when the shops in the West End started opening on a Saturday afternoon, drawing trade away from the suburb. However, the death knell for a number of shops (Jewish and non-Jewish) was the advent of the Brent Cross Shopping Centre on the edge of Golders Green, the opening of which caused great excitement. Children attending the nearby Whitefield School watched in awe as the mall was erected and Golders Green residents recall cars queuing for miles around on the day Brent Cross opened in 1976.[171]

One of the shops to close after the opening of Brent Cross was Henry's Handbags where the staff met to discuss whether to move to the new shopping mall:

> We decided not to. We couldn't believe that such a successful shop situated in such a successful shopping area would be affected by the new development. But business blipped and never rallied. So the shop closed.[172]

Unlike Henry's, a few shops did relocate to Brent Cross, like the fancy goods shop Etcetera, and others hedged their bets and for a while had businesses in both locations, including Lindy's.

Although adversely affected by the opening of Brent Cross for a short time, several of the Jewish-owned clothes shops fought back. The shopkeepers polished their plate-glass windows until they sparkled, filled them with eye-catching goods and deployed their long years of experience to lure shoppers to buy their exclusive, well-made clothes. The Golders Green Traders' Association promoted the area, advertising in tourist and hotel magazines.[173] As a result, some long-standing shops went on trading for many years. A number of new Jewish-run fashion shops also opened and were highly successful. The general trend was to 'go upmarket', consigning the Brent Cross shops to 'middle of the road'. Spacious, light and airy boutiques decked out in pastel shades began to dominate the parades instead of shoe shops. The new 'chic bazaars' included Ruby Sharpe, Le Pop, Beige (run by Barry and Valerie Palache and specialising in clothes for orthodox women), Cream (run by Yvonne Lasky), Chevy (run by Henry Ettinger), specialising in well-cut French clothing and Cherubion in Hoop Lane which sold designer wear for children. In Temple Fortune Janice Rebuck sold gowns designed by her husband Maurice. Some of the new enterprises were Israeli-run, including Bataya that sold leather garments. The new shop owners hired buyers and salespeople who knew what people wanted and who sought to offer 'something special'.

Golders Green was now considered such a smart place that people dressed up to shop there. A *Jewish Chronicle* columnist commented: 'You go to Golders Green for your *Yom Tov* (festival) outfit and you return there to shop in it.'[174] The artist Abram Games, who lived in a flat overlooking Golders Green Road, said that one of the highlights of his week was watching the free fashion parade that took place at about 4 p.m. on a Saturday afternoon as beautifully dressed people promenaded continental-style along Golders Green Road, window shopping.[175] However, some Jewish residents bemoaned the lack of an old-fashioned fish and chip shop, a junk shop, a second-hand bookshop and a 'decent pub'.[176]

The shops that succeeded were mainly clothes shops, but there were a number of others that thrived by being 'quirky' (for example, Kernels Nut House) and those selling luxury goods (for example, Nadia's 'luscious' hand-made chocolates run by Millie Rothbart and her daughter Shirley Claff). Some Jewish shops survived by offering greater personal service than at Brent Cross. One of these shops was Warman-Freed, the chemist. Ivor Warman-Freed had come to Golders Green from Wales in the 1940s and initially started a photography and pharmacy business at 82 Golders Green Road[177] but then set up a larger pharmacy at 57 Golders Green.[178] The shop opened for long hours. According to Michael McIntyre:

You know when the Harry Potter books are released and people of all ages queue around the block? Well I. Warman-Freed pharmacy counter was like that twenty-four hours a day.[179]

A particularly busy time for Warman-Freed was at *Motzei Shabbat* (the end of the Sabbath) when those who had been taken ill over *Shabbat* joined the queue for medicines, often double- and triple-parking outside the shop.[180]

Another Jewish-owned shop that survived for a further generation by meeting customer needs was the Golders Green Pet Bureau situated in Broadwalk Lane. Having previously worked in the shop, Pamela Nenk took over its ownership in 1981 following a fire that had sadly killed a number of animals.[181] Mrs Nenk made a particular point of catering for the strictly orthodox community by stocking the correct animal foods for *Pesach*:

> I phoned my own rabbi, I phoned the manufacturers of Trill birdseed, and they came back to me and said it had to be plain grass seed and plain grass seed is plain canary seed. So that's what we got in.[182]

The shop eventually closed in 1994.

Franks made major investments in updating its 'look' and, like the pet shop, started to cater for the increasing number of strictly orthodox customers living locally, selling clothes with high necks and long sleeves. Hazel Sheldon recalls: 'Sheitels started to appear on the changing room floors when the ladies were trying on clothes'.[183] The children's outfitters, Jeffries, which had initially traded in Temple Fortune before moving to Golders Green Road, survived due to its specialism in *Bar Mitzvah* suits for which there was an ongoing demand.[184] Belmondo Hats in Russell Parade, owned by Marcel Pruwer and Jul Kornbluth, continued to do a robust trade, especially after the shop began stocking hats for the growing orthodox community.

As a result of this drive, innovation and specialisation, after just a brief spell in the doldrums Golders Green had bounced back.[185] Gradually Jewish shops started to open on Sundays, sometimes in addition to Saturdays,[186] and non-Jewish shops followed suit so that Sundays became one of the busiest times of the week in Golders Green. According to one commentator, 'the number of customers on a Sunday was just phenomenal'.[187] The Jewish businesses opening on a Sunday included a branch of Bank Leumi, the Israeli bank that came to the area in 1983.[188]

In the end, far more damaging to the shopping parades than Brent Cross were the four-fold rent increases occurring at the end of the 1980s. The rises were instigated by the Ecclesiastical Commissioners who owned many of the shop freeholds; they increased rents and other landlords following their lead. When leases ended they were not renewed and shops closed. Independent businesses, many of them Jewish, suffered most. Ominous 'closing down' signs appeared up and down Golders Green Road.[189] One of the first shops to close was Lady M in 1989, followed shortly afterwards by Pullen's jewellers. Wage levels were also rising and the family traders struggled to afford them. Franks gradually reduced its staff from sixty to twelve and began using 'freelancers' rather than employing permanent staff to carry out specialist tasks such as window dressing.[190] Some of the Jewish shops moved to Temple Fortune (for example, Beige and M&M shoe shop), where rents were cheaper. The parades there became the main area for 'domestic shopping'.[191]

Several men's shops, such as Geoffrey Davis's, stayed in business for a while longer because of the personal service they offered. However, ultimately they were unable to compete with the high-quality suits and other 'value-for-money' menswear available at Marks and Spencer's. By the turn of the twenty-first century, men were only buying the very expensive suits the shop stocked (such as Chester Barry suits originally retailing for £800) when they were discounted.[192] Some of the long-established shops found it increasingly difficult to keep up with market trends. After almost eighty years of trading, Franks finally closed in 2008. Hazel Sheldon recalls:

> I was getting older and I didn't really understand about fashion for young people. I was very good with the older people though. I remember one older woman who came into the shop once a year to stock up her wardrobe. When she was 99 she came in and bought more clothes than usual. She confided in me: 'I've spent rather more than I intended but I've decided it's not worth saving for my old age'.[193]

The arrival in Golders Green of an increasing number of strictly orthodox families created a demand for more kosher food shops. This development coincided with an upsurge in Jewish identity resulting from the Israeli victories in the Six Day and Yom Kippur wars.[194] As a result, starting in the mid-1970s, there was a rapid growth of stores selling kosher produce and shops selling Judaica (literature, art, or ritual items associated with Judaism) in both Golders Green and Temple Fortune.[195]

The kosher food shops increased not only in number but also in size. In the 1970s Mac Market moved into the area promoting self-service, signalling a move away from the traditional Jewish delicatessen and butchers shop. The transition was hastened by the advent of deep freezers, making it possible for shops to store larger quantities of kosher products, and the rise of the 'two-car family' allowed people to transport bigger shopping loads. Some of the Jewish delicatessens like Cohen's Smoked Salmon expanded and refurbished but they were eclipsed by stores such as the discount supermarket Country Market, established in 1980 and run by Paul Louizou, a former manager with MacFisheries, and the Kosher Freezer Centre owned by the strictly orthodox Jew David Rokach. The new stores increased the availability of kosher produce and created keen competition that helped to make the price of kosher food more affordable. They also led to fewer complaints about 'unfit' products. Up until this time there had been periodic prosecutions for 'rotten' meat and 'unclean' premises.[196]

The expertise of traditional kosher butchers and delicatessen managers was also challenged with the opening of shops run by non-Jewish businesspeople; they marketed and sold kosher goods using business acumen gained in retailing non-kosher food. Country Market was bought by Europa Foods whose Managing Director was Mr J.M. Patel; the shop was run by his son, Chandresh. Dr Raj Kadiwar took over the small shop vacated by Mr Flax in Russell Parade, then the oldest kosher store in the country.[197] He later opened a much bigger store, Raj's Superstore, which by 1992 was one of the largest all-kosher stores in the UK.[198] It ran in close proximity to Kosher King, the enlarged and relocated store run by David Rokach. Although the arrival of the Asian grocers selling pre-packed products initially caused some consternation, their relationship with Jewish shopkeepers gradually became more harmonious. They operated successfully for several years before they were hit by new Sunday trading laws that came into force in 1994. The Asian shop owners were now able to open for only six hours on a Sunday whereas the Jewish shops could trade all day.[199] They started to open for longer hours during the week to compensate, but had ceased trading by the end of the 1990s.

The kosher food business in Golders Green continued to expand even during the economic recession of the 1980s. Much of the expansion was pioneered by Israelis. By the mid-1990s Golders Green had been dubbed the country's 'kosher capital'.[200] With a great flourish in the *Jewish Chronicle* in 1988 a new 'food centre' opened at what was named Lincoln Parade (the former premises of Woolworths), which included Israeli-run Yarden supplying dried, frozen and chilled food from Israel.[201] Within six years Yarden (now B Kosher) relocated to much larger premises on the opposite side of Golders Green Road. Competition was very fierce, especially at *Pesach*. This benefited customers because of the downward pressure on prices. However, shopkeepers, like the owners of kosher grocery store Maxine's, complained that the long hours they had to trade in order to compete was adversely affecting their quality of life.[202]

Even more remarkable than the growth of kosher supermarkets was the veritable explosion of Israeli-owned kosher cafés and restaurants offering a wide variety of cuisine. This explosion, which commenced in the 1980s led to the southern end of Golders Green Road being dubbed as 'Little Tel Aviv'.[203] One prominent local resident commented that the area had become a place that 'exists simply for the body – food for the inside and clothes for the outside'.[204] In addition to the growth of the *haredi* community, the rapid expansion was due to changes in lifestyle; eating out was now much more prevalent. Also influential was the arrival in Golders Green of Israelis seeking eateries with a Middle Eastern flavour. They disliked the Eastern European Jewish food, which until now was largely what was on offer, finding it devoid of taste. They wanted what they saw as healthy food like Israeli salads.[205]

Long-standing Golders Green restaurants such as the Italian Villa Dei Fiori and Redfords, which offered food 'like Booba and Zeida (grandmother and grandfather) used to make', retained their clientele for several decades. However, diners were quickly attracted to new eateries like Zaki's with its exotic mezzes and hitherto little-known dishes such as hummus and tabbouleh. Not only were the menus of the Israeli establishments totally different, so too were their atmosphere, décor, waiters and music. Israeli-owned Rothschild's in Temple Fortune broke new ground (not just in Golders Green but in the country) by offering Chinese food that had a Kedassia licence alongside more traditional fare, aiming to attract *haredi* customers.[206] The type of kosher food available was extended even further when in 1987 Indian-born Triffiene Gottlieb opened Sababa in Temple Fortune, then the only kosher Indian restaurant in Europe.[207]

Slightly later arrivals included Dizengoff, Taboon, SOYO (serving Israeli breakfasts) and Pita. However, one of the most popular of the new wave of Israeli restaurants was Solly's Sephardi kosher restaurant, which opened in 1991. Its pitta filled with succulent lamb, chicken and beef, hummus, grilled aubergine and tahini, thick-cut chips and chicken soup, soon made Solly's a 'foodie favourite'. Within just three years of trading in Golders Green, Solly Sade expanded the business onto the upper floor. Solly's Exclusive, a 100-seat restaurant, which attracted customers from all over London. Photographs adorned the walls picturing Sade with celebrities like Uri Geller, Peter Ustinov and Maureen Lipman, as well as Rabbi Ovadia Yosef, the late Shas spiritual leader, and Rabbi Israeli Meir Lau, Israel's former Ashkenazi Chief Rabbi.[208] As a result of its fame, the restaurant became 'very pricey'. In 2000 Sade tragically died aged 56. His English-born widow Linda took over the business and the restaurant remained a popular eatery. In the very narrow downstairs café people were able to 'grab one of the few stools only if they were really lucky'.[209] But seven years later, tragedy struck again when Solly's was damaged by fire. The café and takeaway reopened just months later but Solly's Exclusive remained closed and the eatery eventually ceased trading altogether in 2014.

In addition to these sit-down restaurants there were many new Israeli takeaways including Pizza Pitta, popular with children and adults alike. The biggest hit was Carmelli's, which opened in 1987. Motti Carmelli, a builder by trade, had the simple but instantly successful idea of selling bagels and other products freshly-baked on the premises, using the aroma to attract customers. People flocked to Carmelli's and soon Motti and his wife Janice were producing 3,000 bagels a day. Grodzinski's and other traditional bakers opened hot bread departments to compete.[210] In its early years of trading in Golders Green, Carmelli's stayed open all Saturday night, attracting crowds of young people.[211]

Many of the new food shops and eateries took over the premises of businesses that closed following the opening of Brent Cross and the later rent rises. However, over time, the main focus of Jewish businesses shifted from the shopping areas at the intersection of Finchley Road and Golders Green Road to the parades nearer the streets to which a large proportion of the *haredi* community had gravitated at the North Circular end of Golders Green Road. While this change in focus eased the pressure on parking along Golders Green Road, it apparently did little to improve driving standards in the commercial areas. By then the Jewish community had apparently developed its own driving code. Newly arrived residents adopted the bad habits and blithely ignored parking regulations: 'They thought "this is how it's done here"!'[212] An article in the *Jewish Chronicle* suggested that driving and parking skills were no better in Temple Fortune, claiming that buses routed through the area sometimes stopped for thirty minutes to treat passengers to the spectacle of the 'outrageous parking manoeuvres laid on by the residents for the benefit of passers-by'. These included 'the enduringly popular sight of the BMW reversing into a space vacated by a moped' and 'the famous Temple Fortune ten-point turn – seen only during rush hour'.[213]

Over the last twenty years the number of kosher supermarkets in Golders Green has continued to expand and now includes two very large undertakings: Kay's and

Kosher Kingdom. Kay's has two outlets in Golders Green, the main store in Prince's Parade and Kay's Local in Hamilton Road. The business evolved from a small grocery store (Sam Kay's) set up by Victor Langberg at 2 Prince's Parade in 1953.[214] Kay's has recently been extended to incorporate a fish counter and delicatessen. Although well-known locally, the owners continue to live in Stamford Hill. Kosher Kingdom in Russell Parade is the successor to Kosher King, and is run by David Rokach and his partners. A fire destroyed Kosher Kingdom in the summer of 2008, but in September 2009 it opened an even larger store, which claims to be Europe's largest kosher supermarket[215] and regularly improves its repertoire to retain customers. It currently has a sushi counter, serves hot drinks and is open several days a week from 7 a.m. until midnight.

The new generation of kosher supermarkets import produce from all over the world, especially from well-known companies in Israel and New York specialising in kosher produce. They also use French and Swiss companies for goods such as cheese, yogurt, chocolate and alcohol. However, meat products are mainly purchased locally from sources approved by Kedassia. Despite the scale on which the supermarkets operate, the kosher food they sell is still more expensive than non-kosher food because of import costs and the costs of rabbinical supervision. While traditional Ashkenazi goods still predominate, Sephardi food is also sold.

Today there are many kosher butchers and delicatessens in Golders Green, including a number that are *glatt* kosher such as Menachem's, located in the premises formerly occupied by Flax's. It is run by Moroccan-born Menachem Haziza, previously a manager at Frohwein's, and sells Sephardi-style specialties as well as a range of meat and poultry. Kosher Deli in Golders Green Road is also a family-run butcher that sells salads and kugel (a savoury pudding made with potato).

The kosher food shops close an hour before the start of *Shabbat* and open again very early on a Sunday morning, when business is very brisk. However, the shops are at their busiest as *Shabbat* approaches. As early as Wednesday evenings trade starts to increase as families begin to stock up, but the peak times are Thursdays and Fridays, which are akin to Saturday afternoons in Brent Cross. At these times Golders Green Road bustles 'like some Marrakesh street market'.[216] By contrast, on Saturdays the shopping areas of Golders Green are comparatively quiet until nightfall when they burst into life again with the re-opening of the eateries.

The arrival of French Jews in Golders Green is proving to be as influential as the Israelis were a generation ago. Their increasing presence in Golders Green is reflected in the produce now available in local shops. Several kosher grocery shops stock Tunisian delicacies like merguez, briques and jars of sauce for making p'kalla, 'at a price to give a Tunisian grandmother a heart attack!'[217] Several stores advertise the availability of 'French specialities' including B Kosher, which has French-Jewish owners who stock an extensive range of French kosher products.[218] The French penchant for eating out has also led to the opening of new cafés and restaurants where they form the main clientele,[219] including La Maison, which has a French décor and serves Tunisian and Moroccan dishes.

Non-food Jewish shops are also a prominent feature of modern-day Golders Green. They include Torah Treasures, selling Judaica and religious and secular Jewish books. There is also a range of specialist shops catering specifically for the *haredi* community. In the last decade there has been a growth of businesses selling 'modest clothing' for women and 'Shabbos outfits' like Miri's in Temple Fortune and Dynasty for childrenswear in Russell Parade. Several of these businesses are located in residential roads rather than in the main shopping parades (for example, Gorgeous Gowns in Highcroft Gardens and Leeside Lingerie in Leeside Crescent).[220] There are also *heimische* shops selling children's clothes and nursery equipment like Yummy Kids and many dry cleaners specialising in cleaning and repairing *tzitzit* and *tallitot*.

Up and down Golders Green Road there are a number of (mainly Jewish) charity shops. In some areas the arrival of charity shops has heralded the decline of an area but in Golders Green this is not the case; they are a symbol of the presence of a sizeable Jewish community, which places a great deal of emphasis on charitable giving and raising money for charitable purposes. Since the neighbourhood is generally quite affluent, the merchandise on sale in the well-laid-out charity shops is often high quality, attracting middle-class shoppers in search of bargains.

In combination these Jewish businesses have made Golders Green much more culturally Jewish than it ever has been. Although kosher eateries and Judaica stores compete for space alongside Polish grocery shops, Korean supermarkets and Turkish restaurants, it is unquestionably now a hub for all things Jewish. People travel considerable distances for a 'kosher eating experience' and for kosher shopping, particularly at *Pesach*.[221] The widely known restaurants, which are either meat or dairy,[222] include Novellino (Italian), La Fiesta (a steakhouse), Met Su Yan (Oriental).

Some of the more recent Jewish shops, takeaways and restaurants are very modern in their décor. They co-exist alongside shops that are reminders of years gone by. The continental-style strictly kosher Parkway Patisserie has been in Golders Green for approaching fifty years. Gold's Outlet Shop ('the big red building') originates from Petticoat Lane market where Warren Gold started work as a 'barrow boy'. He went on to become the renowned Lord John of Carnaby Street. He was still serving in the shop (which caters for all sizes including 'the portly man') until shortly before his death in the summer of 2015, taking pride in being able to 'outfit anyone'.[223]

Mirroring developments in Golders Green Road, the shops at Temple Fortune have also become more Jewish. The parades there include a number of recent additions including Matok, a modern kosher bakery, which opened in 2010 on the corner of Bridge Lane and Finchley Road and sells Jewish specialities like rugelach and borekas (both types of pastries), the mini supermarket Kosher Paradise and Eckstein's delicatessen. They sit comfortably alongside the Jewish shops that have been in Temple Fortune for many decades: Susser's wine merchant, D. and M. Cohen jewellers, Daniel's bakery, which attracts lengthy bustling queues on Fridays and Sunday mornings, and the legendary Shutler's, which continues to stock *Shabbat* urns among its hardware. There are two Jewish bookshops, which also sell Judaica: Joseph's, where there are regular author events, and the long-established Aisenthal's. The area has become a haven for 'ladies who lunch' and 'yummy mummies'[224] visiting its high-end boutiques such as Genevieve. The increasing number of Jewish food and coffee shops are much appreciated alike by local residents and *haredi* women who drive over from Stamford Hill.[225]

Opinions are divided on whether the changes in the shopping areas of Golders Green are a 'good thing' or not. Some people who knew the area when the fashion shops were at their height perceive that the current retail outlets, cafés and restaurants lack the 'touch of elegance' of Golders Green's in its 'glory days'.[226] Some older people find the modern environment quite hostile. Others, particularly people who are relatively new to Golders Green, relish the cosmopolitan and international atmosphere the shopping areas have assumed. However, most people are pragmatic and recognise that places evolve to meet new needs and different outlooks. Even some longer-standing residents take pride in the ability of Jewish businesses to reinvent themselves, adapting to the needs of new generations and maintaining the vibrancy of Golders Green. Although many of the shops in Golders Green and Temple Fortune look very different from fifty years ago and several offer online services, many shoppers still believe there is nothing to beat the experience of standing chatting in the *challah* queue or savouring the aroma of the Jewish bakeries and other food stores.[227]

13

Leisure Times

Prior to the arrival of the railway line in Golders Green the area had been a place of leisure. Many people from inner London came to the small hamlet to enjoy the fresh air and open countryside. The tearoom at the White Swan Tavern and the Royal Oak public house in Temple Fortune were very popular with Londoners, as was walking in Golders Hill Park with its surrounding paths and lanes. After the station opened in 1907 these attractions became even more accessible. Londoners now took the Tube train to sample the ale at the Royal Oak[1] and to enjoy the band that sometimes played on the station forecourt. So popular did these outings become that the train service from Charing Cross was sometimes increased from twelve- to four-minute intervals.[2] The mansion house tearooms in Golders Hill Park were packed on Sundays and Bank Holidays.[3]

For the first few years of the suburb's existence there were few forms of entertainment for the new Jewish residents outside the home other than enjoying the open spaces and parks that had drawn them to live in Golders Green. Before all the roads were built it was much quicker than it is today for people living in Golders Green to walk to Hampstead Heath, although at that time Kenwood House and its lake were not yet open to the public.[4] Within just a few years the situation had changed. In May 1913 Golders Green's first cinema, the Ionic, opened in Finchley Road, its name being derived from the ionic pillars at the front of the building.[5] On Boxing Day in the same year the Hippodrome theatre opened adjacent to the underground station.

Despite substantial opposition from some churchmen and traders in the area, who objected to the showing of films on Sundays,[6] the Ionic was soon joined by other cinemas. The Lido opened in Golders Green Road in 1929 and was the first 'talkie-equipped' suburban 'supercinema'.[7] It became the ABC in 1959. The Regal Cinema in Finchley Road, owned by Odeon, began as an ice rink in 1929 and was converted into a cinema in 1932.[8] It closed in 1956 and reopened as a bowling alley in 1960, the first in the country.[9] In 1933 a second theatre, the Orpheum, was built in Temple Fortune; it became the Odeon cinema in the 1960s.[10]

Along with their non-Jewish neighbours and many visitors from outside the area, the early Jewish residents of Golders Green flocked to the newly established theatres

Regal Cinema,
Hippodrome etc.

Beverley-Jane Stewart.

and cinemas. The Hippodrome was a particular favourite with Jewish families. Advertisements in the *Jewish Chronicle* encouraging Jews to move to Golders Green specifically mentioned the theatre, describing it as 'the largest and most handsome Suburban Theatre'.[11] Designed by the architect Bertie Crewe, the Hippodrome was built to a very high standard. It had a grand entrance hall with mosaic floors and a marble staircase. Originally there were over 3,500 seats, making it larger than many West End theatres.[12] Initially it was run as a music hall with films on a Sunday accompanied by a full orchestra. However, in the 1920s a 90ft stage was introduced, reducing the seating capacity but allowing the Hippodrome to stage major shows. By the latter part of the decade it had become the venue for travelling productions either bound for the West End or which had just played there. It was also the venue for touring opera performances and variety shows:

I remember going to the Hippodrome to see Robert Donat. I also remember two glorious ballets performed by the Ballet Russe de Monte Carlo – 'Les Sylphides' and 'Scheherazade' – and a performance of 'The Yeoman of the Guard' produced by the British National Opera Company. I have one very vivid memory of a striptease! In those days performers were allowed to strip but they weren't allowed to move. I blushed furiously.[13]

In addition to these prominent productions, the Hippodrome was used as a venue for activities of specific interest to the Jewish community, such as the 1927 event 'Young Palestine: Eretz Yisrael' organised by the local Zionist organisations. It was chaired by Councillor Albert Naar and Reverend Livingstone was one of the main speakers.[14]

The Hippodrome reached its heyday in the 1950s when world-famous performers were appearing there. Raymond Gubbay, the well-known Jewish impresario who grew up in Golders Green, was inspired by his visits to the Hippodrome where he saw *The Prime of Miss Jean Brodie* starring Vanessa Redgrave, Margot Fonteyn and Rudolf Nureyev in *Giselle* and many other well-known performers like Marlene Dietrich and Tommy Cooper.[15] The Hippodrome was the first theatre in London to reopen after the closure caused by the declaration of war in 1939.[16] It became the home of the Boy Scout Gang Show produced by Ralph Reader and staged a number of D'Oyly Carte productions and shows arranged by Carol Levis, the Jewish talent scout and impresario.[17] Some Hippodrome productions featured well-known Jewish actors such as *Romanoff and Juliet* staged in May 1956, which starred David Hurst (né Hirsch), who came to the country on the Kindertransport.[18] The Hippodrome Christmas pantomimes were 'must-sees' for many Jewish children.[19] Performances at the Hippodrome were almost continuous and many Jewish families went there each time the show changed, prepared to sit in the hard seats in the gallery if necessary to see the productions.[20]

However, by the early 1960s there were signs that the Hippodrome was 'played out'. Now in competition with other forms of entertainment, its seats were rarely filled and it became uneconomic to run. When in 1968 the BBC bought the building as a home for its concert orchestra and a venue for the BBC Big Band and the BBC Radio Orchestra,[21] Jewish residents attended the concerts being recorded there, and listened to them on the radio. Especially popular was *Friday Night is Music Night*. Many were 'heartbroken' when the Hippodrome closed in 2003.[22]

The Orpheum Theatre was built on the site of a former racecourse at Temple Fortune and the ring where the horses were once exercised was still visible in the theatre car park.[23] Even though a high explosive bomb was dropped on the car park in 1940,[24] the Orpheum remained open for much of the war, staging plays and concerts. In particular, people recall the 'entrancing ballets' produced at the Orpheum during the war.[25]

By the 1930s the Golders Green cinemas were playing the films of Hollywood's epic years to increasingly full houses. Before the days of radio and television, the cinema quickly became a social institution and Jewish (and non-Jewish) residents of Golders Green often went to the cinema two or three times a week:

> The Lido cinema was something fantastic. I would rush down my supper and go and stand in the queue to try and get in. Often I had to go home disappointed. This was back in the days when there were two films for each show. I saw my first x-rated film, *The War of the Worlds*, at the Ionic.[26]

Although they are remembered as 'fuggy' places, thick with smoke from cigarettes and pipes, they were considered to be quite safe. Julia Chain recalls being dropped at the ABC cinema by her grandparents and left on her own to watch the film.[27] The Regal Cinema had such a loyal Jewish following that in 1934 a Jewish Golders Green and Hendon Film and Social Club was formed, which met in the cinema on Tuesday evenings.[28] Younger Jewish viewers, including the writer Brian Glanville, joined the Regal's Micky Mouse Club.[29] The cinemas stayed open during the war. If there was a bombing raid a notice came up on the screen, giving people the option of leaving if they wanted to go to air-raid shelters.[30]

The railway that had brought Jewish residents to Golders Green also gave them easy access to the entertainment and leisure facilities in central London. As early as 1910 the railway company was running a special late-night 'Theatre Express' from Leicester Square. It bypassed several stations to reach Golders Green in just fifteen minutes where electric tramcars were waiting to transport those living in Temple Fortune.[31] As the train service became even more frequent and also cheaper, trips to the West End became more popular:

> There were clubs you know but I don't think we did very much with them. We went to the theatre. I liked ballet and opera. We went into town a lot. We could go to Covent Garden for half a crown. I saw all the best performances in the old days including the Russian Ballet before they split up. It was lovely. And we went to the theatre in London a lot with school friends.[32]

A local venue popular with Jewish clientele from the 1930s onwards was the fashionable Brent Bridge Hotel, just across the North Circular Road from Golders Green. It was a large eighteenth-century private house that became a hotel and sports club just before the First World War. In the 1920s the hotel was taken over by Hermann Appenrodt, who also ran a kosher delicatessen in Golders Green Road.[33] The hotel had a kosher licence enabling it to cater for weddings and *B'nai Mitzvah* but its main draw was its ballroom.[34] Despite complaints about a swastika being displayed at a function held in the hotel,[35] dances organised by bodies such as the New Future Club[36] were very popular with young Jews from Golders Green.

During the 1930s well-attended dances organised by the Jewish Hawthorn Social Club were also held at Hawthorn Hall in Bridge Lane. The Regal Ballroom in

Finchley Road had its 'Grand Opening' in October 1933.[37] For many decades dances were held there organised by a succession of Jewish societies and clubs starting with the North-West Senior Social and Literary Society and then groups such as the Golders Green Social and Sports Club. Some groups that organised dances at the ballroom did so for charitable purposes as well as for entertainment like the Golders Green Havana Club, which met on Thursday evenings for dancing and to raise money for refugee charities.[38]

In 1929 the Foster family bought a property at 1011 Finchley Road, which proved too large for their needs. Aida Foster opened what became a highly successful business venture, the Aida Foster Stage School, that contributed to the careers of many famous people, including celebrities such as Jean Simmons, Barbara Windsor, Shirley Eaton and Jean Marsh. The attached dance school attracted many local Jewish children, including Jocelyne Tobin and her sister Eileen. They later transferred to a rival school run by Nancy Evans, a former teacher at the Aida Foster School. The new school staged productions in the West End in which the sisters took part.[39]

Even during the Great Depression, upwardly mobile Jews in Golders Green were enrolling their children for secular after-school pursuits such as those provided by Aida Foster. Some of the fee-paying schools, including North London Collegiate School, frowned on these activities because they interfered with schoolwork.[40] Opportunities for 'extra-curricular' recreations raised other dilemmas. Some young people found it difficult to decide between religion school classes and other weekend pastimes available locally, such as the horse-riding lessons held at the stables on the site of the former Gloucester Lodge.[41]

Some Jewish children spent a great deal of time on their own reading books. Naomi Rose recalls reading for 'hours and hours' in the spare room of her grandparent's house in Basing Hill, working her way through the *Just William* series.[42] When it opened in 1935, the Golders Green public library was greeted with a great deal of enthusiasm by many Jewish children who visited not only to do their school homework, but also to meet up with friends and to read the book collections.[43]

Despite the growing number of local amenities, Jewish families continued to enjoy the nearby open spaces. In many households it became a tradition for whole families to go to Golders Hill Park on Sundays to watch the peacocks strutting around the grounds of Golders Hill House.[44] Many families also went for long walks on Hampstead Heath, especially those who did not have the money to spare for the cinema or the theatre.[45] Young people would walk unaccompanied 'quite fearlessly' across the Heath.[46] Children also played in the fields that had not yet been built over. Barbara Michaels recalls that her sister Nancie once ate deadly nightshade she found while playing in the fields at the bottom of the road where they lived, Golders Gardens.[47]

Since there were very few cars at that time, children also often played in the streets. During the 1950s the large mansion, The Oaks (formerly owned by Reuben

Lincoln who has been mentioned in previous chapters), was demolished. Until then, its grounds were a favourite haunt for Jewish children living in nearby roads such as Beechcroft Avenue.[48] Child's Hill Park behind Dunstan Road had a tennis court where Jewish young people played regular matches, but they also went to be entertained by the well-known elderly actor O.B. Clarence, who gave impromptu open-air performances when walking his dog in the park.[49]

Within easy reach of Golders Green was the Hertfordshire countryside and in the days when it was safer for young people to travel by themselves, they sometimes cycled to places such as St Albans.[50] The advent of the Green Line bus company, which ran a number of services from Golders Green, enabled families to visit Whipsnade Zoo, Welwyn Garden City, Hemel Hempstead, Croydon and Chertsey.

As well as enjoying the amenities open to all, before the Second World War the Jewish community spent some of their leisure time participating in specifically Jewish activities. Although many families had moved to Golders Green from the East End of London, they did not seek to replicate the forms of entertainment that they had enjoyed there – the Yiddish theatre, the Jewish sports and social clubs and the 'Whitechapel Parade'.[51] Most of the first Jewish families to arrive in the suburb still had relatives living in the East End and Sunday afternoons were often devoted to visiting them there.[52] As they put down firmer roots, Jewish families started to develop pastimes they felt were more in keeping with their new environment. As early as 1916 a Jewish Literary Society was set up, followed four years later by a Jewish Study Circle, mainly aimed at young people.[53] Although the community that became Dunstan Road Synagogue convened them,[54] these societies were open to others and also to non-Jewish members; two local vicars who were regular attendees. For many years the Literary Society held fortnightly meetings at Lyndale Hall, loaned to the group by Miss Chapman, a founding member.[55]

In keeping with Jewish tradition, much leisure time of the new suburban dwellers was spent on charitable activities. Pearl Pollack's father, who was among the first people to make the move from the East End, recalls that he would often travel back to the East End and make arrangements to take children (Jewish and non-Jewish) out to the country for the day. He also identified the most affluent households in Golders Green and its vicinity, like the families living in nearby Bishops Avenue, knocked on their doors and asked for unwanted clothes that he distributed to those in need. Pearl helped her father to pack up and label clothes parcels.[56] Shortly after Dunstan Road Synagogue opened, the congregation established the Golders Green Orphans' Aid Society, which raised large sums for the Jews' Hospital and the Orphan Asylum (Norwood).[57]

During the 1920s and 1930s many leisure pursuits were centred on the home: 'We made our own entertainment in those days'.[58] Among these home-based activities, music featured very prominently. The Jewish impresario Robert Gubbay recalls:

My parents were very musical. My father played violin and my mother played piano and would have gone on to be a professional pianist if the Second World War hadn't intervened. She kept her music going and there was always music in the house.[59]

In September 1919, Gertrude Azulay advertised in the *Jewish Chronicle* to say that she had set up a centre in Golders Green for the 'teaching of pianoforte'.[60] The pupils occasionally held concerts at St Alban's Hall like the one held in November 1922 featuring the offspring of several prominent members of Dunstan Road Synagogue.[61] There was clearly a demand for this kind of activity in the growing community. In January 1923 Professor Kordy started advertising piano and singing lessons,[62] and in 1924 Miss Helena Gosschalk, a well-known Jewish elocutionist, established a drama studio in Golders Green.[63]

Emulating their non-Jewish neighbours, Jews in Golders Green took up card-playing; both Bridge and Solo became popular pastimes. Some of the card-playing circles that sprang up in the suburb consisted of Jewish families, but sometimes Jews and non-Jews played together.[64] Table tennis ('ping-pong') was also a favourite activity in these years,[65] and young people developed networks of friends based on their parents' friendships.[66] These networks were almost exclusively Jewish, but the young people sometimes made non-Jewish friends when they transferred to secondary schools outside the area. They visited these friends at their homes: 'It wasn't like today when people won't eat anything in non-Jewish homes'.[67]

The *Jewish Chronicle* carried advertisements for young people, including those living in Golders Green, seeking to become 'pen-pals' with young Jews living in London and other parts of the country. For example, in 1923, Becky Isaacs (living in The Grove) was anxious to have letters from 'London cousins aged 16–18 years' interested in music and photography.[68]

The early Jewish community of Golders Green was generally pro-Zionist in its outlook, particularly the members of Dunstan Road Synagogue, where both adults and young people were involved in Zionist bodies. During the 1920s the synagogue became the base for several Zionist societies, which were open to members and non-members, including the Golders Green Young Israel Society, the North-West London Junior Israel Society, the Women's Zionist Society, the Golders Green Young Zionist Society (known as Halapid, the Torah), which all held literary meetings, dances and other social activities, lectures and debates. Some of these societies organised rambles and carried out 'practical work for the Zionist cause'.[69] The synagogue convened a Jewish National Fund Commission that raised money for Palestine by holding social events.

From their inception, both Dunstan Road and Alyth Gardens synagogues organised social and cultural activities to engage their adult members. The drama society at Dunstan Road Synaogue regularly staged performances, concerts, dances and other events in the Joseph Freedman Hall attached to the synagogue.[70] At Alyth, a Social Activities Committee organised dances and brains trusts (a panel of experts giving answers to impromtu questions). There was also a Fellowship for single people, which attracted additional young members, and a Young Marrieds' Circle that held talks in the winter and social activities in the summer.[71] Both synagogues had women's societies, which in addition to their charitable activities organised social functions.

For all of the early Golders Green synagogues, their main priority was promoting activities for young people. In 1926 a Golders Green Company of the Jewish Lads' Brigade[72] (later Lads' and Girls' Brigade) was formed at Dunstan Road Synagogue to 'train its members in habits of cleanliness and orderliness, so that in learning to respect themselves they would be a credit to their community'. Although it was initially greeted with 'almost hostility', the company grew and its regular 'parades' included boxing, first aid, chess, physical training and outings to places of interest.[73] A Young Jewish Culturists Society was also formed at Dunstan Road Synagogue for 15 to 18 year olds wishing to further their Jewish education and interest in Jewish affairs.[74]

Both Dunstan Road and Alyth synagogues established Girl Guide companies and Alyth set up a Brownie pack, a Scout troop and a Cubs group. The Alyth uniformed groups were particularly successful. They continued to meet during the war years and ran for approaching fifty years.[75] The early Scout leaders of the 11th Golders Green Scouts Group at Alyth were Jeffery Rose and his brother Alan. They had joined the group when it was formed in 1938 but soon found themselves having to take over its running when its first leaders were called up to fight in the war.[76] Lola Rodin recalls:

> I asked my parents if we could join Alyth rather than Dunstan Road because my tendency was more in that direction and the decorum there was much better. I joined the Girl Guides because I thought that I might get to meet the nice boys in the Scout troop there. I fell in love with a couple of the Scouts.[77]

People have very fond memories of the Alyth Jewish Brownie pack, the 3rd Temple Fortune Brownies, where some lifelong friendships were formed. In the 1960s, the various groups wore their uniforms to services once a month.[78]

During the Second World War the Golders Green synagogues devoted a great deal of effort to organising activities for teenagers remaining in London, such as the Senior Literary and Social Club formed at Dunstan Road Synagogue. However, with many young men called up for National Service, the ratio between boys and girls was often unbalanced, so some young women found their own entertainment:

> Once in a while we went dancing at Covent Garden's hugely popular ballroom, which gave us females the opportunity of dressing up in our best outfits – the 'make-do-and-mend' variety, and to wear those incredibly high-heeled platform shoes – smart but lethal if one was trying to 'jive' – a new American craze to hit the dance floor at the time.[79]

Most successful of the wartime synagogue-based activities was the Golders Green Jewish Youth Club, set up at Dunstan Road Synagogue by David Manuel in 1943. As many young people attended the club whose families were not synagogue members, congregants' children met a wider group of friends, including the children of continental refugees, which exposed them to the realities of Nazism.[80]

By comparison, in the war years there was little organised entertainment for Jewish adults in Golders Green apart from events aimed at raising money for the victims of Nazi persecution such as the concert that took place at the Hippodrome in April 1940, convened by the Golders Green Women's Committee of which Mrs Livingstone was a leading member.[81] Whereas in the pre-war years the communal hall at Dunstan Road Synagogue had been the base for many social activities, these were greatly reduced when the hall was taken over by the local authority at the beginning of the war as a 'rest centre'. Some adult activities were kept alive by holding 'at-homes' in synagogue members' homes.[82]

In the post-war years the Alyth youth clubs were very active. The Junior Youth Club formed in 1946 for 13 to 17 year olds, offered socials, discussions, games, PT, dramatics, music and photography as well as cricket, rambles, swimming and tennis, in which young people could participate for a subscription of just 6*d* a week.[83] The Alyth Fellowship for the over-16s organised a range of social events, including dances.[84] In 1954 a third youth group for younger children was launched. Its first leaders included Lionel Blue, who was to become a household name.[85] Some young people were involved in the Reform Movement's Youth Association of Synagogues of Great Britain, which offered an impressive range of activities.[86]

In addition to its burgeoning youth club, Dunstan Road Synagogue organised a social club for young people returning from war service. The SIGMA club was held in the Joseph Freedman Hall and many couples who met there later married.[87] Also very popular was the young peoples' debating club in which Simon Schama was a prominent member and which he found a useful training for his future career. He recalls that when he participated in debates, his father would stand at the back of the hall and shout 'louder, Simon!'[88]

In the pre-war years the youth clubs organised at Munk's shul, the Ezra Movement, were mixed sex but as the shul became more orthodox in the post-war years, young people were segregated for social and cultural activities at the age of 11. They came together for specific occasions, but these became increasingly rare.[89] This move did not increase membership of the clubs. Senior Ezra went into decline due initially to lack of suitable leaders and then because an increasing number of young people were going away to *yeshivot* and seminaries and had little interest in resuming the youth movements on their return.[90] Nothing appeared immediately to take the place of Ezra and some young people from Munk's shul started to attend youth clubs outside the synagogue, such as the Zionist B'nei Akiva, which had been founded in Golders Green in 1941, and the thriving Sinai Youth Club founded in 1955 as a religious, cultural and non-political centre for young people. Its sessions were devoted to Torah studies as well as to fundraising for charity.[91]

Whereas prior to the war most activities for young Jews were centred on the synagogues, after the war a wide variety of social activities were established in alternative venues across Golders Green. In addition to the dances held at the Regal Ballroom previously mentioned, The Refectory restaurant began to host dances organised by Jewish clubs and societies, many of them with charitable objectives, the first of which was the Jewish Aid for All Society that raised money for Jewish prisoners of war.[92] A few years later the Cavalier Club organised by the Youth Jewish National Fund opened in 292 Golders Green Road.[93]

Over time these various dance venues gained a reputation as 'cattle markets' and were 'avoided like the plague'.[94] Even before then some Jewish young people were looking for new types of experience and wanted to do something different:

> A girl friend of mine took me to an Italian restaurant in Hampstead. I didn't know how to eat the Spaghetti Bolognese, but I enjoyed the experience and soon learned! I also liked going to the bamboo coffee bar next to The Refectory restaurant next door. It's where all of the au pairs and nannies from Hampstead gathered and you could always be sure of getting a date. Like my father, I was a bit of a renegade![95]

Simon Schama spent 'more time hanging round the Golders Green telephone booths … angling for long-lashed girls rather than pondering the Talmud'.[96] Car ownership for young people was still some way off, but some were becoming more mobile. Jeff Alexander had a motorbike, which helped to broaden his social life: 'I used to take myself off to dances held in Compayne Gardens, NW6 and in the Mayfair Rooms opposite Willesden Green station.'[97]

The post-war leisure activities specifically organised for Jewish adults included a high-profile social club for the over-35s, opened in March 1955 by the Mayor of Hendon, Alderman Naar. The club met for many years at the Benmore Hall in Accommodation Road behind the shopping parades. There were already many clubs for older people, including the over-60s friendship club that had met regularly at Dunstan Road Synagogue since 1950 under the leadership of Nettie Winton. The Benmore Hall club was the first to cater for middle-aged people.[98] Within a year it had a membership approaching 200. Its activities included visiting the sick and older people, both Jewish and non-Jewish.[99] Other popular activities for adults included the Golders Green kosher cookery classes sponsored by Mrs Brodie, the Chief Rabbi's wife, which met four evenings a week at Dunstan Road Synagogue and included a 'brides class',[100] and the meetings of the Golders Green League of Jewish Women. The Jewish community was obviously now more confident about its identity since the entertainment on offer in the post-war years included Yiddish theatre, including a performance of *The Happy Bride* in Yiddish at the Hodford Hall.[101]

During the 1930s interest in Zionism had grown significantly in Golders Green, a reaction to events in Europe. A number of new Zionist bodies were formed in which an increasing number of residents became involved in their leisure time, such as the Golders Green Mizrachi Society, established in September 1939. The Mizrachi Society became very active in the lead-up to the founding of the State of Israel in 1948. Its meetings were mainly attended by more observant Jews due to the emphasis placed on inculcating Judaism in the development of Palestine.[102] Habonim, which met in Eton Avenue, Swiss Cottage (and later Finchley Road) was very popular with young people from Golders Green. Many of its members were German refugees who had come to England on the Kindertransport.[103]

An interesting feature of post-war life in Golders Green was the range of social and cultural activities of the former continental refugees. While the offspring of continental Jews who were born in Britain, or who had arrived as very young people, became immersed in the leisure activities surrounding them, the 'in-between generation' sought to combine elements of life from both the old and new societies.[104] This led to the creation in 1948 of a social club called The Hyphen catering for the 21–35 age group. It operated under the auspices of the Association of Jewish Refugees (AJR) based in Swiss Cottage but was run for many years by Miss L. Metzger, who lived in Golders Green Road.[105] Many single people met their future partners through The Hyphen, which organised outdoor activities, talks and social events, including dances held at the Regal Ballroom.[106]

Music permeated the cultural life of the former refugees and many of the activities they organised related to music. In addition to the London-wide events promoted by the AJR, there were also regular local musical events organised by the Golders Green AJR branch chaired by Dr Jacob Salz,[107] which grew out of the friendship club founded by Leo Wolff during the war.[108] It met at Dunstan Road Synagogue and was one of the first self-help refugee organisations in the country. At the AJR branch's inaugural meeting there was a music recital given by the synagogue's *chazzan*, Reverend Taschlicky and Polly Jonas formerly of the Staatsoper in Vienna.[109]

After the war, the AJR branch held regular concerts like the chamber music and song recital that took place the Hodford Hall in February 1946, featuring Fritz Berend playing piano and the soprano Inge Markowitz.[110] It also ran a young people's opera group that gave occasional performances,[111] and organised talks on topical issues such as the Nuremberg trials[112] and Palestine.[113] These activities continued for several decades but gradually ceased as their organisers died and their children's cultural interests became indistinguishable from those of their British peers.

As the 'Swinging 60s' progressed, more and more young people were lured away from organised Jewish activities. Although they still mainly associated with other Jews, they now wanted to spend their leisure time more informally. Graduate accountant Jeremy Packman, aged 23, living in Golders Green in 1969 was quoted in the *Jewish Chronicle* as saying: 'Everyone I know is looking for new scenes, new thrills, for something round the corner'.[114] By the mid-1960s a big Jewish social scene for young people had centred itself on Golders Green station with which the well-financed Jewish youth clubs found themselves unable to compete. The

Jewish Youth Cub at Dunstan Road Synagogue had fluctuated from high to low attendance and was even closed for a time after its activities became the scene of 'rowdiness' and 'violent incidents'.[115] The young people who gathered at the station were mainly drawn from affluent second and third-generation Jewish families:

> Every Saturday night without fail we would meet at 7 at Golders Green station. …
> About 150 kids would turn up and say: 'Right, what are we doing tonight then?'
> Someone would always know about a party in Temple Fortune.[116]

The atmosphere emanating from the crowds of young people was sometimes 'carnival like', causing concern in the Jewish press. However, it was generally recognised that it was, for the most part, harmless adolescent fun that occasionally spilled over into under-age drinking and soft drug use.[117] Those involved considered themselves to be stylish. Typically both sexes had long curly hair and wore polo-necked jumpers and bomber jackets.[118] The activities of the young people gathering at the station from various parts of north-west London were exciting for some of the younger residents of Golders Green, like Robert Papier, who 'joined the throng'.[119] Others were less comfortable with the large groups, finding them 'a bit unpleasant',[120] or 'too Becky'.[121] They were an anathema to young people from strictly orthodox families living in Golders Green like Michael Halvien, who attended Menorah Grammar School. Interviewed by the *Jewish Chronicle*, he said that he much preferred to attend the religious youth group Pirchim that met in Stamford Hill. Danny Fluss, who did not mix with non-observant Jews, thought the 'Becks' were 'a million miles away' from him in their style, temperament and attitude.[122]

The shopping parades of Golders Green were a magnet for young Jews living locally and also for those from outside the area. A favourite pastime was simply walking up and down Golders Green Road:

> We were flash, there is no other word for it, although my Dad said I was turning into a 'spiv'. I used to walk along Golders Green Road in my Beatles boots, and for some reason there was a particularly cool way you had to wear your coat …
> I always made sure that I was seen walking.[123]

Simon Schama recalls skipping school at lunchtime and frequenting the salt beef bar in Golders Green Road.[124] Young people had their favourite cafés such as the Penguin Coffee Bar (now the White House), one of the few with Italian coffee machines at that time. It was run by an older Jewish couple. The husband was 'a rather grumpy man' who shooed out the teenagers regularly gathering there when they became rowdy.[125] Later on the 'in place' was Orange Julius, where young people would sit six to a table sharing one drink for two hours. One former patron commented: 'needless to say, they went out of business!'[126] Some less observant

Jewish young people were excited when McDonald's arrived in Golders Green, (replacing Lyon's teashop):

> It was fantastic. It was the 'place to be seen'. We thought we were very grown up going in there to buy a hamburger. We didn't think about the ham bit! The American-type service really appealed to us.[127]

Although they were less enthusiastic about synagogue based activities, many young people did not ignore developments in the Jewish world and maintained some Jewish involvement, especially in Zionist activities. Simon Schama recalls:'for much of my teen years, being Jewish meant Zionist socialism on the Finchley Road'.[128] At the age of 12 Selma Shrank 'became impassioned' about Israel, having read *The Exodus* by Leon Uris. Even before the Six Day War had raised Jewish consciousness, in 1965 she spent nine months on a kibbutz.[129]

By the 1970s the teenage social scene had moved on to Edgware and young Jews were beginning to re-engage with synagogue activities as a result of the heightened Jewish consciousness following the Six Day War.[130] Young people were encouraged to celebrate the start of *Shabbat* with their families: 'Friday nights were not clubbing nights'.[131] The Jewish youth groups in Golders Green were once again playing a prominent part in the lives of many teenagers, especially at Alyth, where dedicated youth workers had been appointed and a youth centre had opened, providing a base for activities for different age groups. While Alyth attracted young people interested in cultural activities, Golders Green Youth Club at Dunstan Road was popular for its discotheques.[132] These synagogue-based activities co-existed harmoniously alongside those that took place in a non-Jewish orbit. Robert Papier recalls that, because he attended a non-Jewish school, he had many non-Jewish friends with whom he socialised. He also had a very active Jewish life:'The two didn't conflict.'[133]

The social life of Jewish adults in Golders Green evolved along similar lines. During the 1950s and 1960s many Jewish families belonged to tight-knit circles of friends such as the 'young marrieds' clubs operating at the larger synagogues in the area.[134] Members of the Alyth Young Marrieds' Circle met in each other's homes monthly to hear talks and 'mull over the perennial problems that beset Jewish parents'.[135] The social calendar at Dunstan Road Synagogue now included the annual Gold and Green Ball held at top hotels to raise money for charity. From the late 1950s these were held at the Dorchester Hotel and hosted by synagogue members Frankie Vaughan and his wife.[136]

In 1960 Alyth Synagogue set up a Friendship Club (later the Senior Club) for its older members, which regularly attracted eighty to ninety people. They went on seaside outings in the summer and met in a 'very warm hall' in the winter where, with the wider membership of the synagogue, they enjoyed Alyth Theatre Group productions.[137] Some of the preoccupations of the 1960s were reflected in the other social groups that sprang up at Alyth: Keep Fit and judo classes. The activities of a Circle for the Unattached aimed at single parents in the congregation[138] attracted visitors from many synagogues and became one of Alyth's most successful initiatives.[139] There was also a Women's Guild luncheon and a Friends of Hebrew University society that both invited distinguished speakers to the synagogue.[140]

While some families built their social life around their synagogue, others devoted their leisure time to Jewish charitable bodies:

> I was on the committee for the Jewish Blind Society, which my father was the chair of for fifteen years …We used to have committee meetings in our own homes in those days. There were various houses round the district we would go to. We'd hold card evenings or bring-and-buy sales …There also used to be dances and things to raise money. We used to hold them in places like the Washington Hotel in the West End. We were all married about the same time and we held parties for the children.[141]

Kitty and Hans Freund were very involved in B'nal Brith (literally 'sons of the covenant')[142] and Kitty eventually became president of the Leo Baeck women's lodge, devoting a great deal of time to 'worthy causes'.[143] Golders Green gained a reputation as a place of good causes and it was said that 'if you can't raise money in Golders Green then you can't raise it anywhere'. According to the satirist Chaim Bermant, 'you come to my annual dinner and I'll come to yours' was the opening gambit of conversation in Golders Green and leaders of charities found themselves 'eating *kreplach* (meat-filled parcels) soup and roast chicken five times a week and twice on Sunday'.[144]

Like young people, a lot of informal socialising among adults centred on the shopping parades of Golders Green; Woolworths was a particular focal point: 'People would say "I'll see you in Woolworths", or "Where will you be?" "Oh, I'll probably be popping into Woolworths"'.[145] For entertainment Jewish and non-Jewish people walked up and down Golders Green Road, window-shopping and savouring the sights and smells off the shops. This was the era before supermarkets, and shoppers went from one shop to another gathering all the goods they needed. Between errands they often socialised with friends and acquaintances in the cafés and coffee houses in Golders Green Road.[146] This also happened in Temple Fortune where, in the days when fewer women worked, a circle of friends dropped their children off at nurseries or schools and then met up for coffee in the cafés in Finchley Road.[147] For couples with younger children Golders Hill Park remained a favourite location for informal recreation:

> When my children were young we used to go there quite a lot because they had this lovely animal section in the middle. And on the Day of Atonement, for instance, when I was fasting and I had to do something with the children to keep them happy. I used to push them in the pram up to the park and walked round there.[148]

Some of the other open spaces in Golders Green were now additionally attractive to children because the public air-raid shelters had been grassed over, producing 'mountains' on which young people could play.[149] As a child Selma Shrank played for 'hours and hours' with her friends in Prince's Park, especially during the school holidays.[150]

With the arrival of television in the 1960s, the world of entertainment changed dramatically for both adults and young people. Many local venues where people had previously gathered now closed or changed their activities in a bid to retain custom. Transport improvements and rising disposable income also meant that Jewish families were able to look further afield for leisure pursuits.

In addition to underground trains, people were now also using London buses to access the West End shops and cultural facilities. Pamela Nenk recalled that when she was a child people dressed up in their best clothes to go to central London but by the 1960s trips into town were 'commonplace' and no longer a special occasion.[151] London buses were regarded as a safe form of travel for young people, who used them to go to dances in the West End.[152] As car ownership increased, people drove into London to go to clubs and see shows, because at the time congestion and car parking were not the problems they became by the end of the twentieth century.[153]

The Jewish clubs that operated in the East End from the 1880s encouraged young Jewish men to participate in sporting activities, especially boxing, and by the 1930s the East End boxing scene was dominated by Jews.[154] Regarded as a working-class activity, this was not one that Jews took with them to the suburbs of north-west London. Sporting activities did not generally feature prominently in the lives of most suburban Jews apart from among young people enrolled in independent schools.

Those Jews who did seek to emulate the sporting pastimes of their non-Jewish neighbours sometimes encountered obstacles. In the late 1950s it was revealed that Finchley Golf Club, which was officered by prominent members of the local Conservative Party, was excluding Jews from membership, including those from Golders Green. The club was put 'on probation' by the council but a few years later it became public knowledge that nearby Hendon Golf Club had introduced a Jewish quota. 'We do accept them,' the secretary of the Hendon club was quoted as saying, 'but only a certain number'.[155] A campaign led by Freda Gold of Golders Green and Shirley Porter of Hampstead exposed discrimination by several local golf clubs against Jewish women.[156] The discrimination continued into the 1960s when the barring of Jews from the Templars Lawn Tennis Club in Golders Green became a local political issue that ran for several years.[157] However, Jews who were determined to engage in sports were not deterred; they simply joined Jewish-run clubs such as the highly successful Chandos Tennis Club that had relocated from Neasden to Wellgarth Road in Golders Green and attracted Jewish players from across north-west London.

Since the early days of the suburb, affluent Jewish families in Golders Green had taken regular holidays, including to foreign destinations such as Monte Carlo.[158] However, most summer holidays were taken in British holiday resorts, including Brighton, Shoreham-by-Sea, Westcliff-on-Sea, Cliftonville and Bournemouth. Observant households had kosher food sent to them in the places where they vacationed.[159]

After the Second World War, when taking an annual holiday became more widespread, Bournemouth emerged as resort of choice for Jewish families. Several hotels opened catering specifically for Jewish families. The fashionable East Cliff area of the resort became known as 'Golders Green on Sea'. The Jewish-run hotels there offered luxury accommodation and all-inclusive packages, including high-quality entertainment. One of the Bournemouth hotels visited time and again by Golders Green families was the expensive Green Park Hotel. It organised social events, leading to holiday romances that sometimes developed into lifelong partnerships.[160] Services were held at the hotel on *Shabbat* with people sitting in the lounge armchairs. They were followed by elaborate *Shabbat kiddushim* for which the hotel became renowned.[161]

The Bournemouth hotels were not sufficiently kosher for strictly orthodox families, who rented self-catering apartments in Bournemouth and in other resorts along the south coast. They 'koshered' the kitchen at the beginning of the holiday and took kosher supplies with them. Miriam Levene, whose family were members of Munk's shul, recalls their car being packed with their cooking utensils before they departed for their summer holidays. Her father would join them at intervals, bringing supplies of the kosher goods unavailable in the resorts.[162]

By the 1980s the south coast resorts were losing their attraction. Golders Green families began to take advantage of cheap package holidays now making foreign travel accessible to a wider spectrum of the British population generally. Some orthodox families began taking their holidays in kosher hotels that had sprung up along the Adriatic coast.[163] As early as 1961 the Jewish travel agent, Mr Nelson, set up a branch of his Hampstead business at 16 North End Road where it operated for over forty years, selling holidays to destinations all over the world but specialising in trips to Israel.[164] Nelson's main competitor was Gee Travel Service operated by Mr Weiser at 748 Finchley Road, which was open on Sundays.

According to its historians, the Alyth congregation had always been *avant garde* and a love of the arts characterised its membership. By the late 1970s the synagogue's lecture programme was attracting leading Jewish literary figures of the calibre of Martin Gilbert, Dan Jacobson, Dannie Abse and Bernard Kops.[165] In 1982 a branch of the Jewish Association of Cultural Societies (JACS) opened at the synagogue and soon had 100 people attending each week. It continues to the present day, attracting mainly retired people.[166]

The most successful activities at Alyth during the latter part of the twentieth century were musical events. Since its inception, music had been an important feature of synagogue life promoted by a series of talented and committed organists.

In 1980 Viv Bellos was appointed as Director of Music with a brief 'to get Alyth singing', a role from which she has only recently retired. As well as leading the synagogue choir, Viv Bellos founded the Alyth Kid's Choir and the Alyth Youth Choir, which performed at numerous prestigious events, including one at the Guildhall attended by the then Israeli Prime Minister, Menachem Begin. Under Viv Bellos's direction the Pandemonium Choir for young adults has given concerts on the South Bank as well as many memorable musical productions at Alyth.[167] In 1982 Viv Bellos established the Alyth Choral Society, which gives concerts locally and in venues such as the Royal Festival Hall.[168] In 1994 she set up the Alyth Academy of Performing Arts for 13 to 16 year olds.[169]

The new restaurants and takeaways opening in Golders Green during the late 1980s and 1990s helped to reinvigorate the shopping parades,[170] but they also created some unanticipated difficulties. Young Jewish people who for a decade or so had centred their social life on Edgware station started to drift back to Golders Green, attracted by the wide range of places to eat and drink. The columns of the *Jewish Chronicle* were again filled with commentaries and letters on the phenomenon. Whereas the activities of the previous generation had been fairly harmless, the Golders Green gatherings now had a some worrying aspects – the young people became the target for bullying and beatings by non-Jewish gangs and the general affluence of the young people attracted drug dealers to the area.

Some Jewish grandparents likened the public gatherings to their own day when they walked the streets of the East End in search of partners on a '*shidduch* parade' (marriage parade). Communal leaders took a dimmer view of 'the Becks' being back in Golders Green.[171] Various initiatives were launched to deal with the problems created by the gatherings. Bloom's restaurant stayed open until 3 a.m. on a Sunday morning to provide a safe meeting place for the 500 or so young people 'meeting and eating' in the area and hungry young people 'came marching in about midnight'.[172] On the streets, Maccabi youth workers engaged with the young people, backed by Elaine Sacks, wife of the United Synagogue's Chief Rabbi, who herself did late-night 'walkabouts'.[173] The Chabad movement also launched a project, Drugsline Chabad. They parked a big red taxi outside Carmelli's bakery in a bid to attract the attention of the young people.[174] Today, young people no longer gather on the streets of Golders Green but they do meet up inside its many restaurants and eateries on their way home from the clubs in the West End. Sami's, the White House Express and Carmelli's all stay open, forming a 'food hub' for the late-night revellers.

Due to the extensive leisure opportunities available in London and elsewhere, and the pastimes resulting from the rapid development of new technology and social media, the leisure time of the Jewish community in Golders Green is today less focused on synagogues than it was in previous decades. However, by diversifying, the larger synagogues have continued to provide activities that appeal to a wide range of age groups. Dunstan Road Synagogue has a programme of social activities that includes DRESS, which organises adult social events, a thriving Book Circle,

Junior Events, a club for young families and Chevra, a network for people in their 20s and 30s, which has developed a reputation for its well-attended events.[175]

Building on the earlier work of Viv Bellos, in 2012 Alyth Gardens Synagogue launched its Centre for Jewish Music. It stages a variety of events to showcase the important position of Jewish music and musicians in this country, and to take members of the community to events of interest beyond Alyth. In addition to the Alyth Academy for the Performing Arts there are now also children's drama groups for both 4 to 7 year olds and 7 to 13 year olds. Other socialising opportunities run by the synagogue include bridge, cycling, rambling group and a toddlers' group.[176] Over the years successive Alyth rabbis have been concerned with the loss of young people going away to university and have introduced measures to retain their ties to the synagogue. Recent initiatives include the highly successful A-Team and Jeneration.

While in its early days Munk's shul was largely focused on educational and youth activities, today there is a wider range of communal activities for all ages; it is not just a place to pray.[177]

In addition to these synagogal activities, Jewish residents of Golders Green have been able to benefit from the increasing number of Jewish social and cultural activities taking place in the area. Based in Temple Fortune, the Spiro Institute was formed by Nitza and Robin Spiro in the 1970s to provide courses in Jewish history for students in non-Jewish schools. Due to the commitment and energy of its founders, it gradually expanded its activities to include a wide range of cultural sessions for adults on Jewish literature, philosophy, art, music, drama and Hebrew and Yiddish lessons.

Between 2005 and 2015 the London Jewish Cultural Centre (LJCC), a leading provider of Jewish education and culture, offered a broad range of courses, events and leisure activities for people of all ages and affiliations at Ivy House (the former home of the ballerina Anna Pavlova) in North End Road. Its programme attracted world-renowned speakers and academics. LJCC historians and guides also led walks to places of Jewish interest. In September 2014 it was announced that the LJCC would merge with JW3, a Jewish cultural centre, and move into the modern, custom-built space in Finchley Road where the LJCC and JW3 programmes have been integrated since July 2015.

A small but loyal proportion of the community participate in the activities of the Jewish Vegetarian Society (JVS), located in Finchley Road. The JVS was founded in the 1960s by Vivien Pick and her father Philip Pick. It originally met in people's homes, then in small premises in Swiss Cottage but settled in Golders Green in 1971 in premises that were funded mainly by donations raised by Philip Pick. It flourished in the 1970s and in the 1980s a Members' Dining Room was established. The Pick family are no longer involved, but the society has recently started to grow again after a period of stagnation. Its membership includes strictly orthodox Jews and non-Jews.[178]

The *haredim* who constitute a significant and growing proportion of the local Jewish community[179] spend their leisure time differently from other Jews in

Golders Green. Family life is paramount in the *haredi* community, and a great deal of emphasis is placed in socialising with close relatives, especially between different generations.[180] *Shabbat* in particular is a time to be spent with one's family and on Saturday afternoons the roads of Golders Green are filled with families walking around the area at a leisurely pace or who are on their way to the celebrations, which also feature prominently in the *haredi* lifestyle.[181] As they walk and talk, parents are often surrounded by several children. A great deal of time is devoted to staying in touch with family members dispersed across the country and across the world.

On weekdays young *haredi* boys have limited time for leisure pursuits because of their study regime,[182] and those in which they do participate, such as summer camps like Camp Yashar and the activities run by the London Jewish Family Centre (Tzivos Hashem) in Golders Green Road, are strictly segregated. Since 2010 a branch of the Orthodox boys' club, Chaverim (friends) has operated in Golders Green, providing facilities such as a computer room and pool and snooker.[183] A certain amount of informal networking also occurs on the streets of Golders Green as young men move from one activity to another and in the strictly kosher eateries such as Slice.[184] Groups of young *haredi* children play in the open spaces around Golders Green, especially in Prince's Park, which has one of the few kosher park cafés in the country.

Few *haredi* adults regularly participate in cultural activities like concerts and the theatre and there is limited social interaction between *haredim* and the wider Jewish community.[185] However, as the *haredi* community has become generally wealthier, an increasing number of *haredi* families have been travelling for leisure purposes and taking holidays abroad in hotels that have been developed to suit the requirements of the *haredi* community. There are hotels in Austria, Switzerland, France and, more recently, Greece, that offer *glatt* kosher meals, segregated leisure facilities and organised outings as well as hotel-based entertainment programmes, *shiurim* and lectures, and 'kids' clubs'.[186]

Increasing prosperity has had a particular impact on the social lives of *haredi* women by allowing them to buy labour-saving devices and to employ domestic help to create more leisure time. In the comparatively liberal environment of Golders Green, increasing numbers of *haredi* women are driving, which is still generally frowned on as 'immodest' in Stamford Hill, expanding their leisure possibilities.[187] When the Golders Green *haredi* community was still quite small, there were few informal gatherings of observant Jews such as the Hamishmerai Hatzeira group for 20 to 35 year olds that operated in the late 1970s.[188] However, there are now a number of commercial and communal opportunities for *haredi* women to socialise. Coffee mornings with invited speakers for 'mums and mums-to-be' take place at the Reich's Banqueting Suite in Prince's Parade,[189] and the London Jewish Family Centre runs a variety of sessions for women.[190] Recently many cultural activities have sprung up in Golders Green specifically targeted at *haredi* women, such as writing workshops, art, drawing and photography lessons and fitness training.[191]

The general picture, therefore, is that, although still separate, the leisure activities of the different Jewish groupings in Golders Green are becoming more similar, with strictly orthodox Jews starting to pursue some of the activities enjoyed by other elements of the community who are spending more of their leisure time on learning and study. A member of Munk's shul commented: 'previously people used to go out to the theatre and concerts on a Saturday night; now this doesn't happen, they study instead.'[192] The growth of Jewish education and learning is the focus of the next chapter.

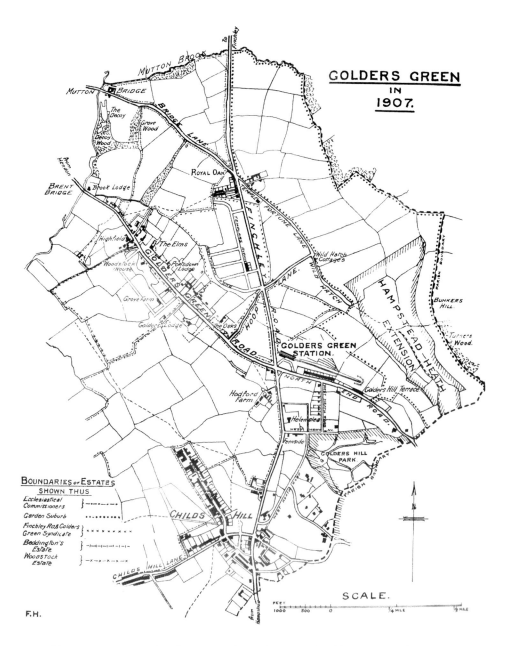

1. Golders Green in 1907 taken from F. Howkins, *The Story of Golders Green and Its Remarkable Development.* (Reproduction courtesy of Barnet Local Studies Centre)

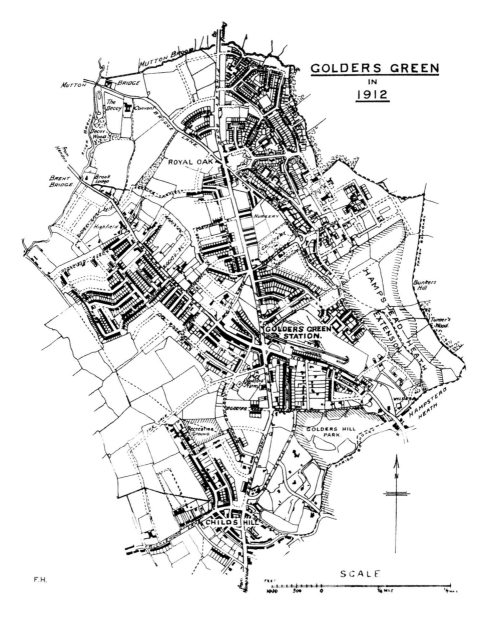

2. Golders Green in 1912 taken from F. Howkins, *The Story of Golders Green and Its Remarkable Development.* (Reproduction courtesy of Barnet Local Studies Centre)

3. Golders Green in 1923 taken from F. Howkins, *The Story of Golders Green and Its Remarkable Development.* (Reproduction courtesy of Barnet Local Studies Centre)

4. Sir Joseph Joel Duveen (1843–1908), first Jewish resident of Golders Green (see p.22) (1903). Artist Emil Fuchs (1866–1929). (Photograph ©Tate, London 2016)

5. The Hawthorns, home of Sir Joseph Joel Duveen, the first Jewish resident of Golders Green (1908). It stood close to the intersection of Finchley Road and Golders Green Road (see p.22). In the picture is an advertising hoarding for the estate agent Ernest Owers, who purchased the property in 1908 on the death of its owner, used it temporarily for his office and sold it for building purposes. (Photograph courtesy of Barnet Local Studies Centre)

6. The Parade, the first shopping parade to be completed in Golders Green. It was built on the site of The Hawthorns, previously owned by Sir Joseph Joel Duveen (see figs 4 and 5) (c. 1920). (Photograph courtesy of Barnet Local Studies Centre)

7. The crossroads at Golders Green before the underground opened in 1907 (1904). To the right is a sign saying land has been purchased by the London Underground Electric Railways Company of London Ltd. In the centre is an estate agents' sign advertising the availability of building plots. In the background is a crematorium in Hoop Lane. (Photograph courtesy of Barnet Local Studies Centre)

8. Recently opened Golders Green Station (*c.* 1908), which brought many Jewish families to the area (see p.23). (Photograph courtesy of Barnet Local Studies Centre)

9. The Golders Green Hippodrome, which was very popular with Jewish families (see p.142) (*c.*1913). (Postcard courtesy of Pat Hasenson)

10. Golders Hill Park where many early Jewish residents spent their leisure time (*c.*1920). (Photograph courtesy of Barnet Local Studies Centre)

11. Recently completed Golders Green Synagogue in Dunstan Road (see p.80, 1927. (Photograph courtesy of Golders Green Synagogue)

12. Reverend Isaac Livingstone, long-standing rabbi of Golders Green Synagogue (see chapter 10) (*c.* 1960). (Photograph courtesy of Barbara Michaels)

13. Importers Retail Salesrooms, a Jewish-owned shop, which traded in Golders Green for over sixty years (see p.125) (1928). It is now the Imperial Café. (Photograph courtesy of Jeff Alexander (see index for his contributions to the book))

14. Isaac Walker (né Taflowitz), seated centre with his family (c. 1928). He was one of the early Jewish shop owners in Golders Green (see p.119). (Photograph courtesy of the Walker family)

15. Golders Green Road, *c*. 1935. Franks lingerie shop, which traded for eighty years in Golders Green Road, can be seen in bottom right of photo (see index for mentions). (Photograph courtesy of Hazel Sheldon (née Franks))

16. *Left*: Ballet production staged at the Phoenix Theatre in central London by Nancy Evans School of Dancing in Golders Green (*c*. 1937). Jocelyne Tobin, former resident of Golders Green, is pictured third from right, (see p.145). (Photograph courtesy of Jocelyne Tobin (née Prevezer))

17. *Below*: Rachel Glassman, secretary to Sir William Duthie MP (see p.189) (*c*. 1950). (Photograph courtesy of Selina Gellert)

18. Dramatic production staged by Golders Green Jewish Youth Club (see p.149) (*c.* 1944). (Photograph courtesy of Jeremy Manuel)

HAVE YOU ANY FOOD PROBLEMS?
LET US FREE YOU OF THIS WORRY

YOU TOO, CAN SMILE LIKE

PARTIES
CATERED FOR
Strictly Kosher Cuisine

Lunches - 12.15-3.0 p.m.

Dinners & Late Suppers
6.15-10.45 p.m.

OUR CHEF

If you Lunch & Dine at

RESTAURANT

130 GOLDERS GREEN ROAD, N.W.11
(Near Woolworth's). SPE. 2832

19. Advertisement for Silver's, the first kosher restaurant in Golders Green (see p.126) (*c.* 1947). The chef shown in the advertisement is Herbert Bruck, who set up the restaurant. (Photograph courtesy of the Bruck family)

20. Martin Sulzbacher, owner of a bookshop in Golders Green (see p.42) (*c.* 1975). (Photograph courtesy of Eva Seliger (née Sulzbacher)

21. Grodzinski bakers, Finchley Road (see p.126). (*c.* 1965). (Photograph courtesy of Jonathan Grodzinski)

22. Rabbi Eugene Newman, rabbi at Golders Green Synagogue (see p.93) protesting at the treatment of Russian Jews outside the Russian Embassy in London in the 1970s. (Photograph courtesy of the Newman family)

23. Women from the Golders Green office of the Women's Campaign for Soviet Jewry ('The 35s') outside the Soviet Embassy demonstrating in support of Alexander Feldman on trial for alleged hooliganism (1973). (Photograph courtesy of One to One (formerly the Women's Campaign for Soviet Jewry))

24. *Left*: Pamela Nenk at the door of Golders Green Pet Bureau (see p.134) (1981). (Photograph courtesy of Beverley Mautner (née Nenk)

25. *Right*: Bernard Benarroch, scribe (see p.200) (2009). (Photograph courtesy of Bernard Benarroch)

26. *Left*: Bloom's kosher restaurant in Golders Green Road (see pp.126–27) (2010). (Photograph courtesy of David Sax, Save the Deli)

27. *Right*: Leon Nicholas, waiter at Bloom's restaurant, Golders Green for forty years (2006). (Photograph © Rena Pearl/ Jewish Museum, London)

28. Rabbi Lord Jonathan Sacks at the opening of Rimon School (2013). (Photograph courtesy of Golders Green Synagogue)

29. *Above*: Kosher shops in Temple Fortune (2013). (Photograph © John R. Rifkin, photographer)

30. *Left*: Rabbi Chuna Halpern (d.2015), Beth Shmuel Beth Hamedrash, Golders Green (see p.74). *Jewish Chronicle*, 27 February 2015. (Photograph courtesy of the *Jewish Chronicle*)

31. Thousands gathering for the funeral of Rabbi Chuna Halpern, *Jewish Chronicle*, 20 February 2015. (Photograph courtesy of the *Jewish Chronicle*)

32. Processing of new scroll to be installed in the Sage nursing home, Golders Green Road (11 October 2015). (Photograph by the author)

33. Alyth Youth Singers conducted by Viv Bellos (see p.157) (2015). (Photograph courtesy of North Western Reform Synagogue)

34. Torah scrolls at Ohel David Eastern Synagogue, Golders Green (2015).
(Photograph by the author)

35. *Brit melia*, circumcision ceremony at Ohel David Eastern Synagogue (2016).
(Photograph courtesy of Ohel David Synagogue)

Education and Study

Early years in Golders Green

The value of education is deeply embedded in Jewish culture and one of the basic duties of Jewish parents is to provide for the instruction of their children.[1] However, Jews moving to Golders Green in the early part of the twentieth century encountered challenges in respect of both the religious and secular education of their offspring. Many of the first Jews to arrive had been educated at state-funded schools run by the London School Board,[2] but there was no such provision when they arrived in north-west London since Golders Green was almost an entirely new settlement. Until the opening of Wessex Gardens School by Hendon Urban District Council in 1920,[3] residents were almost entirely dependent on the dame schools in the area. Nancie Craig recalled attending one in Beechcroft Avenue:

> It was absolutely marvellous. It was two little huts and, whenever the weather was nice, we were out in the air. It was really quite unusual. I was there until I was eight. When they extended the railway to Hendon, the school had to close.[4]

Once Wessex Gardens School became established, many Jewish parents sent their children there, which meant that it was 'almost empty' on Jewish festivals and holidays.[5] In 1934 arrangements were made to provide the Jewish children attending the school with instruction in Hebrew and Jewish Religion at Dunstan Road Synagogue during the 'scripture period'.[6] These sessions were known as the 'withdrawal classes'. Naomi Rose, who attended the school, retains fond memories of her time there:

> I remember when the whole school came out onto the playground in May 1934 to see King George and Queen Mary passing by the school on their way to open Hendon Police Training College. The car slowed down so we could wave.[7]

In Temple Fortune some newly middle-class Jewish families were initially reluctant for their children to attend Child's Way School (later Garden Suburb School), but as it gained a reputation for providing a good education, even affluent Jewish parents began to send their children there. Jacqueline Morris, whose well-to-do family lived in Cranbourne Gardens, recalls:

> The rest of the family thought that my father [was] very peculiar for sending my sister and me to a council school but he argued that it provided a perfectly decent education, which he paid for through local taxes![8]

Some upwardly mobile Jews chose to educate their children at the fee-paying schools that sprang up in this middle-class suburb, still not quite trusting a school run by the council, whatever its reputation. These schools included the co-educational Golders Hill pre-preparatory school in Finchley Road. Founded in 1908, by the 1920s the school's intake included a high proportion of Jewish children.[9] St Dunstan's School, a small preparatory school on the corner of Finchley Road and Hodford Road, opened just before the First World War. The school was run by Miss Arthur and Miss Forder, who had previously worked as missionaries.[10] By the time it was attended by Jocelyne Tobin in the 1930s, it was teaching many Jewish children whose families were closely connected socially.[11]

Other schools attended by children of the early Jewish families were the privately run Woodstock School, which was demolished when Eagle Lodge was built in 1930,[12] and Buchler House School, located initially in West Hampstead but later in Golders Green.[13] In addition, preparatory schools situated in surrounding areas sought to recruit Jewish children living in Golders Green, including Townley Castle School in Eton Avenue, NW3, which advertised in local publications that it offered 'a High-Class Modern Education combined with Hebrew and Religious Instruction, a Hebrew Speaking Class and Bar Mitzvah Preparation'.[14]

While some recently relocated Jews were focused on assimilating socially, a number of more orthodox families were concerned that the existing schools would not safeguard the Jewish identity of their children. In 1929 Beatrice Cohen established a 'Hebrew Kindergarten and Day School' in Wentworth Road.[15] It appears that this school did not remain open for long but from 1930 the more successful West Hampstead Jewish Day School in Minster Road was arranging private transport to the school for children living in Golders Green.[16] By 1938 this school was not meeting the demand for places and parents were writing to the *Jewish Chronicle* calling for a Jewish school to be set up in Golders Green.[17]

The inter-war years

Between the two world wars the statutory school-leaving age remained at 14. Seeing secondary education as key to social mobility, ambitious Jewish families in Golders Green with the means to do so sent their children to the best post-primary independent schools they could afford. The most popular schools for girls were St Paul's School, North London Collegiate School and South Hampstead High School.

The favoured independent schools for boys were University College School, Highgate School and City of London Boys' School.[18] From the age of 8 Nancie Craig travelled to North London Collegiate School on the Tube, accompanied by older girls from Golders Green attending the school. Later she marvelled at the daily journey she made, which involved crossing major roads.[19]

Despite their intake of growing numbers of Jewish pupils, some of the independent schools were not free from discrimination:

> As far as anti-Semitism was concerned, it was always there because it was a Christian school. I can remember one particular boy making some rude comments, so I punched him and broke his nose.[20]

However, other schools went to great lengths to make Jewish children feel welcome. The headmistress at North London Collegiate School during the 1930s was concerned that the Jewish children should have a hot meal rather than take sandwiches. The school introduced vegetarian lunches, which were apparently 'absolutely frightful, appalling, all running with water', but because of the trouble taken 'had to be eaten'.[21]

Before the Second World War an increasing proportion of Jewish children competed successfully for the growing number of grammar school places available by examination at the age of 11 ('the scholarship'). Many local Jewish girls like Lola Rodin were awarded scholarships to attend Henrietta Barnett School in Hampstead Garden Suburb.[22] At this time only a small proportion (about 2 per cent) of young people went on to higher education, but an increasing number of these students were Jewish (mainly young men) for whom a university education was starting to provide a route into the professions, especially medicine and accountancy.[23] For example, Harold Langdon, whose family lived in Golders Manor Drive, attended Westminster City School for which he had won a foundation scholarship,[24] before going on to study at the London School of Economics in 1934:

> In the first year I did not do very much and took intermediate exams. I became very good at table tennis, became secretary of the banking society and a member of the Israel Society. I took a banking and accountancy degree for which I got honours.[25]

Attending university in the inter-war years was not always easy for Jewish young people because there were a limited number of local authority awards and few university scholarships. Louis Westell, whose family was one of the very first to come to Golders Green, won an 'exhibition' to study at Cambridge having excelled in languages at Haberdashers School. His family were unable to afford to pay for him to take up the place, but his uncles who were involved in the diamond trade stepped in to support him financially.[26]

Religious education

During the nineteenth century a variety of provision was made for the religious education of children in the main areas of Jewish settlement to supplement the secular studies most were receiving in non-denominational schools. Some of this religious education took place in classes attached to synagogues and state-funded schools. Other children attended privately organised *chedarim* (religion schools) akin to those that immigrants had previously known in East Europe.[27] However, when Jews arrived in Golders Green there was no provision for the religious education of Jewish children. Until the first synagogues were established, Jewish education was provided privately and usually only for boys.[28] As early as 1910 an advert appeared in the *Jewish Chronicle* for a teacher to prepare a boy living in Golders Green for his *Bar Mitzvah*: 'Gentleman to teach boy of 12 Hebrew at Golders Green. One who can teach the scrolls (in Hebrew). One lesson per week.'[29]

In 1913 a local resident wrote to the *Jewish Chronicle* expressing concern about the lack of religious education for young people in Golders Green.[30] Within two years his call for action had been heeded. The embryonic community that became Golders Green Synagogue[31] started religion classes in 1915 held on Sunday mornings at St Alban's Hall. Just twenty-seven children enrolled for the first classes, but through the efforts of the Ladies' Canvassing Committee the classes developed into a well-attended *cheder* (religion school) for both boys and girls up to the age of 13 affiliated to the United Synagogue's Union of Hebrew and Religion.[32] By 1928 the roll had risen to 120, and by 1933 to 226.[33]

Naomi Rose recalls that during the 1920s the religion classes (the 'Hebrew classes') were held at 5 p.m. on Tuesdays and Thursdays as well as Sunday mornings. She was taught by the 'utterly dedicated' teacher Mattie Cohen who had lost her husband in the First World War and 'gave her life to teaching'. Mrs Cohen worked her students very hard and expected them to arrive early for her classes. She was so committed that she was still teaching when Naomi Rose's daughter attended the *cheder*.[34] Harold Langdon (see page 163), whose family were early members of Dunstan Road Synagogue, attended the *cheder* at the same time as Reverend Livingstone's two daughters,[35] but he also went to religion classes held at the Western Synagogue in Alfred Place in central London. Reverend Livingstone taught him in preparation for his *Bar Mitzvah* in the Livingstone family home.[36] Barbara Michaels (née Livingstone) recalls that she and her sister used to sit on the stairs listening to boys practising their *Bar Mitzvah* portions: 'Not all of them had good voices and sometimes they made us laugh'.[37]

When Alyth Gardens Synagogue was established in 1933, its membership was mainly young families.[38] The congregation initially made use of the religion classes held at West London Synagogue, but also held its own classes twice a week in the Hawthorn Hall in Bridge Lane or in members' homes. Shortage of funding meant that teachers worked for 'a pittance' or on a voluntary basis.[39] Jeffery Rose, who attended the first Alyth religion classes, remembered that the education was somewhat remote and formal:

We were trained to read the *Haftorah* [*sic*] [reading from the Prophets], to declaim it as a dramatic reading, not as an event of religious significance. I learnt little at classes. The lessons in religious philosophy were way above my head.[40]

While Golders Green Beth Hamedrash was in the process of being established,[41] space for religion classes was rented in the Beeches School in Bridge Lane and then in the Broadwalk Hall, renamed the Lincoln Institute after the premises were renovated.[42] Teachers were engaged for both *Shabbat* afternoon and Sunday morning classes which evolved into a Talmud Torah providing more extensive Jewish education.[43] Rabbi Munk taught the older children, who were apparently eager to attend his lessons:

> He would never give the impression of a hurried teacher, pressed to get through a standard syllabus or lots of book learning. Often he started a *shiur* by asking the participants, who had come direct from their secular schools, what they had learnt that day and whether any problems had arisen. He then carefully analysed each problem or challenge, expounding traditional Jewish values and interpretations of sources in relation to the problems raised. He was particularly successful when dealing with such controversial subjects as evolution and Bible criticism.[44]

In 1935 representatives from the three main synagogues in Golders Green, together with representatives from Hampstead Garden Suburb congregation and Hendon Synagogue, met at Dunstan Road to discuss co-operating in providing religious education. However, the conclusion of the meeting was that this was not a practical proposition.[45] With some of the communities being recently formed and intent on forging their own identities, it was probably too early for them to work together on a matter as fundamental as religious education.

Some young people continued to receive their Jewish education privately. Ronald Friedman did not go to *cheder* due to the fact that he attended Highgate School which, like some others, held a 'Saturday school'. His parents thought that six days of education a week was sufficient. However, when he needed to prepare for his *Bar Mitzvah* he was taught by a 'Palestinian Sabra' studying law in England.[46]

The Second World War

During the Second World War the Jewish education of children was reduced to a minimum despite the best efforts of communal organisations, which worked together in attempting to retain the engagement of children billeted in non-Jewish homes. Writing two years after the end of the war, Reverend Livingstone recalled that on the eve of war attendance at the Dunstan Road religion classes was 181 pupils, but just a week after war was declared there were only six pupils with no teachers and not even a headmaster. Mr Bloom, who had headed the school for several years, had been evacuated.[47] Emergency arrangements were put in place with the help of three past pupils, including Reverend Livingstone's daughter Barbara.

At the height of the bombing, attendance at the Dunstan Road classes was just five pupils. However, by 1943 the school roll had risen again to over 100. More than seventy children from Wessex Gardens School were also attending classes held at the synagogue on three mornings a week.[48] Because of the other demands on Reverend Livingstone's time a new head teacher, Mr Hyams, was appointed.[49] The picture was similar at Alyth, where the outbreak of the Second World War temporarily curtailed teaching because of the lack of pupils. As families returned to London, the classes resumed in the autumn of 1941.[50] They were held in a room at the synagogue that had been turned into an ARP shelter. Children still living outside London were taught by correspondence.[51]

The secular education of some Jewish children was also disrupted by the war. Henrietta Barnett School was temporarily closed because of bombs exploding around Hampstead Heath. Hazel Sheldon, a pupil at the school, was evacuated to Henley-on-Thames where she dropped behind in her studies and was never able to make it back to the school.[52] Occasionally the war had unexpected consequences. Jacqueline Pinto, whose family lived in Wycombe Gardens, recalls that she was due to sit a maths exam as part of her school matriculation in 1940. She was worried because she found maths especially difficult. During the exam there was a particularly heavy bombing raid. It was decided that because the raid had been so disruptive, all the pupils should automatically be given a pass. She was very relieved. Had it not been for the bombing she does not think she would have passed the exam.[53]

The post-war years

After the war ended, the experience of dealing with education under evacuation conditions led communal leaders to reappraise the aims and structure of Jewish education. The Holocaust made Anglo-Jewry more receptive to expanding educational provision. Prolonged discussions produced a new system of Jewish education which, according to Reverend Livingstone, 'combin[ed] a central directive authority for the whole of British Jewry, with plenty of fruitful scope for local initiative and enthusiasm'.[54] His optimistic assessment was to prove premature.

With the upsurge in synagogue membership following the end of the war, Alyth gave priority to ensuring that its young people grew up in a Jewish environment, but it was some time before its ambitions were to be fully realised. The austerity of the immediate post-war years meant that religious teaching took place in unprepossessing conditions:

> Our class progressed through a jumble of rooms at the top of the stairs in the front of the building. The final step was the choir room, a delight because it gave a

view over the sanctuary and offered a chance, should the teacher be called away, of playing the organ. Usually this took the form of make-believe music, since actual notes soon brought disciplinary wrath. The higher up the school one advanced, the less work was done on Sunday mornings, particularly after Bar Mitzvah. Nevertheless, over the years a fair amount of miscellaneous knowledge stuck, particularly that obtained on the rare occasions when we did homework – yes homework – which the optimistic teacher assigned weekly.[55]

With the opening of the new Leo Baeck Centre in 1959,[56] the Alyth religion school eventually moved into a self-contained home of its own. In the 'light and airy building' attendance now stood at 350 pupils.[57] There were nine classes, two *Bar Mitzvah* classes and a Confirmation class,[58] held on Sundays and Wednesdays. Many of the teachers were former religion school pupils.[59]

On the other side of Golders Green, Dunstan Road Synagogue continued to provide religious education for Jewish pupils attending Wessex Gardens School. The classes, which were led by a Mrs Rose from Hendon, were now very large. Ian Torrance, who attended the classes in the early 1950s, recalls that two thirds of his class at Wessex Gardens School attended the classes.[60] In addition, he attended the *cheder*, which had increased its provision. A second floor was added to the 'classes block' attached to the synagogue[61] where classes were held on Sundays, and on three evenings a week. Now headed by Samuel Kramer, the *cheder* left an indelible impression on some of its post-war pupils:

> [I] learnt to read Hebrew when I was quite small, had even gone on to teach it at the local synagogue Sunday school. So when, on the Sabbath, I grasped the silver *yad*, the pointer made in the form of a finger to remind us that the only aspect of the disembodied God revealed was the finger that, according to Leviticus, had written directly on to the stone tablets at Sinai, I became, through the mere act of chanted reading from the Torah, connected to the great chain of endurance embodied in Hebrew writing.[62]

In 1942 the Talmud Torah associated with Munk's shul moved to 680 Golders Green Road, Elka Segal House,[63] which was also used for other communal activities. Pupils were expected to attend for an hour and a quarter after school on two or three evenings a week and for two hours on Sunday. In addition to Rabbi Munk, the Talmud Torah now had five teachers who taught fifty boys and thirty-six girls in separate classes.[64] The upper classes prepared boys successfully for entry into *yeshivot*. However, during the weekday sessions it was sometimes difficult to motivate the children who were not at their freshest after they had been at school all day. The teachers also found it difficult to address the varying educational needs of the pupils now attending the new Jewish schools (see below) and those attending non-Jewish schools.[65] Rabbi Munk continued to give regular *shiurim* to mixed audiences of boys and girls in communal premises and in his home.[66]

By the 1960s Dunstan Road Synagogue was no longer offering 'withdrawal classes' but did ensure that Jewish children at Wessex Garden School had kosher lunches as part of the London-wide Kosher School Meals Service.[67] Each day a coach would transport Jewish children from the school to Dunstan Road for lunch in the synagogue hall. Some children apparently believed that they were called kosher dinners 'because you went to get them on a coach'.[68] Steven Derby remembers missing his non-Jewish classmates during the lunch hour[69] and Michael Rutstein recalls that he was quite relieved when the meals stopped:

> The portions veered on the small side and I often left the table hungry. It was a joy when I started having school dinners at Wessex Gardens, leading to the discovery of stodgy puddings and custard. This made me realise that up until this point I'd had a deprived childhood from a culinary point of view.[70]

The emergence of Jewish schools

The first Jewish day school to open its doors in Golders Green was Menorah Primary School in October 1944. Its founding was overseen by a group of members of the Munk's shul who formed the Golders Green Schools Committee. Led by Rabbi Munk, the committee experienced some difficulty in obtaining support for the school, including from members of their own community who had not attended a Jewish school and did not intend to send their children to one.[71]

Menorah Primary School was based initially at Elka Segal House; its first intake was just eight pupils.[72] It grew quickly and 4 and 5 The Drive were purchased to provide more spacious accommodation. Walls were taken down to construct classrooms and a pre-fabricated shed was attached to the rear of the houses to provide a hall for communal activities.[73] Outside, the fences between the houses were removed to construct a playground.[74] By the late 1950s there were approaching 300 children in the school and it was necessary to secure larger premises. Although the school was chronically short of funding, in 1970 a purpose-built school was erected at 1–3 The Drive. The school has now been incorporated into what is called the Wohl Campus on this site.

Menorah Primary School was modelled on English preparatory schools, but with Jewish studies forming a major element of the curriculum, differentiating it from the pre-war West Hampstead Day School that had concentrated on preparing Jewish children for public schools.[75] The school's ethos was *Torah im Derech Eretz* (literally 'Torah within the way of the land') aimed at achieving 'a harmonious combination of traditional Jewish learning and observance with a sound and adequate secular education'.[76]

Rabbi Munk was the principal of the school, and its first headteacher was Aron Shapiro, known by the pupils as 'Shaps'. According to a number of commentators, Mr Shapiro was a strict disciplinarian and, like many headteachers of the time, believed in corporal punishment even for relatively minor offences. Rabbi Munk and Mr Shapiro are said to have had differences of opinion about the disciplining of children.[77] Despite his 'mercurial temper', pupils admired Mr Shapiro. Selma Shrank, a pupil at the school in the 1950s, remembers that Mr Shapiro kindled her love of poetry and music.[78] Stephen Colman, who attended the school in the 1960s, recalls Mr Shapiro's 'unparalleled' assemblies:

> They were worth all of the other lessons put together. He taught us about music. He gave us an explanation of a piece and then played the music, such as 'Flight of the Bumble Bee', on an old-fashioned gramophone record player.[79]

The teachers at the school were 'very upright women', mainly with a German background.[80] The school had very high standards and children who were not academic or who needed learning support sometimes struggled to keep up.[81]

Some pupils entered Menorah Primary School having first attended other schools in Golders Green:

> Denied a complete education because of the frugal circumstances that her generation endured, my mother wanted the best education possible for me. She initially sent me to Golders Hill School but after just a little while she took fright when she saw how anglicised I was becoming. She quickly moved me to Menorah Primary School where I was totally bewildered by the level of orthodoxy in the school and out of sync with the *Mitteleuropean* culture that prevailed in the school at the time. A lot of the children came from that culture and it was a big jump to make for a boy from a Yiddish family. It took me about a year to make the transition.[82]

In its early years, the school roll included many pupils who were related. Miriam Levene (née Bentley) recalls that at one stage she had a sibling or a cousin in each form in the school.[83] She also recalls that although the school was primarily intended to serve the Munk's community, it took a number of children from orthodox Sephardi families living in Golders Green because at the time there were so few Jewish schools in the vicinity. However, there were also a number of pupils who were 'less frum'.[84] As the emphasis on Jewish learning became more pronounced, the school introduced after-school sessions led by Rabbi Refoel Bersich. The sessions took the form of a club with games and rewards to encourage attendance.[85]

By the 1970s the school had become the largest Jewish primary school in north-west London and, despite high house prices, was attracting Golders Green young couples seeking for their children 'a good secular education combined with Jewish learning of a similarly high quality'.[86] There was keen competition for places at the school and in 1986 an extension was set up in Burnt Oak. Initially referred to as 'The Annex', in 1990 it adopted the name Menorah Foundation School. The ethos and approach to education was the same as Menorah Primary School and its intake largely from Golders Green.

Concerned by the deterioration of Jewish education, in 1929 Rabbi Dr Victor Schonfeld, leader of the strictly orthodox Adath Yisroel community in Stamford Hill, founded an independent Jewish secondary school, which was led after his death by his son, Rabbi Solomon Schonfeld. It formed the basis of the Jewish Secondary Schools Movement (JSSM)[87] and was the model for Hasmonean Grammar School, the second Jewish school in Golders Green. It opened with separate departments for boys and girls in The Drive in 1945.

Rabbi Schonfeld also planned to set up a Hasmonean primary school but, after protracted negotiations with the Golders Green Schools Committee, it was agreed that this school would not open until eighteen months after Menorah Primary School so that the two schools did not compete for pupils. It opened in Hendon in 1947. It was also agreed that Menorah Primary School would feed into Hasmonean Grammar School and would be loosely associated with JSSM.[88] The boys' department of the grammar school relocated to Holders Hill Road in Hendon in 1947 and the girls' school followed suit, relocating in 1952 to a nearby site in Parson's Street (and later to Page Street, Mill Hill). In their early days the Hasmonean schools were firmly anti-Zionist in their stance.[89]

The curriculum of Hasmonean Grammar School was heavily influenced by Rabbi Munk, who initially taught the senior classes at the school.[90] Its curriculum included ninety minutes a day of Jewish studies and Hebrew. The first teachers at the school, who were mostly members of Munk's shul, included Mr Levene, the English teacher; Mr Frank, who taught Latin; Mr Grossman, who taught maths and was a fierce disciplinarian; and Mr Myer, who taught Modern Hebrew.[91] Some of the early pupils were the sons of 'Golders Green wealthy dynasties' such as the Klugg and Loftus families who were generous communal benefactors.[92]

After becoming a voluntary aided state school in 1957, Hasmonean Grammar School introduced an after-school *yeshivah* stream offering a more intensive curriculum studying Talmud and other texts and doubling the time available for Jewish studies. This enabled alumni to enter the higher classes in the prestigious *yeshivah* in Gateshead. The *yeshivah* stream ran from 4.15 to 5.45 p.m. during the week and on Sunday mornings. According to one source, children were strongly encouraged to attend the Sunday session, although at times this provision is said to have been a 'religiously divisive' influence in the school.[93]

Not all of the pupils from Menorah Primary School went on to Hasmonean Grammar School. A number of boys transferred to Hendon County Grammar School, which had high academic standards. Its headmaster, Mr Maynard-Potts, was devoted to the school and to the advancement of students from all backgrounds. However, he had a reputation for being ill at ease with the school's large Jewish intake and the leave of absence the Jewish boys required for festival observances.[94] For pupils who had lived 'a totally Jewish life' before transferring to Hendon County, the school's Christian-dominated environment came as something of a shock. In the early 1950s Reverend Livingstone met with the headmaster to discuss the school's lack of religious education for Jewish pupils.[95]

While Hasmonean Grammar School had quickly gained a reputation for providing a high quality of both Jewish and secular education, to begin with Hasmonean Girls' School was 'less academic', mainly focusing on preparing its pupils to be 'good Jewish housewives'. Girls from Menorah Primary School who passed the 11-plus examination usually attended the high-achieving Henrietta Barnett School or Copthall Grammar School in Mill Hill.[96] Some students from Hasmonean Girls' School transferred to Henrietta Barnett to take A-levels, especially if they wished to study science subjects, which were not offered at Hasmonean.[97] By the 1960s Henrietta Barnett was much more Jewish in its intake than it had been thirty years earlier. The teachers were apparently sometimes puzzled by the varying degrees of observance by the Jewish girls attending the school.[98] Later standards at Hasmonean Girls' School started to rise and religious leaders encouraged parents to send their daughters there to learn 'to lead a good Jewish life'.[99]

In 1984 Hasmonean Grammar School merged with Hasmonean Girls' School organisationally, but the two schools remained on separate sites. The Hasmonean School, which continues to serve Golders Green, now has academy status. It has a *Beth Hamedrash* programme for boys in years 11 to 13 and a *Midrasha* programme for sixth-form girls.[100] A large proportion of Hasmonean students go on to some form of tertiary education. Most boys study at a *yeshivah* and girls at seminary followed by courses at university or professional training institutions. Among the more orthodox alumni, higher studies are increasingly being deferred until after marriage to help ensure that young people are not affected by the secularising influences and liberal morals seen to be associated with university life.[101]

Established in 1959, the Mathilda Marks-Kennedy Jewish Primary School was named after the daughter of Michael Marks, one of the founders of Marks and Spencer. Mathilda Marks-Kennedy was a renowned philanthropist and was particularly generous in her support of educational and medical causes.[102] The school, which was Zionist in orientation,[103] was originally located at 783 Finchley Road and was known to many parents and pupils as 'Barclay House School'. Its first head teacher was the South African educationalist Dolly Elias, and its honorary principal was Rabbi Newman from Dunstan Road Synagogue. Over time, it attracted a large proportion of Israeli children living in the area. Special tuition was arranged to enable their integration to the English curriculum. From its inception the school was always cramped for space and almost closed at one point. New premises were eventually secured in Mill Hill in 1991.

The growth in Jewish schooling in Golders Green included provision for young children. A few years after Menorah Primary School opened, a playgroup for under-5s was set up by Munk's shul at the Lincoln Institute in Broadwalk Lane. This became Menorah Kindergarten, based at Elka Segal House in Finchley Road under the headship of Mrs Wilsack, which fed into the primary school. On the advice of HM Inspector of Schools, the kindergarten later moved to the same site as the primary school.[104] In 1947 a Jewish nursery school opened in Elmcroft Avenue. Founded by Anny Schwarzbart, it provided kosher meals.[105]

Non-Jewish schooling after the war

In the two decades following the Second World War, Wessex Gardens School continued to educate a large number of Jewish children. In his autobiography, the poet Dannie Abse recalls that his daughter Keren who attended the school, believed that because of the preponderance of her Jewish classmates, Jews in Britain were in the majority. He also recalls that his other daughter Susanah once came home from school and asked, 'Dad, who is Leonardo de Vinsky?'[106]

At the same time as Jewish schools were developing, some Jewish parents were finding Wessex Gardens School less attractive:

> In the 1980s the Japanese started to come to the country to sell cars and televisions and Golders Green was a good place to rent a house. Their children flooded into Wessex Gardens, changing the character of the school. When there are a lot of children in a school whose first language is not English, it can't help but have an impact on the school.[107]

Children from Wessex Gardens School (and also Garden Suburb School) began to transfer into the new Jewish primary schools and into independent primary schools seen as providing a 'good education'. One of these schools was La Sagesse Convent School situated just off Golders Green Road in premises incorporating the former Woodstock House.[108] It took a certain number of Jewish children and the influences to which they were exposed sometimes raised issues for parents:

> I came home from school one day and said I wanted a rosary. A friend of mine had come into school with a rosary made up of purple beads. I thought it was very pretty. My mother said that I could have one but I would have to give up my gold magendovid [star of David]. Since I loved playing with the chain on the magendovid, I decided on balance that I would keep the magendovid, I wasn't prepared to sacrifice it. Years afterwards we used to laugh about this.[109]

Having mainly been educated locally at primary level, Jewish children transferred to a variety of secondary schools further afield. A significant proportion of Jewish children continued to attend fee-paying schools but some of the schools, including Channing School in Highgate[110] and Haberdashers School in Cricklewood,[111] had introduced quotas to ensure they did not become dominated by Jewish children. Some Jewish families took advantage of the free places at grammar schools that had become available following the 1944 Education Act, including at Orange Hill Grammar School in Burnt Oak. Christ's College School in Hendon Lane was a very popular school for Jewish boys. Michael Rutstein, who was brought up in Garrick Avenue, recalls that when he attended the school in the 1970s, a third of the boys in his class were Jewish.[112]

Jewish families living in Golders Green were also keen to grasp the opportunities provided by the rapid expansion of tertiary and higher education that took place during the 1960s. Naomi Rose, who studied at Cambridge during the Second World War, had been among a small minority of women who had a university education.[113] by the 1960s equal proportions of Jewish men and women were obtaining degrees.[114]

Supplementary education

Despite the opening of Jewish schools in Golders Green, up until the 1980s most young people in the area continued to receive their Jewish education by attending a *cheder*. Sometimes they were not thoroughly enamoured with the experience and found that it competed for time with a growing variety of non-religious activities and forms of entertainment. Michael Rutstein recalls that Mrs Abramski, his teacher at the Sunday morning Hebrew classes at Dunstan Road Synagogue, was very good in engaging with children. However, the timing of the classes meant that he missed the first part of the TV programme *Thunderbirds*: 'I was devoted to the adventures of my heroes Virgil and Brains and I really resented not seeing how they started'.[115]

Following the appointment of Rabbi Marmur, the Alyth religion school became a friendlier and more informal place, with less emphasis on text book learning and closer links with the synagogue. During the 1970s Alyth prioritised investment in education over other much-needed improvements.[116] The syllabus for the school had now been extended to include tuition in music, arts and crafts by specialist teachers, a 'far cry' from the rote learning that epitomised the early religion classes.[117] As a result, the number of children in the religion school grew and outstripped the accommodation available. Classes overflowed into the nearby Garden Suburb School.

At Dunstan Road Synagogue the picture was quite different. During the 1970s participation in the religion school dwindled to just a few children due to the aging membership of the synagogue. The quality of the teaching at the *cheder* was criticised publicly.[118] Sponsored by the United Synagogue, in 1978 a new initiative was launched, the Brent Cross Teenage Centre, which sought to retain the involvement of young people in education after the age of 13. The teenage centre became very popular and transferred from the synagogue to the Sobell Centre in 1983.[119] It ran over twenty-five courses attended by children and young people from across north-west London, mainly those attending non-Jewish schools. Such was its success that its activities extended into Machzikei Hadath Synagogue. However, the teenage centre closed after the United Synagogue divested itself of its education functions and no longer paid the wages of teachers at the centre.[120] Some synagogues attempted to reopen *chedarim* to replace the provision of the teenage centre but few were successful. Dunstan Road Synagogue set up a short-lived joint *cheder* with Hampstead Synagogue.[121] The classes, which were held at Hampstead Synagogue, soon stopped due to the lack of students, as most children in the two congregations were now receiving their religious education in Jewish schools.

Expansion of Jewish schools

In 1971 the Chief Rabbi of the United Synagogue, Rabbi Immanuel Jakobovits (later Lord Jakobovits), launched the Jewish Educational Development Trust, aimed at raising the profile of Jewish education and encouraging fundraising for educational purposes. As a result of this initiative, which was reinforced by messages on Jewish continuity delivered by Rabbi Jonathan Sacks when he succeeded Rabbi Jakobovits,[122] the Jewish educational scene changed dramatically. Whereas in 1975 less than 20 per cent of Jewish children attended Jewish day schools, thirty years later the proportion had increased to 60 per cent.[123] Moreover, while the Jewish schools set up in the nineteenth century had promoted integration into wider society, the new wave of schools placed an emphasis on encouraging a sense of Jewish identity in the context of a multicultural society.

For families living in Golders Green this development meant that a new generation of children experienced an education system very different from that which had existed for the preceding generation. Growing up in the 1960s in a practising Jewish family in Temple Fortune, Rabbi Amanda Golby went to Laneside Nursery School that met at St Barnabas Church in Cranbourne Gardens[124] and received her secular education aged 4–18 in non-denominational schools. Her Jewish education took place at Alyth Gardens Synagogue. A generation later her nieces attended the Alyth kindergarten and went on to Akiva School in Finchley, both founded under the leadership of Rabbi Marmur and modelled along Reform principles, where they received both a Jewish and secular education. The experience of many of their peers in the locality was similar.[125]

Under the leadership of Eva Jacobs,[126] the Alyth kindergarten thrived and became an institution with wide parental involvement. Since priority for places was given to the children of synagogue members, young families joined the synagogue as Rabbi Marmur had hoped.[127] The kindergarten, which has now been operating for over forty years, has received several generations of Golders Green Jewish children. Children at the kindergarten often provide entertainment for the Alyth Senior Club and the nearby Clare Nehab Care Home.[128]

As Jewish schooling became the preference of an increasing proportion of Jewish families, children from Golders Green began attending Jewish day schools serving a plurality of denominations such as the Zionist-Orthodox Independent Jewish Day School, founded in Hendon in 1979[129] and the Jews' Free School (JFS), founded in the early nineteenth century, which moved from Camden to Kenton in

2002. In the last decade a number of new pluralist Jewish schools have opened in London, including the Jewish Community Secondary School (JCoSS) in Barnet,[130] the catchment of which covers Golders Green. Even more recently, members of Dunstan Road Synagogue led and oversaw the setting up of a 'free school' attached to the synagogue. Rimon Primary School, which opened in 2012, is 'Modern Orthodox' in outlook, but caters for a diversity of Jewish denominations and also for 'all other faiths and none'.[131] It was the brainchild of the former chairman Benny Chain and his daughter, Rachel Clark, who became the school's first chair of governors. It is committed to the study of Jewish texts and preservation of the environment. By 2015 the school was over-subscribed.[132]

Haredi schools

The most dramatic growth in Jewish schools has been in those serving the burgeoning *haredi* community of Golders Green, for whom the existing Jewish schools were not sufficiently observant. In recent years a number of new strictly orthodox schools have opened in the area, which are all over-subscribed due to the high birth rate among *haredim*.

A *haredi* boy from Golders Green nowadays typically starts school at either Pardes House Primary School (established in 1954 with just four pupils in Sneath Avenue by Rabbi Halpern;[133] shortly afterwards it moved to West Heath Road and later to East End Road in East Finchley before transferring to its present location in Finchley),[134] or Avigdor Hirsch Torah Temimah Primary School (set up in 1989 in Hillcrest Crescent but now in Dollis Hill). Primary school provision for *haredi* boys also includes Talmud Torah Tiferes Shlomo in Golders Green Road catering for boys aged 3–7 years, and Torah Vodaas Primary School in West Hendon Broadway, which takes boys aged 5–11. At secondary age, *haredi* boys usually transfer to Hasmonean Grammar School, Menorah Grammar School (set up in 1978 and initially located in premises formerly occupied by La Sagesse Convent School),[135] or Pardes House Grammar School (established in 1974).[136] In terms of its orthodoxy, Menorah Grammar School sits between Hasmonean School and Pardes House.

The first *haredi* girls' primary school in the area was Beis Yaakov, the brainchild of Benzion Freshwater.[137] It was founded in 1972 in the attic of 835 Finchley Road before moving to the premises in West Heath Road vacated by Pardes House School. It later moved to the former premises of the Kilburn Polytechnic annex at 373 Edgware Road. At one time it was linked to Pardes House Primary School to enable the schools to become voluntary aided, but subsequently 'de-merged'.[138] The other *haredi* girls' primary schools serving Golders Green are Beis Soroh Schneirer School in Hendon (set up in 1996), and the more recently established Peninim School, which opened in Golders Green in 2010; like other schools started in the area, it subsequently moved to new premises in Green Lane, Hendon in 2013 due to the lack of affordable property or development sites. *Haredi* girls usually transfer to either London Jewish Girls' High School (Tiferes) in Hendon, Beth Jacob Grammar School for Girls (which was founded in 1980 in two adjoining houses in Finchley Road owned by the Freshwater family and moved to purpose-built premises in Hendon in 1998), or Menorah High School in Dollis Hill, established in 2001.

The way in which *haredi* schools are structured is different from other Jewish day schools and the system for boys' education differs from that of girls. Aged 5, *haredi* boys start learning Torah and Mishnah. When they are 9, intensive teaching of the Talmud commences.[139] At the most orthodox secondary schools, such as Pardes House, boys take A-levels (usually only two subjects) aged 15 in just one year so that they can concentrate on Jewish learning. Some boys would like to do more A-levels, but this is not generally encouraged. They sometimes take additional A-levels at a later stage. In *haredi* boys' schools a limited range of secular subjects is taught. Creative subjects such as art seldom form part of the curriculum and sporting activities are a low priority.[140] Certain subjects such as church history and geological structure are avoided.[141]

At primary school level *haredi* girls study Torah, Rashi's traditional commentary, Hebrew grammar, liturgy and Jewish history up to the destruction of the Second Temple.[142] At secondary level, girls continue with their secular education and also study ethics and the Prophets but not Talmud. Most are entered for GCSEs and an increasing number go on to sit A-levels, often in foreign languages. This assists them in obtaining employment because they are sometimes the main breadwinners.[143] At some of the girls' schools, older pupils are taught Modern Hebrew outside school hours and 'off campus'.[144] This is to help prepare them for seminary in Israel or marriage to an Israeli.[145]

Some of the *haredi* primary schools are voluntary aided, but most are small and financed by fees and donations so that they can maintain freedom over admissions and the curriculum. As *haredi* families are often large, finances are sometimes strained. However, no child is turned away from a *haredi* school due to lack of means.[146] The schools are run on very tight budgets and some have accrued large deficits which have been met by generous benefactors such as William Stern[147] and the Freshwater family.[148] Some of the *haredi* schools (notably Pardes House Grammar School and Menorah Grammar School) have sometimes had to start afresh.

When *haredi* schools have become voluntary aided, Ofsted has asked for secular and religious studies to be interspersed throughout the day. However, at the Pardes House schools that have remained staunchly independent, Jewish studies continue to take priority over secular studies and are taught in the morning when the children are more alert.[149] Secular subjects are usually taught in English but until recently religious studies were taught in Yiddish, even though some of the pupils were from Munk's shul and had a German rather than a Yiddish-speaking background.[150] Since fewer *haredi* children are now speaking Yiddish at home,[151] some schools have started to depart from the tradition of teaching in Yiddish. However, a few schools, notably Pardes House[152] and Tiferes Shlomo, continue to teach religious studies almost exclusively in Yiddish. Torah Vodath and the Peninim girls' school use a mixture of English and Yiddish.[153]

Haredi boys' schools are led by rabbis. Men and women teach secular studies, but only men teach religious studies.[154] Some of the *haredi* boys' schools would prefer male-only teaching, but male teachers are in short supply because teaching is not a lucrative occupation for people supporting large families. At times problems can arise in the continuity of teaching because women in the *haredi* community tend to marry young and may leave teaching after just a few years to join their husbands outside the area or to care for their children.[155] For many years the privately funded Massoret Institute based in Golders Green helped to fill the gap in the supply of teachers by training strictly orthodox women to become teachers. The institute relocated to Hendon and became the MST College but in 2008 was forced to close when its backers withdrew funding.[156] Discussions are currently taking place on the opening of similar establishments in the area.[157]

The small numbers of Lubavitch children living in Golders Green mostly attend Lubavitch schools in Stamford Hill, but there is a small Lubavitch school at 1 Bridge Lane. The growing number of Sephardi children who live in Golders Green attend a variety of schools, including the Sephardic Od Yoseph Chai schools, which range from a relatively new kindergarten to a *yeshivah*. However, some strictly orthodox Sephardi families send their children to the Ashkenazi *haredi* schools.[158]

Kisharon Day School in Finchley Road is the only Jewish special needs school in north-west London. The school was set up in 1976 in the former premises of the Montefiore College, under the headship of Chava Lehman, who had previously taught a 'remedial class' at Menorah Primary School.[159] The school welcomes children from all Jewish denominations, but it operates along strictly orthodox lines. It caters for a wide range of educational needs, from moderate learning difficulties and autistic spectrum disorders to more severe, profound and multiple learning difficulties.[160] In a nearby building Tuffkid, an integrated nursery, accommodates children from 2 years of age. Children with special needs play and learn alongside mainstream children.

Post-school *haredi* education

A girls' seminary known as Carmel Girls' Seminary was set up in Golders Green in 1969 under the headship of Rabbi O. Schonthal with five full-time and fifteen part-time students, some of whom boarded with local families.[161] The seminary provided an intensive twelve-month course in orthodox Jewish studies but this initiative was short lived. A large proportion of *haredi* girls now go on from secondary school to study at seminaries ('sems'), either in Manchester or in Gateshead where there are two seminaries. One is a teacher training seminary and the other is more vocational. Some girls attend seminaries in Switzerland or in Israel, usually for nine months. It is uncommon for *haredi* girls to study at university, but some take Open University or other distance-learning courses, usually after they are married.[162]

Most *haredi* boys transfer from school to *yeshivot* where the curriculum is entirely Talmud and *halachah*. The first move to set up a *yeshivah* in Golders Green was made by Rabbi Munk in 1946. Sha'are Zion (Gates of Zion), which grew out of the Munk's shul Talmud Torah,[163] was criticised in the Anglo-Jewish press because it departed from the tradition of teaching in Yiddish to accommodate the married men living in Golders Green.[164] Rabbi Munk defended the use of English, stressing that his aim was not to train future rabbis, but to educate English Jews. Perhaps because of the controversy it created, the *yeshivah*, headed by the then unknown Rabbi Louis Jacobs,[165] only lasted for two years.[166] After Rabbi Jacobs accepted a rabbinic post in Manchester, the *yeshivah* was discontinued and Munk's shul established the Ohel Shem Society, led by Mr Bendix, and employed Rabbi Tarshish to lead regular study sessions at Elka Segal House.

The first *yeshivah* in Golders Green to endure was Yeshivas Chayei Olam, set up in 1957 under the leadership of Rabbi Eleazer Wahraftig,[167] who had also been prominent in establishing the Munk's *yeshivah*. Chayei Olam's beginnings were very humble. At first there were only two students, who studied in the Sassover Beth Hamedrash in Finchley Road.[168] Rabbi Rakow, who had previously taught at Yesodei Hatorah School in Stamford Hill, became the *Rosh Yeshivah* (head of the *yeshivah*). Even after the first *yeshivah* students had moved on, Rabbi Rakow was determined to persevere and over the next twenty-five years hundreds of young men came to study at the *yeshivah*, which relocated to Rabbi Halpern's shul in Golders Green Road,[169] and eventually to a permanent home at 961 Finchley Road.[170] Rabbi Rakow was much loved by his students, and also in the wider community.[171] After his death, his position was taken over initially by Rabbi Knopfler from Sinai shul in Woodstock Avenue and then by Rabbi Freshwater from the Sassover shul in Helenslea Avenue, who remains the *Rosh Yeshivah*.[172]

Today there are a number of other *yeshivot* in Golders Green providing a range of study opportunities. Etz Chaim Yeshivah in Bridge Lane (formerly in the East End), led by Rabbi Zvi Rabi, caters mainly for young married men who learn there in the morning.[173] Yeshivah Yad Halevi, led by Rabbi Yosef Bamberger, specialises in teaching young men who 'do not fit into the large *yeshivot*'.[174] There is also a Lubavitch *yeshivah*, Yeshivah Gedolah, in Temple Fortune.

Young *haredi* men generally experience more educational transitions than young women. The usual pattern is for boys to enter the Golders Green *yeshivah* in Finchley Road when they are 15 or 16, which is considered too young for them to leave home. When they are 17 or 18 they study at the *yeshivah* in Gateshead until they are 20 or 21, when they transfer to a *yeshivah* in Israel. Often young men are not able to study at *yeshivot* for as long as they would wish because of the expense involved.[175] In recent years young men have returned from Israel earlier than they planned because they can no longer afford to stay there, even when they have wives who work, because of changes in the benefits system.[176] An increasing (but very small) number of post-*yeshivah* young men in Golders Green have enrolled at mainstream universities.[177] *Yeshivot* still discourage further secular education, mainly for religious reasons.[178]

Recent developments in synagogue-based education

With an increasing number of its young people attending Jewish day schools, Alyth Gardens Synagogue sought ways of engaging with young people to retain their interest in synagogue life. In 2002 the synagogue introduced SatCh (an acronym for Saturday *cheder*) as an alternative to Sunday morning classes for younger children. Based on an American model of family education, SatCh became a committed group of parents who learned alongside their children.[179] Through a mixture of study, singing, drama, art and discussion, families learned about their heritage and culture and to read Hebrew. Classes for children approaching *B'nai Mitzvah* also moved to *Shabbat* morning followed by service attendance. More recently, the learning and engagement programme for young people called *Galim* (literally 'waves') has been expanded to include specialist provision for those attending Jewish day schools including services, day trips, festival-based sleepovers and residential study sessions.[180]

Adult learning

The history of adult Jewish learning in Golders Green has mirrored that of the education of young people. As it grew in membership, Dunstan Road Synagogue organised a variety of activities for adults,[181] but to start with they were largely secular. Some of the male members of the synagogue made their own arrangements to study together privately, such as Mr Prevezer, Mr Kaye and Mr Serkes, who studied in each other's homes on Saturday afternoons.[182] However, by the 1930s Reverend Livingstone had organised a Talmud Study Circle, which met every evening and sometimes also invited guest speakers on a Sunday.[183]

When the strictly orthodox Golders Green Beth Hamedrash was set up in 1933, its activities included study sessions for men and women, as well as lectures given by highly regarded speakers.[184] Rabbi Munk had said that he did not want 'an ignorant laity'[185] and devoted the whole of *Shabbat* to learning with various groups of young people.

Speaking at the laying of the foundation stone for the Alyth Gardens Synagogue in January 1936, the first chairman, Mr J.A. Wolfe, expressed the hope that it would become 'a home of education',[186] and from its inception the synagogue has had a full adult learning programme. Early educational activities included a Saturday afternoon study circle when Jewish scholars led sessions, which were typified by their 'intimate and friendly atmosphere'.[187] *Shiurim* also took place at the first *shtieblech* established in Golders Green just before and during the Second World War.[188]

Just as there was a major upturn in Jewish education for young people, after the war there was a significant expansion in Jewish learning for adults living in the area. In the late 1940s, Rabbi Y. Beck ran Golders Green Orthodox Study Circle in Temple Gardens,[189] the forerunner for *Chovevai Torah* (Lovers of Torah) set up at Elka Segal House in Finchley Road in 1955. *Chovevei Torah* was sponsored by a number of prominent individuals from various congregations in the area seeking to co-ordinate and supplement existing synagogue provision.[190] Lectures and *shiurim* took place most evenings, but the main events were held on Mondays when there were usually visiting speakers. Some of the speakers delivered to male-only audiences. However, there was also dedicated provision for women. The Monday lectures covered *Midrash* (interpreting biblical stories), *halachah* and Jewish ethics and were often filled to capacity.[191]

A number of the study sessions that took place in Golders Green between 1950 and 1980 were organised by informal groups of people living in the area such as the meetings of the London branch of the Association of Orthodox Jewish Scientists, which focused on the inter-relationship between science and Judaism. Professors, scientists and doctors met in various halls and private homes in Golders Green. There were also various study groups attached to the Zionist organisations that met at PAI House[192] in Alba Gardens. B'nei Akiva, which in previous decades had concentrated on Zionist activities, now focused almost exclusively on learning sessions featuring top Jewish lecturers aimed at sixth-formers and college and university students.[193]

As mentioned in Chapter 7, in 1972 Jews' College opened a branch in Golders Green named the Brodie Institute.[194] A variety of educational activities were established at the institute, including a Midrasha centre for women and a Torah Youth Centre opened by former Chief Rabbi Brodie in 1974, offering courses held on a Sunday morning leading to O- and A-levels in Modern and Classical Hebrew and Jewish Religious Studies. The Brodie Institute was hailed as 'a further milestone in the history of the service rendered to Jewish education by Jews' College'.[195] However, within four years the premises were sold to the Montefiore College to meet a major deficit in the Jews' College budget.[196] The college's first intake of twenty-six students came from countries as diverse as Tunisia, Southern Rhodesia (Zimbabwe), Holland and Iran, as well as Britain.[197] In 1975 Rabbi Meir Rogosnitzky, previously principal of Liverpool Yeshivah, founded an academy for Jewish learning catering for former *yeshivah* students based at Ohel David Synagogue,[198] and in 1980 the Bachad Federation set up lecture courses in Hallswelle Road.[199] A year later the Bachad Federation in partnership with Jews' College and the Mizrachi Federation established the Midrasha Institute for Israel Studies at the Montefiore College.[200]

However, all of these initiatives proved insufficient to meet the growing demand for adult learning. Some *haredi* men were regularly travelling to Stamford Hill to study. One *haredi* man recalls that he devised many different routes between Golders Green and Stamford Hill to break the monotony of the journey.[201] Individual shuls and *shtieblech* in Golders Green started to provide facilities for more *shiurim* and *bechevruta* (supported study sessions).

Much of the growing demand for study came from young men returning from *yeshivot* who wanted to continue their studies alongside their employment. To meet this need, a *Bet Hatalmud* (centre for Talmud study) was set up in Hendon where young men could study texts of their choice with other local young men, usually friends or acquaintances with similar backgrounds and interests.[202] The same sort of facility was later established for young women returning from seminaries.[203]

These developments heralded a change in the approach taken to learning. Instead of formal lectures with the audience taking notes, the main approach was *chevruta* (learning with a partner); as one commentator described it, 'the emphasis was now much more on a guide at the side rather than a sage on the stage'.[204] *Chevruta* was supported by locally based, experienced scholars and community rabbis like Rabbi Kimche of Ner Yisrael Synagogue in Hendon and Rabbi Pearlman from Machzikei Hadath Synagogue.[205] *Chevruta* is now the preferred form of study for most *haredi* men in Golders Green. Daily study sessions commence as early as 6 a.m., which men attend before they recite the morning service. However, most *shiurim* or *chevruta* still take place in the evenings and at weekends. Developments in information technology have further extended learning opportunities. Using applications such as Skype, some men learn regularly with partners in other countries, including in Israel and Germany.[206]

Many *haredi* women also study, often becoming very proficient in their learning. They study *halachah*, Bible texts, philosophy but not Talmud, since it is not considered suitable for study by women.[207] Learning for *haredi* women tends to be more ad hoc because of their family responsibilities. It is also more seasonal, with most study sessions being organised around the main Jewish festivals. Some *haredi* women study at home, but there are also classes for women in local shuls such as the study sessions that take place at Machzikei Hadath Synagogue on Tuesday mornings where there is also a programme of special events for women, sometimes with visiting speakers. Munk's shul holds fortnightly study sessions for older women, which they attend with their carers. At Jewish Care, Orah, an organisation promoting learning for post-seminary women, runs a programme of Saturday evening learning opportunities.[208] Some women have study partners, with whom they learn by telephone ('Phone and Learn').[209] However, *Haredi* women rarely attend the same study sessions as men and learning for women generally continues to be regarded as secondary to that of men.[210]

On the whole, the Sephardi shuls place less emphasis on learning than the Ashkenazi shuls and religious values are normally imparted in the home environment, although some Sephardi women in Golders Green attend study sessions organised by Chabad.[211] However, Yehezkel Beth Hamedrash organises a monthly *shiur* for women and plans to start a class on educational skills to enable parents to pass on Sephardi traditions to their children.

There are a number of organisations referred to as *kiruv* serving Golders Green. They are concerned with educating Jewish people with little Jewish involvement, particularly young people. Seed is a body based in Edgware that organises adult and family Jewish education across the UK through formal study events and informal learning experiences.[212] Some Jewish families living in Golders Green partner with those who know relatively little about Judaism, meeting with them in informal settings to share their knowledge. Seed might, for example, take a family away to a hotel over a weekend so that the family can learn about *Shabbat*, which would be followed by Jewish study sessions led by tutors. Jewish families in the area also assist with sessions organised by Aish, an organisation promoting understanding of Judaism, aimed at secular Jews seeking to learn about Judaism.[213]

A similar organisation operating locally is the Jewish Learning Exchange (JLE), a branch of the Israeli *yeshivah*, Ohr Someach. Located since 1996 in Golders Green Road, JLE holds over eighty classes attended by around 1,000 people each week and has seen its team grow from two dedicated couples to a faculty of eighteen full-time and thirty part-time educators from a range of backgrounds.[214] Many of the activities organised by JLE are social in nature like the monthly Friday night 'Meet & Eats' at which around 150 young Jews eat together prior to a seminar. There are also one-to-one learning sessions open to both men and women. For newly married couples there are regular social and educational gatherings, as well as pre-marriage and parenting courses. Well-known lecturers and authors frequently speak at JLE events and up to 200 people attend the Wednesday evening lectures on 'Spiritual and Philosophical Ideas Within Judaism' led by Rabbi Dr Akiva Tatz, senior lecturer at JLE.[215]

Since opening the doors of the Kesher Community Centre at 933 Finchley Road in 2004, Rabbi Rashi Simon and his wife, Ruthie (founders of JLE), have created a community that caters for Jews of all levels of observance. Kesher's learning opportunities are particularly targeted at couples and young families. Ruthie Simon runs courses for women and couples held in people's homes featuring a range of international guest speakers as well as her own insights into a woman's role in Judaism.[216] Knesset Yehezkel has also conducted outreach work to help reconnect families with their Sephardi origins and to develop learning skills among those who have engaged in relatively little study.[217]

Over the last decade there has been a major expansion in the number of *kollelim* in Golders Green where married men devote themselves to studying either on a full- or part-time basis. These are not vocational institutes for training rabbis but follow the time-honoured Jewish tradition of learning Torah for its own sake. Some people have the means to support themselves while they study; others rely on donations. The Golders Green *kollelim* are Kollel Harabonim at Beth Yisochor Dov Beth Hamedrash ('Hager's shul'), Kollel Baalai Batim at Ohel Moshe shul, Kollel Be'er Simcha at Etz Chaim Yeshivah, Kollel Boker at Beis Hamedrash Shaarei Tefillah, Kollel Kesser at Yisroel Beis Hamedrash Ohr, Kollel Brura Etz Chaim Yeshivah, and Kollel Tiferes Zvi. Each of these *kollelim* has a different programme.

Munk's shul runs a *kollel* for retired people on certain weekday mornings and Knesset Yehezkel Beth Hamedrash has a *kollel* where both young married and retired people study each morning.

The upsurge of interest in Jewish learning was not confined to the orthodox sections of Anglo-Jewry. By the time that Alyth Gardens Synagogue celebrated its 50th anniversary in 1983, over 200 adults were participating in an adult leaning programme, which had been given a new lease of life by the appointment in 1978 of the synagogue's first Director of Education, Joseph Schiff.[218] The programme included Hebrew classes, courses in Jewish history and Jewish life and worship together with workshops on Jewish London and Israel.[219] Today the synagogue's adult learning programme, *Otzar*, includes a regular 'Scholar in Residence' session at which rabbis, scholars and cantors share their knowledge and thoughts, a monthly study group that examines topical and ethical issues, a Home Study Group bringing members together in a home environment to extend their understanding of Judaism, a programme of lectures, *Moreinu*, from internationally recognised speakers, special study sessions for festivals, a pre-service *Shabbat Shiurim*, a Talmud class and an Introduction to Judaism class.[220]

Following the retirement of Reverend Livingstone, the rabbis who succeeded him at Dunstan Road Synagogue introduced progressively more extensive learning programmes. Rabbi Newman ran *shiurim* on weekday mornings and a Talmud *shiur* on Saturday afternoons.[221] Rabbi Sacks placed more emphasis on study of texts and introduced an innovative programme of adult learning, including Tuesday evening study sessions (the Synagogue Education Centre).[222] However, the pace of change was too fast for some members of the congregation, including the very traditional Dayan Moshe Swift, who sometimes sat in the front row of the synagogue 'with his lips pursed because he didn't like Rabbi Sacks using non-Jewish sources and interspersing philosophy with his study of texts'.[223] Dayan Swift gave his own regular flamboyant lectures on 'authentic Judaism', which were apparently a source of entertainment.[224]

Rabbi Ivan Binstock introduced a termly adult education lecture series, but learning opportunities were somewhat in abeyance during the Dunstan Road Synagogue's period of turbulence.[225] However, in recent years there has been a major increase in adult learning under the leadership of Rabbi Belovski, who is a highly regarded educator in Anglo-Jewry and has attracted to the congregation many academics.[226] The current weekly programme includes a Sunday morning session, Contemporary Conundrums, a Monday evening *shiur* on Gemara, a *Shabbat* morning session on issues in Jewish theology, a *Shabbat* afternoon session on Rabbinic Authority and Halachic Multiplicity. A programme of guest *shiurim* and *Shabbatonim* (Saturday afternoon learning events) is open to the wider community.[227]

Taking all of these learning opportunities together, some educators in Golders Green consider that there may be an over-provision of some types of educational activities. Shuls are competing with each other and often prayer meetings and study sessions are not well attended.[228] The recent opening of the Jewish Cultural Centre

(JW3), in Hampstead, which is starting to draw people away from the area, may prove to be the catalyst for some form of reorganisation.

This chapter has underlined how much Jewish learning is based on the study of texts and the extent to which study is a social activity for Jews. However, education has also been a route to financial well-being, as the next chapter will show.

15

Earning a Living

For several centuries after the readmission of the Jews to Britain in 1656 their means of earning a living were confined to a restricted range of occupations, mainly in trading and finance. As society modernised, these restrictions lessened and Jews started to enter a wider range of occupations. By the early nineteenth century a small number of Jews had penetrated the professions but it was not until the latter part of the century that the last of the formal restrictions constraining Jewish employment opportunities were finally lifted. Until then the Jewish community specialised in light manufacturing businesses producing jewellery, clothing and furniture or dealing in imported goods, including food and tobacco. Even after Jewish emancipation some constraints remained. Some of the limitations resulted from *Shabbat* and festival prohibitions but often they were caused by the hostility of non-Jews. Some Jews changed their names to obtain jobs, especially middle-class occupations.

Few employment opportunities were open to the large number of Jews who came to Britain from Eastern Europe during the late nineteenth and early twentieth century since they arrived with few skills and little English. They were mostly employed in tailoring, cabinet-making, cigarette manufacturing and boot-, shoe-, cap- and hat-making. They often worked as 'sweated labour' in appalling conditions and for very low wages. Women were also employed in the East End workshops, but generally in the least skilled jobs and for even lower rates of pay. With their preference for self-employment, which allowed them to observe the Sabbath and Jewish festivals, many immigrants rented market stalls or set up shops, largely selling goods to the Jewish community. Bread, butcher and grocery shops were the most common types of Jewish retailing. However, these forms of employment were transitional. As the community developed from one dominated by recent immigrants to being mainly British-born, there was both a widening of the occupational experience of Jews and a rise in their socio-economic status. The move of Jews to the suburbs was a stimulus to and a manifestation of changing employment patterns.

Some of the very first Jews to settle in Golders Green were the owners of successful businesses trading in the sectors in which Jews had traditionally been employed: a kosher butcher (Isaac Cohen, living in Park Drive); a gentlemen's tailor

(Carl Klipstein, 10 Hamilton Road); a theatrical outfitter (William Elkan, living in Hodford Road); a cabinet-maker (Frank Morgenstern, 39 Montpelier Rise); a Russian jeweller and watchmaker (Francis Ephraim Hieger, living in St John's Road). The first families also included a Jewish music-hall artist (Harry Simms, 32 Hamilton Road) – an occupation that was becoming more common for Jews as a way out of the 'ghetto' based on their early experience of singing in synagogue and the strong theatrical tradition in the Jewish community – a Russian writer (Dr Samuel Max Melamed);[1] an antiques dealer (Reuben Shenker, who was born in Russia but had previously lived in Grimsby, one of the destinations for immigrants who came by ships from Baltic ports); an Hungarian gentlemen's tailor (Julius Becko) and a Dutch piano importer (Abram van Leeuwen, living in Golders Green Crescent).[2]

It is interesting to note that among the early arrivals there were a number of German-Jewish families, who, like others in London at this time, had come to take advantage of increasing trading opportunities, often having gained experience in family firms before their arrival.[3] These residents included Albert Tannenbaum, a jewellery broker at 21a Golders Green Parade; Samuel Kuhn, an importer of Eastern Art at 20 Powis Gardens; John Lotz, a diamond trader living in Golders Green Road; and Ludwig Heil, a baker living in Hodford Mansions.[4] There were also some professionals from Germany and Austria including Moritz Kahn, a civil engineer at 20 Ravenscroft Avenue, and Jacob Schumer, at 103 Hodford Road, who trained as a doctor in Vienna.[5]

These early settlers were soon joined by a number of Jewish entrepreneurs, whose businesses had expanded as a result of introducing modern methods of large-scale production and distribution, including Benjamin Drage (né Cohen) who lived in Woodstock Road.[6] Mr Drage owned a furniture retailing business that had relocated from Spitalfields to Oxford Street. He was a pioneer in 'easy payment' on credit[7] and is said to have been wealthy before he arrived in Golders Green.[8]

Among the Jews who came to Golders Green in greater numbers from 1914 were a number of East End entrepreneurs who had become prosperous during the First World War.[9] Some had been involved in the clothing industry and had obtained lucrative government contracts to make uniforms for the armed forces, the so-called 'khaki-boom'. Others had been cabinet-makers who had obtained orders for ammunition boxes, pre-fabricated huts and furniture for barracks.[10] The successful traders from the East End included the son of a successful hardware merchant, Solomon (Sol) Karet, and Mr M.K. Greidinger, who had an egg and a general provisions business operating in Mile End and close to Tower Bridge.[11] Both of these successful merchants, like Benjamin Drage mentioned above, were prominent in the establishment of Dunstan Road Synagogue.[12]

The Jews who arrived in Golders Green either during or immediately after the First World War also included a number of clothing manufacturers who had relocated their workshops to the West End to be close to the showrooms and warehouses that had grown up there, and those running shoemaking businesses,

which had moved to north London as they had grown and outstripped the
space available in the cramped streets of the East End. There were, however, a
few professional people who came from other parts of London and outside the
capital, such as Alfred Ackerman, a civil engineer at 9 Rotherwick Road who had
previously lived in Fulham, and Dr William Feldman, who had previously lived in
Whitechapel Road.[13]

The occupations of the early Jewish settlers were distinguishable from those
people who had lived in Golders Green before the opening of the railway station
and the non-Jewish people who bought the new suburban housing. Until the 1930s
there remained in Golders Green several small cottages, rows of terraced houses and
farm properties housing people engaged in rural and agricultural occupations – farm
labourers, dairymen, Mr Suckling the farrier, Mr Hudgell the wheelwright and
Mr Segeren, a horse dealer – and those working in the brickworks that had been
the main industry in the area. Among the non-Jewish people settling in the area
were many who were employed as civil servants and in senior clerical occupations,
commissioned members of the armed forces, bank managers, barristers and company
directors. There were also a significant number of non-Jews with 'private means'.[14]
The general prosperity of the new suburb was a stark contrast to the poverty and
unemployment experienced in other parts of the country during the 1920s.

Many of the successful Jewish shopkeepers and entrepreneurs who came to
Golders Green during the first two decades of the twentieth century had previously
lived 'over the shop' or in close proximity to their workplaces. They initially became
commuters, travelling daily to their places of business, like Hyman Hovsha, a dentist
who travelled to his practice in Commercial Road.[15] However, by the late 1920s
an increasing number of Jews were establishing businesses in Golders Green, either
in the well-established shopping parades, based in their homes or in nearby retail
areas,[16] including some Jewish professionals like Dr Israel Feldman, who had a
medical practice in Hodford Road,[17] and Ralph Pinto, who had set up a chartered
accountant's office at 25 The Parade.[18] Living alongside the numerous tailors,
costumiers and outfitters who set up shops in Golders Green in the 1920s[19] were
Jews who had succeeded in the world of property, such as Reuben Lincoln who, in
addition to his holdings elsewhere, gradually acquired the freeholds of a significant
proportion of the commercial property in Golders Green.[20]

Despite the Great Depression, by the 1930s the Golders Green Jewish community
was becoming increasingly prosperous:

When my family moved to Golders Green in the 1920s they had a gown
workshop with a showroom in Great Portland Street. The business, the BP Gown
Company, had relocated there from Bishopsgate. They employed designers and
a lot of outdoor workers. In the 1930s the business was doing so well that my
parents were able to employ a chauffeur. At this time there was quite a lot of peer
pressure in the Jewish community to succeed in business and to make enough
money to finance a decent lifestyle.[21]

Although some Jews may have been content with becoming successful businessmen in traditional Jewish arenas, this is not what they wanted for their children. The middle-class aspirations of Jews had been raised by their move to suburbia and, as we have already seen, parents were placing a great deal of emphasis on education as a means for improving the upward mobility of their offspring. As a result, younger people were now moving into a variety of occupations such as insurance brokering, pharmacy, engineering and property. Boris Prevezer, whose family lived in Dunstan Road, became a successful estate agent trading in South Molton Street.[22] A small number of men made it into the professions including Mr Sharpe (né Shapiro), the son of an East End cabinet-maker, who became a successful accountant.[23] Others did not quite make it into the professions. Having obtained a degree in economics, Harold Langdon worked with the accountancy firm Peat Marwick Mitchell during the 1930s. He did not become a qualified accountant but took over the running of the family clothing business during the 1940s.[24] The widening horizons of suburban young people in the inter-war years were a stark contrast to the prospects for young Jews still living in the East End who were now often working in different occupations from their parents but not ones that improved their socio-economic status.[25]

The socio-economic profile of the Jewish community of Golders Green was changed significantly by the arrival of the refugees from Central Europe. A large proportion of the refugees were professionals, academics, artists and industrialists. Government restrictions were placed on the employment of the refugees whose skills were not generally welcomed in Britain, especially those of doctors and dentists. Many highly experienced practitioners were required by the Home Office to 're-qualify' and professional associations, intent on defending the interests of their members, allowed only a handful of doctors and dentists to be registered.[26] One of the few doctors able to overcome all the hurdles was Dr Avraham Adler, whose famed Leipzig medical practice and university research had led to his skills being in demand throughout Europe. Although the British medical profession supported his move to the country in 1937, he was nevertheless obliged to retrain at Guy's Hospital before setting up his practice in Golders Green.[27] He and another refugee, Dr M. Seckbach, became well known in the area and attracted a high proportion of patients with a continental background.[28] This possibly allayed any fears there might have been about their taking patients away from existing practices in the area.

The continental refugees arriving in Britain before 1938 generally fared better economically than those who came immediately before the war, since by then the refugees were unable to bring any assets with them, and the government had introduced even tighter restrictions on their employment.[29] Some of the early refugee businesses set up in Golders Green in the mid-1930s included those that made use of their proprietor's connections in Europe, including the continental food importing business established by Erwin Kallir at his home in Russell Gardens.[30] Although only a small number of refugee businesses were well established before war commenced, some were successful enough to employ other continental refugees.

Herbert Landsberg, who arrived in Golders Green in 1935, obtained employment in his uncle's costume jewellery business.[31] Harry Morton (né Helmut Moser), who lived with an aunt and uncle in Golders Green, worked for two and a half years making truffles in the chocolate business founded by his aunt that operated from the kitchen of her home.[32] Robert Goldman from Frankfurt registered for military service and was issued with a temporary work permit he used to work as a delivery boy at the kosher butchers set up by the Frohwein family. The Frohweins had arrived relatively recently themselves, but already needed help on Thursdays and Fridays as *Shabbat* approached.[33]

By 1938 many continental refugees who had been used to a comfortable middle-class existence were forced to accept work as domestic servants or sweeping factory floors. These were among the few jobs for which they were able to obtain a visa to gain entry to Britain. To acquire these positions they either advertised themselves, or friends and acquaintances did so on their behalf. A typical advertisement in the *Jewish Chronicle* read: 'German Jew, single, speaks English, drives car, desires post as manservant or similar, c/o 2a Hoop Lane, NW11'.[34]

Some refugees employed in Jewish households in Golders Green were given a warm welcome; others had less happy experiences. Viennese refugee Lotte Hümbelin lived for a while in Golders Green with an émigré family from Vienna. Despite being Social Democrats, they apparently expected her to work fifteen hours a day indulging their whims and those of their guests.[35] While younger refugees were able to accept the loss of status as a temporary measure and remained optimistic they would eventually find situations matching their aspirations, older people with long and successful careers found menial jobs hard to bear, such as the former judge who worked with his wife as housekeepers to the Sharpe family in Dunstan Road.[36]

Traditionally young Jewish women had worked close to home until they married, typically in occupations such as millinery and dressmaking. With the move to the suburbs young women began to work in what were regarded as the more refined occupations such as secretaries and shorthand typists. Before the Second World War most women still ceased working when they married, but a small number were continuing their employment until they had children.[37] Most Jewish parents still regarded the careers of their sons as being more important than those of their daughters. By the 1930s a few Jewish women were employed in non-traditional occupations and had very successful careers, especially those who did not marry. After a short career working in repertory theatre, Jacqueline Morris became an interpreter, having learned French from the au pairs employed by her family. She obtained a well-paid position in the External Telephone Executive, translating messages to be relayed to people in other countries.[38] Selina Gellert's two great-aunts who did not marry had fulfilling careers. One became secretary to the MP Sir William Duthie and the other worked for a film company. Very unusual indeed however, was the experience of Maria Phillips (née Westell) whose family settled in Heath Close in about 1908. After leaving South Hampstead High School, where she had been head girl, Maria Phillips was encouraged by her father to train as a barrister. Having studied at Middle Temple, she became one of the first women barristers in the country, a career that ended with her marriage in 1925.[39]

Since they were not bound by the same traditions and because of their generally greater level of assimilation and education, a large proportion of the women continental refugees who came to Golders Green prior to the Second World War worked in a wider range of occupations than indigenous Jewish women. Either by choice or due to economic necessity, they were sometimes the main wage earners.[40] Historical accounts suggest that, on the whole, women refugees adapted better to life in a new country and were more flexible in their employment patterns than some of their spouses, especially women over the age of 45.[41]

Examples of the resourcefulness of continental refugee women in Golders Green include the story of Marion Kreindler's mother, who arrived just a few months before the Second World War and who had the foresight to take a course in corsetry and buy a sewing machine to start a business shortly before leaving Germany. She had to leave behind the jewellery and collection of antiques built up by her father, but was able to bring the sewing machine with her to England. Alongside her corsetry business she worked in a canteen and as a housekeeper to make ends meet.[42] As a married woman Kathe Trenter was unable to obtain a work permit. However, she met a young Russian girl and her mother outside the baker's near where she was living in Highcroft Gardens. The mother employed Kathe, who was 'practically penniless', to look after her daughter.[43] The woman who established the chocolate business mentioned above did so after learning the skills involved from another woman refugee. According to her nephew, she worked fifteen hours a day, seven days a week to build up the business and was 'ruthless' in her business dealings.[44]

During the Second World War Jews from Golders Green were very active in all of the armed services. This enabled some people, both men and women, to gain new skills and experience, like Boris Prevezer who joined the army and trained as a radiographer. However, some careers were interrupted by the war. Lola Rodin's husband started training as an accountant. He was called up at the age of 21 and he had to take a refresher course when he was demobbed before he could resume his career.[45] Some Jews were employed in what were classified as 'reserved occupations', including Nancie Craig, who was working as a secretary with Rothschilds, which meant that she could not serve full time in the armed services. However, she gained additional experience by joining the St John Ambulance Brigade.[46]

While some businesses struggled in wartime conditions, others found new niches:

> During the war my family switched to selling hosiery wholesale. The new business initially operated from the front dining room in our home. My father acquired batches of seconds that sold really well. He employed me to match the stockings in pairs. I earned one half penny for each dozen pairs I matched. I once managed to make 5 shillings. That was a lot of money![47]

The development of many fledgling refugee businesses was curtailed when their owners were interned, especially when people were away for some time. On their release from internment some refugees joined the non-combatant Pioneer Corps, which had several 'aliens' companies. Later both men and women refugees were accepted into a variety of active service units where some found themselves in the peculiar position of returning to Germany as liberators. Following his internment, Harry Morton joined the Pioneer Corps and subsequently the Royal Artillery, Anti-Aircraft Regiment 81.[48] The refugees who joined the Pioneer Corps were obliged to change their names. Steven Derby's father joined the Pioneer Corps in 1939. When he was stationed at Newmarket he was told that he could not keep the name Schachter in case Germans captured him and treated him as a traitor rather than a prisoner of war. So he chose the name Derby because he knew that Newmarket had something to do with horses and a well-known horserace was the Derby.[49]

A number of refugees who did not join the armed forces were drafted into war work such as working in factories, which was sometimes an improvement on the positions they had occupied pre-war but still not the type of work to which they had previously been accustomed.[50] However, a few worked in high-profile positions, including Markus Schillaj, who fled from Frankfurt and settled in Golders Green in 1937. During the Blitz he worked as a special envoy for food importation for which he won many awards.[51]

Some women who would have preferred to continue working after they were married came into their own during the war when they took on stimulating voluntary occupations:

> My mother was highly intelligent and very educated. She was quite bored not working but in those days married women who did not need to work stayed at home. She felt needed during the war when she joined the Women's Voluntary Service and was in charge of National Savings Schemes for the area working from a shop in Golders Green Road. It was such a waste of her talents when she had to stop![52]

Having served in the armed forces, some indigenous Jewish men found it difficult to obtain employment after the war. Ronald Friedman, who returned to Golders Green in 1948, recalls:

> I couldn't get a job. I tried to get into the film studios but one had to be a union member and the union was not taking new members until the old ones had their jobs back. I then tried to get into advertising but ended up at the Law Society School in Lancaster Place. I did three years' articles instead of five because of war service.[53]

In the immediate post-war years many of the continental refugees living in Golders Green also struggled to find a foothold to build a secure existence, even after they were naturalised and restrictions on their employment were lifted:

My father worked in business with my grandfather for several years but there was not enough income for two families. He eventually became a salesman in the plastics industry after an interlude trying to run a shop in Notting Hill. It was a general type of corner store. Someone else ran it on *Shabbat* and took profits for that day. My mother worked with him and we had an au pair for a few years.[54]

Employers tended to give preference to British applicants returning from war service over 'foreigners' with stilted English.[55] Becoming established was often not straightforward for people who had not completed their education before they were uprooted. Isca Wittenberg recalls:

The Jewish Refugee Committee sent me to Yorkshire to train as a nursery nurse. The place where I did my training was cold and there were mice running up and down the curtains. The matron welcomed me by saying that as the committee had paid half the fees I needed to work twice as hard. I was thoroughly miserable but decided to stay when I became very attached to a little boy I was caring for who had a heart condition. Later the Jewish Refugee Committee obtained a scholarship for me to go to Birmingham University where I studied to become a social worker. Once I had qualified, I was invited back as a lecturer.[56]

By the 1950s the economic position of the continental Jews was clearly changing. The education, skills and ambition that many of the ex-refugees had brought with them had obviously stood them in good stead. Although they could never compensate for their suffering, restitution payments from West Germany alleviated the position of some of those who had previously struggled. Professional people living in Golders Green were now engaged in their own successful practices or in well-paid positions in local firms. For example, Mr M. Schwab had a thriving dental practice attached to his home in Bridge Lane,[57] and Ellis and Co., located at 52 Golders Green Road, advertised in the journal of the Association of Jewish Refugees (AJR) to say that they had appointed 'Mr H. Reichenbach, formerly of Berlin'.[58] By 1960 there were at least twelve medical practitioners living in Golders Green with German-Jewish names, two of whom were women doctors.[59]

A number of ex-refugees set up businesses, mainly in the fields of fancy goods, leatherwear, stationery, toys, bags, clothing and textiles,[60] which were beginning to produce a reasonable income. A number of the businesses springing up in Golders Green in the 1950s had a distinctly continental feel to them, like M. Oberlander & Son at 783 Finchley Road, 'caterers with that fine continental touch'.[61] Sometimes these businesses were quite small scale, like the honey-bottling business established by the Bentley family, some of the processes for which were carried out on the kitchen table in their home in Prince's Park Avenue.[62] By comparison, another refugee family, who had arrived in Golders Green from Frankfurt in 1935, set up a vinyl printing company based in Crouch End. It was highly successful and by the 1950s had contracts with some major non-Jewish clients. Some of the businesses run by the continental refugees in Golders Green were quite innovative for the time, such as the photocopying service Golders Trading Company that operated for several years at 54 Golders Gardens.[63]

By the end of the decade some ex-refugee families who had initially held low-status jobs were now sufficiently prosperous to employ post-war immigrants from continental countries in the sorts of roles they had occupied just twenty years earlier.[64] The columns of AJR newsletter *Information* regularly included advertisements for domestic assistance needed by families in Golders Green, such as the one appearing in June 1957 seeking part-time help to assist a housewife with weekend tea parties.[65] The children of Jewish refugees born in Britain were acquiring an education and qualifications that would equip them for the new job opportunities that emerged in the affluent 1960s. Victor Hochhauser, whose family came from Slovakia, became one of the youngest impresarios in the country. He started promoting artists and stage shows when he was just 22 and by the time he was 34 he was touring the country with Mario Lanza and had options on appearances of both the Bolshoi and Leningrad ballet companies.[66]

According to the historian Anthony Grenville, no account of the post-war employment patterns of the former refugees is complete without a mention of the boarding houses set up for refugees by other refugees. They were oases of continental culture as well as a source of income for those who ran them.[67] Prime examples of these boarding houses in Golders Green were those run by Mr W. Halberstadt (a member of Munk's shul) at 38 West Heath Drive ('permanent guests and visitors are welcome; meals optional'),[68] by Mr A. Joelson at 7a Basing Hill and by S. Fleishmann at 10 West Heath Drive.[69] These continental boarding houses were later replaced by a new generation of hotels run by the offspring of ex-refugees like the kosher Croft Court Hotel that opened in Ravenscroft Avenue in the 1970s run by Mr and Mrs Shapira.

However, some ex-refugee families continued to live in straitened circumstances and may have been reliant on the AJR Employment Agency, which not only helped people to find jobs but also organised training courses to help people move up the social ladder.[70] Some of those still arriving from the continent to join former refugees already settled in Golders Green took a while to establish their career:

> When I came to England in 1956 I initially worked in a well-known bookshop in the East End, Shapiro/Vallentine. I catalogued books and my experience enabled me to get a job at the Wiener Library. I then worked for a while as a numismatist in Hatton Garden before going on to catalogue a collection of books for the famous book collector, Jack Lunzer. I made such a good job of it that he recommended me for a job as the librarian at Jews' College where I worked for twenty years.[71]

On the whole, the Indian Jews who started to come to Golders Green in the 1950s did not fare as well economically as the continental refugees. Although they fitted in better culturally, they had little or no capital and their former qualifications and experience were of little relevance. Many of the newcomers found themselves working in factories or selling merchandise on market stalls to earn a living, including David Elias, who became a local communal leader.[72] The Egyptian Jews who arrived in Golders Green shortly after the Indian Jews initially found themselves under-employed – bankers became office clerks, students became shop assistants – but some of them later became quite affluent. This was attributed to the fact that, unlike the Indian Jews, they were financially compensated by the British government for the loss of their homes in Egypt.[73]

The Iraqi Jews who settled in Golders Green starting in the 1970s were mainly business people who had shops and clothing enterprises in the East End and in Regent Street. Their offspring took over the businesses but often either changed the direction of the businesses or had second careers. However, a large proportion of the second- and third-generation Iraqi Jews, who have mostly had a university education, are now mainly working in the professions rather than in business. Nadia Nathan, who came to Golders Green in 1972, raised two sons, one of whom became a lawyer and the other a lobbyist: 'My sons' generation rarely think of working for themselves, having seen the collapse of prominent Iraqi businesses in the East End'.[74] Although a small number of Iraqi Jews living in Golders Green are still business people, there are very few Iraqi businesses based in the area apart from the Golders Green Hotel run by the Kattan family, Sami's restaurant and Taboon bakery and takeaway.[75] Most of the South Africans who arrived in Golders Green during the 1960s and 1970s were professional people – dentists, lawyers, academics[76] – including Abraham Adelstein, who lived in Dunstan Road and served as the medical statistician in the General Register Office.[77]

Although traditional Jewish occupations were abandoned with rapidity in the post-war years,[78] people continued to arrive in Golders Green who were employed in longstanding Jewish occupations, including a number of tailors. Some of these tailors established businesses in the area or close by, like Gerald Peters's father, who set up a tailoring business in Child's Hill.[79] However, a number retained their businesses in their original locations, especially those with well-established contacts:

> My father, like his father before him, was a tailor – he made jackets for Saville Row tailors. He shared premises in Foley Street with a number of other tailors who each had their own tables. They used old-fashioned gas irons to press the jackets that they made. He came home for dinner but soon afterwards he would start work again. I used to thread needles for him. It was a hard life but there was sometimes laughter. My father sold jackets to a tailor in The Cut near Waterloo and I remember going there with him in a taxi to make deliveries. These visits were one of the highlights of my childhood – the banter in the shop was hilarious![80]

At Dunstan Road Synagogue, the post-war congregation was largely made up of tradespeople, including jewellers, furriers, tailors and milliners,[81] but the younger generation were not encouraged to follow such trades. The desideratum of the early

Golders Green families was the professions, which represented status, independence and economic security, all of which were very important to former immigrants.[82] After the Second World War there was a significant rise in the number of young people who trained as doctors, dentists, lawyers and accountants. Some of those who entered the professions in the post-war years became very prominent, including David Freeman who has been described as 'one of the most successful and well-connected solicitors in London'.[83] His family had moved to Golders Green from the East End in the 1940s. After leaving Christ's College School he had been intent on reading history at Oxford but was advised by his father to 'get a job'. He took articles and founded the successful law firm D.J. Freeman in 1952 shortly after he qualified, which became a leading law firm in the City.

Not all young people in Golders Green went into the professions. Increasingly attractive were careers in local government, teaching (including university lecturers and professors), and the expanding caring professions. Some young people were also keen to pursue careers in the arts and entertainment. Whereas Mr Manuel, a prominent member of Dunstan Road Synagogue, ran a fruit and vegetable business in Covent Garden, his son Michael attended the Royal Academy of Arts and after working as the stage manager for the Royal Ballet became head of the Metropolitan Opera in America.[84] Another example of talent emerging from Golders Green is Raymond Gubbay. After leaving University College School in Hampstead, Raymond Gubbay worked briefly with his father, a chartered accountant, which he 'detested', and then Pathé News before founding in 1966 his own firm of concert promoters arranging events at major London venues.[85] Gubbay is noted for popularising the arts and for founding the London Concert Orchestra.[86] Via a circuitous route, Norman Myers also found himself working as an entertainer:

> What I really wanted to do was to work in films so in 1949 I started my own company, Greville Films. In time Greville Films began showing movies after tea at children's parties. This in turn eventually led to my becoming a full-time party entertainer in the 1950s.[87]

Other young people were entrepreneurs, finding niche markets and demonstrating the business flair reminiscent of their foreign-born grandparents:

> I didn't want to go into the family factory based in the East End, which made walking sticks and umbrellas. I did an HNC in mechanical engineering and got involved in selling cars before setting up a business in Sardinia. When I came home after I married, I had a business printing business cards for cab companies. I found a little factory in Euston and someone gave me a print machine, which I paid for gradually. I was the only specialist card printer in London, doing all the artwork myself. Then I started a plumbing company and after that a mini cab business. When I discovered that there wasn't anywhere for plumbers to go to get a decent cup of tea, I opened a café in West Hampstead. All my businesses were successful.[88]

By the 1960s there was an important colony of Jewish poets and writers living in Golders Green, including the well-known doctor-poet Dannie Abse, his neighbour, the South African novelist and critic Dan Jacobson,[89] and Simon Blumenfeld, author and journalist, who lived in Wessex Gardens. There were also a number of artists, perhaps the most famous of whom was the designer and poster artist Abram Games who lived in The Vale for many decades. The son of immigrants from Russia who moved to Golders Green from the East End, Games designed the emblem for the United Synagogue, the motif for the *Encyclopaedia Britannica*, one of the early BBC logos and the Festival of Britain Symbol, working from a studio attached to his home.[90] The roll call of well-known Jewish residents at this time also included several prominent musicians and singers, including the viola player Leo Birney (né Birnbaum)[91] and Frankie Vaughan (né Abelson), who lived in Western Avenue.

After the war employment patterns changed dramatically for women. As a result of the increased number going to university, some women embarked on high-powered careers in non-traditional fields. During the Second World War Naomi Rose read chemistry at Oxford and became a research scientist studying water pollution, while Barbara Michaels obtained a degree in psychology at Birkbeck College and became an educational psychologist.[92] Hazel Sheldon went to college to learn shorthand after her education was disrupted by the war. She worked as a personal assistant but was 'totally bored', so she entered the family business, the Franks lingerie shop in Golders Green,[93] which she took to 'like a duck to water', especially after she started buying for the store.[94] In line with the changes taking place in the workforce generally, many more Jewish women were now working after they married and returned to work, usually on a part-time basis, after raising their children.

Although they lagged behind young men, from the 1960s onwards an increasing number of young women from Golders Green became doctors and lawyers. Selina Gellert recalls how her parents changed the school she attended to ensure that she obtained the academic background she needed to become a doctor.[95] She made it to medical school but not without overcoming some hurdles – some medical schools still had quotas for the number of women that they would admit. The progress made by Jewish women over three generations was clearly discernible:

> My grandmother had a job at Harrods. My mother's generation were encouraged to work but even more so my generation. We were told that, like men, we could be lawyers and dentists and carry on working after we had our families.[96]

The entrepreneurial spirit that women refugees had demonstrated in the pre-war years was fully evident by the 1950s. Madame Leiberg and her Finchley Road store selling ladies' foundation garments had a high profile across London. However, equally successful was another corsetiere, Mrs E. Sonnenfeld, who worked from her home at 24 St John's Road;[97] and Mrs Frieda Freiwal, living at 24 Gainsborough Gardens, who set up a mobile chiropody business using 'modern appliances'.[98]

Hilde Galton opened a flower shop at 75 Golders Green Road in 1948, her previous shop in Berlin having been destroyed on *Kristallnacht*. Her daughter, Brita Wolff, who also became a florist and worked in the business, recalls that some very well-known continental people frequented the shop like Lady Zahava Kohn, Lucie Rie (ceramist), Sigi Nissel (Amadeus String Quartet), and Lord Ludwig Schon.[99] The shop remained open until 2009, when the Brent Cross branch of the business became the main store.[100]

Some former refugee women also pursued highly successful artistic careers, including Ruth Aaronson and Lucy Press. Ruth Aaronson came as a refugee to Golders Green from Leipzig aged 6 months in 1938. Having been educated at Orange Hill Grammar School, she went on to St Martins School of Art. She was discouraged by her family from becoming a singer but eventually made it into broadcasting and became 'the hostess with the mostest' on a Canadian TV show.[101] Born in Warsaw, Lucy Press came to Golders Green in 1937 and studied at the Arts and Crafts School in Southampton Row and St Martins School of Art. She became a successful designer with her work being exhibited at the Ben Uri Gallery.[102]

The number of both men and women entering occupations that differed vastly from those of their grandparents reached its zenith in the 1980s. From that time onwards the economic profile of the Jewish community began to change again. This was partly because young people were moving away from the area to the outer London suburbs, leaving behind older people who either worked in more traditional occupations or who were retired. The other factor that affected the economic profile of the community was the arrival in increasing numbers of *haredim*, among whom there were fewer working women. Although Golders Green was still a haven for middle-class professionals, it was less so than neighbouring Hampstead Garden Suburb and Finchley,[103] and there were fewer women who were economically active.[104]

Employment patterns for the *haredim* in Britain differ from the wider Anglo-Jewish community. There are also different occupational structures for the various elements that make up the *haredim*.[105] Since Munk's shul was founded, many of its members have earned their livings as merchants, industrialists, doctors, lawyers and academics.[106] Benjamin Sachs, who grew up in the Munk's community, feels privileged that as a child he would spend Friday nights listening to intense secular and non-secular discussions with his extended family that included the 'intellectual giants' Rabbi Dr Joseph Rosenwasser, a keeper of Semitics at the British Museum, and Siegfried Stein, founder of the Hebrew Department at University College London.[107] In the past a common pattern was for Germanic *haredim* to defer marriage to enable them both to spend time on religious studies at a *yeshivah* and subsequently to gain the skills required to pursue careers providing a secure income.[108] However, more recently, some younger Munk's members have been marrying earlier and continuing their university and professional careers afterwards to counteract the risks and temptations seen as being associated with mixed-sex educational and training establishments.[109]

One of the best-known and revered Munk's congregants was Dr Shlomo Adler, the son of Avraham Adler (see page 188), who trained as a doctor at Guy's Hospital during the Second World War while studying in London's Etz Chaim *yeshivah*, then located in the East End. Rabbi Leib Gurwicz, Adler's learning partner, later recounted that even during the dash to the shelters when the sirens sounded, the young medical student did not stop learning.[110] Following his father's untimely death just after the war, Dr Shlomo Adler inherited the widely respected practices his father had established in Golders Green and in Bryanston Square.[111] His daily routine was seemingly superhuman: he would conduct his surgery for long hours – people were prepared to wait until midnight if necessary in order to see him[112] – and then, after snatching a quick meal, he would commence his night visits, which could continue until the early hours of the morning without respite.[113] Dr Adler had patients in Stamford Hill as well as in Golders Green and he treated many prominent Hassidic rabbis: 'People came from miles around to consult him'.[114]

Today a number of the accountancy, architectural and other practices operating from home offices or from small business premises in Golders Green are run by orthodox Jews of German origin. There are also some German orthodox dental surgeries and opticians, either located in the main shopping parades or in premises attached to private houses.[115] For example, for many years Nathan Gluck, the *chazzan* at Munk's shul, has operated the Hearing Aid Centre in Wentworth Road.

Litvishe Jews have historically been engaged in occupations akin to those of the wider Anglo-Jewish community. When they first arrived in Britain they generally worked as skilled and semi-skilled tradespeople and then entered middle-class occupations, especially the professions and careers in education. However, more recently, respect for and involvement in the professions among *Litvishe* Jews has decreased. The shift has been particularly noticeable among those families who have 'moved right' and have become more orthodox:

> My generation were all encouraged to become professionals. I trained as a lawyer and one of my brothers as an accountant. Now *yeshivot* steer young men away from becoming professionals because this means going to university, which are both secular and mixed sex which is frowned upon. Some orthodox young people do become accountants because they can study for that online but that's not the case for becoming a doctor.[116]

While professional occupations may no longer be attractive to *Litvishe* men living in Golders Green, they are not generally content with unskilled work like labouring or driving, or with entering the blue-collar trades such as plumbing. As a result, young *Litvishe* men often prepare for the world of work by obtaining vocational qualifications, such as in surveying, mainly through distance learning while still studying at *yeshivah* or shortly after they leave.[117]

Traditionally Hassidic Jews in London relied for a living on small businesses and trades that did not need secular education or professional training with which, in comparison with both the German and *Litvishe haredim*, the community had no historical association.[118] However, over the years, there has been a diversification of employment as Hassidic Jews have become more committed to the Torah learning, formerly the preserve of the Germanic and *Litvishe* Jews. While some Hassidic Jews were able to commit themselves to a life of learning by relying on family and philanthropic support, others have found occupations that have allowed them to combine learning and earning: working within the *haredi* community (for example as religious functionaries, or as teachers in *haredi* schools), in the diamond and jewellery industries, in property, and in retail services.[119]

Chapter 9 described how Hassidic Jews moving to Golders Green have become more open to the pressures of consumerism. As a result, some Hassidic Jews living in the area have sought ways of earning a living that will enable them to become 'men of means' without compromising their *haredi* lifestyle.[120] In recent years an increasing number of *Hassidim* have begun to engage in part-time work while they are still studying, not only as a source of income but also to develop skills that will be of use when they enter the workforce full time. However, compared to the Germanic and *Litvishe* Jews, Hassidic Jews still spend less time preparing themselves for full-time earning. Their entry to the labour market is often much more abrupt and their choice of occupations therefore more limited.[121]

Today a proportion of Hassidic Jews living in Golders Green earn their living by running companies that have passed from one generation to another,[122] by working in property, or more recently in IT. Some of the businesses operated by Hassidic Jews are still located in Stamford Hill, to which, like the early Jewish arrivals to Golders Green from the East End, they travel each day. This is because their clientele and lines of business are difficult to reproduce in another setting.[123] Employment in the diamond trade has decreased rapidly as this sector has become dominated by the Asian community,[124] while employment in the food industry is becoming more common.[125] Small numbers of young *Hassidim* are seeking employment in the wider world, although the majority still prefer working for Hassidic employers because they are sensitive to the norms of behaviour in *haredi* society: Hassidic dress, the daily prayer schedule, and trips to see relatives abroad. These roles are generally low paid. It appears that Hassidic employers also tend to prefer employing workers with the same background. One Jewish employee who has worked for a number of different kosher supermarkets in Golders Green explains:

> In these stores there is no role for employee recruitment. They first employ people who have a similar cultural identity. For example, if someone is from a certain town, like Satmar, he will first try to employ a Satmar, then, if he cannot, he will employ the person who is closest to his ways and traditions. It is easier to get a job from them if you are in their group.[126]

According to one interviewee, some young Hassidic men have started to acquire marketable skills such as in accountancy, which they have used to secure jobs in the financial sector or in large property companies run by Hassidic Jews to which they add expertise which sometimes previously had to be brought in from outside the *haredi* community.[127] These young men are sometimes referred to within the community as 'the yuppies of the *haredi* world'.[128] However, the pressures to earn money quickly, which become greater with marriage and a growing number of children, have led to a preference for self-employment, perceived as offering a faster route to improving one's economic situation.[129] There has also been an increased interest in skilled trades (such as plumbers and electricians) that were formerly avoided in Britain but which have been more popular in Hassidic communities in America.

At present there are resources within the Golders Green *haredi* community to support young men wishing to study either full time or part time. However, some members of the community have recognised that this situation is not sustainable and that the recent diversification in occupations is likely to become more prevalent among future generations.[130] Communal bodies are beginning to respond to the situation. For example, the *kollel* Ohr Hatorah in Golders Green offers accredited external degree courses in subjects such as mathematics and business studies alongside religious text studies, with the aim of equipping young men with the skills to obtain more lucrative employment.

The world of work is also changing for *haredi* women in Golders Green. In previous generations young *haredi* women were largely employed in family businesses or as teachers for the brief time between their leaving seminary and marrying, at which point they stopped working. Now more *haredi* women work after they are married in order to contribute to family finances, and they are also starting to pursue more demanding forms of employment. In some Hassidic households, women are generating a significant income by running businesses, often at night when their children are in bed. Some use the Internet to recruit clients and to operate on an international basis.[131]

Strictly orthodox Sephardi Jews living in Golders Green pursue a variety of occupations. Several operate the kosher businesses they have set up in the area; others are professionals, working in the jewellery trade or in property.[132]

From its early days as a suburb, Jews in Golders Green have been employed in occupations serving the needs of the local Jewish community. Initially these occupations were mainly confined to meeting the dietary needs of the community. However, by the late 1920s there was also a Jewish bookseller, E.J. Cox, located at 28 North End Road, who was supplying Jewish literature such as 'The Pentateuch and Lessons from the Prophets (*Haftorahs*) For use in Synagogue, School and Home'.[133] He was joined after the Second World War by Mr Sulzbacher in Sneath Avenue and by Matanot at 4 Russell Parade, which sold books and 'all kinds of religious articles'.[134] From 1970 Mr Rogosnitzky ran the Hebrew and Bar Mitzvah bookshop from 20 The Drive.[135]

As the *haredi* community has grown, the 'Jewish economy' has become both much more significant and diverse. From 1989 Bernard Benarroch operated from his home in Russell Gardens as a scribe using traditional methods handed down through generations. His first encounter with scrolls was when as a small child he crawled on to his father's workbench and, knocking over a bottle of ink, destroyed a whole section of a scroll, which had to be repaired by his father. He has a strong artistic bent and loves his work even though it is not a 'money spinner'. When he is writing, he feels the handwritten words speak to him.[136] He has recently moved his business into a new shop, Sofer Stam, in Russell Parade.

During the 1960s Mr Cohen ran an importing business for the *Arba minim* (the four species for *Sukkot*),[137] which operated from his sitting room in Leeside Crescent. The enterprise subsequently moved to the Machzikei Hadath Synagogue in Highfield Road before being taken over first by David Brager and then Stephen Colman at Munk's shul where the imported *Arba minim* are stored and sold. Some of the imports are marketed on various temporary stalls erected along Golders Green Road. In the last five years or so local entrepreneurs have set up temporary businesses selling *sukkahs*.

There are at least six local *sheitel* firms, many *mohellim* (Jews trained to perform circumcisions), mainly associated with the Union of Orthodox Hebrew Congregations, and traders specialising in *haredi* celebrations – event managers, florists, caterers, entertainers, filming and photographic services.[138] There are also a number of firms providing transport for the *haredi* community – private car hire and minibuses, transport for women. The expanding number of kosher eateries and shops provide an ever-increasing source of employment. Some of these enterprises have proved to be so successful that people have left professional jobs to enter the businesses, such as one of the sons of Mr Bendahan, who trained as a doctor but is now involved in the running of the Kosher Deli in Golders Green Road.[139]

Today there are fewer extremely wealthy Jewish business people than there were during the early years of the development of Golders Green. The wealthy people are mainly confined to the *haredi* community, and particularly the Hassidic community. A number of the grandchildren and great-grandchildren of the original Jewish families who settled in Golders Green have moved on from being professionals and business people to become politicians, MPs and academics living in new locations. As with other aspects of their lives, the *haredim* and Jews from other denominations within the Golders Green Jewish community are becoming more similar in their occupations and economic profile.

16

Conclusion

This history has described a series of waves of Jewish groups settling in Golders Green. The constant arrival of Jews with different national and religious backgrounds has meant that the community has always been very diverse. This feature distinguishes it from the homogeneous communities living in the Jewish ghettos of the past, and from some more modern Jewish enclaves such as Stamford Hill.

At different points in its evolution, particular Jewish groupings have dominated the community. In the early years when it was becoming established, there was a preponderance of Jewish families who had moved to Golders Green from the East End, often via Stamford Hill. In the last two decades the community has become noted for its large *haredi* element. However, while different groupings may have predominated at certain points, the community overall has remained richly diverse. The former East Enders joined families who had come to Golders Green from different parts of London, from outside the capital and from abroad. Although the *haredim* may be very visible because of their distinctive dress and lifestyles, the Jewish population today includes more sects, sub-groups and families originating from different countries than ever before.

In addition, any apparent dominance by particular groupings has proved to be transitional. The prominence of former East End Jews was reduced by the arrival of continental refugees, whose largely Germanic culture was very different from those with Eastern European backgrounds who had settled in Golders Green before the 1930s. Likewise, although the local *haredi* population is not diminishing, there are already signs of a new wave of settlement: Jews with Sephardi backgrounds are becoming an increasingly powerful force in the area.

The diversity of the Jewish community of Golders Green is not only its most outstanding feature; it also accounts for its endurance. Few Jews have felt excluded from living in Golders Green and, over the decades, different groups have moved into the area confident that their national characteristics or forms of religious beliefs would not be compromised or diluted. Existing Jewish residents have often been proactive in helping new groups of their co-religionists to make their home in the area.

Many other factors have sustained this internationally recognised Jewish community, including those leading to its establishment in this part of north-west London in the first place, which are mainly non-religious. Jews originally came to Golders Green because it was an attractive area, surrounded by open spaces, with good transport links, and close to central London's many attractions and amenities. The housing stock was generally of a high standard and there were no intrusive or unsightly industries. However, in combination, these assets have also acted as a brake on local development. Because it is a desirable area, housing in Golders Green has always been fairly expensive, not as expensive as nearby Hampstead and St John's Wood maybe, but nonetheless beyond the means of many who aspire to live in the area. Although there are now more flats and smaller properties than previously, the housing is still mainly suitable for established families rather than other household types.

The impact of this brake on expansion is twofold. The cost of housing in Golders Green and its lack of variety have limited the number of Jewish people moving to the area. This has prevented it becoming overwhelmingly Jewish and being seen as a modern-day 'ghetto'. Had this happened, it might have decreased the attractiveness of the area to Jews and non-Jews alike. In addition, although many Jews like living close to other Jews, over the years there has been a continuous outflow of Jews from Golders Green, mainly due to property prices and lack of suitable accommodation. Although this has worried communal leaders, it has created a sense of dynamism and opportunities for new Jewish residents to inject fresh perspectives and different ways of living. As a result, unlike the early Jewish suburbs (for example Maida Vale, Willesden, Brondesbury), Golders Green has never stagnated or been through a cycle of rise, peak and decline.

The establishment of the Golders Green Jewish community and its endurance are also due to historical timing. In his seminal study of the growth of Jewish suburbia during the nineteenth century, Lipman described how, following in the footsteps of non-Jewish people, some Jews began to leave the East End London and settle in the more salubrious and fashionable areas of west and north London.[1] The numbers doing so were small because few Jews at that time could afford to make the move. However, between 1900 and 1910 major changes started to take place in the overall nature of Anglo-Jewry. It became more affluent and assimilated and Jews began leaving the East End and other areas of first settlement in much larger numbers. These changes occurred just as Golders Green was developing into a residential suburb, a significant historical coincidence; it was in the right place at the right time.

The timing of the development of Golders Green not only explains why the area became the location for a significant Jewish community; it also contains the seeds of its sustainability. House building in Golders Green continued well into the First World War, years during which the Jewish community in general became more economically secure and some Jews achieved affluence, enabling them to buy the substantial houses erected in Golders Green. Some of the first wave of Jewish settlers had the resources and influence to establish communal facilities such as a

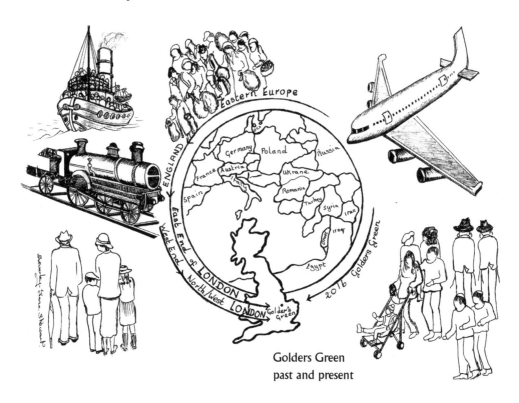

Golders Green
past and present

synagogue, Jewish education classes, charitable activities, social and literary societies, and a kosher butcher. This communal infrastructure was important in enabling the early Jewish families to retain their Jewish heritage and was also pivotal in attracting more Jewish families. Over the years the nature of this communal infrastructure has changed significantly, adapting to the needs of successive generations of Jews and new arrivals. However, the initial investment made by the first Jewish families is a key to the lasting viability of the community.

The Jewish community of Golders Green is undeniably more segmented and polarised than it was in previous times, yet it retains a certain amount of cohesion, with its component parts sharing more than a common heritage. From the early days there have been tensions between sections of the community with different backgrounds (for example, during the 1930s, between indigenous Jews and the continental refugees) and with different religious outlooks (for example, between Dunstan Road Synagogue and the new shuls established during the 1930s). There have also always been sections of the community that have been more self-sufficient than others. Iraqi and Israeli Jews for example, have tended to be more inward looking than the South Africans. Nevertheless, throughout the community's history there have been strong, though not always immediately obvious links between the different groupings: families have inter-married across religious and social divides, extended families have moved to the areas *en masse*, Sephardi Jews worship in

Ashkenazi shuls and vice versa, people often socialise or study together despite their religious and cultural differences. The close-knit nature of the community is illustrated by people interviewed for this book who made remarks such as 'in Golders Green everybody has a cousin living in the area', and 'It sometimes takes me an hour to walk from my house to the shops just around the corner because I meet so many people I know'.

The social connections contributing to the coherence of the community are reinforced by geographical factors. Compared to adjacent Hendon, where Jews live in pockets across the district, the Golders Green community is much more spatially integrated. The area also has some clear physical boundaries that enhance its identity and while it is not sprawling, Golders Green is sufficiently large for many different strands of Judaism to co-exist.

In addition, despite the disagreements that have erupted from time to time (for example in relation to the *eruv*) and worries that the proliferation of numerous small shuls has splintered the community, when an issue emerges threatening the whole community, animosities and differences have been set aside. This solidarity in the face of adversity was vividly illustrated during the writing of this book when an unashamedly anti-Semitic group announced its intention of staging a demonstration in Golders Green on a *Shabbat* morning in the summer of 2015. A cross-communal forum, Golders Green Together, was formed with the aim of demonstrating the solidarity of the community. It received a massive amount of support and eventually succeeded in convincing the police to relocate the planned demonstration to central London, leaving Golders Green to enjoy a peaceful *Shabbat*.[2]

Golders Green Together highlighted another important feature of the Jewish community: its generally good relationship with non-Jewish residents of the area. The forum was supported not only by a cross-section of the Jewish community but also by other faith groups.[3] While from time to time there have been tensions between Jews and non-Jews in Golders Green (for example, in the lead-up to the establishment of the State of Israel and at times of housing shortages), in general the relationship has been remarkably harmonious. The tone was set by the first Jewish residents, who were either already assimilated or had made the move to Golders Green with the specific intention of becoming part of mainstream society. Although the significant *haredi* community is more separatist than other Jewish groupings that have resided in the locality, they have not been totally immune to the wider influences of the area in which they live.

The Jewish community's relationship with non-Jews in Golders Green has remained harmonious even though the non-Jewish community has, as in society as a whole, changed significantly. When Jews arrived in Golders Green, their neighbours were almost exclusively Christians but since the 1970s Jewish residents have found themselves living in an increasingly multicultural environment. Some Jews were initially fazed by the arrival of different ethnic groups but they quickly developed cordial relationships with their new neighbours. Today the Jewish community exists quite happily as part of an ethnically diverse population. Interfaith activities are a prominent aspect of communal life (as they have always been) and there are many examples of people from very diverse backgrounds working together for the benefit of the local population as a whole.[4] For most Jews living in Golders Green, geographical concentration and the existence of their own communal infrastructure does not mean segregation.

Two clear conclusions emerge from this discussion. First, while the Jewish community of Golders Green has always been a microcosm of Anglo-Jewry, displaying changes taking place at a national level, it also has some quite unique qualities and assets not enjoyed in other areas. As a result, people are likely to continue to aspire to join rather than leave the community. The second conclusion is that the future of the community looks bright. Throughout its history it has been welcoming of new groups and flexible in responding to changing expectations and ideas. Time and again, the community has demonstrated its ability to reinvent itself. This adaptability means that, whatever the challenges of coming years, it is likely to have the capacity not only to survive but also to emerge even stronger and more vibrant than it is today.

Appendix
Explanatory Notes

Denominations of Anglo-Jewry

The Union of Orthodox Hebrew Congregations (UOHC)[1] includes congregations that expect strict adherence to *halachah*. A large proportion of the smaller houses of prayer in Golders Green belong to the UOHC.

The term 'Mainstream Orthodox' covers the United Synagogue led by the Chief Rabbi,[2] the Federation of Synagogues,[3] those regional synagogues that recognise the authority of the Chief Rabbi and a small number of independent Ashkenazi orthodox congregations. Golders Green Synagogue, generally known as Dunstan Road Synagogue, belongs to the United Synagogue and there are two long-standing 'Federation' synagogues (Sinai Synagogue and Machzikei Hadath). Sassover Finchley Road has historically been affiliated to both the Federation and UOHC.

The Spanish and Portuguese Jews' Congregation[4] is the oldest synagogal body in the UK. It includes Bevis Marks Synagogue in the City of London, Maida Vale Synagogue (Lauderdale Road) and the Sephardi synagogue in Wembley. There are an increasing number of small, largely independent Sephardi communities. Their members are mainly North African and Middle Eastern in origin, who do not see themselves as connected to the Spanish and Portuguese Jews. Although there have been a number of abortive moves to unite the small Sephardi shuls, there is apparently little desire among them to form a movement akin to the Shas movement in Israel.[5] There are a growing number of independent Sephardi shuls in Golders Green.

Liberal synagogues are brought together under the umbrella of Liberal Judaism (previously the Union of Liberal and Progressive Synagogues).[6] There are no Liberal congregations in the area. However, since they are not prohibited from driving or using public transport on *Shabbat*, a number of Liberal Jews have always resided in Golders Green. More traditional 'Reform' synagogues are co-ordinated by the Movement for Reform Judaism (MRJ).[7] North-Western Reform Synagogue (Alyth Gardens) in Temple Fortune is a member of the MRJ. Masorti[8] congregations are mainly to be found in Greater London. Their theological position sits between Mainstream Orthodox and Reform Judaism. There are no Masorti communities in Golders Green but some members of Masorti shuls live in the area.

In Golders Green there are a number of synagogues which, either throughout or for parts of their history, have remained independent of any denominational organisation. The long-established Golders Green Beth Hamedrash (Munk's shul) is an example of such a community but a number of the smaller, strictly orthodox shuls that have been set up in recent years are also independent.

Houses of prayer

Houses of prayer in Britain are often referred to as a synagogue (Greek for assembly), shul (Yiddish for school), *shtiebl* (Yiddish for small room), or *beth hamedrash* (house of study). The term synagogue is usually applied to larger communities housed in sizeable purpose-built premises and the word *shtiebl* is applied to the smaller, orthodox communities. However, as Anglo-Jewry has become more traditional, synagogues are widely referred to as shuls, including by progressive communities.

Most strictly orthodox houses of prayer have a Hebrew name that includes *beth hamedrash*, signifying the emphasis placed on learning. Many are very small and it is therefore appropriate to refer to them as *shtieblech*. However, some have become quite large and it is therefore more appropriate to refer to them as shuls.

A *minyan* is a group of people (in Jewish law ten men or more) who come together informally to pray. A *minyan* does not require a dedicated building or a religious leader.

In this history of Golders Green 'community' and 'congregation' are used interchangeably to refer to those who belong to or worship in a house of prayer.

Notes

Abbreviations, conventions and notes

AJR: Association of Jewish Refugees
JC: *Jewish Chronicle*
JML: Jewish Museum of London
UOHC: Union of Orthodox Hebrew Congregations

All interviews were conducted by the author unless otherwise specified.

References to the census for the relevant years refer to the decennial Census of Population carried out by the Office for National Statistics, available online at Ancestry.co.uk, where it is reproduced with the permission of the National Archive, London.

Rabbi Ofir Ronen, who is quoted on a number of occasions, contributed on a personal rather than an official basis.

Preface

1   This situation changed with the publication of Helen Fry's book on the 100-year history of the Golders Green Synagogue (Dunstan Road).

Chapter 1

1   'Golders' was formerly spelt with an apostrophe (Golder's).
2   Ben Weinreb, *The London Encyclopedia* (London: Macmillan, 3rd edition, 2010), pp.328–329.
3   Https://www.barnet.gov.uk/citizen-home/libraries/local-studies-and-archives/pocket-histories/hendon-and-golders-green/hendon-online-resources.html.
4   Georgia Abrams, 'Golders Green: The Development of the Jewish Community', JML, reference 1900.37, p.1.
5   F. Howkins, *The Story of Golders Green and Its Remarkable Development* (London: Ernest Owers Ltd, 1923), p.35.

6   Https://www.barnet.gov.uk/citizen-home/libraries/local-studies-and-archives/pocket-histories/hendon-and-golders-green/hendon-online-resources.html.
7   See glossary.
8   Hugh Petrie, *Hendon and Golders Green Past* (London: Historical Publications, 2005), p.100.
9   Alan Jackson, *Semi-Detached London, Suburban Development, Life and Transport 1900–39* (London: George Allen Unwin, 1973), p.70.
10   Ibid., pp.70–71.
11   Howkins, *The Story of Golders Green*, p.15.
12   Pronounced Yer-kees. He built the 'elevated railways' in Philadelphia and Chicago. He died in 1905 so did not live to see his vision realised. Given his role in the development of Golders Green, it is surprising that no road is named after him.
13   Jackson, *Semi-Detached London*, p.73.
14   Howkins, *The Story of Golders Green*, p.31.
15   Jackson, *Semi-Detached London*, p.74.
16   Ibid., p.74.
17   Ibid., p.75.
18   Ibid., p.76.
19   Howkins, *The Story of Golders Green*, p.19. It is now the Central Hotel.
20   'Hendon: Growth After 1850' in A History of the County of Middlesex: http://www.british-history.ac.uk/vch/middx/vol5/pp.11–16.
21   Mathew Hopkins, *A History of Hendon* (London: Hendon Borough Council, 1964), p.60.
22   Jackson, *Semi-Detached London*, p.75.
23   Ibid., p.76.
24   Ibid., p.75. 477 and 432 houses were built in 1914 and 1915 respectively.
25   'Hendon: Growth After 1850', pp.11–16.
26   Jackson, *Semi-Detached London*, p.76.

Chapter 2

1   Https://en.wikipedia.org/wiki/Joseph_Duveen,_1st_Baron_Duveen.
2   Kelly's Directory for Middlesex Hill, 1890. His name did not appear in the directory for 1887.
3   See Chapter 12.
4   1901 census.
5   For example, Geoffrey Alderman says the first Jewish inhabitants: 'generally came from the East End rather than from the west of London'. Geoffrey Alderman, *Modern British Jewry* (Oxford: Clarendon Press, 1998) p.234.
6   See Chapter 15.
7   Information for paragraph taken from 1901 and 1911 censuses.
8   H.S. Levin and S.S. Levin, *Jubilee at Finchley: 1926–1975, Story of a Congregation* (London: Finchley Synagogue, 1976), pp.2–3.
9   1911 census.
10   Elaine Rosa Smith, *East End Jews in Politics, 1918-39: A Study in Class and Ethnicity* (PhD thesis, University of Leicester, 1990), p.24.
11   Anne J. Kershen, 'The Jewish Community in London' in Nick Merriman (ed.), *The Peopling of London: Fifteen Thousand Years of Settlement From Overseas* (London: Museum of London, 1993), p.142.
12   *JC*, 26.9.1912, p.4.
13   See Chapter 15.
14   According to Pearl Pollack, whose family came to the area in the 1920s, some early residents were 'older people' who owned properties in the South of France. They were

'Russians' who later moved 'to the country'. Interview with Pearl Pollack, JML, Audio 195.

15   Alan Jackson, *Semi-Detached London, Suburban Development, Life and Transport 1900–39* (London: George Allen Unwin, 1973), p.82.

16   Kershen 'The Jewish Community in London', p.145.

17   *JC*, 15.4.1910, p.6.

18   Maria Alice Philips in *Jewish Memories of the Twentieth Century by Members of the North-Western Reform Synagogue London*, recorded and collated by David Stebbing, compiled by Evelyn Kent (London: Evelyn Kent Associates, 2003), p.214.

19   See Chapter 10.

20   *JC*, 20.7.1917, p.11.

21   Georgia Abrams, 'Golders Green: The Development of the Jewish Community', JML, reference 1900.37, p.6.

22   Ibid., p.7.

23   Rev. Isaac Livingstone, *History of the Golders Green Synagogue* (London: Golders Green Synagogue, 1949), p.3.

24   Ibid., p.2.

25   *JC*, 26.1.1917,p.5. Other young Jewish men from Golders Green who lost their lives include Samuel Cohen, Jack Glass, Moss Levy, Stanley Levine and Bernard Torrance. See memorial at Golders Green Synagogue.

Chapter 3

1   Clive R. Smith and John P. Hall, *The Story of Golders Green* (London: Ernest Owers/Cornwell Developments, 1979), p.56.

2   Alan Jackson, *Semi-Detached London, Suburban Development, Life and Transport 1900–39* (London: George Allen Unwin, 1973), p.88.

3   Smith and Hall, *The Story of Golders Green*, p.56.

4   Ibid, p.57

5   For example robbery reported in *JC*, 30.3.1928, p.28.

6   *JC*, 30.9.27, p.8.

7   'Nostalgia or Pain,' *Manchester Evening Gazette*, 28.9.1979.

8   Interview with Selina Gellert.

9   Interview with Jocelyne Tobin.

10   *JC*, 2.5.1919, p.2. Miss Lewisohn lived in Garrick Avenue and belonged to the community that became Dunstan Road Synagogue. Another elocution teacher in Golders Green during the 1920s was Clarice Hyams. *JC*,16.4.1926, p.11.

11   See article in *JC*, 2.10.1981, p.22.

12   Georgia Abrams, 'Golders Green: The Development of the Jewish Community', JML, reference 1900.37, p.4.

13   *JC*, 31.7.1925, p.28.

14   *JC*, 22.6.1923, p.23.

15   *JC*, 23.4.1926, p.28.

16   Abrams, 'Golders Green', p.5.

17   Ibid., p.5.

18   Interview with Barbara Michaels.

19   Interview with Naomi Rose.

20   Abrams, 'Golders Green', p.5.

21   Ibid., p.5.

22   Participant in a group discussion at Hammerson House care home, 24.6.2015.

23   See Chapter 12 for information on the difficulties of securing a kosher butcher.

24   Interview with Nancie Craig, JML, Audio 191.

25   Interview with Jocelyne Tobin.

26   Ibid. Observant Jews do not do anything that involves lighting a flame on *Shabbat* but a non-Jew can be employed to perform tasks if the arrangement and the payment are made prior to *Shabbat*.

27   Ibid.

28   Conversation with Susan Pollack, 10 March 2015. During Passover, it is essential that milk is free from leavened products. To ensure this some observant Jews bought milk directly from the cow.

29   Interview with Pearl Pollack, JML, Audio 195.

30   See Chapter 10.

31   *JC*, 21.11.1980, p.iii.

Chapter 4

1   It was designed by a Polish architect who carved the Polish eagle into the façade, giving the block its name.

2   Hugh Petrie, *Hendon and Golders Green Past* (London: Historical Publications, 2005), p.114.

3   Interview with Jacqueline Morris. The Selman family owned pubs across London, including the Royal Oak in Temple Fortune.

4   Petrie, *Hendon and Golders Green Past*, p.114.

5   Clive R. Smith and John P. Hall, *The Story of Golders Green* (London: Ernest Owers and Williams with Cornwell Developments Ltd, 1979), p.60.

6   Ibid., p.60.

7   See Chapter 13.

8   *JC*, 21.10.1932, p.27.

9   The Kindertransport was an organised rescue effort in the nine months before the Second World War. See https://en.wikipedia.org/wiki/Kindertransport.

10   Robert B. Goldmann, *Wayward Threads* (Evanston, IL: Northwestern University Press, 1997), p.53.

11   See Chapter 15.

12   See Chapter 10.

13   June Rose, *50 Years of 'Alyth', A Short History of the North-Western Reform Synagogue* (London: North-Western Reform Synagogue, 1983), p.16.

14   Ibid., p.16. Rosa Freedman became a prominent councillor and was Mayor of Barnet in 1981-2.

15   Interview with Jocelyne Tobin.

16   See Chapter 10.

17   Ibid.

18   Georgia Abrams, 'Golders Green: The Development of the Jewish Community', JML, reference 1900.37, p.13. The shul was sometimes referred to as 'Frankfurt in Exile'.

19   Report of Hendon Borough Library Service, quoted in Petrie, *Hendon and Golders Green Past*, p.65.

20   *JC*, 25.5.1934, p.28. The initiative was led by Mrs Wright who lived in Golders Green Road.

21   Anthony Grenville, *Continental Britons, Jewish Refugees From Nazi Germany* (London: Association of Jewish Refugees and JML; 1st Edition 2002), p.10.

22   *Kristallnacht* (night of the broken glass) was a coordinated attack on Jews and their property throughout the German Reich on the night of 9 November 1938.

23   Interview with Benjamin Sachs.

24   See Chapter 15 on how they made a living.

25   Marcelle Robinson in Ellen Stein, Marcelle Robinson, Daisy Roessler, *...and then there were four: Berlin Memories – 1930s and Beyond* (ebook, available at Xlibris.com © 2006).

26   Werner Rosenstock, 'The German Refugees, Some Facts' in *Britain's New Citizens,*

the Story of the Refugees from Germany and Austria, Tenth Anniversary Publication of the
Association of Jewish Refugees in Great Britain (London: AJR, 1951), p.19.

27   Cecil Roth in AJR Information, October 1962.

28   Vivian D. Lipman, 'Anglo-Jewish Attitudes' in Britain's New Citizens, p.528.

29   JC, 19.1.1979, p.17.

30   Esther Judith Baumel, 'The Jewish Refugee Children in Great Britain, 1938-1945'
      p. 276. See: www.jewishvirtuallibrary.org/jsource/Holocaust/advertisement.html.

31   Interview with Marion Kreindler, 'Jewish Survivors of the Holocaust', British Library,
      C830/094/01.

32   Interview with Naomi Rose. After the war the family set up home in Croydon.

33   Interview with Rachel Konigsberg, 'Jewish Survivors of the Holocaust', British Library,
      C830/034/01-02.

34   Interview with Lola Rodin.

35   Professor Nicolas Daniel Reis in Bertha Leverton and Shmuel Lowensohn, I Came Alone:
      The Stories of the Kindertransports (London: Book Guild Publishing Ltd, 1990), p.256.

36   Interview with Jacqueline Morris.

37   Ibid.

38   Quoted in David Cesarani, 'A Funny Thing Happened on the Way to the Suburbs:
      Social Change in Anglo-Jewry Between the Wars, 1914–1945', Jewish Culture and History,
      Vol.1, No.1, p.19.

39   Abrams, 'Golders Green', p.12.

40   JC, 30.10.1936, p.18. It was led by Mrs E. Levy of Hendon Way, Golders Green.

41   Quoted in JC, 19.2.1937, p.55.

42   This practice continued for several decades. Interview with Beverley Mautner. Next
      door to the house where she grew up two sisters lived with their respective spouses –
      one couple lived upstairs and the other downstairs.

43   Cesarani, 'A Funny Thing Happened', p.22. The Jewish Chronicle small ads section in the
      1930s included many from people seeking to let rooms in Golders Green.

44   Interview with Gordon Greenfield.

45   Interview with Gerald Peters. From their time living together in Berwick Street, the
      Peters family knew the Franks family who opened a lingerie shop in Golders Green. See
      Chapter 12.

46   'MF' quoted in Howard M. Brotz, 'The outlines of Jewish society in London',
      in Maurice Freedman (ed.), A Minority in Britain, Social Studies of the Anglo-Jewish
      Community (London; Vallentine Mitchell, 1955), p.148.

47   Information from Michael Jolles.

48   Geoffrey Alderman, British Jewry Since Emancipation (Buckingham: University of
      Buckingham Press, 2014), p.210.

49   Interview with Jocelyne Tobin.

50   Joan Harris in Jewish Memories of the Twentieth Century by Members of the North-Western
      Reform Synagogue London, recorded and collated by David Stebbing, compiled by Evelyn
      Kent (London: Evelyn Kent Associates, 2003), p.111.

51   Interview with Naomi Rose.

52   Simon Blumenfeld, Jew Boy (London: Lawrence and Wishart Ltd, 1986), pp.131–143.

53   Rev. Isaac Livingstone, History of the Golders Green Synagogue (London: Golders Green
      Synagogue, 1949), p.16. The two councillors were Councillor Rosenthal and Councillor
      Somper, later Mayor of Stepney.

54   The Synagogue Review (Golders Green Synagogue), Vol.1, No.2, October 1929, p.13.

55   See http://archives.ucl.ac.uk/DServe/dserve.exe?dsqIni=Dserve.ini&dsqApp=Archive&d
      sqDb=Catalog&dsqCmd=NaviTree.tcl&dsqField=RefNo&dsqItem=GASTER.

56   JC, 10.3.1922, p.34. The name of the house, Hatikvah, was the Zionist anthem.

57   Geoffrey Alderman, The Jewish Community in British Politics (Oxford: Clarendon Press,
      1982), p.172. The other councillor was Mr L. Hirshfield. See JC, 28.4.1989, p.3.

58   Http://archive.org/stream/
      OurDutiesAsCitizensSermonPreachedAtTheGoldersGreenSynagogue.
59   Daniel Weinbran, 'Hendon Labour Party 1924–1992': http://www.microform.co.uk/
      guides/R97559.pdf_p.5.
60   Ibid., p.5.
61   Ibid., p.6. Lewis was confirmed as the local candidate for Golders Green but lost the
      election. Mrs Henderson resigned from the party.
62   Cesarani, 'A Funny Thing Happened', p.22.

Chapter 5

1   Clive R. Smith and John P. Hall, *The Story of Golders Green* (London: Ernest Owers and
     Williams/ Cornwell Developments Ltd, 1979), p.64.
2   Ibid., p.64.
3   *JC*, 27.5.1938, p.16.
4   *JC*, 3.6.1938, p.15.
5   See Chapter 11.
6   Georgia Abrams, 'Golders Green: The Development of the Jewish Community', JML,
     reference 1900.37, p.15.
7   Interview with Jocelyne Tobin.
8   Interview with Jeff Alexander.
9   Rita Brodie in *Jewish Memories of the Twentieth Century by Members of the North-Western
     Reform Synagogue London*, recorded and collated by David Stebbing, compiled by Evelyn
     Kent (London: Evelyn Kent Associates, 2003), p.20.
10   Smith and Hall, *The Story of Golders Green*, p.64.
11   Interview with Barbara Michaels.
12   Interview with Nancie Craig, JML.
13   Telephone conversation with Peter Hobbins, 11.5.2015.
14   *The Blessing of Eliyahu, A volume dedicated in memory of Rabbi Doctor Eliyahu Munk*
     (London: Golders Green Beth Hamedrash, 1982), p.92.
15   Hugh Petrie, *Hendon and Golders Green Past* (London: Historical Publications, 2005),
     p.148.
16   BBC World War Two People's War, online archive of wartime memories. Story
     contributed by Bill Kendall, Article ID. A4625705. See bbc.co.uk/ww2peopleswar.
17   *The Blessing of Eliyahu*, p.39.
18   Interview with Lola Rodin.
19   Joan Harris in *Jewish Memories of the Twentieth Century*, p.112.
20   Interview with Naomi Rutstein.
21   For further information on the evacuation of Kindertransport children see Dr Judith
     Grunfeld, *Shefford: A Story of a Jewish School Community in Evacuation 1939–1945*
     (Jerusalem: Feldheim Publishers, 2004).
22   This hostel was headed by Mr Shapiro who went on to become the first head of
     Menorah Primary School in Golders Green. See Chapter 14.
23   See Chapter 11.
24   Obituary for Rabbi Rubin, *The Times*, 24.6.2003.
25   Interview with Jocelyne Tobin.
26   BBC World War Two People's War, an online archive of wartime memories. Story
     contributed by Pearl Dalby, Article ID. A3288521. See bbc.co.uk/ww2peopleswar.
27   Interview with Jocelyne Tobin.
28   Ibid.
29   Interview with Selina Gellert.
30   Joan Harris in *Jewish Memories of the Twentieth Century*, p.114.
31   Interview with Jocelyne Tobin.

32 Interview with Nancie Craig, JML, Audio 191.
33 Petrie, *Hendon and Golders Green Past*, p.64.
34 Interview with Jeff Alexander.
35 Interview with Jocelyne Tobin.
36 Interview with Nancie Craig, JML.
37 Ibid.
38 Percy Reboul and John Heathfield, *Days of Darkness, The London Borough of Barnet at War* (Stroud: Sutton Publishing, 1995), p.vi.
39 Petrie, *Hendon and Golders Green Past*, p.64.
40 Ibid., p.64.
41 Interview with Rabbi Amanda Golby and Helen Golby.
42 Reboul and Heathfield, *Days of Darkness*, p.vii.
43 Second World War oral histories, Imperial War Museum, Edwin Stanley Hudson, catalogue number 25044, production date 2003-04-30.
44 Kathe Trenter in *Jewish Memories of the Twentieth Century*, p.305.
45 The SS *Arandora Star* was a British passenger ship of the Blue Star Line, which was requisitioned as a troopship in the Second World War. In June 1940 it transported German and Italian internees and prisoners of war to Canada bound for internment camps. On 2 July 1940 it was sunk in controversial circumstances by a German U-boat with large loss of life.
46 Interview with Esra Kahn.
47 'Acceptance of Suffering' in Rabbi Nachman Seltzer, *True stories of people who brought the 48 ways of Torah wisdom to life* (Brooklyn, NY: Sharr Press, 2014), pp.179–193.
48 Letter from his son, Max Sulzbacher, *AJR Journal*, September 2009.
49 Ibid.
50 See Chapter 15 for further information on 'enemy aliens' in the armed forces.
51 Irene White, *I Came as a Stranger* (London: Hazelwood, 1991), p.34.
52 Reboul and Heathfield, *Days of Darkness*, p.100.
53 *JC*, 14.3.1941, p.18.
54 Interview with Jocelyne Tobin.
55 Stamford Hill is generally used as an umbrella term for a number of adjacent neighbourhoods – Stamford Hill itself plus South Tottenham, Stoke Newington and Upper Clapton - all with a high proportion of Jewish residents.
56 Interview with Jeff Alexander.
57 See Chapter 11.
58 The right of admission for refugees fleeing persecution was not lifted until the Geneva Convention, 1951.

Chapter 6

1 Simon Schama, 'Matzo ball memories', *Financial Times*, 17.2.2012.
2 *JC*, 21.11.1947, p.6.
3 Lady Henriques quoted in *The Blessing of Eliyahu, A volume dedicated in memory of Rabbi Doctor Eliyahu Munk* (London: Golders Green Beth Hamedrash, 1982), p.41.
4 Martin Gilbert, *The Boys: Triumph Over Adversity* (London: Phoenix, 2003), p.358. Some young people who stayed in the hostel were amongst the early pupils of Hasmonean Grammar School. See Chapter 14.
5 Interview with Barbara Michaels.
6 Interview with Naomi Rose.
7 Anonymous interviewee.
8 The pages of *The London Gazette, Official Public Record* abound with instances of Golders Green residents who changed their names in the immediate post-war years.
9 Interview with Miriam Levene.

10   Interview with Steven Derby.
11   Anonymous interviewee.
12   Interview with Naomi Rutstein.
13   Interview with Kitty and David Freund.
14   Email from Benjamin Sachs, 1.2.2016.
15   Ibid.
16   See Chapter 13.
17   Interview with Peter Englander.
18   Interview with Hazel Sheldon.
19   Interview with Rachel Deutsch.
20   Ibid. Sadly her father, who was sent to Belsen, did not survive.
21   Pam Fox, *A Place to Call My Jewish Home, Memories of the Liberal Jewish Synagogue 1911–2011* (London:Vallentine Mitchell, 2011), p.22.
22   Clive R. Smith and John P. Hall, *The Story of Golders Green* (London: Ernest Owers and Williams/Cornwell Developments Ltd, 1979), p.74.
23   See *AJR Information*, December 1947.
24   It was named after the benefactor Charles Barclay, a prominent member of Golders Green Synagogue and a Hendon councillor.
25   *JC*, 9 .7.1948, p.16.
26   See Chapter 14.
27   Sonita Sarker (ed.), Esha Niyogi De (ed.), Philippa Levine (contributor), Nihal Perera (contributor), *Trans-Status Subjects: Gender in the Globalization of South and Southeast Asia* (Durham, NC: Duke University Press Books, 2002), p.259.
28   See glossary for explanation of Ashkenazi and Sephardi Jews.
29   The influx from Shanghai was due to the rise of communism, which banned religious services.
30   Interview with Sarah and David Elias, 10 March 1992, JML, Audio 233.
31   Sarker et al., *Trans-Status Subjects*, p.259.
32   Interview with Sarah and David Elias, JML.
33   Ibid.
34   Sarker et al., *Trans-Status Subjects*, p.259.
35   Interview with Sarah and David Elias, JML.
36   Percy S. Gourgey, 'Tribute to David Elias', *The Scribe*, Issue 76, Spring 2003.
37   *AJR Information*, May 1959.
38   *JC*, 25.8.1978, p.8.
39   Gourgey, 'Tribute to David Elias'.
40   Ibid.
41   See Chapter 11.
42   *JC*, 2.10.1987, *London Extra*, p.2.
43   Interview with Selina Gellert.
44   At the beginning of the twentieth century the East End contained about 125,000 Jews but no more than 30,000 Jews were left after the Second World War. Http://www.jewishvirtuallibrary.org/jsource/judaica/ejud_0002_0013_0_12735.html.
45   Howard M. Brotz, 'The outlines of Jewish society in London', in Maurice Freedman (ed.), *A Minority in Britain, Social Studies of the Anglo-Jewish Community* (London: Vallentine Mitchell, 1955), p.141.
46   Ibid., p.143.
47   Ibid., p.142.
48   Simon Schama, 'Matzo ball memories'.
49   Interview with Pearl Pollack, JML, Audio 195.
50   Interview with Maurice Sheldon, JML, Audio 192.
51   In the post-war years the lists of proceedings against those who had been declared bankrupt recorded in *The London Gazette, Official Public Record* included several residents of Golders Green.

52   Interview with Nancie Craig, 8.3.1989, JML, Audio 191.
53   Interview with Pearl Pollack, JML.
54   Interview with Naomi Rose.
55   Daniel Weinbran, 'Hendon Labour Party 1924–1992'. Http://www.microform.co.uk/ guides/R97559.pdf, p.15.
56   Smith and Hall, *The Story of Golders Green*, p.68.
57   David Cesarani, 'A Funny Thing Happened on the Way to the Suburbs: Social Change in Anglo-Jewry Between the Wars, 1914–1945', *Jewish Culture and History*, Vol.1, No.1, p.23.
58   Geoffrey Alderman, *London Jewry and London Politics*, 1889-1986 (London and New York: Routledge, 1988), fn. p.172
59   Interview with Beverley Mautner.
60   Schama, 'Matzo ball memories'.
61   Interview with Beverley Mautner.
62   Ibid.
63   See http://www.jewishvirtuallibrary.org/jsource/judaica/ejud_0002_0013_0_12735.html
64   'S.R.', Golders Green resident, quoted in Howard M. Brotz, 'The outlines of Jewish society in London', in Maurice Freedman (ed.), *A Minority in Britain, Social Studies of the Anglo-Jewish Community* (London; Vallentine Mitchell, 1955), p.149.
65   See Chapter 12.
66   Interview with Maurice Sheldon, JML.
67   Schama, 'Matzo ball memories'.
68   Hugh Petrie, *Hendon and Golders Green Past* (London: Historical Publications, 2005), p.63.
69   Interview with Esra Kahn.
70   Ibid.
71   Interview with Ian Torrance.
72   Ibid.

Chapter 7

1   Dr Gerry Black, *Jewish London an Illustrated History* (Derby: Breedon Books Publishing, 2007), p.165.
2   Stanley Waterman and Barry Kosmin, *British Jewry in the Eighties, A statistical and geographical study* (London: Board of Deputies, 1986), p.16. The loss was not just the people who went to Israel but also their children.
3   David Cesarani, 'A Funny Thing Happened on the Way to the Suburbs: Social Change in Anglo-Jewry Between the Wars, 1914–1945', *Jewish Culture and History*, Vol.1, No.1, pp.5–26.
4   Anonymous interviewee.
5   *JC*, 30.10.1964, p.iii.
6   Interview with Jeff Alexander. A readership survey carried out by the *Jewish Chronicle* in 1959 suggested that suburban Jews were taking up modern lifestyles more quickly than their non-Jewish neighbours. See *JC*, 6.3.1959, pp.12–13 and 13.3.1959, pp.30–31.
7   See Chapter 12.
8   *JC*, 30.7.1976, p.6.
9   See Chapter 14.
10   Anonymous interviewee. As the Eastern European *Hassidim* were moving into Stamford Hill, they were prepared to pay high prices for property to be close to family and others from the same sects. This encouraged longer-standing German Orthodox households to sell their homes and move to more fashionable and spacious areas such as Golders Green. See Amiram Gonen, *Between Torah Learning and Wage Earning* (tr. Jessica Bonn) (Jerusalem: Floersheimer Institute for Policy Studies, 2006), p.18.
11   Interview with Esra Kahn.

12   Amiram Gonen, *Between Torah Learning and Wage Earning* tr. Jessica Bonn (Jerusalem: Floersheimer Institute for Policy Studies, 2006), p.19. See Chapter 11 for further information on the strictly orthodox community.

13   Barry A. Kosmin and Nigel Grizzard, *Jews in an inner London borough: a study of the Jewish population of the London Borough of Hackney based on the 1971 census* (London: The Board of Deputies, 1975), p.33.

14   Simon Schama, 'Matzo ball memories', *Financial Times*, 17.2.2012.

15   Ibid.

16   Interview with Kitty and David Freund.

17   Interview with Robert Papier.

18   Interview with Lucille Sher.

19   Ibid.

20   Interview with Kitty and David Freund.

21   *JC*, 1.9.1961, p.42.

22   Monazzam Samyah in *Jewish Memories of the Twentieth Century by Members of the North-Western Reform Synagogue London*, recorded and collated by David Stebbing, compiled by Evelyn Kent (London: Evelyn Kent Associates, 2003), p.271.

23   Interview with Nadia Nathan.

24   Interview with Beverley Mautner.

25   See Chapter 14.

26   Interview with Michelle Huberman.

27   Schama, 'Matzo ball memories'.

28   Interview with Peter Englander.

29   Email from Benjamin Sacks, 1.2.2016.

30   Interview with Beverley Mautner.

31   Interview with Robert Papier.

32   Interview with Jeff Alexander.

33   Interview with Michelle Huberman.

34   Interiew with Rabbi Amanda and Helen Golby.

35   *JC*, 2.10.1981, p.22.

36   *JC*, 21.7.1967, p.8.

37   *JC*, 6.6.1969, p.16.

38   *JC*, 23.2.1979, p.30.

39   *JC*, 5.5.1978, p.8.

40   Anonymous interviewee.

41   *JC*, 5.12.1958, p.35.

42   Clive R. Smith and John P. Hall, *The Story of Golders Green* (London: Ernest Owers/ Cornwell Developments, 1979), p.59.

43   June Rose, *50 Years of 'Alyth', A Short History of the North-Western Reform Synagogue* (London: North-Western Reform Synagogue, 1983), p.33.

44   *AJR Information*, September 1965.

45   Ibid., August 1964.

46   Ibid., March 1965.

47   Daniel Weinbran, 'Hendon Labour Party 1924–1992'. Http://www.microform.co.uk/ guides/R97559.pdf, p.9.

48   See Chapter 14.

49   Interview with Beverley Mautner.

50   Interview with Ian Torrance.

51   Palwin is the name of the first kosher and Israeli wine brand.

52   Peter Gilbey in *Jewish Memories of the Twentieth Century*, p.75.

53   Dannie Abse, *Goodbye, Twentieth Century: The Autobiography of Dannie Abse* (London: Pimlico, 2001, ebook).

54   Dannie Abse, *Poems: Golders Green* (London: Hutchinson & Co., 1962), p.23.

55   'The Golem of Golders Green', *Jewish Quarterly*, Vol. 38, Issue 2 (1991), pp.38–40.

56   Efraim Sicher, *Beyond Marginality, Anglo-Jewish Literature After the Holocaust* (Albany, NY:

State University of New York Press, 1985), p.117.
57 *JC*, 6.3.1992, p.13.
58 *JC*, 2.6.1961, p.22.

Chapter 8

1   Marlena Schmool and Frances Cohen, *A Profile of British Jewry, Patterns and Trends at the Turn of the Twentieth Century* (London: Board of Deputies, 1998), p.5.
2   See Chapter 14.
3   Lionel S. Kochan, 'Anglo-Jewry Since World War II', *The American Jewish Year Book*, Vol.78 (1978), p.341.
4   Ibid., p.346.
5   See Chapter 11 for information on the make-up of the orthodox community.
6   See Chapter 11.
7   Interview with Rabbi Refoel and Loli Berisch. *Haredi* Jews usually wear dark clothes with a white shirt.
8   See glossary for explanation of these terms.
9   *JC*, 28.5.1976, p.21.
10 See Chapter 14.
11 At the onset of *Chanukkah* a giant *chanukkia* is erected outside Golders Green station. At *Sukkot*, canvas *sukkahs* line the main thoroughfares outside the kosher restaurants. See glossary for definitions.
12 See Chapter 11.
13 Quoted in interview with Gabriel Goldstein.
14 Interview with Julia Chain.
15 See Chapter 14.
16 Bnei Brak, east of Tel Aviv, is a centre of strict Jewish orthodoxy.
17 Interview with Lola Rodin.
18 Anonymous interviewee.
19 Interview with Robert Papier.
20 Interview with Rabbi Charles Emanuel.
21 Interview with Rabbi Alexandra Wright.
22 Interview with Hannah Jacobs.
23 Ibid.
24 Anonymous interviewee.
25 Anonymous interviewee.
26 Interview with Esra Kahn. This is a quote from Rabbi Samson Raphael Hirsch (see Chapter 11).
27 *JC*, 7.7.1989, p.1.
28 See note 161, Chapter 10.
29 For further information see Daphne Gerlis, *Those Wonderful Women in Black, The Story of the Women's Campaign for Soviet Jewry* (Montreux, London, Washington: Minerva Press, 1996).
30 Interview with Margaret Rigal, Rita Eker and Joanna Aron.
31 Ibid.
32 During *Pesach*, observant Jews do not consume leavened food and their homes must be leaven-free.
33 *JC*, 28.4.1989, p.26.
34 In 2014 the *eruv* was extended to cover an area of Cricklewood on the western side of the Hendon Way where a number of Golders Green Synagogue members live.
35 The *Guardian*, 16.1.1993.
36 *JC*, 10.7.1992, *Community Chronicle*, p.1.
37 *JC*, 8.2.2013, p.25.
38 Although there is no information on numbers for Golders Green alone, the ratio can be seen from general figures produced by the Israeli Bureau of Statistics. While 7,468 British Jews emigrated from Britain to Israel in 1979–1983, only 314 Israelis immigrated

to Britain. Quoted in Schmool and Cohen, *A Profile of British Jewry*, p.31.

39 R. Linn and N. Barkan-Ascher, *Permanent Impermanence: Israeli Expatriation in non-event transition, Jewish Journal of Sociology*, 38 (1), 1996, p.7.

40 According to census figures there was a 50 per cent increase in the number of Israelis living in Britain between 1981 and 1991. A disproportionate number of these residents lived in Barnet, which includes Golders Green. Schmool and Cohen, *A Profile of British Jewry*, p.29.

41 Steven Gold and Rona Hart, *Transnational Ties During a Time of Crisis; Israeli Emigration, 2000 to 2004* (Oxford: Blackwell Publishing Ltd, 2009), p.6.

42 They were usually young married couples with a non-working wife. Schmool and Cohen, *A Profile of British Jewry*, p.30.

43 Interview with Ofer Ronen.

44 See glossary.

45 Interview with Bernard Benarroch.

46 Interview with Robert Papier.

47 BBC News Born Abroad, South Africa. Http://news.bbc.co.uk/1/shared/spl/hi/uk/05/born_abroad/countries/html/south_africa.stm.

48 Interview with Hazel Sheldon.

49 Email from Simon Walters, 1 June 2015.

50 Eulogy for Miriam Burke, http://www.karbatznick.com/wp-content/uploads/2012/03/eulogy-miriam-burke-2000-by-alexander.pdf.

51 S. Waterman *The 'return' of Jews to London* in A. Kershen (ed.), *The Promised Land? – The Migrant Experience in a Capital City* (Aldershot: Avebury, 1997), pp.143-160.

52 Hugh Petrie, *Hendon and Golders Green Past* (London: Historical Publications, 2005), p.65.

53 Interview with Selina Gellert. This was the first Hindu temple to be built in Europe. It was established in the home of its founder, Aajibai Banarse, in 1965. Https://sushilshirbhate.wordpress.com/aajibai-banarse-london/.

54 Interview with Viki Minsky.

55 Interview with Steven Derby.

56 See Chapter 12.

Chapter 9

1 David Graham, *A tale of two Jewish populations, Census results 2011 (England and Wales)* (London: Institute for Jewish Policy Research, 2013), p.9. The *haredi* community is made up of a number of sub-populations. See Chapter 11.

2 The official figure based on the religion question in the census was 6,795. The larger figure of 7,661 has been estimated by IJPR, ibid., adding people who did not answer the question.

3 Ibid., p.3.

4 Michel S. Laguerre, *Global Neighborhoods, Jewish Quarters in Paris, London, and Berlin* (Albany: State University of New York Press, 2008), p.64.

5 Interview with Gabriel Goldstein. See chapters 10 and 11.

6 Interview with Hannah Jacobs.

7 Anonymous interviewee.

8 Ibid.

9 See: http://en.wikipedia.org/wiki/Shomrim_(neighborhood_watch_group).

10 See Chapter 14.

11 Ibid.

12 *JC*, 2.3.2008, p.1. An inquest found that he had taken cocaine before the accident.

13 Information from Michael Jolles.

14 Anonymous interviewee. For example, she paid £50 for a wedding dress worth £3,000, which she gave back after she had worn it.

15   Anonymous interviewee.
16   Anonymous interviewee.
17   Interview with Rachel Deutsch.
18   Ibid.
19   Interview with Rabbi Refoel and Loli Berisch.
20   See Chapter 12.
21   Strictly orthodox households do not use crockery and cutlery unless it has first been cleansed in a *mikveh*.
22   The Torah (Leviticus 19:19 and Deuteronomy 22:9–11) prohibits the wearing of wool and linen fabrics in one garment. See http://en.wikipedia.org/wiki/Shatnez.
23   See Chapter 11.
24   Anonymous interviewee.
25   See Chapter 11.
26   Geoffrey Alderman, *JC*, 20.3.2015, p.43.
27   Anonymous interviewee.
28   *Beth Din* - see glossary. The Golders Green *Beth Din* is not yet fully developed, taking largely 'lower level' decisions. It is a symbol of the independence of the Golders Green community from Stamford Hill.
29   Interview with Michael Cohen.
30   Laguerre, *Global Neighborhoods*, p.77.
31   Bruce Mitchell, *Language Politics and Survival: Yiddish Amongst the Haredim in Post-War Britain* (Leuven: Peeters Publishers, 2006), p.118.
32   Amiram Gonen, *Between Torah Learning and Wage Earning* tr. Jessica Bonn (Jerusalem: Floersheimer Institute for Policy Studies, 2006), p.27.
33   *New York Times*, 6.11.2013.
34   Anonymous interviewee.
35   Interview with Michael Cohen.
36   The *shadchan* is not usually paid a fee for his or her services. However it is a custom to present a *shadchan* with a 'gift' in the event of a successful match being arranged.
37   Anonymous interviewee.
38   Interview with Michael Cohen.
39   Ibid.
40   Interview with Rabbi Refoel and Loli Berisch.
41   Cited in Laguerre, *Global Neighborhoods*, p.64.
42   Interview with Michael Cohen.
43   Interview with Bernard Benarroch.
44   Interview with Michael Cohen.
45   Ibid.
46   Anonymous interviewee.
47   Anonymous interviewee.
48   See for example, *JC*, 22.2.2013, p.12.
49   *JC*, 27.2.2015, p.6.
50   Interview with Rabbi Refoel and Loli Berisch.
51   Interview with Ofer Ronen.
52   Interview with Dov Softi.
53   Ibid.
54   Interview with Ofer Ronen.
55   Interview with Dov Softi.
56   Interview with Ofer Ronen.
57   *JC*, 17.7.2015, special supplement on Golders Green.
58   Speaker at Limmud Conference, 2014.
59   *JC*, 16.4.1999, p.29.
60   Interview with Dov Softi.
61   An Israeli newspaper advertising jobs and accommodation available to the Israelis.

62   Quoted in Amiram Barkat, 'Israelis in London prefer their own', *Jewish Telegraph*, 30.3.2008.
63   Interview with Dov Softi.
64   *JC*, 16.4.1999, p.29.
65   Interview with Dov Softi.
66   This group includes a high proportion of highly qualified people leading to concerns about a 'brain drain' from Israel. Speaker at Limmud Conference, 2014.
67   Ibid.
68   Interview with Benny Chain.
69   'Octogenarian Olim', *Golders Green Synagogue Journal*, Issue 2, March 2013, p.17. The couple have sadly since died.
70   Interview with Eva and Lionel Blumenthal.
71   Michelle Huberman, 'Les Feujs a Londres – French Jews in London', *Jewish News*, 20 January 2015. Http://www.jewishnews.co.uk/opinion-les-feujs-londres-french-jews-london/.
72   See Chapter 14.
73   See Chapter 11.
74   Interview with Rabbi Bassous.
75   *AJR Journal*, July 2008.
76   Interview with Jeff Alexander.
77   See chapters 11 and 14.
78   Alex Brummer, *JC*, 2.8.2013, p.22.
79   The strong links between Golders Green and the Antwerp Jewish community are demonstrated by the daily mini-bus service that operates between Golders Green and Antwerp.
80   Laguerre, *Global Neighborhoods*, p.182.

Chapter 10

1   V.D. Lipman, 'The Development of London Jewry' in S.S. Levin (ed.), *A Century of Anglo-Jewish Life 1870–1970* (London: United Synagogue Publications, 1970), p.54.
2   *JC*, 10.3.1911, p.17.
3   1911 census.
4   *JC*, 28.2.1913, p.32.
5   Clive R. Smith and John P. Hall, *The Story of Golders Green* (London: Ernest Owers and Williams/Cornwell Developments, 1979), p.58.
6   See Pam Fox, *Israel Isidor Mattuck, Architect of Liberal Judaism* (London: Vallentine Mitchell, 2014).
7   *JC*, 1.5.1914, p.20.
8   *JC*, 9.10.1914, p.2.
9   Rev. Isaac Livingstone, *History of the Golders Green Synagogue* (London: Golders Green Synagogue, 1949), p.1.
10   Aubrey Newman, *The United Synagogue 1870–1970* (London: Routledge, 1977), pp.87–88.
11   See Chapter 13.
12   He was knighted for his services to the Imperial Institute and the Empire Marketing Fund.
13   Livingstone, *History of the Golders Green Synagogue*, p.2.
14   Lynne Fertleman, 'The Establishment of Golders Green Synagogue', http://www.jewishgen.org/jcr-uk/london/golders/history11_consecration.htm. The church was not completed until 1937, fifteen years after the synagogue.
15   *JC*, 19.6.2015, p.15.
16   Quoted in Georgia Abrams, 'Golders Green: The Development of the Jewish

Community', JML, reference 1900.37, p.9.

17   Rev. I. Livingstone, 'The District and the Community, Some Notes', *The Synagogue Review*, Vol.1, No.2, October 1929, p.4.

18   At this time ministers ordained in the United Synagogue were given the title of reverend rather than rabbi even though they were highly qualified in Jewish law.

19   *Golders Green Synagogue Journal*, Centenary Edition, Issue 6, September 2015, p.18.

20   Livingstone, *History of the Golders Green Synagogue*, p.3. Rev. Livingstone is commonly referred to as the first minister of the community but in fact he was the second.

21   Obituary, *JC*, 28.9.1979, p.28.

22   Interview with Nancie Craig, 8.3.1989, JML, Audio 191.

23   Ibid.

24   Quoted in Smith and Hall, *The Story of Golders Green*, p.58.

25   Interview with Nancie Craig, JML.

26   Interview with Barbara Michaels.

27   Interview with Nancie Craig, JML.

28   *JC*, 30.3.1917.

29   Helen Fry in *Golders Green Synagogue Journal*, Issue 6, September 2015, p.22.

30   *JC*, 21.10.1921, p.2.

31   Livingstone, 'The District and the Community', p.4.

32   *JC*, 29.11.1918, p.22.

33   The building was designed by Digby L. Solomon.

34   Paul Lindsay, *The Synagogues of London* (London: Vallentine Mitchell, 1993), p.113.

35   Helen Fry, *Golders Green Synagogue, The First Hundred Years* (Wellington: Halsgrove, 2016), p.58.

36   Livingstone, 'The District and the Community', p.4.

37   The *minyan* included men from Hampstead as well as Golders Green.

38   *JC*, 19.10.1928, p.28. See note 20, Chapter 15.

39   Unless otherwise specified, the early history of Golders Green Beth Hamedrash is based on information in *The Blessing of Eliyahu, A volume dedicated in memory of Rabbi Doctor Eliyahu Munk* (London: Golders Green Beth Hamedrash, 1982).

40   *Golders Green Beth Hamedrash, 75th Anniversary Gala Dinner* (London: Golders Green Beth Hamedrash, 2009).

41   Rabbi Munk was born in Königsberg. He studied at Berlin University, Marburg University (doctoral thesis on Wordsworth) and at the Hildesheimer Rabbinerseminar, and officiated at the Fransecki Strasse private synagogue, Berlin.

42   *Golders Green Beth Hamedrash, 75th Anniversary Gala Dinner*.

43   Because of its origins, the community was never referred to as a synagogue.

44   Dedicated to the memory of Reuben Lincoln and his wife, Fanny's, parents. The Institute was designed by one of the Lincolns' sons, the architect Wolfe Lincoln.

45   See Chapter 14.

46   Unless otherwise stated the history of North-Western Reform Synagogue is taken from: Leonard Hyman, *A Short History of the North-Western Reform Synagogue, 1933–1958* (London: North-Western Reform Synagogue 1958); June Rose, *50 Years of 'Alyth', A Short History of the North-Western Reform Synagogue* (London: North-Western Reform Synagogue, 1983); Gill and Jon Epstein (eds), *Alyth 1933–2008, The Last 25 Years* (London: North-Western Reform Synagogue, 2008). Where people are quoted, the publication from which the quote came is cited.

47   *JC*, 23.6.1933, p.15. Mr King Hamilton later resigned due to his misgivings about the financial viability of the new synagogue so the first chairman was Mr Wolfe.

48   See Chapter 14 for information on the early religion classes.

49   Interview with Jeffery Rose.

50   See glossary.

51   The *Ner Tamid* (see glossary) is attributed to Benno Elkan (who also designed the

menorah outside the Knesset in Israel) but this has not been evidenced. It is still used in the synagogue.

52   *JC*, 17.7.1936, p.45.

53   Interview with Barbara Michaels. Sidney Ellis was employed by the congregation in its early days to assist Rev. Livingstone.

54   See Chapter 11.

55   *JC*, 30.3.1934, p.24.

56   *The Blessing of Eliyahu*, p.46.

57   Interview with Barbara Michaels.

58   Ibid.

59   Interview with Nancie Craig, JML.

60   Livingstone, *History of the Golders Green Synagogue*, p.10.

61   Michael Wallach, 'No Job for a Jewish Boy', *The Observer Supplement*, 1969. Undated cutting kindly loaned by Barbara Michaels.

62   He had subsequently worked at the Bayswater and the Great Synagogue.

63   Interview with Nancie Craig, JML.

64   Ibid.

65   Interview with Esra Kahn.

66   Pam Fox, *A Place to Call My Jewish Home, Memories of the Liberal Jewish Synagogue 1911–2011* (London: Vallentine Mitchell, 2011), p.158.

67   It included a number of wealthy families from Hendon that did not yet have a 'United' synagogue.

68   See Chapter 14.

69   See Chapter 13.

70   Ibid.

71   Livingstone, *History of the Golders Green Synagogue*, p.13. For further information on social activities in the synagogue see Chapter 13.

72   Ibid., p.18.

73   Ibid., p.11.

74   Interview with Barbara Michaels.

75   Livingstone, *History of the Golders Green Synagogue*, p.13. Rev. Taschlicky also gave public performances outside the synagogue.

76   David Rurka Ra'anna in the *Golders Green Synagogue Journal*, Issue 6, September 2015, p.8.

77   Jonathan Weissbart, 'Our Musical Heritage', in ibid., p.16.

78   *JC*, 17.6.1932, p.10.

79   Interview with Nancie Craig, JML.

80   Ibid.

81   Abrams, 'Golders Green', p.10.

82   *JC*, 24.6.1932, p.13.

83   Livingstone, *History of the Golders Green Synagogue*, p.15.

84   *JC*, 12.5.1933, p.22. Sidney Bolsom was a successful estate agent whose Hampstead office covered Golders Green.

85   See Chapter 14.

86   After the war he went on to become Chief Rabbi of the Jewish Community of Belfast and Northern Ireland.

87   Email from Benjamin Sachs, 1.2.2016.

88   Quoted in Rose, *50 Years of 'Alyth'*, p.18.

89   It is interesting to note that despite this, subscription rates were different for men and women (5 guineas and 4 guineas respectively) and for single men and single women (2.5 guineas and 1.5 guineas respectively).

90   Livingstone, *History of the Golders Green Synagogue*, p.4.

91   *JC*, 24.5.1935, p.10.

92   Whittingehame Farm School, which operated between 1939 and 1941, was located in East Lothian, Scotland. It was part of the Kindertransport mission. See Chapter 4.

93   Quoted in Rose, *50 Years of 'Alyth'*, p.16.

94   Rev. M. Perlzweig in Leonard Hyman, *A Short History of the North-Western Reform Synagogue*, p.24.

95   See Chapter 13.

96   Interview with Naomi Rose.

97   See Chapter 5.

98   He was interned for eighteen months at Kitchener Camp in Kent and later in Mooragh Camp on the Isle of Man. *JC*, 17.9.1982, p.67.

99   Interview with Marion Kreindler, Jewish Survivors of the Holocaust, British Library, C830/094/01.

100   He was recruited by the World Jewish Congress to undertake speaking tours for which he was in much demand.

101   *JC*, 17.9.1982, p.67.

102   *Golders Green Beth Hamedrash, 75th Anniversary Gala Dinner*.

103   Ibid.

104   'Memories – Mr Alex Halberstadt' in *Golders Green Beth Hamedrash, 75th Anniversary Gala Dinner*.

105   Ibid.

106   See Chapter 6.

107   Ibid.

108   Interview with Miriam Levene.

109   *JC*, 14.5.1948, p.14.

110   Interview with Julia Chain.

111   Public ddiscussion between Rabbi Lord Sacks and Simon Schama held at Golders Green Synagogue, 7.12.2015.

112   Interview with Jeff Alexander.

113   Quoted in Rose, *50 Years of 'Alyth'*, p.21.

114   See Chapter 13 for further information on synagogue activities for young people.

115   Dr Henry Cohn quoted in Rose, *50 Years of 'Alyth'*, p.24.

116   Simon Schama, 'Matzo ball memories', *Financial Times*, 17.2.2012.

117   Monty Brahams in *Golders Green Synagogue Journal*, Issue 6, September 2015, p.9.

118   Interview with Nancie Craig, JML. She was referring to the festival of *Simchat Torah*. See glossary.

119   *The Blessing of Eliyahu*, p.28.

120   Robin Summers, in the *Golders Green Synagogue Journal*, Issue 6, September 2015, p.8.

121   *Golders Green Beth Hamedrash, 75th Anniversary Gala Dinner*.

122   Interview with Esra Kahn. In keeping with Jewish tradition, the fruit trees were all saved and planted in the gardens of shul members.

123   The site was purchased by Sam Kahn's nephew Bernard with money he had received from Germany. Interview with Esra Kahn.

124   See You-Tube video of the processing of the scrolls: https://www.youtube.com/watch?v=z-LOIVLfTWA.

125   'Memory of Dr Solomon Adler' in *Golders Green Beth Hamedrash, 75th Anniversary Gala Dinner*.

126   *JC*, 26.7.1963, p.12.

127   Youth Association of Synagogues of Great Britain.

128   It was initially known as the Jewish Theological College but the name was changed following Rabbi Leo Baeck's death in 1956.

129   The rabbinic college was inaugurated in September 1956. Leo Baeck was too ill to attend.

130   See Chapter 14.

131   He had previously served at the Portsmouth and Southsea Synagogue.

132   In orthodox synagogues reading desks were central but in the nineteenth century, the 'end' desk was introduced to make more space.

133   Interview with Benny Chain.

134   This was Rabbi Sack's first rabbinic appointment. After leaving Dunstan Road, Rabbi Sacks was at Marble Arch Synagogue.

135   For example, *JC*, 21.11.1980, p.ii.

136   Dayan Ivan Binstock in *Golders Green Synagogue Journal*, Issue 6, September 2015, p.14.

137   The exact rate of decline is difficult to assess because some members were counted as families and others as individuals.

138   Interview with Naomi Rose.

139   Ibid.

140   Interview with Nancie Craig, JML.

141   The *Austrittesgemeinde* communities provided a range of ancillary, particularly educational, services necessary for an orthodox community in a modern world.

142   Interview with Rachel Deutsch.

143   Rabbi Feldman quoted in *Golders Green Beth Hamedrash, 75th Anniversary Gala Dinner*.

144   Dr Solomon Adler quoted in ibid.

145   Ibid.

146   Interview with Miriam Levene.

147   Ibid.

148   'Memories – Mr Alex Halberstadt', *Golders Green Beth Hamedrash, 75th Anniversary Gala Dinner*.

149   Ibid.

150   *JC*, 14.8.1964, p.12.

151   Ibid.

152   *The Blessing of Eliyahu*, p.62.

153   *Golders Green Beth Hamedrash, 75th Anniversary Gala Dinner*.

154   Rabbi Munk's first wife died in 1951. He married a widow with two girls who gave him 'a great deal of joy'. *The Blessing of Eliyahu*, p.50.

155   Ibid., p.71.

156   Interview with Esra Kahn.

157   Ibid.

158   Ibid.

159   Professor Bentwich was a former Attorney General in Palestine and Professor of International Relations at the Hebrew University in Jerusalem. As Director of the League of Nations High Commission for Refugees between 1933–36, he rescued thousands from Nazi persecution.

160   Later the Joint Israel Appeal.

161   Interview with Selina Gellert. The Refuseniks were professed Jews living in the former Soviet Union debarred from emigrating to Israel and entering the professions.

162   Joyce Rose, 'I remember, I remember', *Centre* (synagogue newsletter), July 2008.

163   Ibid. See glossary for explanation of *Simchat Torah*.

164   Information provided by Jon Epstein.

165   See Chapter 11.

166   Interview with Eva and Lionel Blumenthal.

167   Interview with Julia Chain.

168   Interview with Benny Chain.

169   Ibid.

170   Ibid.

171   *JC*, 22.1.1999, p.25.

172   Interview with Eva and Lionel Blumenthal.

173   *JC*, 19.3.1999, p.38.

174   Interview with Eva and Lionel Blumenthal.

175   *Golders Green Beth Hamedrash, 75th Anniversary Gala Dinner*.

176 Ibid.
177 Http://www.alyth.org.uk/about-us/our-members/.
178 See glossary.
179 This contact was maintained until 1999 when it was replaced with support for the Jewish community in Kerch in the Crimea, which was highly influential in its renaissance.
180 See chapters 7 and 8 for information on South Africans in Golders Green.
181 Peter Galgut, 'The South African Jewish Community' in Epsteins, *Alyth 1933–2008*, pp.73–74.
182 Ibid.
183 Conversation with Rabbi Mark Goldsmith, March 2015.
184 Interview with Eva and Lionel Blumenthal. Rabbi Belovski was previously at Ilford Federation Synagogue.
185 Interview with Benny Chain.
186 Interview with Eva and Lionel Blumenthal.
187 See Chapter 14.
188 Interview with Benny Chain.
189 This vision was set out in Building for the Future, *The Redevelopment of the Golders Green Synagogue and its Community* (London: Golders Green Synagogue 2011).
190 The Lebetkin Hall was added in the 1950s.
191 Interview with Naomi Rose.
192 *The Golders Green Synagogue Journal*, No. 2, March 2013, p.6.
193 See various issues of *The Golders Green Synagogue Journal*.
194 Fry, *The Golders Green Synagogue Journal*, p.133.
195 *JC*, 9.5.2014, p.27
196 *JC*, 7.9.2014, pp.10–11.
197 Article by Rabbi Belovski, *JC*, 13.3.2015, p.40.
198 Interview with Julia Chain.
199 Daniel Greenberg in *The Golders Green Synagogue Journal*, No.1, September 2012, p.16.
200 *JC*, 19.6.2015, p.15.
201 Interview with Julia Chain.
202 *Golders Green Beth Hamedrash, 80th Anniversary*.
203 See Chapter 14.
204 Discussion during visit to the shul, 13.12.2015.
205 Interview with Rabbi Refoel and Loli Berisch.
206 Discussion during visit to the shul, 13.12.15. Many younger men have been ordained but do not practice as rabbis.
207 Interview with Rabbi Refoel and Loli Berisch.
208 Rabbi Emanuel's contribution to 75th Anniversary issue of *Centre* (synagogue newsletter).
209 The theme of the windows is 'The Celebration of Life' depicting scenes of Israel, images of nature and inscriptions from the Bible.
210 With windows on the theme of Night designed by Ardyn Halter. Information provided by Jon Epstein.
211 Information provided by Jon Epstein.
212 Http://www.alyth.org.uk/wp-content/uploads/2015/07/Around-Alyth-July-August.pdf.

Chapter 11

1 Yekke is German for jacket. It refers to the formal jackets the Jews of German origin typically wore but also alludes to their culture – they are seen as being pedantic and focused on orderliness.
2 High Holyday services were held in the Broadwalk Hall off Golders Green Road. *JC*,

15.9.1933, p.iii. The community was sufficiently formed by this time to have a religion school.

3   *JC*, 16.5.1975, p.17.
4   *JC*, 20.10.1933, p.32.
5   Ibid.
6   *JC*, 18.11.1938, p.39.
7   Interview with Gerald Peters.
8   Rabbi Rosenfeld's brother, Rabbi Abraham Rosenfeld, the *chazzan* at Finchley United Synagogue, was well known for his compendium of *Selichot* prayers.
9   *JC*, 4.5.1934, p.43.
10 *JC*, 23.6.1939, p.54.
11 *JC*, 15.6.1945, p.18.
12 Interview with Gerald Peters.
13 *JC*, 30.10.1964, p.xi.
14 Interview with Gerald Peters.
15 Interview with Gordon Greenfield.
16 Interview with Gerald Peters.
17 Interview with Gordon Greenfield.
18 Interview with Gerald Peters.
19 A S'phardish shul is one where the liturgy incorporates some elements of Sephardi liturgy. See http://www.jewishgen.org/Sephardic/differ.HTM.
20 *JC*, 5.8.1938, p.13.
21 Harry Rabinowicz, *A World Apart, The Story of the Chasidim in Britain* (London and Portland, Or: Vallentine Mitchell 1997), p.150.
22 Vizhnitzer *Hassidim* are uniquely dressed in that they are the only group – besides the Stropkover *Hassidim* – who wear their hat bow on the right side rather than the left.
23 Interview with Steven Derby.
24 Rabinowicz, *A World Apart*, p.150.
25 Ibid., pp.150–151.
26 Ibid., p.151.
27 Anonymous interviewee.
28 When he died the title passed to Gershon Hager.
29 Rabinowicz, *A World Apart*, p.151. He attended Hasmonean School and completed his studies at Gateshead and Hebron *yeshivot*.
30 Anonymous interviewee.
31 Ibid., p.151.
32 See Chapter 14.
33 Anonymous interviewee.
34 Ibid.
35 Ibid.
36 Amiram Gonen, *Between Torah Learning and Wage Earning* tr. Jessica Bonn (Jerusalem: Floersheimer Institute for Policy studies, 2006), p.60.
37 Anonymous interviewee.
38 Rabinowicz, *A World Apart*, p.148.
39 Ibid., p.149.
40 Ibid., p.148.
41 Ibid., p.148.
42 Anonymous interviewee.
43 *Jewish News*, 19.2.2015.
44 See Chapter 14.
45 Rabinowicz, *A World Apart*, p.149.
46 *JC*, 5.10.1951, p.6.
47 Rabinowicz, *A World Apart*, p.149.
48 *Jewish News*, 19.2.2015.

49 *The Times*, 26.6.2003. He was head of a dynasty stretching back to the eighteenth century rabbi, Moshe Leib, who had made his home in Sassov. Rabbi Leib could trace his family back to the founder of Hassidism, the Baal Shem Tov.

50 Rabinowicz, *A World Apart*, p.79.

51 Ibid., p.79. Apparently he was not a very successful businessman.

52 *JC*, 291.1988, p.2.

53 *The Times*, 25.6.2003.

54 Ibid.

55 Rabinowicz, *A World Apart*, p.81.

56 Interview with Michael Cohen.

57 Rabinowicz, *A World Apart*, p.80.

58 *Jewish Tribune*, 17.8.1985, p.5.

59 Ibid, 4.7.1991, p.9.

60 Ibid, 5.5.1988, p.5.

61 Quoted in Rabinowicz, *A World Apart*, p.79.

62 He is also the head of the Chayei Olam *yeshiva* in Golders Green. See Chapter 14. Although the Rubin family belonged to a Hassidic dynasty, leadership of the community did not pass to Rabbi Rubin's son as the family reputation was rocked by the scandal surrounding the business dealings of Rabbi Rubin's son David. *JC*, 2.8.1991, p.16.

63 He did not take on the title of the Sassover rabbi, which was reserved for Rabbi Rubin's grandson who lives in Israel.

64 In 1978 William Stern was declared bankrupt owing millions but rose again to be a successful businessman and generous benefactor.

65 Rabinowicz, *A World Apart*, p.82.

66 Interview with Michael Cohen.

67 Rabinowicz, *A World Apart*, p.82.

68 Anonymous interviewee.

69 *Hakohol* 5775-2015, UOHC, 2015, p.52.

70 Ibid., p.52.

71 Rabinowicz, *A World Apart*, p.131.

72 Ibid., p. 131.

73 Ibid., p.132.

74 85 Bridge Lane was purchased and joined to number 83 to form premises for the Yeshiva, Etz Chaim. See Chapter 14.

75 At one stage there were a number of members from South America. *JC*, 3.11.1989, p.2.

76 *JC*, 6.3.1981, p.2.

77 Interview with Peter Colman.

78 Ibid.

79 Http://blbh.shulcloud.com/history-of-the-shul.html.

80 In 1979, Rabbi Ehrentreu suffered a stroke and spent the remainder of his life at the Jewish Hospital and Home in Tottenham. *JC*, 6.3.1981, p.2.

81 *JC*, 26.6.1987, p.19.

82 Http://blbh.shulcloud.com/history-of-the-shul.html.

83 Interview with Peter Colman.

84 Interview with Rachel Deutsch.

85 Carmel College in Oxfordshire, now closed, was a co-educational Jewish equivalent of Eton. Mr Rosen, Rabbi Winegarten's uncle, was the head teacher.

86 Interview with Michael Cohen.

87 Ibid.

88 North London Beth Hamedrash did not subscribe to the agreement and several years later in 1909 became the Adath Yisroel Community under Rabbi Dr Victor Schonfeld in Green Lanes.

89 Machzikei Hadath also had a property in Bridge Lane but was not able to convert it for worship for many years due to lack of funds. *JC*, 12.3.1971, p.viii.

90 The building was made possible because a small piece of land that the president, Bernard Homa, had bought on the North Circular Road many years previously for £5,000 had by the 1980s appreciated to nearly £200,000. The proceeds of the sale went partly to Etz Chaim *yeshiva* and partly to build the synagogue.

91 Anonymous interviewee.

92 Rabinowicz, *A World Apart*, p.148.

93 Paul Lindsay, *The Synagogues of London* (London: Vallentine Mitchell, 1993), p.116.

94 Ibid., p.116.

95 For many years the shul struggled with the planning authorities objecting to services being conducted in a house.

96 Rabbi Knopfler is a member of a famous rabbinic family. His brother is a well-known figure in the Manchester Orthodox community.

97 *JC*, 18.8.1989, p.2.

98 *JC*, 22.9.1989, p.2.

99 Interview with Michael Cohen.

100 Ibid.

101 Rabinowicz, *A World Apart*, p.193.

102 Anonymous interviewee.

103 *JC*, 7.2.986, p.1.

104 Rabinowicz, *A World Apart*, p.194. Until recently, Rabbi Chuna Halpern was the honorary rabbi of the shul.

105 Interview with Michal Cohen. Another son, Rabbi David Halpern, leads Hendon Beth Hamedrash.

106 Interview with Michael Cohen.

107 See Chapter 14.

108 Ibid.

109 Interview with Michael Cohen.

110 Interview with Esther Colman.

111 Interview with Eli Cohen.

112 Interview with Michael Cohen.

113 Http://www.ohrchodosh.org/.

114 Anonymous interviewee.

115 Interview with Michael Cohen.

116 Obituary, *JC*, 20.12. 2002, p.16.

117 Interview with Sophie and David Elias, 10 March 1992, JML, Audio 233.

118 Obituary, *JC*, 20.12.2002, p.16.

119 *JC*, 15.4.1988, p.18.

120 See Chapter 7.

121 *JC*, 25.8.1978, p8.

122 The scrolls, which are still in use in the shul, were brought from India but they originated in Babylonia.

123 Interview with Sophie and David Elias, JML.

124 *JC*, 13.9.1963, p.20.

125 Interview with Sophie and David Elias, JML.

126 *JC*, 23.7.2010, p.24.

127 See Chapter 7.

128 Interview with Nadia Nathan.

129 *JC*, 25.12.2015, 'Community', p.21.

130 Interview with Nadia Nathan.

131 *JC*, 19.8.1988, p.8.

132 Interview with Rabbi Bassous.

133 Ibid.

134 Ibid

135 Interview with Rabbi Ofir Ronen.

136 Ibid.
137 Interview with Rabbi Refoel and Loli Berisch
138 See Chapter 14 for information on both bodies.
139 Interview with Michael Cohen.
140 The benefactor also pays for people to learn. Mrs Soriano works with secular Israelis living in the area.
141 Interview with Michael Cohen.
142 Interview with Rabbi Ofir Ronen.
143 Gonen, *Between Torah Learning and Wage Earning*, p.77.
144 Ibid., p.76.
145 Anonymous interviewee.
146 Rabbi Shoshana Boyd Gelfand 'Post-denominational communities: finding a home for serious Jews' in *New Conceptions of Community* (London: Institute for Jewish Policy Research, 2010), p.8.
147 Anonymous interviewee.
148 Interview with Rabbi Ofir Ronen.
149 Ibid.
150 Interview with Rabbi Refoel and Loli Berisch.

Chapter 12

1 Hugh Petrie, *Hendon and Golders Green Past* (London: Historical Publications, 2005), p.28.
2 Sucklings remained in business until well after the Second World War by which time the firm was selling and repairing lawn mowers and making security grilles. Interview with Peter Colman.
3 Kelly's Directory for Middlesex, 1899.
4 Petrie, *Hendon and Golders Green Past*, p.113.
5 Alan Jackson, *Semi-Detached London, Suburban Development, Life and Transport 1900–39* (London: George Allen Unwin, 1973), p.75.
6 Ibid., p.86.
7 Ibid., p.86.
8 Petrie, *Hendon and Golders Green Past*, p.113.
9 The Refectory, now a public house, still exists at the same location.
10 Petrie, *Hendon and Golders Green Past*, p.143.
11 See Chapter 15.
12 *Hendon and Finchley Time*, 19.1.1962, p.1. He continued to commute for the remainder of his life.
13 Hilary S. and Salmond S. Levin, *Jubilee at Finchley, The story of the congregation* (London: Finchley Synagogue, 1976), p.3.
14 Kelly's Directory for Middlesex, 1914. To be included in the 1914 edition, it must have been established in 1913.
15 *JC*, 26.11.1915, p.5. According to Kelly's Directory for Middlesex, 1937, the Cope brothers' shop (one of several branches) was still operating twenty-two years later at 83 Golders Green Road.
16 Interview with Barbara Michaels.
17 See Chapter 9.
18 *JC*, 28.12.1917, p.25.
19 Interestingly this suggestion was opposed by Paul Goodman, a leading synagogue member in his role of secretary to the Shechita Board. *JC*, 8.7.1921, p.16.
20 Lynne Fertleman, 'The Establishment of Golders Green Synagogue'. Http://www.jewishgen.org/jcr-uk/london/golders. In 1925 Mr Nathan transferred the business from his earlier shop to his shop in Golders Green. *JC*, 2.10.1925, p.25.
21 Georgia Abrams, 'Golders Green: The Development of the Jewish Community', JML, reference 1900.37, p.6.

22 Hermann Appenrodt also ran the Brent Bridge Hotel across the road from Golders Green, which had a kosher licence as well as a 'model factory' in north London and a business in Coventry Street in the West End importing 'continental delicacies'. Mr Appenrodt, who came to the country from Poland, used to stand at the front of the shop in an immaculate suit and greet everyone by name, 'He knew everyone'. Interview with Jeff Alexander.

23 Advertisements in *The Synagogue Review* (Golders Green Synagogue), Vol.1, No.2, October 1929, p.2. Since Mr Rosen was advertising as 'the only Jewish fishmonger in Golders Green' it is possible that the Cope brothers' establishment was not kosher.

24 The store later moved to Temple Fortune. Mendel Susser was apparently known by young people as 'Mr Shusher' because during services at Dunstan Road Synagogue (where he was the Beadle) he would walk around asking people to 'shush'. Interview with Jeff Alexander.

25 Interview with Pamela Nenk, 28.2.1989, JML, Audio 194.

26 Information from rate books for Golders Green in the Barnet local history archives.

27 Kelly's Directory for Middlesex, 1927.

28 Information from Lindsey Walker. The family later had a chain of shops in various towns.

29 Interview with Barbara Michaels.

30 Interview with Nancie Craig, 8.3.1989, JML, Audio 191.

31 Kelly's Directory for Middlesex, 1937, pp.218–225.

32 Advertisements in 1940s programmes for the Golders Green Hippodrome kindly loaned by Pat Hasenson.

33 Kelly's Directory for Middlesex, 1937, pp.220–221.

34 Interview with Jacqueline Morris.

35 The Shaftesbury Avenue store was opened in 1897. Details taken from advertisement in a programme for the Golders Green Hippodrome in the 1950s kindly loaned by Pat Hasenson.

36 Https://en.wikipedia.org/wiki/Montague_Burton.

37 Interview with Hazel Sheldon, daughter of Mrs Franks. The Franks, who lived in Dunstan Road, bought the freehold and still own the shop, which is now let.

38 The Franks came to England from Poland. They eventually set up shops in Shaftesbury Avenue, Hammersmith, Edgware and Slough, which were run as separate businesses by different members of the family. Interview with Maurice Sheldon, 9.3.1989, JML, Audio 192. When the Shaftesbury Avenue shop closed, the headquarters of the Franks' business was relocated to premises in Broadwalk Lane off Golders Green Road. Interview with Hazel Sheldon.

39 Interview with Hazel Sheldon.

40 Ibid.

41 Reported in interview with Maurice Sheldon, JML. Despite the Depression, commercial rents in Golders Green Road maintained their high levels. *JC*, 5.2.1932, p.26.

42 Kelly's Directory for Middlesex, 1937, p.221.

43 *JC*, 28.11.1930, p.6.

44 Interview with Viki Minsky.

45 This involved steeping the meat in water for an hour and then salting it to remove all traces of blood. Today this process is carried out by the shop or the wholesaler.

46 *JC*, 16.3.1934, p.47.

47 Ibid. It later moved to 46 Golders Green Road.

48 The family firm also provided catering and had its own suite of rooms for hire in Aldgate as well as bakery outlets in Middlesex Street in the East End and in Stamford Hill. Later there were ten shops and a restaurant business managed by different parts of the family, which originally came from Monnickendam in Holland. Conversation with Philip Monnickendam, grandson of the founder of the business, 7.9.2015.

49 *JC*, 26.8.1938, p.6.

50 See Chapter 10.

51 Rabbi Solomon Schonfeld was the son of Rabbi Dr Victor Schonfeld, rabbi of the Adath Yisroel Synagogue. He was honoured for his work in rescuing Holocaust victims. Https://en.wikipedia.org/wiki/Solomon_Schonfeld.

52 During the late nineteenth and early twentieth centuries the Spitalfields Great Synagogue, later known as Machzikei Hadath, fought a long battle with the London Beth Din and the Chief Rabbi about the lax approach to *kashrut* and eventually established its own systems for guaranteeing *kashrut*. Http://machzikehadath.com/history/.

53 *The Blessing of Eliyahu, A volume dedicated to the memory of Rabbi Dr Eliyahu Munk*, (London: Golders Green Beth Hamedrash, 1982), p.92.

54 Interview with Naomi Rose.

55 Interview with Peter Colman. Members of the Frohwein family still live in Golders Green.

56 The family also ran a 10,000 square foot factory in Paddington producing kosher cooked meats and canned goods and an abattoir in Luton. They were at one time the largest meat wholesaler in Europe. *JC*, 29.1.1988, p.vii.

57 The *Kedassia* decided that the shops could not hold both *Kedassia* and the London Board for Shechitah licenses. The family's traditions were taken forward in a chain of shops named Kosher Deli owned by the Bendahan family, descendants of the Frohweins, *JC*, 19.10.2007, p.17.

58 Interview with Jacqueline Morris.

59 Clive R. Smith and John P. Hall, *The Story of Golders Green* (London: Ernest Owers and Williams/ Cornwell Developments Ltd, 1979), pp.64–65.

60 Ibid., p.67.

61 Notice in the *London Gazette*, 22.5.1942, p.2275.

62 *JC*, 7.4.1989, p.vii.

63 Interview with Jeff Alexander.

64 Interview with Maurice Sheldon, JML.

65 Ibid.

66 Interview with Viki Minsky.

67 Interview with Maurice Sheldon, JML.

68 Interview with Hazel Sheldon.

69 Interview with Kitty and David Freund.

70 Conversation with Sybil Marcus-Kanner, 24.6.2015.

71 Interview with Beverley Mautner.

72 Not to be confused with the Jews' Free School.

73 Information in this paragraph taken from 'Our Story: From Russia With Love', http://www.karbatznick.com/?page_id=12.

74 Ibid.

75 See Chapter 3.

76 Https://www.thegazette.co.uk/London/issue/49247/page/1228/data.pdf and http://www.ajr.org.uk/journal/issue.Mar15/article.16792.

77 The business moved to 1179 Finchley Road, Temple Fortune during the 1970s to be run by a descendant. The shop is still trading but is no longer owned by the Leiberg family.

78 Interview with Hazel Sheldon. Madam Leiberg was the main competitor for Franks lingerie shop.

79 See Chapter 5 for further information on Mr Sulzbacher.

80 Interview with Peter Colman. A Morrison shelter was a sealed table that many families installed in their dining rooms. The shelters were designed to be slept under at night and used as a table at other times.

81 Interview with Ben Sachs.

82 *AJR Information*, October 1959.

83   Ibid., April 1953.
84   *JC*, 30.10.1964, p.ii.
85   *JC*, 8.3.1985, p.xv.
86   Jackson, *Semi-detached London*, p.86.
87   Simon Schama, 'Matzo ball memories', *Financial Times*, 17.2.2012.
88   Interview with Esra Kahn.
89   Interview with Viki Minsky.
90   Interview with Gordon Greenfield.
91   Interview with Naomi Rose.
92   Interview with Jeff Alexander. This system was in use in several of the larger shops in Golders Green in the post-war years.
93   Ibid.
94   Ibid. The shop was part of a chain of eight outlets.
95   Interview with Selina Gellert.
96   Interview with Michael Rutstein.
97   The walls of the café are adorned with historic photos of Golders Green.
98   The chain of famous tea houses was founded by Isidore and Samuel Montague Gluckstein, Barnett Balmon and Joseph Lyons. Http://www.gracesguide.co.uk/J._Lyons_and_Co.
99   Interview with Pamela Nenk, JML.
100   Interview with Jeff Alexander.
101   Ibid.
102   Group discussion at Alyth Gardens Synagogue, 29.6.2015.
103   Interview with Eva and Lionel Blumenthal.
104   Ibid. During *Pesach* not only are Jews prohibited from eating *chametz*, but they are also prohibited from having any *chametz* in their possession. To comply with these requirements shops selling kosher goods have to be specially cleaned to ensure that they are *chametz*-free. Many of the kosher shops in Golders Green closed (and some still do) during *Pesach* to avoid carrying out the intensive cleaning required.
105   Interview with Michelle Huberman.
106   Michael McIntyre, *Life and Laughing: My Story* (London: Penguin, 2011), p.92.
107   Green Flag *Jewish Travel Guide*, 1957, p.39.
108   Information from Pat Hasenson. Biedak's also had a branch in Piccadilly.
109   *JC*, 18.10.1963, p.24.
110   Information from his son Stephen and grandson Jonathan.
111   The restaurant advertised in the Green Flag *Jewish Travel Guide*. See 1952 edition, p.31. It appears to have been linked to a kosher guesthouse.
112   See Green Flag *Jewish Travel Guide*, 1957, p.39. This restaurant was linked to a small hotel. See Chapter 15.
113   The East End restaurant closed in 1996 due to the changing nature of the area.
114   Julian Kossof, the *Telegraph*, 28.6.2010.
115   Conversation with Jon Pollins, 28.12.2015.
116   Vanessa Feltz, *JC*, 18.6.2010, p.23.
117   Interview with Selina Gellert.
118   Ibid.
119   The new owner was Jonathan Tapper, grandson of the founder.
120   Julian Kossof, the *Telegraph*, 28.6.2010.
121   *JC*, 27.9.2009, p.37.
122   *JC*, 30.10.1964, p.iii.
123   Many of the shoe shops later became part of the British Shoe Corporation owned by the Jewish property magnate and philanthropist, Charles Clore.
124   *JC*, 18.10.1974, p.22.
125   Interview with Naomi Rose.
126   Interview with Michele Huberman.

127 *JC* 16 .5.1969, p.27.
128 Interview with Nin Saunders.
129 Interview with Eva and Lionel Blumenthal.
130 Interview with Josephine Oliver.
131 Interview with Michele Huberman.
132 Interview with Selina Gellert.
133 Interview with Josephine Oliver.
134 Stephen Corren, tailor, interviewed by Matthew Linfoot, 20.5.2005, BBC 'Millenium Memory Bank', reference C900/05156.
135 Ibid. The West End tailors, who largely served non-Jewish clients and the showbusiness community, were mainly based around Soho.
136 Geoffrey Davis was the son of a famous East End menswear retailer, Morry Davis. Having learned his trade from his father and working in Harrods, he opened a store in Regent Street. He subsequently had stores in New Cavendish Street and then in Golders Green where he later opened a second shop. For many years he chaired the Golders Green Chamber of Commerce. Conversation with Cyril Savage, 27.8.2015.
137 The shops were owned by two Jewish families, the Blooms and the Segals, who had started out in the East End.
138 *JC*, 30.10.1964, p.iii.
139 *JC*, 14.12.1962, p.4.
140 JC, 10.9.1971, p.25.
141 He started in business as a tobacconist before moving into leather goods in the City. Information taken from electoral registers and telephone directories, Ancestry.co.uk.
142 Interview with Nin Saunders.
143 Ibid.
144 Ibid.
145 *JC*, 11.11.1977, p.ix.
146 Interview with Michelle Huberman.
147 *JC*, 19.11.1976, p.28.
148 *JC*, 24.12.1971, p.22.
149 Email from Simon Walters, 1.6.2015.
150 *JC*, 19.11.1976, p.29.
151 Now occupied by Caffe Nero. The ornate tiling at the entrance, in which the name Chinacraft is embedded, has been retained.
152 Interview with Michal Rutstein.
153 *JC*, 23.5.1952, p.19.
154 *JC*, 28.10.1955, p.20.
155 *JC*, 30.10.1964, p.ii.
156 Interview with Rabbi Amanda Golby and Helen Golby.
157 Interview with Gordon Greenfield.
158 Interview with Michael Rutstein.
159 Interview with Peter Colman.
160 Interview with Jeff Alexander.
161 Interview with Peter Colman.
162 Sam Stoller had previously had a stall on Ridley Road market in the East End.
163 Interview with Rabbi Amanda Golby and Helen Golby.
164 Interview with Esra Kahn.
165 *JC*, 5.2.1965, p.iii.
166 Smith and Hall, *The Story of Golders Green*, p.75.
167 Interview with Maurice Sheldon, JML.
168 Ibid.
169 Conversation with Sybil Marcus-Kanner, 24.6.2015.
170 Interview with Maurice Sheldon, JML.
171 For example, interview with Selina Gellert.

172   Interview with Nin Saunders.
173   *JC*, 19.11.1976, p.27.
174   *JC*, 23.11.1979, p.xi.
175   JC, 21.11.1980, p.iii.
176   Ibid.
177   Advertisement in 1950s programme for Golders Green Hippodrome kindly loaned by Pat Hasenson.
178   The business passed to Ivor Warman-Freed's son when he died in 1977.
179   McIntyre, *Life and Laughing*, p.92.
180   Interview with Steven Derby.
181   *Times and Post*, 23.7.1981. Pamela Nenk initially worked with a partner, Brian Lee, and later as a sole trader.
182   Interview with Pamela Nenk, JML.
183   Interview with Hazel Sheldon.
184   Conversation with Cyril Savage, 27.8.2015.
185   *JC*, 8.3.1985, p.xv.
186   Once registered under the 1950 Shops Act, Jewish shops were able to open on a Sunday, but opening on both Saturdays and Sundays contravened the legislation.
187   Conversation with Cyril Savage, 27.8.2015.
188   *JC*, 11.2.1976, p.11. It was the first bank in Britain to open on a Sunday but it was not open on Saturdays.
189   *JC*, 2.6.1989, p.2.
190   Interview with Maurice Sheldon, JML.
191   Ibid.
192   Conversation with Cyril Savage, 27.8.2015.
193   Interview with Hazel Sheldon.
194   See Chapter 7.
195   A kosher establishment is one that complies with Jewish dietary laws (*kashrut*). To be approved by one of the rabbinical licensing bodies, these shops must also comply with other Jewish laws such as not opening on *Shabbat* and on Jewish holidays.
196   *JC*, 26.6.1987, p.1.
197   *JC*, 27.3.1992, p.ii
198   See for example the proceedings against Frohwein's butchers. *JC*, 19.6.1987, p.1.
199   *JC*, 2.9.1994, p.12.
200   *JC*, 29.1.1993, p.i. The influx of Israeli food stores included Elite kosher chocolates.
201   *JC*, 18.11.1988, p.ix. Yarden later moved to 123 Golders Green Road where it was run for several years by a South African couple, the Teimans, who expanded the business into two shop fronts. The shop has recently been renamed B Kosher, specialising in Israeli, South African and French kosher foods.
202   *JC*, 18.11.1988, p.ii.
203   *JC*, 21.11.1980, p.iii.
204   Ibid.
205   Interview with Ofer Ronen.
206   *JC*, 30.1.1987, p.vii.
207   *JC*, 20.11.1987, p.xiv.
208   *JC*, 6.6.2014, p.3.
209   Interview with Hannah Jacobs.
210   *JC*, 10.3.1989, p.12.
211   See Chapter 9.
212   Interview with Hannah Jacobs.
213   *JC*, 20.11.1992, p.iii.
214   *JC*, 21.8.1953, p.11.
215   Http://www.kosherkingdom.co.uk/site/.
216   Https://ginaingoldersgreen.wordpress.com/category/recent-posts/.

217 Michelle Huberman, 'Les Feujs a Londres – French Jews in London', *Jewish News*,
     20.1.2015. 'Feujs' is French slang for Jews used by the French Jews themselves.
218 Interview with Michelle Huberman.
219 Huberman, 'Les Feujs a Londres'.
220 Information in *The North-West Connection 8, Shomer Shabbos Telephone and Business
     Directory*.
221 Interview with Hannah Jacobs.
222 According to the laws of *kashrut*, meat (the flesh of birds and mammals) cannot be eaten
     with dairy foods, which means that kosher restaurants and other eateries are categorised
     as being either meat or dairy.
223 Visit to the shop 15.1.2016. In the shop there are many photos of Warren Gold taken
     with the pop stars who frequented his Carnaby Street store in the 1960s. Warren Gold
     was a lifelong philanthropist. http://blog.atomretro.com/2015/06/dedicated-followers-
     of-fashion-warren.html.
224 *JC*, 18.7.2014, p.51.
225 Interview with Rachel Deutsch.
226 Interview with Michael Rutstein.
227 Author's conversations with several interviewees.

Chapter 13

 1 By the 1920s the pub was owned by a Jewish family, the Selmans, who had completely
    refurbished the pub. Interview with Jacqueline Morris. There were very few pubs
    in Golders Green because much of the land had been owned by the Ecclesiastical
    Commissioners, who when they sold the land, included clauses precluding usages
    involving alcohol.
 2 Alan Jackson, *Semi-Detached London, Suburban Development, Life and Transport 1900–39*
    (London: George Allen Unwin, 1973), p.70.
 3 The decision to open public parks for public recreation was not taken until 1933 and
    even then 'play' did not commence until after 1 p.m.
 4 Interview with Pearl Pollack, JML, Audio 195.
 5 It was opened by Anna Pavlova, a local resident. Its 700-seat auditorium had a
    double-vaulted ceiling and its wall panels were decorated with Grecian and Italian Lake
    scenery. It was demolished in 1975 and replaced with a Sainsbury's supermarket. A
    smaller Ionic cinema operated above the supermarket until 1999.
 6 There was considerable debate locally on whether Sunday cinema should be banned but
    at a poll at the Congregational Hall in 1929, the vote was 13,895 for Sunday cinema
    and 3,511 against. Hugh Petrie, *Hendon and Golders Green Past* (London: Historical
    Publications, 2005), fn.8, p.130.
 7 Jackson, *Semi-Detached London*, p.177. It stood on the site now occupied by the Sage
    nursing home
 8 To children's glee, it had attached to it a sweet shop.
 9 Now an apartment block.
10 It was closed in 1974 and demolished in the 1980s to make way for a Marks and
    Spencer foodstore.
11 *JC*, 30.9.1927, p.8.
12 Jackson, *Semi-Detached London*, p.86.
13 Interview with Jocelyne Tobin.
14 *JC*, 9.12.1927, p.19. The national body, Keren Hayesod, was established at the World
    Zionist Conference held in London in 1920 to provide the Zionist movement with
    resources needed for the Jewish people to return to the Land of Israel.
15 Raymond Gubbay interviewed in the *Eastern Daily Press*, 10.2.2011.
16 Clive R. Smith and John P. Hall, *The Story of Golders Green* (London: Ernest Owers/
    Cornwell Developments, 1979), p.61.

17 Interview with Viki Minsky.
18 *AJR Information*, April 1957.
19 Interview with Pamela Nenk, 28.2.1989, JML, Audio 194.
20 Interview with Barbara Michaels.
21 Although space was much reduced because of the installation of a studio, a number of pop concerts took place, TV shows were recorded and plays were staged in the concert area.
22 Interview with Pamela Nenk, JML. In 2007, despite being Grade II Listed, the theatre's status hung in the balance, and was placed on English Heritage's buildings at risk register. Eventually the El Shaddai International Christian Centre bought the theatre and has used the building ever since.
23 The racecourse, which operated until the 1860s, is said to have been of 'some importance'. Petrie, *Hendon and Golders Green Past,* fn.2, p.130.
24 Smith and Hall, *The Story of Golders Green*, p.66.
25 Interview with Naomi Rose.
26 Interview with Jeff Alexander. Seats cost 1s 9d at the front and 2s 3d upstairs.
27 Interview with Julia Chain.
28 *JC*, 9.3.1934, p.53.
29 *JC*, 14.6.1963, p.vii.
30 Interview with Jacqueline Morris.
31 Jackson, *Semi-Detached London*, p.83.
32 Interview with Nancie Craig, JML.
33 Petrie, *Hendon and Golders Green Past*, p.29. In 1969 a fire damaged the hotel. It reopened but finally closed in 1975.
34 In advertisements encouraging Jewish people to relocate to Golders Green it was referred to as a 'Palais de Danse'. *JC*, 30.9.1927, p.8.
35 *JC*, 11.9.1936, p.56.
36 For example, *JC*, 6.1.1933, p.35.
37 *JC*, 20.10.1933, p.11.
38 *JC*, 3.3.1939, p.46.
39 Interview with Jocelyne Tobin.
40 Interview with Nancie Craig, JML. The only after-school activities that were encouraged was involvement in charitable activities at a settlement in the East End arranged by the school. Interview with Barbara Michaels.
41 Mr Wasser, a member of Golders Green Synagogue, quoted in Georgia Abrams, 'Golders Green: The Development of the Jewish Community', JML, reference 1900.37, p.7.
42 Interview with Naomi Rose.
43 Ibid.
44 It was destroyed by bombing in the Second World War.
45 Interview with Nancie Craig, JML.
46 Interview with Pearl Pollack, JML.
47 Interview with Barbara Michaels.
48 Interview with Jeff Alexander.
49 Interview with Jocelyne Tobin.
50 Ibid.
51 David Cesarani, 'A Funny Thing Happened on the Way to the Suburbs: Social Change in Anglo-Jewry Between the Wars, 1914–1945', *Jewish Culture and History*, Vol.1, No.1, p.16. The Whitechapel parade was a *shidduch* parade, involving people walking up and down Whitechapel Road with a view to identifying future partners.
52 Interview with Pearl Pollack, JML.
53 *JC*, 17.11.1916, p.27 and 15.10.1920, p.10. The Literary Society meetings were held in a room in a private home in Finchley Road, Hampstead.
54 See Chapter 10.
55 Rev. I. Livingstone, 'The District and the Community, Some Notes', *The Synagogue*

Review, Vol.1, No.2, October 1929, p.14.

56   Interview with Pearl Pollack, JML.

57   *JC,* 28.10.1927, p.31.

58   Interview with Barbara Michaels.

59   Raymond Gubbay interviewed in the *Eastern Daily Press,* 10.2.2011.

60   *JC,* 26.9.1919, p.2.

61   *JC,* 24.11.1922, p.29.

62   *JC,* 5.1.1923, p.30.

63   *JC,* 2.5.1924, p.29.

64   Interview with Jocelyne Tobin.

65   Ibid.

66   Ibid.

67   Interview with Nancie Craig, JML.

68   *JC,* 14.12.1923, p.36.

69   Rev. I. Livingstone, 'The District and the Community, Some Notes', *The Synagogue Review,* Vol.1, No.2, October 1929, pp.9–13.

70   Interview with Barbara Michaels.

71   Leonard Hyman, *A Short History of North-Western Reform Synagogue* (London: North-Western Reform Synagogue, 1958), pp.19–20.

72   The Jewish Lads' and Girls' Brigade is the UK's oldest Jewish youth movement. It was founded in 1895 as the Jewish Lads' Brigade by Colonel Albert E.W. Goldsmid, a senior army officer, to provide an interest for children of the many poor Jewish immigrant families. The first company was launched in London's East End but others soon appeared throughout the city and the provinces.

73   Livingstone, 'The District and the Community', p.15. The initial hostility may have been due to the fact that it was associated with the East End, which the new suburban dwellers wanted to leave behind them.

74   *JC,* 12.1.1934, p.9.

75   Gill and Jon Epstein (eds), *Alyth 1933–2008, The Last 25 Years* (London: North-Western Reform Synagogue, 2008), p.28.

76   Interview with Jeffery Rose.

77   Interview with Lola Rodin.

78   Interview with Amanda and Helen Golby.

79   Joan Harris in *Jewish Memories of the Twentieth Century by Members of the North-Western Reform Synagogue London,* recorded and collated by David Stebbing, compiled by Evelyn Kent (London: Evelyn Kent Associates, 2003), p.112.

80   Ronald (Roy) Friedman in ibid., p.60.

81   *JC,* 5.4.1940, p.28.

82   *JC,* 21.2.1941, p.20.

83   June Rose, *50 Years of 'Alyth', A Short History of the North-Western Reform Synagogue* (London: North-Western Reform Synagogue, 1983), p.21.

84   Ibid., p.22.

85   Rabbi Lionel Blue was well known for his contribution to religious programmes.

86   Interview with Selina Gellert.

87   Letter from Irene Prevezer kindly loaned by Jocelyne Tobin.

88   Public discussion between Rabbi Lord Sacks and Simon Schama held at Golders Green Synagogue, 7 December 2015.

89   *The Blessing of Eliyahu, A volume dedicated in memory of Rabbi Doctor Eliyahu Munk* (London: Golders Green Beth Hamedrash, 1982), p.62.

90   See Chapter 14.

91   *JC,* 22.12.1961, p.20.

92   *JC,* 9.2.1945, p.24.

93   Held in a room of the Prince Albert Public House in Golders Green Road.

94   *JC,* 2.5.1969, p.47.

95   Interview with Jeff Alexander.
96   Simon Schama, 'Matzo ball memories', *Financial Times*, 17.2.2012.
97   Interview with Jeff Alexander.
98   *JC*, 25.3.1955, p.30.
99   *JC*, 3.2.1956, p.11. It was later replaced by the Rendez-Vous Club
100 *JC*, 26.8.1955, p.22.
101 *JC*, 22.10.1948, p.22.
102 *JC*, 4.7.1947, p.15.
103 Interview with Jocelyne Tobin. Habonim is a socialist Zionist, culturally Jewish youth movement.
104 Kenneth Ambrose, 'The Second Generation', *AJR Information*, February 1949.
105 Ibid., June 1953.
106 Ibid., October 1952.
107 Ibid., April 1950. He was also its voluntary legal adviser.
108 Leo Wolff was formerly President of the Berlin Jewish community. In Germany he had been a judge but his career foundered as a result of the move to Britain.
109 *JC*, 22.3.1940, p.13.
110 *AJR Information*, February 1946.
111 Ibid., March 1948.
112 Ibid., April 1946.
113 Ibid., September 1946.
114 *JC*, 2.5.1969, p.47.
115 *JC*, 30.10.1959, p.18.
116 Gerald Ratner, *Gerald Ratner: The Rise and Fall...and Rise Again* (Chichester: Capstone Publishing, 2007), p.17.
117 Fiona Factor and Kevin Stenson, 'At the end of the line' in *Youth in Society* (Journal of the National Youth Bureau), January 1987, p.16.
118 *JC*, 28.3.2008, p.28.
119 Interview with Robert Papier.
120 Interview with Selina Gellert.
121 Interview with Hannah Jacobs. The term Becky was applied to young people who were overly concerned with outward appearances.
122 *JC*, 18.11.1983, p.v.
123 Ratner, *Gerald Ratner*, p.18.
124 Simon Schama interviewed in the *Telegraph*, 22.2.2014.
125 Interview with Jeff Alexander.
126 Interview with Michelle Huberman.
127 Interview with Jeff Alexander. The Golders Green MacDonald's was one of the first in the UK.
128 Schama, 'Matzo ball memories'.
129 Interview with Selma Shrank.
130 See Chapter 7.
131 Interview with Robert Papier.
132 *JC*, 18.11.1988, p.xv.
133 Interview with Robert Papier.
134 Interview with Selina Gellert.
135 Rose, *50 Years of 'Alyth'*, p.30.
136 Helen Fry, *Golders Green Synagogue, The First Hundred Years* (Wellington: Halsgrove, 2016), p.88.
137 Rose, *50 Years of 'Alyth'*, p.29.
138 Ibid., p.29.
139 Ibid., pp.29–30.
140 Ibid., pp.32–33.

141 Interview with Pamela Nenk, JML.
142 A Jewish organisation founded in New York in 1843, which pursues educational, humanitarian, and cultural activities and attempts to safeguard the rights and interests of Jews around the world.
143 Interview with Kitty and David Freund.
144 Chaim Bermant, *JC*, 30.10.1964, p.iii.
145 Interview with Pamela Nenk, JML.
146 See Chapter 12.
147 Interview with Rabbi Amanda Golby and Helen Golby.
148 Interview with Pamela Nenk, JML.
149 Interview with Rabbi Amanda Golby and Helen Golby. Rabbi Golby's memory relates to Prince's Park but there were 'mountains' in other parks in Golders Green.
150 Interview with Selma Shrank.
151 Interview with Pamela Nenk, JML.
152 Interview with Hazel Sheldon.
153 Anonymous interviewee.
154 Cesarani, 'A Funny Thing Happened', p.17.
155 Daniel Weinbran, 'Hendon Labour Party 1924–1992'. Http://www.microform.co.uk/guides/R97559.pdf, p.9.
156 *JC*, 18.3.1960, p.12.
157 *JC*, 25.3.1966, p.16.
158 Interview with Selina Gellert.
159 Interview with Jocelyne Tobin.
160 Interview with Hazel Sheldon.
161 Interview with Rachel Deutsch.
162 Interview with Miriam Levene.
163 *JC*, 30.1.1987, p.xii.
164 *JC*, 7.7.1961, p.29.
165 Rose, *50 Years of 'Alyth'*, p.45.
166 JACS is an independent organisation that uses the synagogue as a base.
167 Epsteins, *Alyth 1933–2008*, pp.56–59.
168 It remains the only Jewish choral society as opposed to choir.
169 Epsteins, *Alyth 1933–2008*, pp.57–58.
170 See Chapter 12.
171 *JC*, 17.6.1988, p.8.
172 *JC*, 31.5.1991, p.1.
173 *JC*, 11.6.1993, *Community Chronicle*, p.1.
174 *JC*, 16.2.1996, p.13.
175 Http://www.goldersgreenshul.org.uk/connect.
176 Http://www.alyth.org.uk/.
177 Interview with Rabbi Refoel and Loli Berisch.
178 Interview with Lara Smallman conducted by Rosita Rosenberg 19.5.2015.
179 See Chapter 9.
180 Interview with Eli Cohen.
181 Anonymous interviewee.
182 See Chapter 14.
183 It currently operated from Hager's Beth Hamedrash in Highfield Avenue.
184 Witnessed by the author.
185 Anonymous interviewee.
186 Advertisements in *The Local News*, a Jewish advertising circular for North-West London.
187 Interview with Michael Cohen.
188 *JC*, 6.1.1978, p.24.
189 Advertisements in *The Local News*.
190 Http://www.ljfc.com/. The centre is run by the Lubavitch movement.

191 See advertisements in *The Local News*.
192 Anonymous interviewee.

Chapter 14

1   The Talmud attaches great importance to the *Tinokot shel beth Rabban* (the children [who study] at the Rabbi's house), stating that the world continues to exist for their learning and that even for the rebuilding of the Temple in Jerusalem classes are not to be interrupted (tractate Shabbat 119b).
2   Https://en.wikipedia.org/wiki/London_School_Board.
3   Http://www.british-history.ac.uk/vch/middx/vol5/pp43-48#h3-0003.
4   Interview with Nancie Craig, 8.3.1989, JML, Audio 191.
5   Ibid.
6   Under educational legislation at this time denominational education could not be given on school premises but arrangements could be made for children to receive instruction at nearby accommodation. Jewish parents could also ask for their children to be excused from non-Jewish instruction or worship.
7   Interview with Naomi Rose.
8   Interview with Jacqueline Morris.
9   Interview with Hazel Sheldon.
10 Interview with Jocelyne Tobin. The premises later became Barclay House and accommodated the Mathilde Marks-Kennedy School. See Chapter 14.
11 Ibid.
12 Hugh Petrie, *Hendon and Golders Green Past* (London: Historical Publications, 2005), p.87.
13 *JC*, 13.5.1927, p.3.
14 Advertisement in *The Synagogue Review* (Golders Green Synagogue), Vol.1, No.2, October 1929, p.14.
15 *JC*, 7.6.1929, p.16.
16 For example, *JC*, 16.1.1931, p.3.
17 Letter from S. May, *JC*, 5.8.1938, p.10.
18 Interview with Jocelyne Tobin.
19 Interview with Nancie Craig, JML.
20 Ronald (Roy) Friedman in *Jewish Memories of the Twentieth Century by Members of the North-Western Reform Synagogue London*, recorded and collated by David Stebbing, compiled by Evelyn Kent (London: Evelyn Kent Associates, 2003), p.60.
21 Interview with Nancie Craig, JML.
22 Interview with Lola Rodin.
23 V.D. Lipman, *A History of the Jews in Britain Since 1858* (Leicester: Leicester University Press, 1990), p.212.
24 While he was at this school, his family changed his surname (but not their own) by deed poll from Lazarus to Langdon, which may have been a result of anti-Semitism he experienced at the school. Interview with Selina Gellert (Harold Langdon's daughter).
25 Harold Langdon in *Jewish Memories of the Twentieth Century*, p.171.
26 Maria Alice Phillips in ibid., p.215.
27 Salmond S. Levin, 'The changing pattern of Jewish Education' in Salmond S. Levin (ed.), *A Century of Anglo-Jewish Life 1870–1970* (London: United Synagogue, 1971), pp.64–55.
28 Interview with Gabriel Goldstein. It is also possible that they attended *cheder* at Brondesbury or Hampstead synagogues.
29 *JC*, 10.6.1910, p.3.
30 *JC*, 28.2.1913, p.32.
31 See Chapter 10.
32 Rev. I. Livingstone, *History of the Golders Green Synagogue* (London: Golders Green Synagogue, 1949), p.6.

33   Ibid., p.6.
34   Interview with Naomi Rose.
35   There were three classes led for several years by Rev. Livingstone himself, Mr Orler and Miss Shaer. The top class was mainly boys preparing for their *Bar Mitzvah*. Despite their title, the classes actually covered the full gamut of Jewish education. Interview with Barbara Michaels.
36   Harold Langdon in *Jewish Memories of the Twentieth Century*, p.171.
37   Interview with Barbara Michaels.
38   See Chapter 10.
39   June Rose, *50 Years of 'Alyth', A Short History of the North-Western Reform Synagogue* (London: North-Western Reform Synagogue, 1993), p.11.
40   Ibid., p.12.
41   See Chapter 10.
42   Ibid.
43   *The Blessing of Eliyahu, A volume dedicated in memory of Rabbi Doctor Eliyahu Munk* (London: Golders Green Beth Hamedrash, 1982), p.35.
44   Ibid., p.36.
45   Helen Fry, *Golders Green Synagogue, The First Hundred Years* (Wellington: Halsgrove, 2016), p.68.
46   Ronald (Roy) Friedman in *Jewish Memories of the Twentieth Century*, p.59.
47   Livingstone, *History of the Golders Green Synagogue*, p.7.
48   Ibid., p.7.
49   Ibid., p.8.
50   Rose, *50 Years of 'Alyth'*, p.17.
51   Ibid., p.21.
52   Interview with Hazel Sheldon.
53   Conversation with Jacqueline Pinto, 27.3.2015.
54   Livingstone, *History of the Golders Green Synagogue*, p.8.
55   Memory of Henry Cohn, son of Professor Ernst Cohn who later became president of the synagogue, Rose, *50 Years of 'Alyth'*, p.22.
56   It was opened by Alderman Joseph Freedman, a former synagogue chairman.
57   Rose, *50 Years of 'Alyth'*, p.28.
58   In the early part of the twentieth century many progressive synagogues did not have *B'nai Mitzvah* for 13 year olds but instead had a Confirmation service for children aged 16. After the war, *B'nai Mitzvah* were gradually reintroduced.
59   Leonard Hyman, *A Short History of North-Western Reform Synagogue* (London: North-Western Reform Synagogue, 1958), p.21.
60   Interview with Ian Torrance.
61   Interview with Naomi Rose.
62   Simon Schama, 'Matzo ball memories', *Financial Times*, 17.2.2012.
63   Named after the wife of the congregant who purchased the premises.
64   *The Blessing of Eliyahu*, p.57.
65   Interview with Gabriel Goldstein.
66   *The Blessing of Eliyahu*, p.33.
67   Initially the synagogue was the only centre for kosher lunches, providing nearly 400 meals each weekday. The responsibility was later shared with Hendon Synagogue. *JC*, 31.1.1958, p.5.
68   Penna Bowman, 'My youth in the community', *Golders Green Synagogue Journal*, Issue 6, September 2015, p.11.
69   Interview with Steven Derby.
70   Interview with Michael Rutstein.
71   *The Blessing of Eliyahu*,, p.43.
72   Ibid., p.44.
73   Interview with Peter Colman.

74   Interview with Gordon Greenfield.
75   *JC*, 10.1.1947, p.10.
76   Aron Shapiro, first head teacher of the school, quoted in *The Blessing of Eliyahu*, p.44.
77   *The Blessing of Eliyahu*, p.45.
78   Interview with Selma Shrank.
79   Conversation with Stephen Colman, 15.3.2015.
80   Interview with Gerald Peters.
81   Ibid.
82   Ibid.
83   Interview with Miriam Levene.
84   Interview with Selma Shrank.
85   Interview with Rabbi Refoel and Loli Berisch. The sessions were held twice during the week and on Sunday mornings.
86   Rabbi Israel Cohen, quoted in Clive R. Smith and John P. Hall, *The Story of Golders Green* (London: Ernest Owers and Williams/Cornwell Developments, 1979), p.59.
87   The movement was set up on the third night of Chanukkah 1944, hence the name Hasmonean and the origin of the school badge depicting the menorah.
88   *The Blessing of Eliyahu*, p.43.
89   *JC*, 23.7.1999, p.3.
90   *The Blessing of Eliyahu*, p.44.
91   Interview with Peter Colman.
92   Ibid.
93   Interview with Gabriel Goldstein.
94   Interview with Gerald Peters.
95   *JC*, 9.5.1952, p.19.
96   Interview with Miriam Levene.
97   Interview with Rachel Deutsch.
98   Interview with Rabbi Amanda Golby and Helen Golby.
99   Ibid.
100   Http://en.wikipedia.org/wiki/Hasmonean_High_School.
101   Interview with Esra Kahn.
102   She was married late in life to Terence Kennedy.
103   *AJR Information*, November 1959.
104   *The Blessing of Eliyahu*, p.93.
105   *JC*, 7.11.1947, p.3, and later by Mrs Davis.
106   Dannie Abse, *Goodbye, Twentieth Century: Autobiography of Dannie Abse* (London: Pimlico, 2001, ebook).
107   Interview with Naomi Rose.
108   It was founded in 1910 by the Daughters of Wisdom, a Catholic community established in 1904. It later became a special needs school before closing in 1976.
109   Interview with Beverley Mautner.
110   Ibid.
111   Interview with Ian Torrance. When Ian Torrance entered Haberdashers School in 1953 the quota was ten per cent, but by the time he left it had been raised to 15 per cent.
112   Interview with Michael Rutstein.
113   Interview with Naomi Rose.
114   Marlena Schmool and Frances Cohen, *A Profile of British Jewry: Patterns and Trends at the Turn of the Century* (London: Board of Deputies of British Jews, 1998), p.23.
115   Interview with Michael Rutstein.
116   Rose, *50 Years of 'Alyth'*, pp.35–36.
117   Ibid. p.46.
118   *JC*, 17.10.1969, p.19.
119   *JC*, 9.9.1988, p.32.
120   Interview with Michael Cohen.

121 Interview with Benny Chain.

122 Jonathan Sacks, *Will We Have Jewish Grand Children* (London: Vallentine Mitchell, 1994).

123 Helena Miller, 'Supplementary Jewish Education in Britain: Facts and issues of the cheder system', *International Journal of Jewish Education Research*, 2010 (1), p.98. This was mainly a result of raised Jewish consciousness but also a desire by some Jews not to send their children to the new comprehensive schools.

124 It was not a Jewish school but most of the children were Jewish.

125 Interview with Rabbi Amanda Golby and Helen Golby.

126 Later Lucille Sher and Ruth Weiner and now Cindy Summer.

127 Interview with Lucille Sher.

128 Lucille Sher in Gill and Jon Epstein (eds), *Alyth 1933–2008: The Last 25 Years* (London: North Western-Reform Synagogue, 2008), p.54.

129 The school employed Israeli teachers who taught in *Ivrit*. Interview with Rachel Deutsch.

130 The school opened in 2010.

131 Http://www.rimonschool.org.uk.

132 Public discussion between Rabbi Lord Sacks and Simon Schama at Golders Green Synagogue, 7.12. 2015.

133 See Chapter 11.

134 Harry Rabinowicz, *A World Apart, The Story of the Chasidim in Britain* (London and Portland, Or: Vallentine Mitchell 1997), p.144.

135 *AJR Journal*, January 1978.

136 It was set up in West Heath Drive in 1974, later moved to East Finchley and temporarily back to West Heath Road. It moved in 1992 to the former premises of Christ College in Finchley, which were purchased for £2.5 million. Some of the students come from Stamford Hill as well as Golders Green and other parts of North-West London.

137 Rabinowicz, *A World Apart*, p.146. Although not labelled Hassidic, many of the students come from Hassidic families.

138 According to an anonymous interviewee 'the relationship didn't work well but they stayed together for the sake of the children. Eventually they were divorced.' Although they are no longer linked operationally, they remain part of the same charitable foundation.

139 Rabinowicz, *A World Apart*, p.145.

140 Ibid., p.145.

141 Ibid., p.145.

142 Ibid., p.147.

143 Simeon D. Baumel, 'Black Hats and Holy Tongues: language and culture among British Haredim', *European Judaism: A journal for New Europe*, Vol.36, No.2 (Autumn 2003), p.106.

144 Ibid., p.104.

145 Modern Hebrew is not a mainstream subject because some *haredi* groups are anti-Zionist and are therefore ambivalent about it being taught.

146 Rabinowicz, *A World Apart*, p.146.

147 William Stern is the Hungarian-born, Harvard-educated son-in-law of Osias Freshwater. William D. Rubinstein, Michael A. Jolles , Hilary L. Rubinstein (eds), *The Palgrave Dictionary of Anglo-Jewish History* (London: Palgrave Macmillan, 2011), p.299.

148 Rabinowicz, *A World Apart*, p.146.

149 Anonymous interviewee.

150 Bruce Mitchell, *Language Politics and Survival: Yiddish Amongst the Haredim in Post-War Britain* (Leuven: Peeters Publishers, 2006) p.128.

151 See Chapter 9.

152 Rabbi Halpern, who as instrumental in setting up Pardes House School, was committed to Jewish studies being taught in Yiddish.

153 Anonymous interviewee.

154 Anonymous interviewee.

155 Interview with Gabriel Goldstein.
156 Interview with Michael Cohen.
157 Ibid.
158 Baumel, 'Black Hats and Holy Tongues', p.103.
159 *JC*, 21.6.1985, p.22.
160 See www.kisharon.org.uk.
161 *JC*, 10.10.1969, p.19.
162 Interview with Eli Cohen.
163 *The Blessing of Eliyahu*, p.93.
164 *JC*, 26.7.1946, p.18.
165 Rabbi Jacob's writings were later to lead to a major controversy in Anglo-Jewry. Https://
     en.wikipedia.org/wiki/Louis_Jacobs.
166 See Julius Carelebach, 'Orthodoxy' in Werner Mosse (ed.), *Second Chance, Two Centuries
     of German-Speaking Jews in the United Kingdom* (Tubingen: J.C.B. Mohr, 1991), p.421.
167 Rabbi Wahraftig was a German refugee prominent in the Munk's community.
168 See Chapter 11.
169 Rabinowicz, *A World Apart*, p.79. See Chapter 11 for further information on Rabbi
     Halpern.
170 Ibid., p.80.   —
171 Http://www.chareidi.org/archives5762/EKV62features.htm.
172 Interview with Rabbi Refoel and Loli Berisch.
173 This *yeshiva* was formerly located in the East End under the leadership of Rabbi Altman.
     Its alumni include former Chief Rabbi Lord Jakobovitz and former Chief Rabbi
     Jonathan Sacks.
174 Http://www.frumlondon.co.uk/directorylisting.asp?abcid=A&CategoryID=911.
175 Interview with Rabbi Refoel and Loli Berisch.
176 Ibid.
177 Anonymous interviewee.
178 Interview with Michael Cohen.
179 Epsteins, *Alyth 1933–2008*, p.27.
180 Http://www.alyth.org.uk.
181 See Chapter 13.
182 Interview with Jocelyne Tobin.
183 *JC*, 8.1.1932, p.8.
184 *Golders Green Beth Hamedrash, 80th Anniversary.*
185 *JC*, 7.6.1935, p.38.
186 Rose, *50 Years of 'Alyth'*, p.7.
187 Hyman, *A Short History of North-Western Reform Synagogue*, p.19.
188 See Chapter 11.
189 *JC*, 16 .7.1948, p.6.
190 *JC*, 18.2.1955, p.16.
191 Interview with Gabriel Goldstein.
192 PAI is the abbreviation for the Zionist movement Poale Agudat Israel.
193 *JC*, 20.2.1987, p.3.
194 See Chapter 7.
195 *AJR Information*, February 1972.
196 *JC*, 2.4.1976, p.12. Although the premises were sold, for a number of years educational
     activities (talks and lectures) continued to take place in the building under the collective
     name of the Brodie Institute.
197 *JC*, 1.7.1977, p.4.
198 *JC*, 6.6.1975, p.6.
199 *JC*, 1.8.1980, p.7.
200 *JC*, 27.3.1981, p.10.
201 Anonymous interviewee.

202 The *Bet Hatalmud* was overseen by Rabbi Kaplin and Rabbi Karnovsky. See *The Blessing of Eliyahu*, p.93.
203 Interview with Gabriel Goldstein.
204 Ibid.
205 See Chapter 11.
206 Interview with Gabriel Goldstein.
207 Interview with Michael Cohen.
208 See www.Orah.org.uk.
209 JC, 29.6.12, p.25.
210 Interview with Michael Cohen.
211 Interview with Rabbi Ofir Ronen. Chabad, also known as Lubavitch, is a Hassidic movement known for its outreach activities. It is the largest Jewish religious organisation in the world.
212 It was established in the mid-1980s. The local Seed centre for Golders Green is located in Edgware.
213 See www.aish.org.uk.
214 Http://jle.org.uk.
215 Ibid.
216 See http://kesher.org.uk/about-kesher/.
217 Interview with Rabbi Bassous.
218 He was followed by Rabbi Michael Heilbron, Jeremy Collick and Jan Roseman and more recently by Lawrence Cohen, Michael Morri Camille and Bebe Jacobs.
219 Rose, *50 Years of 'Alyth'*, p.46.
220 Http://www.alyth.org.uk.
221 Helen Fry, *Golders Green Synagogue*, p.97.
222 Ruth and Moshe Cohn, 'Strength to Strength' in the *Golders Green Synagogue Journal*, Issue 6, September 2015, p.20.
223 Interview with Benny Chain. Dayan Swift briefly led the synagogue prior to the appointment of Rabbi Sacks.
224 Daniel Greenberg in *The Golders Green Journal*, No. 1, September 2012, p.16.
225 See Chapter 10.
226 Fry, *The First Hundred Years*, p.139.
227 Http://www.goldersgreenshul.org.uk/learn/.
228 Interview with Gabriel Goldstein.

Chapter 15

1 Dr Melamed was a contributor to the *JC*. For example, *JC*, 17.2.1911, p.16, letter protesting at what he saw as laxities in Jewish observance.
2 Information for this paragraph taken from 1911 census and Kelly's Directory for Middlesex, 1911 which would have been compiled in 1910.
3 Todd Edelmann, 'German Jewish Settlement in Victorian England' in Werner Mosse (ed.), *Second Chance, Two Centuries of German-Speaking Jews in the United Kingdom*, (Tubingen: J.C.B. Mohr, 1991), p.38.
4 He had a shop at 1 Buckingham Mansions, Kelly's Directory for Middlesex, 1911. He previously lived in Brentford (1901 census).
5 1911 census.
6 See Chapter 10. Benjamin Drage became President of Golders Green Synagogue.
7 William D. Rubinstein, Michael A. Jolles, Hilary L. Rubinstein (eds), *The Palgrave Dictionary of Anglo-Jewish History* (London: Palgrave Macmillan, 2011), p.228. Benjamin Drage later left Golders Green Synagogue to become a member of West London (Reform) Synagogue.
8 Interview with Nancie Craig, 8.3.1989, JML, Audio 191.

9   Interview with Pearl Pollock, JML, Audio 195.
10 Discussed in David Cesarani, 'A Funny Thing Happened on the Way to the Suburbs: Social Change in Anglo-Jewry Between the Wars, 1914–1945', *Jewish Culture and History*, Vol.1, No.1, p.8.
11 Information from 1901 and 1911 censuses and electoral registers available at Ancestry.co.uk.
12 See consecration stone at Dunstan Road Synagogue.
13 1901 census and Kelly's Directory for Middlesex, 1914.
14 1911 census.
15 Electoral registers for London, 1918 available at Ancestry.co.uk. He eventually relocated his practice to Golders Green Road.
16 Kelly's Directory for Middlesex, 1927. For example, Maurice Kassimoff, a turquoise merchant at 30 Woodville Road.
17 Obituary *JC*, 20.2.1931, p.12. Dr Feldman died aged 37.
18 Kelly's Directory for Middlesex, 1926.
19 See Chapter 12.
20 Reuben Lincoln (né Tribich) trained as a rabbi at Jews' College but after holding several pulpits in the UK and the US he became a solicitor. Until it was demolished after the war, he lived in the 300-year-old manor house 'The Oaks', in Beechcroft Road. The family had moved to Golders Green from Plymouth in 1921. Information provided by Michael Jolles. Rate books for the area show that in the early years much of the property was owned by local estate agents, but by the mid-1920s ownership of a significant number of properties had passed to the Lincoln family.
21 Interview with Jocelyne Tobin. During the 1920s the gown and dress trade began shifting from the East End to central London closer to the show rooms that served the wealthy families living in the West End. Cesarani, 'A Funny Thing Happened', p.9.
22 Ibid.
23 Ibid.
24 Interview with Selina Gellert.
25 Cesarani, 'A Funny Thing Happened', pp.5–26.
26 Anthony Grenville, *Jewish Refugees from Germany and Austria in Britain 1933–1970, Their Image* (London and Portland, OR: Vallentine Mitchell, 2010), p.11.
27 Interview with Rachel Deutsch.
28 *AJR Information*, April 1956. Dr Adler initially saw patients at his home in Hoop Lane as well as in Bryanston Square. He later had a practice at 680 Finchley Road after it had been vacated by Menorah Primary School.
29 Grenville, *Jewish Refugees*, p.25.
30 Kelly's Directory for Middlesex, 1937.
31 Interview with Herbert Landsberg, Imperial War Museum, catalogue number 30631, production date 2008-01.
32 Interview with Harry Morton, in ibid., catalogue number 19100, production date 1999-07-03.
33 Robert B. Goldmann, *Wayward Threads* (Evanston, IL: Northwestern University Press, 1997), p.53.
34 *JC*, 9.5.1939.
35 Anthony Grenville in *AJR Journal*, December 2008.
36 Interview with Jocelyne Tobin.
37 Interview with Nancie Craig, JML.
38 Interview with Jacqueline Morris.
39 Maria Phillips in *Jewish Memories of the Twentieth Century by Members of the North-Western Reform Synagogue London*, recorded and collated by David Stebbing, compiled by Evelyn Kent (London: Evelyn Kent Associates, 2003), p.216.
40 For example, if their husbands were prevented from working because of restrictions on professional practices or because their skills were redundant as was the case for lawyers because of the different legal system in Britain.

41   Charmian Brinson, 'Autobiography in Exile: The Reflections of Women Refugees from Nazism in British Exile, 1933-1945', *Yearbook of the Research Centre for German and Austrian Exile Studies*, 3 (2001), pp.1-21 esp. p.9.

42   Interview with Marion Kreindler, 'Jewish Survivors of the Holocaust', British Library, C830/094/01.

43   Kathe Trenter in *Jewish Memories of the Twentieth Century*, p.305.

44   Interview with Harry Morton, Imperial War Museum.

45   Interview with Lola Rodin.

46   Interview with Nancie Craig, JML.

47   Interview with Jocelyne Tobin.

48   Interview with Harry Morden, Imperial War Museum.

49   Interview with Steven Derby.

50   Brinson, 'Autobiography in Exile', p.8.

51   *JC*, 28.9.2012, p.8.

52   Interview with Jacqueline Morris.

53   Ronald 'Roy' Friedman' in *Jewish Memories of the Twentieth Century*, pp.63–64.

54   Interview with Miriam Levene.

55   Grenville, *Jewish Refugees*, p.137.

56   Interview with Isca Wittenberg.

57   Interview with Peter Colman.

58   *AJR Information*, March 1949.

59   Hendon Borough Directory for 1959–60 (London: Johnston Evans & Co., 1959).

60   Grenville, *Jewish Refugees*, p.147.

61   *AJR Information*, December 1953.

62   Interview with Miriam Levene.

63   See regular adverts in *AJR Information*.

64   Anonymous interviewee.

65   *AJR Information*, June 1957.

66   *JC*, 17.1.1958, p.6.

67   Grenville, *Jewish Refugees*, p.230.

68   *AJR Information*, March 1957.

69   *Jewish Travel Guide* compiled by Green Flag, 1952 edition, p.31.

70   Grenville, *Jewish Refugees*, p.135.

71   Interview with Esra Kahn.

72   *JC*, 20.12.2002, p.16.

73   *JC*, 25.8.1978, p.8.

74   Interview with Nadia Nathan.

75   Ibid.

76   Interview with Lucille Sher.

77   Interview with Kitty and David Freund.

78   Ernest Krausz, 'The Economic and Social Structure of Anglo-Jewry' in Julius Gould and Shaul Esh (eds) *Jewish Life in Modern Britain* (London: Routledge Keegan Paul, 1964), p.29.

79   Interview with Gerald Peters.

80   Interview with Gordon Greenfield.

81   Helen Fry, *Golders Green Synagogue, The First Hundred Years* (Wellington: Halsgrove, 2016), p.88.

82   Interview with Michael Cohen.

83   Obituary, *The Times*, 14.3.2015.

84   Http://www.nytimes.com/1999/04/07/arts/michael-manuel-director-70-worked-at-met.html.

85   *JC*, 4.3.2011, p.34.

86   Rubinstein et al., *The Palgrave Dictionary*, p.381.

87   Norman Myers in *Jewish Memories of the Twentieth Century*, p.213.

88   Interview with Jeff Alexander.
 89   Dannie Abse, *Goodbye Twentieth Century*: The Autobiography (London: Pimlico, 2001, ebook).
 90   *JC*, 19.10.84, p.23.
 91   Information from Michael Jolles.
 92   Interview with Nancie Craig, JML. She trained at Stockwell College in Bromley, the charter for which included educating Jewish students. During her two years there she was provided with kosher meals. Interview with Barbara Michaels.
 93   See Chapter 12.
 94   Interview with Hazel Sheldon.
 95   Interview with Selina Gellert.
 96   Interview with Julia Chain.
 97   See advertisements in *AJR Information*.
 98   *AJR Information*, November 1952.
 99   Ibid., July 2015.
100   *JC*, 2.10.2009, p.10.
101   *JC*, 23.1.1987, p.6.
102   *JC*, 22.3.1986, p.2.
103   Stanley Waterman, *Jews in an Outer London Borough, Barnet*. Research paper number one (London: Department of Geography, Queen Mary College, London, 1989), p.35.
104   Ibid., p.37. This may have been the result of the number of observant Jewish women who were not at that time working after marriage but also because of the high proportion of Israeli men living in the area with non-working wives.
105   See Chapter 11.
106   Mainly in the realm of the natural sciences rather than philosophy and the arts.
107   Email from Benjamin Sachs, 1.2.2016.
108   Interview with Esra Kahn.
109   Ibid.
110   Http://www.vosizneias.com/71577/2010/12/21/.
111   Obituary in *Hamodia*, 23.12.2010, p.A2.
112   Interview with Selina Gellert.
113   Obituary in *Hamodia*.
114   Interview with Selina Gellert. A new room for disabled women, funded by the family, has recently been opened and dedicated in his memory. His son now runs the practice.
115   Information in *The North-West Connection 7, Shomer Shabbos Telephone and Business Directory*.
116   Interview with Michael Cohen.
117   Interview with Eli Cohen.
118   See J. Katz, *Tradition in Crisis: Jewish Society in the Middle Ages* (New York: New York University Press, 1993).
119   Amiram Gonen, *Between Torah Learning and Wage Earning* tr. Jessica Bonn (Jerusalem: Floersheimer Institute for Policy Studies, 2006), p.84.
120   Ibid., p.27.
121   Ibid., p.40.
122   Anonymous interviewee.
123   Michel S. Laguerre, *Global Neighborhoods, Jewish Quarters in Paris, London, and Berlin*, (Albany: State University of New York Press, 2008), p.73.
124   Interview with Esra Kahn.
125   Interview with Michael Cohen.
126   Laguerre, *Global Neighborhoods*, p.96.
127   Anonymous interviewee.
128   Ibid.
129   Laguerrre, *Global Neighborhoods*, p.88.
130   Interview with Michael Cohen.

131 Anonymous interviewee.

132 Interview with Rabbi Bassous.

133 Advertisement in *The Synagogue Review* (Golders Green Synagogue), Vol.1, No.2, October 1929, p.14.

134 *JC*, 2.12.1955, p.13.

135 Now known as the Antique Bookshop.

136 Https://www.youtube.com/watch?v=tqfkYY7W--c.

137 The *etrog* plus the three branches that form the lulav – myrtle, willow and date palm – which are the four plants mentioned in the Torah (Leviticus 23:40) as being relevant to the festival of *Sukkot*.

138 Information in *The North-West Connection 7, Shomer Shabbos telephone and Business Directory*.

139 Interview with Rabbi Refoel and Loli Berisch.

Chapter 16

1 V.D. Lipman, 'The Development of London Jewry' in S.S. Levin (ed.), *A Century of Anglo-Jewish Life 1870–1970* (London: United Synagogue Publications, 1970), pp.78–103.

2 See special supplement, *JC*, 17.7.15, pp.2–3.

3 Ibid.

4 For example, the Friends of Childs Hill Park group which restored the park behind Dunstan Road Synagogue. *JC*, 5.12.2014, p.18.

Appendix

1 Https://en.wikipedia.org/wiki/Union_of_Orthodox_Hebrew_Congregations.

2 Http://www.theus.org.uk.

3 Http://federationofsynagogues.com.

4 Http://www.sandp.org/history.html.

5 See information on abortive attempt to form a union, *JC*, 27.9.1991, p.1.

6 Http://www.liberaljudaism.org.

7 Http://www.reformjudaism.org.uk/.

8 Http://www.masorti.org.uk.

Index